THE
MODERNIZATION
OF
FATHERHOOD

THE ..... MODERNIZATION OF FATHERHOOD

A Social and Political History

RALPH LaROSSA

THE UNIVERSITY OF CHICAGO PRESS
CHICAGO AND LONDON

Ralph LaRossa is professor of sociology at Georgia State University. He is the author of *Conflict and Power in Marriage: Expecting the First Child* (1977) and *Becoming a Parent* (1986); coauthor of *Transition to Parenthood: How Infants Change Families* (1981); editor of *Family Case Studies: A Sociological Perspective* (1984); and coeditor of *Sourcebook of Family Theories and Methods: A Contextual Approach* (1993).

The University of Chicago Press, Chicago 60637
The University of Chicago Press, Ltd., London
© 1997 by The University of Chicago
All rights reserved. Published 1997
Printed in the United States of America
05 04 03 02 01 00 99 98 97   1 2 3 4 5

ISBN 0-226-46903-4 (cloth)
        0-226-46904-2 (paper)

Library of Congress Cataloging-in-Publication Data

LaRossa, Ralph.
    The modernization of fatherhood : a social and political history /
Ralph LaRossa.
        p.   cm.
    Includes bibliographical references (p.   ) and index.
    ISBN 0-226-46903-4 (cloth : alk. paper). — ISBN 0-226-46904-2
(pbk. : alk. paper)
    1. Fatherhood—United States—History.   2. Fatherhood—Social
aspects—United States.   I. Title.
HQ756.L37 1997
306.874′2—dc20   96-25634
                                                                                      CIP

• • • • •

To Maureen, Brian, and Adam

Contents

Illustrations follow page 88

• • • • •

Prologue: 1932

It is Mother's Day. Rain has forced the cancellation of a Parents' Day rally—a counter celebration of sorts—in New York City's Central Park. The following Sunday brings clear skies along with an estimated 10,000 people who show up at the mall to protest the fact that only mothers were honored the week before. The crowd wants fathers to be recognized, too. Both the mayor of New York City and the president of the United States go on record in support of the cause. [1]

Earlier in the year, the Child Study Association of America, a parent education conglomerate with a national membership, publishes an article in its newsletter about a school that stays open on Lincoln's Birthday, when most businesses are closed, so that fathers can spend the day with their children and see, firsthand, how the youngsters are doing. At another school, the fathers have organized themselves into a child study group that meets regularly. And at another, the program for the annual PTA dinner is made up entirely of men who share with the audience the various activities that they have developed to be a presence in their children's lives. [2]

In the summer, the editors of *Parents' Magazine* say that their periodical has so many male readers that "a special department" devoted to fatherhood seems due, and they announce their intention to publish a "For Fathers Only" column and invite men to contribute. The first article in the series is titled, "Confessions of a Newborn Father," and describes the sheer joy one man has experienced while caring for his infant son. "I'll never forget the first time I held my youngster," the author writes. "I had gooseflesh all over and chills down my back." And the hard work that goes along with being a parent? "Well, I admit there's nothing alluring about crawling out of bed at 2 A.M. in mid-winter, getting the bottle out of the refrigerator, heating it up, picking up a twelve-pound, warm, wet bundle, unraveling it, redressing your future heir in a dry one, getting a nipple that has the right size hole in it, and finally sitting for fifteen minutes." But, the father admits, there is something mystical about having those private moments with his infant son. "Watch him go after that nipple.

Watch him go to sleep and keep right on working his suction pump. Listen to him 'grunt' (I know no better word for it) for his highball *de lait,* urging you to hustle along as your clumsy hands adjust the nipple. Hear his sigh of satisfaction when that first spurt of warm milk trickles down his palate. . . . Yes—the first year of baby's life is the hardest for Mother and Father and Baby, but it can be one of the happiest if *you* get into the game."[3]

On the radio, a nationally known educator talks about the importance of fathers, how it is unfortunate that so many "are often strangers in their own house." He tells his listeners that "children want to be fathered as well as mothered," and he cites as an example a child he knows who revels in the knowledge that every Saturday is a day that he and his father spend together. "We go everywhere," the child had boasted. "Sometimes we fish, sometimes we walk, or go to a show, or just stay home and work and talk. We have a grand time."[4] Afterward, a man who had listened to the show sits down and writes a letter to communicate his identification with the program's theme. Proudly admitting to being "over 60 years old," he says that he has five daughters and that he has been a companion to them ever since they were little: "I taught them to walk, to talk, play children's games, play baseball, tennis, cards, checkers, and would play anything with them that would interest and help develop them into healthy intelligent women. Even such a thing as climbing trees."[5] Another man, twenty-one and not yet a father, but also an avid listener, had written the month before to say, "I know that to be a companion to your children is more in life than to make a lot of money."[6]

In the nation's capital, the Children's Bureau, a government agency, has its hands full trying to meet the demand for its enormously popular child-rearing manual, *Infant Care,* now in its fourth edition, and it decides to give the go-ahead to the Government Printing Office to produce more copies. The manual, which is the parenting bible for tens of thousands of fathers and mothers, offers detailed instructions in the "exacting profession" of "the care of the baby." Throughout the book appears the message that men need to be involved with their infant children, that they cannot allow themselves to be absentee fathers. At the bottom of the hour-by-hour schedules recommended during the first twelve months, for example, there is this maxim: "Parents must work together."[7] Many fathers over the years have taken the maxim to heart and written to the Children's Bureau to ask for advice on everything from the nutritional value of powdered milk to the psychological consequences of thumb sucking. This year, however, the American economy is in a depression, and people's concerns are directed elsewhere. One man, who is barely making a living, pleads for advice on what to do about his eight-year-old boy, who is in dire need of extended medical assistance.[8] And a soldier, stationed in Michigan, is trying to help his children by *not* living at home; that way, his wife tells the bureau, there is one less mouth to feed—his.[9]

1 The Modernization of Fatherhood

You modern fathers have no respect for tradition.
Katharine Hepburn, in the
movie *Woman of the Year* (1942)

Every once in a while, in the ebb and flow of human events, there is an era so significant, so cataclysmic, that it forever changes the heart and soul of a country and its people. Such a time was the Machine Age, which, in America, began when World War I ended, and ended when World War II began—the 1920s and 1930s, essentially—two decades that rocked the world.[1]

Much has been written about the Machine Age: about the Roaring Twenties, and the Great Depression; about the technological innovation and the personal devastation; about the national euphoria following the "war to end all wars," and the collective anguish over having to fight another. But the Machine Age was also an important time in the history of American gender relations, particularly in the history of American fatherhood. For it was during the Machine Age that the current image of the father as economic provider, pal, and male role model all rolled into one became institutionalized.[2]

The key word here is *institutionalized*, because all three expectations were around, in one form or another, long before the Machine Age arrived. What happened in the 1920s and 1930s, however, is that economic and cultural events worked to fuse the expectations into a stereotype of fatherhood that, first in the middle class and later in other groups, became America's ideal.

How this fusion took place is essentially the subject of this book. Stated simply and directly, this is the story of how American fatherhood was reshaped and welded during the Machine Age into the configuration that so many have come to know and revere today.[3]

With all that has been written and said about the 1920s and 1930s, and with all the attention that has been given to the subject of fatherhood, one would think that the impact of the Machine Age on American fatherhood would have been pretty well covered—by researchers as well as others. In truth, however, a detailed study of how fatherhood was transformed during the 1920s and 1930s has never been carried out. While the historical study of fatherhood is not a new field, and some fine historical work has been done, fatherhood scholars until now have tended to focus on the pre-1920s (the seventeenth, eighteenth, and nineteenth centuries) or the 1940s to the present. The 1920s and 1930s, by comparison, generally have been ignored or erroneously classified as a deceptively uninspiring and cartoonlike phase in fatherhood annals. The 1930s seem to have been especially misunderstood, often being viewed narrowly and exclusively as a time of crisis for fathers battered by the Depression. Few are aware that while the 1930s may have had a debilitating effect on men's domestic duties and responsibilities, the period also sparked intensified efforts to sanctify men's relationships with children and, on a cultural level at least, may have been less alienating for fathers than the decade before. (Witness the events of 1932 described in the prologue.) Fatherhood scholars who neglect the Machine Age, or who overlook the complex negative *and* positive forces operating during the Depression, thus run the risk of painting at best a limited, and at worst an inaccurate, picture of twentieth-century fatherhood.[4]

The failure to recognize fully the importance of the 1920s and 1930s in the history of fatherhood has meant also that the various theories being developed to explain contemporary men's involvement, or lack of involvement, with children are not as sound as they could be because they lack the proper historical grounding. For example, social commentator David Blankenhorn argues in *Fatherless America* that men's absence from the home has its roots in the nineteenth century, when there was a dramatic reversal in men's and women's parental roles. Before this time, says he, men were seen as the primary parent; beginning in the 1800s, however, women took over this responsibility. What happened, according to Blankenhorn, is that industrialization "led to the physical separation of home and work," which set in motion the "shrinking" of men's involvement in family life ("no longer could fathers be in both places at once"). Blankenhorn also contends that this de-fathering process proceeded nonstop and in a linear fashion. "Not being overly gloomy," Blankenhorn writes, "but in some respects it has been all downhill for fathers since the Industrial Revolution."[5]

Blankenhorn is correct to note that industrialization had a profound effect on father involvement, though the nature of the impact is more intricate than he describes. (I will have more to say about industrialization in chapter 2.) Blankenhorn is wrong, however, when he implies that "it has been all downhill" since the Industrial Revolution. History is rarely, if ever, linear, and it is almost never so neat. Since the 1800s, fatherhood has had both its ups and downs, and the brand of American fatherhood that we see today bears the legacy of these wins and losses. That some of fatherhood's most notable struggles came during the Machine Age means that the 1920s and 1930s cannot be ignored or seen as only a variation on what had come before.

FATHERHOOD AND THE ABSENCE OF A USABLE PAST

As the prologue illustrates, some of the features that we have come to identify with fatherhood today were part of American fatherhood long before now. Thus, while it may be gratifying for men in the late twentieth century to believe that they are the first generation to change a diaper or give a baby a bath, the simple truth is that they are not. Hearing this may be a disappointment to many. Not hearing it, however, may be worse, for lost in the artificially generated excitement of being around when the first caring men happened on the scene is the debilitating effect of not having what historians call a *usable past*.[6]

In her book *The Creation of Feminist Consciousness*, historian Gerda Lerner argues that "the most serious obstacle" to women's "intellectual growth" is that women have been denied a true knowledge of their ancestors. Most women, for example, do not realize that the struggle for women's rights has been going on for centuries, that there were activists at least as far back as A.D. 7 who were writing and speaking out against patriarchy. Without this knowledge, otherwise informed women (and men) locate the beginning of feminist thought in the nineteenth century. Some use the early twentieth century as a benchmark. Still others think that feminism did not really begin until the 1960s. The problem that has resulted from this myopia, according to Lerner, is that "[w]omen [have been] denied knowledge of their history, and thus each woman [has] had to argue as though no woman before her had ever thought or written. Women [have] had to use their energy to reinvent the wheel, over and over again, generation after generation."[7]

Something along the same lines seems to have happened with respect to the history of fatherhood. Back in 1982, historian John Demos said that "[f]atherhood has a very long history, but virtually no historians."[8] That now has changed, and we are beginning to see histories of fatherhood being presented in both articles and books. What remains, however, is some of the myopia that was there before the histories were written, because most of the historical accounts tend to downplay the importance of the Machine Age or depict yesterday's fathers as little more than human toys for their children—or worse, dupes of the child-rearing elite. The possibility that fathers may have been active agents in the most significant transformation in fatherhood in the twentieth century, or that they were involved in not only the expressive but also the instrumental aspects of parenthood remains largely unexplored.[9]

I do not mean to suggest that the absence of a usable past for fathers is equivalent in magnitude or seriousness to the absence of a usable past for women. Clearly, women's oppression is more extreme and more incapacitating. But there is a parallel that is worth noting, and I mention it because men are not the only ones being adversely affected; women are being hurt, too. First, men are harmed because their "intellectual growth," to use Lerner's phrase, is hampered by the belief that yesterday's fathers not only did not want to be involved with their children, but did not even give the subject much thought.[10] ("Fifty years ago, fathers didn't think much about what kind of job they were doing," said one authority a few years back, while two other experts recently proclaimed that the question of what it means to be a father was given "little serious consideration" by the "men of our parents' generation.")[11] In other words, caring and loving men have been denied the value of knowing that there were others before them, others who shared their concept of what good fatherhood meant. Without a valid sense of history, activist men, like activist women, have been forced to "reinvent the wheel," endlessly repeating rather than building on what has come before.[12] Thus, when a father in the 1990s decides to take pen in hand and write about what it means to have sole responsibility for his children while his wife is out of town, there is little sense from the author that this really is not new(s); little sense that many fathers in the past have been in the same situation, and that some have even written about it.[13] There is little recognition, too, that writing about having sole responsibility for the kids while one's wife is away reinforces the gender-based division of labor. Chances are, the article would not have been written if the reporter were a female.

As for women, they are negatively affected by the failure to give credit to yesterday's fathers because when they ask men why the division of child care is so one-sided, with the mothers doing most of the nitty-gritty work, they often are told that they should be happy for "what they get," that men now at least are doing "a lot more than did men in the past."[14] Telling subordinate groups to "be patient," that "change takes time," is one way to put the brakes on a revolution. And braked, or at least slowed, the gender revolution seems to be. For despite all the hoopla about "New Fatherhood" this and "New Fatherhood" that, mothers continue to shoulder most of the child care burden, and increases in father involvement in recent years, while certifiable, continue to be minimal.[15]

Before I go any further, I want to make several things clear. It is not my purpose here to engage in a glorification of the past, to brand the Machine Age the "Golden Age of Fatherhood," as it were. I am intent, however, on getting away from what I think are simplistic contrasts between early- and late-twentieth-century fatherhood, whereby whatever happened then is viewed in the most homogeneous terms (e.g., men were the family breadwinners and their children's pals, nothing more) and whatever is happening now is infinitely complex, with only a superficial resemblance to what has come before. It also is not my intent to go to the other extreme, to imply that the New Fatherhood of today is just a variation on the New Fatherhood of the Machine Age. Without a doubt, events in recent years (e.g., mothers' rising employment, the increase in divorce) have had a profound effect on men's relationships with their children. I do think, however, that the similarities between the two brands of New Fatherhood deserve as much attention as the differences. Until now, the accent has been more on the latter. Why this is so, I am not entirely sure. What I find striking, however, is how much men's identities as fathers seem to hinge on their drawing distinctions between the past and the present. By crafting stories (histories) that depict themselves as different from their predecessors, men engage in what may be termed the politics of self and other. "Other-izing" yesterday's fathers, like "other-izing" another race or gender, allows men to feel better about themselves. This kind of exercise may be pacifying to some, but it is not inconsequential, for as every historian knows, whoever controls the view of the past gains considerable leverage on shaping the present—and the future. Fatherhood researchers must begin to cut through this form of paternal (and paternalistic) egocentrism.[16]

THE CLASH BETWEEN "NEW FATHERHOOD" AND "OLD FATHERHOOD"

The events described in the prologue should give us pause. I, for one, was unaware that New Fatherhood could be traced back to the early twentieth century. Like others, I believed that New Fatherhood started in the 1970s (which was gratifying to me, because that is when I became a father.)

I do have a confession to make, however. In writing the prologue, I did take some license with the texts. First of all, I excluded facts that would have made the fathers appear, shall we say, less radical. I did not mention, for example, that most Americans in 1932 wanted little to do with Parents' Day. Indeed, some thought the idea ludicrous and somehow sacrilegious.[17] I also did not reveal that the newsletter that spoke of men's participation in child study groups included statements like, "Some of those who would educate the father as well as the mother in parenthood start out with the mistaken theory that the father should know as much and the same kind of detail about their children as the mother. It would be very unfortunate if that were so."[18] As for the government manual *Infant Care,* parents may have been told to "cooperate," but it still was the mother whom the Children's Bureau held responsible for the baby's well-being. This was evident, on the one hand, from the fact that the cover had a picture of a mother holding a baby and, on the other, from the staff's decision to phrase the section on the sick baby in terms of "what a mother should note." Finally, the bibliography, which easily could have been called "Helpful Reference Works" or "Selected Readings" was instead titled "Selected Books of Interest to Mothers."[19]

Why, then, use the stories at all? Two reasons. First, I wanted to establish from the beginning that some of the features that we have come to associate with contemporary fatherhood were in evidence long before now. Second, I wanted to illustrate the inconsistency surrounding fatherhood in early-twentieth-century America; to show how one version of fatherhood could coexist with, and be in the same text as, another version of fatherhood.

I would like to say something more about the second point: The fact that there is a New Fatherhood on the block does not mean necessarily that the Old Fatherhood has left. This is clear if we look at New Fatherhood in the present, and it is just as clear if we look at New Fatherhood in the past. Thus, back in 1932, the Child Study Association of America and the Children's Bureau seemed to endorse simultaneously both an old and a new version of fatherhood, even though the two versions would appear to cancel each other out. And by introducing a "For Fathers Only" column, *Parents' Magazine* may have tried to come across as avant-garde, but anyone who read the magazine could see that it was still primarily for women. Most of the advertisements, for instance, continued to be aimed at mothers.

The Machine Age

How much contra-diction (conflict in expression) there is at any moment in history is a variable: sometimes there is a little, sometimes there is a lot. In 1932, it is safe to say there was a lot. But the conflict was not just because of the Depression; it was also and mainly because of the Machine Age.

What exactly was the Machine Age? It was, quite simply, America's second "Revolutionary War," the point at which the United States finally was able to create its own "Way of Life" or "Culture" with a capital *C*.[20]

Architectural historian Richard Guy Wilson described the period in *The Machine Age in America, 1918–1941,* a coffee-table book which accompanied a traveling exhibition on the Machine Age several years ago:

> For many people the period marked a new age, brought into being by the machine. From the clock that awakened one in the morning, to the flicked switch, the faucet handle, the vehicle for transportation, and the radio and motion picture, machines and their products increasingly pervaded all aspects of American life. Machines were everywhere; their impact went beyond the fact of their physical presence to challenge perceptions of both the self and the world. This new consciousness implied a whole new culture that could be built as readily as the machine; history seemed irrelevant, traditional styles and pieties outmoded.[21]

Though the Machine Age ended over half a century ago, the changes that it brought about are still with us. Consider, for example, that it was during the Machine Age that electricity became widespread (used in 24 percent of American homes in 1917 but in 80 percent of homes by 1940); the first radio station started broadcasting (in 1920); the FM band was invented (in 1939); the United States became predominantly urban (over 50 percent in 1920); the Nineteenth Amendment to the Constitution, giving women the right to vote, was passed (again, in 1920); the automobile became the major mode of transportation, marked by a jump from 10 million registrations in 1920 to 32 million registrations in 1940; Charles Lindbergh and later Amelia Earhart flew across the Atlantic; penicillin was discovered and developed as a practical antibiotic; Albert Einstein's theories of relativity were empirically confirmed; both Freudian and behavioristic psychology took hold; the social and behavioral sciences began systematically to use statistics; the forty-hour work week was established as an ideal; the first birth control center opened in New York City; the first jet engine was built; and the first automatic computer was developed. All of this, of course, was in addition to the end of World War I, the beginning of World War II, and the Great Depression. Clearly, it is impossible to have a true understanding of late-twentieth-century culture and social structure without a firm grasp of what happened during the Machine Age.[22]

Modernism

The transformation that inspired and, at the same time, was fueled by the Machine Age was modernism. Generally, when people think of modernism, they think of modern dance, modern art, or modern architecture, but modernism's influence extended beyond the visual or the graphic. Indeed, modernism arguably was the most critical change in the history of twentieth-century culture.[23]

The defining characteristic of modernism was its eschewing of history and tradition; its emphasis on "the here and now." Before the turn of the century, the word *modern* generally meant "contemporary" and was used by each successive generation to talk about its own present. In the early twentieth century, and in the 1920s and 1930s especially, however, the word came to refer to "an identifiable and special sensibility that called for a complete break with the past."[24] Americans have long identified with the notion of progress, but modernism seemed to communicate something deeper. Modernism made the adulation of the present a secular religion. (Auto maker Henry Ford put the attitude in a nutshell when he said, "History is more or less bunk.")[25]

Modernism had other features, too. Aside from being associated with a nonhistorical form of consciousness, modernism also was characterized by a preoccupation with microscopic analysis. It was during the 1920s and 1930s, for example, that the study of the family as a social group was given its impetus. "Unity of interacting personalities" is the definition that University of Chicago sociologist Ernest W. Burgess proposed.[26] Modernists also took seriously the role of language and its influence on personality. Both cognitive research and clinical psychology—and America's entire therapeutic or self-help culture—have strong ties to the Machine Age.[27] Modernism revered science and technology as a basis for truth, which often put it at odds with both theological dogma and practical experience (as in, "I know how to do it because I've been doing it for a while"). Finally, modernists tended to focus on the similarities between objects and people.[28] Modernists, for example, were less likely to view men and women in dichotomous terms, which explains, in part, why the phrase *companionate marriage* became popular in the mid-1920s.[29] "Less likely," of course, does not mean that modernists advocated androgyny (though some did); it signifies simply that modernism was a form of consciousness that was less gender differentiating than, say, Victorianism.

When all these features are considered together, it is easy to understand why a new brand of fatherhood would take shape during the Machine Age. Parents' Day made sense under modernism because it did not polarize gender as Mother's Day did. Similarly, fatherhood study groups, fatherhood lectures, and "For Fathers Only" magazine articles, designed to help men get in touch with their children (and with their own feelings), emphasized both the dual role that parents were supposed to play and the link between family interaction and personal identity. The proliferation of "scientific" child-rearing manuals, written not necessarily by parents but by "experts," was certainly in keeping with modernism, as was the idea that people should feel comfortable writing to a stranger (or, more accurately, "scientific authority") to ask for child-rearing advice or solace. Last but not least, the taken-for-granted assumption of most, if not all, modernistic writers from the 1920s and 1930s was that "contemporary" fathers were significantly more involved with their children. In other words, the same emphasis on "the here and now"—what might be called "modern-*usm*"—that we see in the New Fatherhood of today can be found in the New Fatherhood of the Machine Age.[30]

Although modernism was a powerful force in American society, it did not eradicate what had been there before. First of all, modernism initially was a movement confined to the urban middle class. *Parents' Magazine* may have been a successful venture with a large circulation (it began publication in 1926 and continued, unlike other magazines, to grow in popularity during the Depression), but it had a highly select readership; and fatherhood study groups overwhelmingly were composed of college-educated men—much the same as they are today. Secondly, there were factions among the urban middle class who found modernistic principles threatening. Some clergymen, for example, viewed the movement to replace Mother's Day as a threat to "God's Law" that a woman's true place was in the home, caring for her children.[31]

Given the often uneasy coexistence of modernism with other, more traditional, world views, it is not surprising that we would find inconsistencies in the texts that were supportive, at least to some degree, of New Fatherhood. The fourth edition of *Infant Care* is a perfect example. Influenced by the modernistic idea that child rearing should be a science, and embracing the psychology of the day (behaviorism), the pamphlet incorporated fathers into the schedules that were part of the child's "habit formation." However, because *Infant Care* also was influenced by Victorian and religious beliefs about women's roles, it excluded fathers from one of the most important duties that a parent has: caring for a baby when it is sick.[32]

What begins in the cities and in the middle class often fans out over time to other parts of the country and to other social groups. This is especially true in matters pertaining to gender and family.[33] Thus, as the twentieth century wore on, modernistic notions of fatherhood spread. The diffusion, no doubt, was erratic and uneven, with some ecological areas and some class, racial, and ethnic groups proving to be less porous than others. But today, if we look around, we see not only the same clash between the new and the old, but also a culture where modernistic notions of fatherhood loom large. Granted, we also see tremendous diversity and perhaps the beginning of a new set of principles (postmodernism?), but it is nonetheless empirically verifiable that America's philosophy of fatherhood—its stereotype of what constitutes a good father—is firmly planted in soil tilled sixty to seventy years ago and before.

ECONOMIC AND CULTURAL FORCES
IN THE SHAPING OF FATHERHOOD

When scholars write about fathers and their children during the 1930s, they typically focus on the negative impact of the Depression—on how men's inability to be good economic providers resulted in their physical and psychological withdrawal from their families.[34]

As for New Fatherhood, historians generally contend (1) that the Depression had little or no effect, or (2) that the 1930s essentially were no different than the decade before, or (3) that the Depression "temporarily disrupted" what was in motion before. The possibility that the Depression might also have had a positive impact on New Fatherhood is rarely considered, let alone discussed. Yet this is exactly what happened.

How a downturn in the economy could have both a negative and positive effect will be explained in a moment, but first I want to offer a definition of *fatherhood*. As I see it, fatherhood should be conceptualized as a social role and a sociohistorical institution, and should be said to consist of the norms that men are expected to follow when they become fathers or are about to become fathers; the norms that children and other non-father actors are expected to follow when they pretend to be fathers; the attitudes and sentiments that people have toward fathers; the knowledge, valid or not, of what fathers have done in the past and what they are doing, and are capable of doing, in the present and future; the ceremonies and rituals that honor fathers and, in some cases, marginalize them (for example, Father's Day and Mother's Day); and, finally, the routine activities of men when they are trying to act "fatherly."

Any serious study of fatherhood, historical or otherwise, must keep these different facets in mind and, most important, recognize that the connection among them is complex. Consider, for example, the link between the *culture of fatherhood*, the norms, values, and beliefs surrounding men's parenting, and the *conduct of fatherhood*, what fathers do, their paternal behavior.[35]

Methodologically, the distinction between culture and conduct is relevant because it encourages us to ask whether the data used in a particular study are more indicative of one realm versus the other. A researcher, for example, who relies exclusively on magazine articles to chart changes in early-twentieth-century fatherhood can comment on the norms that people once followed and on the attitudes and beliefs they once held. But the extent to which he or she can discuss how fathers in the past acted, how they behaved in public and private, is something else.

Theoretically, the distinction between culture and conduct is relevant because it invites a discussion of the relationship between thought and deed. We often assume, for example, that the culture and conduct of a society are naturally in sync, when the two are frequently not aligned at all. Some people make it a habit of operating outside the norms. Others do wrong because they do not know any better. And in a rapidly changing society like ours, countervailing forces can result in major changes in culture but not in conduct, and vice versa, or in a scenario where culture changes in one direction while conduct changes in the other. The latter is what happened to fatherhood during the Depression. Here is how.

Consider again the events described in the prologue. All of them occurred in 1932, and all of them offer evidence of New Fatherhood. One might be inclined to suggest that the stories are holdovers from the 1920s, and that very quickly, perhaps beginning in 1933, when the Depression reached its lowest point, things like Parents' Day, fatherhood study groups, and "For Fathers Only" magazine articles would go by the wayside as the country turned its attention to more serious concerns, like avoiding mass starvation. But in fact all of these symbols of New Fatherhood gained a stronger hold on the consciousness and conscience of the educated middle class after 1932. Parents' Day rallies, for instance, continued throughout the 1930s, and at various points were endorsed by the postmaster general, the commander of the American Legion, even the president's mother. Child study organizations seemed to intensify their efforts to involve fathers in the science of child rearing, and the number of books that endorsed New Fatherhood increased. Consider, too, these statistics: From 1920 to 1929, only 35 popular magazine articles were catalogued in the *Reader's Guide to Periodical Literature* under the heading of "father," compared to 84 articles cataloged under the heading of "mother." From 1930 to 1939, however, 123 popular magazine articles were catalogued under the heading of "father," compared to 114 articles catalogued under the heading of "mother." In other words, articles on fathers increased by 251 percent, whereas articles on mothers increased by only 36 percent— and most of the articles on fatherhood or motherhood published from 1930 to 1939 were devoted not to women but to men.[36]

What is to be made of all these symbols of New Fatherhood in the midst of the Depression? First we must recognize that they are just that, *symbols*. Parents' Day, child-rearing books, popular magazine articles, parenting classes, all say something about how the culture of fatherhood changed, but offer only limited insight into what fathers actually were doing, day in and day out. (Recall the last element in the definition of fatherhood: the *routine activities* of men when they are trying to act "fatherly.") So, yes, it appears that the symbols surrounding New Fatherhood increased in both breadth and intensity over the course of the Depression, but what about fathers' conduct? What happened there? The evidence from a variety of sources indicates that during the Depression, men generally became less involved in their children's lives.[37]

This disjunction, or asynchrony, between the culture and conduct of fatherhood, with one going up and the other going down, is not uncommon, and is central to understanding how the Depression affected fatherhood. Overlook it, and you overlook what may be the central story of fatherhood in early-twentieth-century America. Overlook it, and you also miss the opportunity to address one of the most important questions in the social sciences: How do economic and cultural factors intersect?

One answer to what happened during the Depression is that the culture and conduct of fatherhood were each being driven by different forces. Child-rearing books and *Parents' Magazine* were fueled, it could be said, by the almighty dollar. If an idea like New Fatherhood was hot, who cares if it did not help people find food? (There was virtually no mention of the Depression in any of the child-rearing books or magazine articles published during the 1930s.) As for the daily life of fathers, it too was affected by money, but in a different way. Out of work, or preoccupied with keeping their jobs, fathers (who, we may assume, had been socialized into the economic provider role) simply may have been too busy or too psychologically down to spend much time with their kids.[38]

This explanation, to some degree, is valid, but it misses a lot, too. For one thing, it glosses over the variety of interests that contributed to the culture of fatherhood. The Parents' Day organizers, the Child Study Association of America, the Children's Bureau, the publisher and editors of *Parents' Magazine,* the radio personality, for example, all had different agendas and different attitudes toward fathers. Because there were so many players, assessing the contours of New Fatherhood and the rate at which it changed is more difficult than may be immediately apparent, for a careful analysis demands keeping track of *whose* New Fatherhood is being plotted and the *stage or phase* of New Fatherhood that is being zeroed in on.

A comprehensive explanation of the shifts in the culture and conduct of fatherhood during the 1920s and 1930s also must take into account the fact that a poor economy not only "de-presses," it also "ex-presses." When the economy is in a slump, avant-garde ideas like New Fatherhood may seem incidental. "First things first," as they say. But a poor economy also can make new ideas more attractive. This would seem to be especially true if the ideas being circulated provide a respite from financial woes—perhaps because they valorize identities that give less weight to financial responsibility. It was during the 1930s, for example, that more emphasis was given to fathers as masculine caregivers or male role models. Measuring virility and manliness in ways that were *independent* of whether one had a job captured the attention of many.[39] Among other reasons, this theme may have become popular then, because it served to counterbalance the emasculating effect of the Depression. As historians Steven Mintz and Susan Kellogg note in their book *Domestic Revolutions:* "The economic dislocations caused by the depression had a powerful effect on the father's stature as economic provider and disciplinarian. Many fathers were overwhelmed by guilt because they were unable to support their families. One father told a *New York Daily News* reporter: 'I haven't had a steady job in more than two years. Sometimes I feel like a murderer. What's wrong with me, that I can't protect my children?' . . . One wife commented, 'they're not men anymore, if you know what I mean.'"[40]

What we see, therefore, is a complex interweaving of both economic and cultural forces in the social construction of New Fatherhood. Created *before* the Depression, New Fatherhood gained in strength *during* the Depression not only because various interest groups had a stake in its growth (some were able to make money selling the concept), but also because the fathers and mothers who were exposed to its message wanted, more than before, to see men in nonmonetary terms.

THE POLITICS OF PARENTHOOD

Citing the connection between fatherhood and masculinity, made clearer during the Depression, may seem only to restate the obvious, namely, that fathers are men first and parents second. In truth, however, bringing the connection between fatherhood and masculinity to the fore raises a host of questions, the answers to which are not as obvious as some may think.

To the average American, fatherhood can be reduced to a biological state—an extension of what is anatomically a man's destiny. But to social scientists who seriously study the subject, this interpretation is far from sufficient, because what fatherhood is, or is not, social science has shown, is also a product of people's collective imagination.[41]

Contemplate, for a moment, how people generally draw distinctions between the "is" and the "is not." Sociologist Eviatar Zerubavel, author of *The Fine Line,* is helpful in this regard: "Separating entities from their surroundings is what allows us to perceive them in the first place. In order to discern any 'thing,' we must distinguish that which we attend from that which we ignore. Such an inevitable link between differentiation and perception is most apparent in color-blindness tests or camouflage, whereby entities that are not clearly differentiated from their surroundings are practically invisible."[42]

To know what fatherhood "is," in other words—to be able to *see* it—we must be clear about what it "is not." And how is this clarity achieved? Zerubavel contends that we engage in a form of cognitive geography, partitioning the world into "islands of meaning," which become components in the map or schemata that ultimately serves as our guide: "Creating islands of meaning entails two rather different mental processes—lumping and splitting. On the one hand, it involves grouping 'similar' items together in a single mental cluster—sculptors and filmmakers ('artists'), murder and arson ('felonies'), foxes and camels ('animals'). At the same time, it also involves separating in our mind 'different' mental clusters from one another—artists from scientists, felonies from misdemeanors, animals from humans."[43] *Or fatherhood from motherhood.*

To wit: It is not uncommon for people to assume that there is a natural distinction between fatherhood and motherhood. And on a biological level, there may very well be. On a social level, however, the distinction between fatherhood and motherhood is blurred.[44] If, for example, a man is warm and tender to a crying child, is he acting motherly? If a woman patronizes her teenage son with stories of "what it was like in my day," is she being paternalistic? And how, if there are ambiguities like these, do we know where fatherhood ends and motherhood begins, or vice versa? How are we supposed to *see* the difference between the two? By lumping and splitting, Zerubavel would say. In order to create islands of meaning known as "fatherhood" and "motherhood," people will group some items together into a single mental cluster, while separating other items into different mental clusters. Thus, the roles of "economic provider" and "pal" become associated with fatherhood, while "diaper changer" and "child nurse" become associated with motherhood—even though many women are economically supportive of and pals to their children, and many fathers are active diaper changers and medical and emotional nurturers.

From a number of vantage points, in fact, it can be argued that fatherhood and motherhood are more alike than not. Both have something to do with caring for children. Both are valued roles in American society. (Motherhood may be more valued, but that does not mean that fatherhood is not valued at all.) Both cut across racial, ethnic, and class lines. On the other side of the coin, neither has anything to do with the price of tea in China, or with the number of rings around Saturn. Neither is likely to be confused with childhood, brotherhood, or widowhood.

If fatherhood and motherhood exhibit so much similarity, why then is so much attention given to their distinctiveness? The answer comes down to gender politics. Fatherhood and motherhood are intimately tied to societal concepts of masculinity and femininity (what it *means* to be a man and woman), which in turn are products of people's collective imagination—again, lumping and splitting processes. Examined this way, from even a natural standpoint, men and women are closer to each other than to a lot of other things, say, rocks, birds, and plants. Hence, the idea that men and women are dichotomous categories must arise from the application of a cognitive geography, where the similarities between the sexes are ignored, and the differences are accentuated.[45] (Zerubavel talks about "the law of the excluded middle," in which differences in degree are translated into differences in kind by ignoring the commonalities in the middle of the spectrum and exaggerating the differences at the poles.)[46] And where does gender politics enter the equation? Concepts of masculine and feminine are not accidentally constructed, but are politically motivated, for the simple reason that money, status, and power itself are often distributed along gender lines. In a nutshell, men, who have been in the position to control definitions of masculinity and femininity, generally have done so to their own advantage. The fact, for example, that the qualities of being a "good" lawyer, doctor, or politician—professions that can command high salaries—are the same qualities that society associates with masculinity (nonemotionality, aggressiveness, etc.) is hardly coincidental. Connecting masculine traits to these jobs increases the likelihood that men will be recruited for them. And if we look at the percentage of lawyers, doctors, and politicians who are men, the results of this connection cannot be denied.

Thus, why is so much attention given to delineating the distinction between fatherhood and motherhood? Because ultimately people stand to gain or lose on the basis of where the lines are drawn. Here, however, is where the gender politics gets especially sticky. Generally speaking, men have worked the system to their advantage; typically, they have managed to cast themselves as the experts and have been accorded the most respect. Yet in the parental stratification system, the authority structure is more vague. In the social world of parenthood, mothers sometimes (though not always) are seen as the ones who have the knowledge and deserve the honors that go along with it. Fathers, in contrast, are not uncommonly viewed as less informed in the child realm (unless they are child psychologists or pediatricians), and in some circumstances can be perceived as flat-out incompetent.

Some would say that what appears to be a stratification system that periodically favors women is, in actuality, a system that always rewards men. By not having to be in charge of children, men also do not have to be responsible for children. Men thus have more freedom than women to pursue enjoyable and often lucrative tasks, because they are not as tied down to the tasks that go along with parenthood.[47] Certainly, we cannot ignore the fact that men created the overarching cultural framework that gives legitimacy to the idea that women are supposed to be, first and foremost, mothers. (After all, who made the laws, and who published the child-rearing books and magazine articles that hammered this point home?) Still, to assume that men consciously created a world that serves their interests in every conceivable way is to ignore the fact that sometimes there are unintended negative consequences to even the most self-serving actions. Yes, men stand to gain by not having to be as accessible to children, but they lose, too, because parenthood has advantages of which they are deprived. Many fathers are jealous of the love and affection they see their children bestowing upon their wives, and numerous divorced fathers grieve over the loss of their children in custody disputes.

Also, we should not be so quick to assume that mothers have played no part at all in the lumping and splitting of fatherhood and motherhood, for the evidence indicates that when it has been in their best interest, women have worked hard to protect the rights and privileges that go along with the premier status of motherhood. Granted they may have done so in order to protect one of few spheres over which men have permitted them some control, but that does not mean that women have been only reactors or bystanders. To the contrary, they have been actively engaged in the politics of parenthood (though it has often been an uphill battle for them).

Finally, there is the fact that concepts of fatherhood and motherhood not only are being negotiated by men and women on a daily basis but also have changed over time, which means that a true understanding of the politics that goes into the creation of the parental stratification system today depends upon a firm grasp of the politics that went into the creation of the parental stratification system yesterday. One of the reasons that the Machine Age is not only fascinating in its own right but also important to the development of sound theories for why fathers are, or are not, involved with their children is that it was a period when the gender politics surrounding parenthood was especially acute. As I said earlier, the period between World War I and World War II witnessed intensified efforts to sanctify men's relationship with their children and thus constituted a time when the social placement of the American father was very much an issue. The challenge that people faced, however—one that we will see played out repeatedly in the chapters that follow—was finding a new and more honorable place for fathers that did not undermine the privileged place that mothers occupied. The remapping of fatherhood and motherhood during the Machine Age thus puts the political struggle in bold relief. The lumping and the splitting processes could not be sharper.

Consider, for example, this little game of cognitive geography. As you may or may not have noticed, I have yet to use the words, *dad* or *daddy.* That is, up to now, I have not employed these words as substitutes for *father.* The reason for this is that my analysis of various Machine Age texts revealed that *father* and *dad* had different meanings in the 1920s and 1930s; the latter term was more often associated with a diminutive child-rearing role for men.

Central to the course that New Fatherhood took during the Machine Age was the rise (in the 1920s) and fall (in the 1930s) of what I call the *culture of daddyhood;* and the concomitant fall (in the 1920s) and rise (in the 1930s) of men's child-rearing status. This culture of daddyhood was a crucial element in the marginalization that fathers experienced during this time, in that it created a place for fathers that did not overlap with the place of women. Essentially, it framed fathers as children's pals, and by doing so, also framed fathers as trivial and less important. (More will be said about the culture of daddyhood in chapter 6.)[48]

Ironically, the culture of daddyhood also may be framing the way scholars today look at fathers during the Machine Age. Historians of fatherhood who have disproportionately focused on the 1920s when describing Machine Age fatherhood have tended to trivialize yesterday's fathers, seeing them as little more than weekend companions to their school-age kids. In fact, however, although the culture of daddyhood was extremely influential in the 1920s, it had become more diffuse by the 1930s. (What happened after the 1930s is another story.) The culture of daddyhood, to the extent that it can become incorporated into a scholar's mind-set, also may account for why evidence of fathers' undaddylike activities during the Machine Age (e.g., diaper changing, baby feeding, labor-intensive child socializing) has been almost always ignored. Believing is seeing.

METHODOLOGICAL NOTE

The aim of this book is to bring a wealth of primary and secondary data to bear on one basic question: How and why was American fatherhood transformed during the Machine Age? Child-rearing books, popular magazine articles, newspaper reports, personal letters, and the correspondence of some of the leading parent education organizations in the 1920s and 1930s are closely analyzed, with the goal of identifying not only the abstract social forces but also the very concrete and very human players in the transformation process.

As the reader will observe, considerable effort has been made not to view the books, articles, and letters as disembodied texts. Rather, the people behind the texts get significant billing, which explains why most of the chapters tend to be organized primarily around the producers and authors of the texts, and secondarily around the chronology of the texts themselves. (The exception is chapter 2, which offers a history of American fatherhood prior to the Machine Age.) In other words, rather than a chapter on 1920 to 1925 and then another on 1926 to 1929, and so on, there is a chapter on the U.S. Children's Bureau, the most important government agency devoted to "infant care" in the early twentieth century, followed by a chapter on the Children's Bureau's most ardent clients (i.e., the fathers and mothers who wrote the bureau for advice). These are followed by chapters on the fathercraft movement and, in particular, the Child Study Association of America, a private organization that was behind many of the parent education classes popular at the time; on the magazine industry and the development of *Parents' Magazine;* on Angelo Patri, a junior high school principal in New York City who, in the 1920s and 1930s, hosted a radio show on parenthood and wrote a syndicated newspaper column titled "Our Children"; and on the creation of Father's Day in America.

Within each of these chapters, there is a chronology—for example, the Children's Bureau's prescriptions in the 1920s versus its prescriptions in the 1930s—but, again, the chronology is subordinate to the producer/author scheme. What this format allows me to do is demonstrate that, contrary to what has been suggested by others, fatherhood during the Machine Age *was* politicized and contested, in the sense that its making, or remaking, was the result of various "interests" in competition with one another. (Whose agenda prevailed and whose did not, we shall also see, rested on the same factors that make the difference in most battles: resources, organization, cultural capital, charisma, drive, and luck.)[49]

Finally, a word on my decision to accentuate the technological ethic of the Machine Age and the cultural impact of modernism. Some may say that this is a strategic mistake, in that effaces the Depression. I believe, however, that equating the 1930s with the Depression and only the Depression, in the historical study of fatherhood, has itself been a mistake, in that it has prevented scholars from seeing the myriad forces that were at work at the time. Only if we totally ignore the Depression does our attention to the Machine Age and modernism prevent us from acknowledging what is an established fact: that America's economic crisis had a profound negative effect on men's involvement with their children. Keep in mind, however, that I am not proposing that we ignore the Depression. I am proposing only that we steer clear of simple economic determinism. I find it interesting, for example, that the Depression-era fathers who embraced "modern" notions of marital and family life were less likely than others to lose authority inside the home and less likely to decrease their contact with their kids.[50] This confluence of economic and cultural forces—what social scientists would call an interaction effect—makes the point well: Single-variable theories generally are not sufficient to explain much of anything. Finally, we should not forget that one very important reason that the Depression was not only financially but also psychologically devastating was that, within the circumference of the Machine Age and modernism, its very existence was such a disappointment. "How," people wanted to know, "could this happen to us, the most technologically advanced and philosophically supreme country in the world?" In short, the story that I am about to tell does not overlook the Depression. Rather, it contextualizes the Depression. The result, I would argue, is a truer account of the modernization of fatherhood.

2　The Historical Roots of Standard North American Fatherhood

> It is one of the misfortunes of our American way of living that
> the head of the house, the father—he who is the support, the
> mainstay, the highest central figure—should be scarcely able
> to live with his family at all. If he is a busy man, earning their
> daily bread, he must leave them after a hasty breakfast, to
> meet them again at a late dinner with a chance of seeing
> them in the evening; but, if a club man, or anxious for the
> opportunity of going out in the evening for improvement or
> change, he does not see much of his family even then. The
> younger children get to regard him as a feature of Sundays,
> and perhaps associate him with the unpleasant slavery of sit-
> ting still in church. A loving and kind father will, of course,
> impress himself upon his family and earn their affection and
> respect even in these brief intervals; but it is too little for the
> proper emphasis of an affection which should be almost the
> first in our hearts.
>
> From "The Good Father," in *Amenities of Home,*
> one of Appleton's Home Books (1881)

To understand the reconfiguration of fatherhood during the Machine Age, we must have some understanding of the history of fatherhood prior to the Machine Age. For the past is not simply prologue, as Shakespeare suggested; it is seed.[1]

Strictly speaking, however, there is no such thing as "the" history of fatherhood; rather, there are histories of fatherhoods, with an accent on the plural. In the nineteenth century, for example, the strain of father-hood that might be found in a northern industrial state differed from the strain of fatherhood that might be found in a southern agricultural community. Likewise, the strain of fatherhood among Anglo-Saxons in Boston differed from the strain of fatherhood among Chinese or Italian immigrants in Philadelphia or among African slaves in Atlanta.[2] Even these categories minimize the contradictions within locales and groups—consider the differences from one city block to the next, or from one family line to another.

The modernization of fatherhood that transpired during the Machine Age eventually affected a variety of "fatherhoods," but during the Machine Age itself, it was confined largely to the white urban middle class. The roots of the transformation thus will be found not under every cultural tree but under a particular cultural tree—again, that of the white urban middle class.

There is a name for this tree—or at least one has been proposed. Sociologist Dorothy Smith suggests it be called the "Standard North American Family" tree (or SNAF, for short). SNAF, according to Smith, "is a conception of the family as a legally married couple sharing a household. The adult male is in paid employment; his earnings provide the economic basis of the family-household. The adult female may also earn an income, but her primary responsibility is to the care of husband, household, and children. Adult male and female may be parents (in whatever legal sense) of children also resident in the household."[3]

SNAF itself is a descendant of what is commonly referred to as the "nuclear family," a conception that includes a husband and wife and their dependent offspring.[4] The nuclear family is a distinctive western European family pattern that during the Middle Ages was characteristic of England, the Netherlands, and northern France. It was this family model that was brought to the North American colonies in the seventeenth century.[5]

To some, SNAF is the building block of all families, and the ideal against which all family patterns should be measured.[6] To others, SNAF constitutes only one conception of family life, and a very narrow conception at that, as it basically ignores the variations that families exhibit across time, space, race, class, and sexual orientation. Limited or not, SNAF *is* the standard that generally has been used to evaluate the quality of family life in America. Thus, in this country at least, everything from family law to the marital division of labor tends to be "SNAF governed."[7] Men, more so than women, for example, tend to be judged by their ability to provide financially for their families. Women, more so than men, tend to be judged by their ability to care for their children. Only rarely are families outside the heterosexual norm considered to be families at all.

SNAF is so tightly woven into the fabric of North American society that it is basically an "ideological code," analogous to a genetic code, capable of "replicat[ing] its organization in multiple and various sites."[8] Smith confesses, for example, that when she and her colleague, Alison Griffith, embarked on a study of mothers and their children, they unintentionally replicated SNAF by asking questions of the mothers that implicitly assumed that SNAF was the valued norm. Similarly, most efforts to create a New Fatherhood, both during the Machine Age as well as today, have assumed that men occupy households with women, and that whatever men do in the way of child rearing is laudable by virtue of the fact that child rearing is not their accustomed or most accomplished role.

Central to SNAF replication is an interaction process that Griffith and Smith refer to as the "mothering discourse." By *discourse* they mean "an organization of relations among people participating in a conversation mediated by written and printed materials." The mothering discourse includes exchanges among "experts" who teach and do motherhood and childhood research; and magazine articles, books, courses, and the like that orient women to mothers' "work" and communicate how women should grade their performance when they are acting motherly. The mothering discourse, says Smith, "is not reducible to SNAF, [but] it is through and through SNAF-ordered, and indeed may have been, in the course of its historical development, among the carriers that generalized SNAF throughout English-speaking North America."[9]

The modernization of fatherhood during the Machine Age was part of the social construction—and reification—of the Standard North American Family.[10] At the same time that a SNAF-ordered mothering discourse was created, a SNAF-ordered fathering discourse was created as well. The fathering discourse, however, included more than might be supposed from Smith's definitions. In addition to breadwinning responsibilities, there were the expectations that fathers should be pals and male role models to their children. Men's one-on-one parental involvement legitimately could be less than that of their wives (for SNAF assumed, and continues to assume, that men have wives, and women have husbands), but it could not be so secondary as to be ignored. During the Machine Age, for example, SNAF-judged fathers repeatedly were chastised for giving too much attention to breadwinning and too little attention to their responsibilities as playmates and gender socializers.

While the mothering discourse and fathering discourse may have differed in their content, they were similar enough in their structure. The fathering discourse also consisted of ongoing interchanges among "experts" teaching and doing research, and it too instructed men as to how they should grade themselves when they were acting fatherly.

Smith historically situates the development of the mothering discourse in the first two decades of the twentieth century. The fathering discourse that I have outlined here and will describe in some detail in the chapters that follow, however, solidified in the 1920s and 1930s. (The mothering discourse also received a boost in the 1920s and 1930s, as we will see.) Needless to say, neither the mothering discourse, nor the fathering discourse, nor SNAF developed de novo in the early 1900s. All three have roots that are centuries old.

This brings me back to Shakespeare's axiom. The modernization of fatherhood that transpired during the Machine Age sprang from the same sources that served as the foundation for the social construction of the Standard North American Family. It is the genealogy of these sources that we must trace if we are to understand how American fatherhood was modernized in the 1920s and 1930s.[11]

THE COLONIAL ERA

According to popular lore, ever since the first Europeans settled in New England, men in America have been marginal parents. Only recently, so the legend goes, have fathers thought to give any attention to child care. Only recently have they become a presence in their daughters' and sons' lives.

A careful reading of the historical evidence, however, paints a very different and more complex picture. First of all, contrary to what is often assumed, colonial fathers played a very important role in the daily lives of their children. Although mothers may have been responsible for children under the age of three, fathers were the ones who were expected to guide older children and young adults—an age when, in keeping with the psychology of the era, humans were ready to be socialized. Thus, fathers typically made sure that children were learning their lessons, and fathers typically imparted religious instruction. This pattern was especially true when it came to sons.[12]

Some fathers, to be sure, did not wait until their children grew older to have a hand in child rearing. Charles Cotesworth Pinckney, who was born in 1745 and was a delegate to the Constitutional Convention, reported that his father tried to teach him the alphabet by the time he could talk, and had even built him a special set of toys so that he could learn his letters.[13] Pinkney's experience, however, was more the exception than the rule. Most of the evidence that historians have gathered indicates that colonial fathers generally had limited contact with infants.

One measure of men's standing as child socializers is that fathers in the seventeenth and eighteenth century almost always were awarded custody of their children in the event of a divorce. Another measure is that the child-rearing literature then was aimed not at mothers but at fathers.

(Some authors, however, did caution that mothers should not be "exempted.") A third is that, while it is more typical today for children who are living away from home to write to either their mother, or father and mother, in colonial times, children who were serving apprenticeships or on their own generally would direct their correspondence to the male head of the family.[14]

How do we explain the configuration that fatherhood took in the American colonies? It helps first to realize that the western European pattern of fatherhood essentially was a form of "patriarchal fatherhood," with roots going back to ancient times.[15] In early Greece, for example, the father "was the sole lord of his legal wife, children, concubines, and slaves," with responsibilities that included "various priestly duties, as well as the direct or indirect management of all nonreligious affairs in the household." [16] By law, he could reject a child at birth, dictate the marriage of his daughter or son, and kill his wife if he found her guilty of adultery. The ancient Roman father *(pater familias)* had these powers and more. His authority *(patria potestas)* included not only the ability to arrange his children's marriages but also the right to control their earnings after they were married. Legally, he also could "scourge, banish, and even sell his children as slaves." [17] Colonial fatherhood had deep ties to Christianity and its patriarchal tenets. Thus, like God the Father, men as fathers were expected to be both loving and just; and they were religiously bound to be authority figures in the home.[18]

Beliefs and values were not the only factors that played a part in the social construction of fatherhood in the American colonies. Equally important was the fact that the colonists generally lived off the land. With men owning most family property then, fathers had considerable economic hold over their older children. Fathers, for example, could delay when their sons married on the grounds that they still needed a hand to work the farm, and they could influence their daughters' choice of a mate because they were the ones who provided the dowries.[19] Patriarchal fatherhood, in other words, was based on more than ideological prescription; resources were important, too.[20]

Because most families not only lived but worked on farms, fathers and children spent plenty of time together. While today it may be rare for children to see their parents on workdays, in colonial America, family members not only saw each other regularly during the week, they toiled side by side before and after school (which for most children included but a few grades). And during the harvest, parents and children might be with each other even longer, from sunrise to sunset. Many artisans also worked at home or close by and, like farmers, "could be summoned easily whenever household matters required their supervision."[21] Thus, a number of fathers, like many mothers, were psychologically and physically present in their children's lives.

Let me reiterate that my description of American fatherhood in the seventeenth and eighteenth centuries is a sketch of only one particular family pattern, and that even within this pattern, important variations have been ignored. Landless wage laborers, for example, did not have the economic security that farm owners had and often were forced to move from one locale to the next to seek employment. The children of these migrant laborers might work alongside their parents, or they might find themselves in a shop or in the field, far removed from the watchful eyes of their parents.[22]

We should keep in mind, too, the distinction between the culture and the conduct of fatherhood mentioned in chapter 1. We know that the law gave fathers the license to punish their children physically, but we do not know how many fathers actually carried out the deed. We know that child-rearing books in the seventeenth and eighteenth centuries typically were aimed at fathers, but we are less sure whether fathers followed what the books said, or if they even read them. The problem we confront is that no one has yet carried out a full-scale historical study of fatherhood during this early period.

THE REVOLUTIONARY AND INDUSTRIAL ERA

What happened next in the history of the western European strain of American fatherhood is that it modernized. I am not talking here about the modernization that occurred during the Machine Age, but the modernization that occurred over a hundred years before, during the late eighteenth and early nineteenth centuries: the modernization of fatherhood wrought by the Enlightenment and the Industrial Revolution.[23]

The Enlightenment was a philosophical movement originating in England and France that emphasized rational (i.e., scientific) thinking, individual freedom, and democratic rule. The Industrial Revolution was a technological and economic metamorphosis, also with roots in western Europe, that typically is associated with the invention of machines and steam-powered tools and with the rise of mass production.

The manifold effects of the Enlightenment and the Industrial Revolution on American fatherhood were profound. It was the Enlightenment, of course, that provided the intellectual impetus behind both the French and the American Revolutions. But it was the Enlightenment, too, that instigated a revolution of sorts in child-rearing prescriptions, initially in England and France, and later in the new United States. John Locke's *Essay Concerning Human Understanding* (1690) and Jean-Jacques Rousseau's *Emile* (1762), for example, were two books that were popular in the late 1700s; both awakened the colonists to a variety of "illuminating" child-rearing notions. "Drawing on Locke's view of the child's mind as a *tabula rasa*, or 'blank slate' which could be imprinted in an infinite variety of ways, and on Rousseau's conception of children as naturally social and affectionate," say historians Steven Mintz and Susan Kellogg, "novelists and child-rearing experts told their readers that the primary object of child rearing was not to instill submission to authority but to develop a child's conscience and self-government." [24]

One effect of the new child-rearing philosophy was that the culture of fatherhood became more egalitarian. Whereas before fathers were expected to rule with a stern hand, now they were instructed to be more sensitive to the needs and interests of their live-in constituents. What this meant for the conduct of fatherhood is that men who were exposed to the new philosophy deferred to their children more. (Today, we might say that they became more "permissive.") Patriarchal fatherhood was not eliminated, by any means, but it did lose some of its edge. Books, toys, and games designed specifically for children also became more commonplace, and charting children's psychological as well as physical growth assumed greater importance. [25]

The Enlightenment and the Industrial Revolution also altered the relationship that older sons had with their fathers. Caught up in the excitement of a successful rebellion, some sons chose to challenge paternal authority in order to gain earlier control of their fathers' estates. Others opted to strike out on their own, lured by the commercial opportunities that industrialization had spawned. [26]

As important as these changes were, perhaps the most important effect that the Industrial Revolution had on fatherhood was that it shifted *where* fathers worked. Instead of laboring in or near their homes, men began to commute to jobs, leaving wives and mothers alone to care for children. Gone, was the ubiquitous patriarch. In his place was the wage earner who was absent much of the day. The role of "good economic provider" had arrived for men, and Standard North American Fatherhood had taken root. [27]

In time, fathers became "absent" from their children in more ways than one. Previously, men almost always had been awarded custody of their children after a divorce. With the coming of the Enlightenment and the Industrial Revolution, however, judges began to rule against men in custody suits, especially when the children involved were in their "tender years" (infancy and toddlerhood). By the end of the nineteenth century, the reversal was almost complete, with "the great majority" of cases being ruled in the mother's favor.[28]

The fact that the interests of the children were being taken into account at all reflected significant changes in child-rearing philosophy. Judges may have been concerned about the impact of divorce on the emotional life of children, because ministers and advice givers in the 1800s increasingly were saying that the first three years of life were crucial to a child's development. The greater emphasis given to infancy and toddlerhood had the effect of elevating the mother's parental stature, since women all along had been responsible for young children.[29] Similarly, when the prescriptive child-rearing literature in the nineteenth century began to place more value on persuasion and reward rather than on coercion and punishment, the mother's position in child rearing was strengthened, since women were believed to be better skilled than men in the emotional realm. Men, it was felt, could *exact* obedience from children by using corporal punishment and other punitive methods, but women could *entice* obedience with love, sympathy, and understanding.[30]

Although a number of books on the importance of the emotional bond between mothers and children began to appear after the war, with women increasingly being asked to teach the new nation's youth the "proper republican" values,[31] it was not until the 1830s and 1840s that we begin to see an institutionalized set of beliefs—an ideology, if you will—exulting the joys of motherhood.[32] The new set of beliefs made good parenting not only critical to a child's welfare and America's future, but also the cornerstone of a woman's happiness. Reflecting the change in attitude were a host of new magazines focused on the home and family and aimed specifically at women.[33] Because the magazines were relatively inexpensive, they helped to disseminate the motherhood ideology to Americans of lesser means. (The magazine industry played a similar role in the modernization of fatherhood during the Machine Age.)

If we look beyond the child-rearing literature, we find evidence to suggest that the motherhood ideology was part of a larger tapestry. Personal and public writings in the nineteenth century refer to the importance of motherhood, to be sure. But many, if not most, also stressed something more encompassing, something that the moral entrepreneurs at the time called "True Womanhood." According to historian Barbara Welter, "The attributes of True Womanhood, by which a woman judged herself and was judged by her husband, her neighbors, and society could be divided into four cardinal virtues—piety, purity, submissiveness, and domesticity. Put them all together and they spelled mother, daughter, sister, wife— woman. Without them, no matter whether there was fame, achievement, or wealth, all was ashes. With them she was promised happiness and power."[34]

And men? Well, while women were being placed at the center of the family constellation, men, it seems, were being moved to the periphery. At least this is the impression that we get from the child-rearing literature, which increasingly spoke to mothers, and only mothers. If and when fathers were mentioned in the tracts, it was often in reference to their "economic provider" role or to their responsibilities as the family "head."[35] Every now and then, fathers would be told to participate in child care so as to lighten their wives' burden. But these admonishments, if they communicated anything, demonstrated just how peripheral fathers had become in the writings.[36] Thus, whereas in colonial times, mothers were the ones who deserved not to be "exempted," now fathers were the ones who were asked to "pitch in."

Let me stop here for a moment to emphasize two points. The first is that the Enlightenment and the Industrial Revolution did not transform American fatherhood overnight or in a tidy manner. Whether we are talking about this social transformation or any other, the end of one stage always blends with the beginning of another, and different segments of society undergo transitions at different moments and at different speeds. Second, the nineteenth century, without a doubt, was a period of rapid industrialization, but it should not be forgotten that even the people who lived in the largest cities did not have the instantaneous communication and mass transportation to which we are accustomed today. There were no automobiles, no radios, no televisions; in short, no mechanisms for quickly and efficiently creating a nationwide· popular culture. Stating it in the reverse, there was considerable room for diversity, with different pockets of people pursuing their own agendas, seemingly oblivious to what others might be doing miles away.[37] It should come as no surprise, therefore, that "our understanding of nineteenth-century fathers is clouded with contradictions."[38] The simple truth is that the nineteenth century was a very contradictory time.

Clearly, then, the above description of events neglects some important subtleties. For example, nineteenth-century working class women would be less exposed to the "economic provider" father model as well as the motherhood ideology and the cult of True Womanhood because they would be less inclined to read the various child-rearing tracts and more likely to be employed outside the home.[39] Also, we should remember that many women in the nineteenth century, both working class and middle class, if not employed outside the home, were still employed inside the home, producing vegetables and fruits in the family garden, pigs and chickens in the yard, and a variety of medicines and cleansers in the kitchen.[40] Finally, we should remember that America may have been in the throes of industrialization in the nineteenth century, but "as late as 1900, nearly two-thirds of all American families earned their living from the land." Thus, for much of the 1800s, "two systems of work, production on the farm or in the household and production in the factory co-existed."[41]

Nineteenth-century men also were more diverse than my account suggests. On the farm and in the city, one might find any number of fathers who maintained strong emotional ties to their children, interacted with them on a regular basis, and were important sources of guidance and solace.[42] Research shows, too, that during the Civil War, fathers traveled great distances to "render aid and comfort" to their wounded and dying sons. While it might be expected that the war would intensify father-son feelings, it is still surprising (given what was being written in books and magazines) to find such intimacy coming from the male side of the nineteenth-century gender "divide." Thus, in spite of the shifts in the culture of fatherhood that placed men on the outside looking in, some nineteenth-century fathers remained "intimately intertwined" with their children.[43] We should be careful also not to limit our definition of child care to face-to-face tending, for in doing so, we neglect the fact that economic tending is also a form of care.[44] Factory-working fathers, in other words, may have been physically absent more than farm-working fathers, but they still could be psychologically present in their children's lives.

Do these qualifications undermine the proposition that fathers in the nineteenth century generally were less involved in child rearing than were fathers in the two centuries before? I would say no. The qualifications help us to understand that social change is often gradual and uneven, and they awaken us to the complexity of family life, but they do not negate the basic fact that the Enlightenment and the Industrial Revolution ultimately reshaped men's relationships with children.[45]

THE PROGRESSIVE ERA

Toward the end of the nineteenth and the beginning of the twentieth centuries, America became more urbanized and factory oriented, which helped to reinforce the economic provider role.[46] Interestingly enough, around the same time, a new—and, on the surface at least, dissenting— set of expectations for fathers started to emerge.

Aimed primarily at the middle class, the new scripts essentially said that in addition to supporting their families via their jobs, men should also support their families by assuming a larger share of housework and child care. This was not the first time, of course, that fathers had been asked to do more than simply be breadwinners. But it was the first time since the economic provider role had become paramount that men had been asked, on more than an individual basis, to pull a "second shift" when they got home.[47] The ingredients for the new configuration, in other words, were already present; the difference now was in the sequencing and propor- tioning of those ingredients.

Masculine Domesticity and Domestic Masculinity

What exactly was the new "recipe" for men? Historian Margaret Marsh has tried to describe it, and has even given it a name: *masculine domes- ticity*. Masculine domesticity, she admits, is elusive:

> Masculine domesticity is difficult to define; in some ways, it is easier to say what it was *not* than what it was. It was not equivalent to feminism. It was not an equal sharing of all household duties. Nor did it extend to the belief that men and women ought to have identical opportunities in the larger society. It was, however, a model of behavior in which fathers agreed to take on increased responsibility for some of the day-to-day tasks of bringing up children and spent their time away from work in playing with their sons and daughters, teaching them, taking them on trips. A domestic man also made his wife, rather than his male cronies, his regular companion on evenings out. And while he might not dust the mantel or make the bed except in special circumstances, he would take a significantly greater interest in the details of running the house- hold and caring for the children than his father had been expected to do."[48]

Thus, more so than before, popular magazines admonished men for failing to pay sufficient attention to their children ("father and son [should] . . . take their social enjoyments *en famille*," said one author in 1906). Increasingly, fathers were asked to "chum up" with their charges, especially with their sons (some might say that the founding of the Boy Scouts in 1910 was one concrete illustration of this shift). Kate Wiggen, who eventually went on to write *Rebecca of Sunnybrook Farm,* but who started her professional career around the turn of the century as a kinder- garten teacher, reportedly asked her male students to participate in "doll's day," and taught the rudiments of fatherhood by having the boys rock a toy infant to sleep. Wiggen wrote a widely circulated teaching manual outlining these and other techniques, which she said were designed to instill "the father spirit" in young males. Bernarr Macfadden, who owned the *New York Daily News* as well as *True Story* and *True Romance* (popular periodicals), published *Manhood and Marriage,* in which he insisted that men should be present at the birth of their children. "Whenever you find a man who is without an innate love for children," said Macfadden, "you may rest assured that there is something wrong with his character."[49]

As to the impact of masculine domesticity on fathers, there is some disagreement. Historian E. Anthony Rotundo contends in his book *American Manhood* that masculine domesticity spelled trouble for men: "Within the governing metaphors of gender, masculine domesticity was a contradiction in terms. It presumed that men could—and should—carry out female tasks for which their male nature did not fit them. If a man was spending more time at home exercising the skills which supposedly belonged to women, what kind of a man was he?"[50] Marsh, on the other hand, believes that masculine domesticity did not necessarily imply a conflict: "The concepts of masculine domesticity and 'manliness' were in many ways more complementary than antithetical"[51]

Who is right? They both may be, because each may be talking about two different socially constructed realities. An interesting transposition puts the controversy in some perspective. In the same book where Marsh's essay appears, there is another essay that also discusses masculine domesticity, but uses a different term : *domestic masculinity.* (Why the adjectives are inverted is not made clear.)[52]

Masculine domesticity. Domestic masculinity. Two nomenclatures, seemingly identical—and yet not. If we grammatically dissect the phrase *masculine domesticity,* we would say that it means "doing domestic activities in a masculine way." If we do the same for *domestic masculinity,* however, we come up with another translation. Now it appears that we are talking about "domesticating someone who is masculine." This is more than a play on words. In early-twentieth-century American culture, doing domestic activities in a masculine way meant doing child care and housework in a manly or virile manner. Fathers taking their sons hunting for the sake of instilling the masculine virtues of aggressiveness, competitiveness, and dominion over nature would be exhibiting masculine domesticity. So would fathers who did housework the macho way, or the military way, or the corporate capitalist way, since all of these imply either a manly disposition or a manly world. But domesticating someone who is masculine is something else. According to the dictionary, "to domesticate" denotes essentially one of three things: to bring into the home, to civilize, or to tame. If we are talking about men spending more time with their families, then we are talking about one definition of domestic masculinity. There is evidence to indicate that around the turn of the century, American middle-class men were less likely than those before them to spend evenings "out with the guys," preferring to pursue their leisure with their wives and children.[53] If we are talking about men becoming refined, then we are talking about a second definition of domestic masculinity. After abandoning their male cronies, men did increase their participation in couple-oriented literary societies and science clubs. Finally, if we are talking about men having their "native wildness" subdued, then we are talking about a third definition of domestic masculinity. To the extent that child care and housework were seen as docile activities, the fact that men were playing with their children more could be interpreted as a sign that they were doing things that were alien to them; that is, alien to their very being.

So, let's pose the question again: Is masculine domesticity a contradiction in terms? No. Or at least not as much as domestic masculinity is. Masculine domesticity valorizes masculinity. It says that men have a "special something" garnered from nature or nurture, or both, that allows them to make a unique and, depending on your perspective, positive contribution to an activity. Domestic masculinity, however, communicates another message. It can be—and has been—trouble for men, if by trouble we mean an increase in men's feelings of alienation and anomie, and a decrease in their privilege and power. When domestic is equated with feminine, and feminine is seen as the antithesis of masculine, the contradiction is especially pronounced, for then staying home, joining coed literary clubs, and spending time with one's children are defined as emasculating activities, and the question, "What kind of man would do such a thing?" is more likely to come up. In short, Marsh is correct. There is little to no contradiction between domesticity and manliness, if we are talking about masculine domesticity. But Rotundo is also correct, in that there is the potential for contradiction, if we are talking about men's domestication, or domestic masculinity.

Separating masculine domesticity from domestic masculinity is important because it allows us to see that in the late nineteenth and early twentieth centuries, there were not just two, but three expectations for middle class men. The first centered on the economic provider role. By far the most dominant, it said that men should be a family's sole, or at least primary, wage earner. The second was masculine domesticity, which I suggest we define as the norm that men should interject their manliness into domestic work. The third was domestic masculinity, or the maxim that men's manliness needed to be placed under house arrest (at least in the evening), civilized, or tamed. Bear in mind that these expectations are not mutually exclusive (that is, the presence of one does not preclude the presence of another). Hence, it is possible to have periods of high masculine domesticity and high domestic masculinity, and other periods of low masculine domesticity and low domestic masculinity. Similarly, the emphasis given to economic provision may wax and wane.

Separating masculine domesticity from domestic masculinity allows us to view with additional clarity the lumping and splitting process that characterizes the politics of parenthood described in chapter 1. New Fatherhood, besides associating men with the domestic sphere, calls into question the connection between fatherhood and masculinity and the supposed (for some) disconnection between fatherhood and motherhood. Thus, the referents for fatherhood and motherhood, masculinity and femininity, and the domestic and nondomestic spheres become at one moment blurred and at another moment resolute, as various interest groups work to give meaning to their world—and to their lives. When we get to our discussion of fatherhood during the Machine Age, we shall see this sense-making process up close.

Democratization, Economic Fluctuation, and Suburbanization

The roots of the economic provider role may be clear from what I have said earlier about the impact of industrialization, but where, it may be asked, did the ideals of masculine domesticity and domesticity masculinity come from? The answer is that both, in part, were outgrowths of "enlightened" efforts to "democratize" marriage.

The rules for a democratic marriage were that couples should be lifelong friends as well as procreators and coprotectors of the young. Hence, "mutual esteem, mutual friendship, [and] mutual confidence" were defined as the hallmarks of a good union, and "personal happiness" and "love" were its by-products.[54] As an ideal, democratic marriage has had a long history, but the concept did not begin to gain a significant footing in America until the early to mid 1800s; and, as a *practice,* it did not become institutionalized, even among the urban middle class, until the end of the nineteenth and beginning of the twentieth centuries.[55] Democratic marriage, as both an ideal and as a practice, contributed to the development of masculine domesticity and domestic masculinity because it raised questions about the permeability of the boundaries between men's and women's roles.[56] The more the middle class viewed marriage as a partnership, the more it pondered the role of women in the masculine world (outside the home) and the role of men in the feminine world (inside the home). Contemplating these role reversals did not mean domestic equality (or tranquillity, for that matter), but it did mean growing expectations that men would help more with the kids and around the house.[57]

Still, we may ask, If both masculine domesticity and domestic masculinity grew out of ideals that had been around for decades, how do we account for their appearance at the end of the nineteenth century rather than before? Marsh suggests that two factors were involved: one was economic; the other was ecological.

In the business world of the 1800s, American middle-class men, for the most part, were entrepreneurs and independent professionals whose financial situation often changed from one year to the next. By the end of the 1800s, however, increasing numbers of male workers were executives employed by companies large enough to offer stable incomes. The security of a predictable salary gave many fathers the freedom to focus more attention on their families, to be present in both body and mind for their children and wives. Interestingly enough, this financial security was not without its ups and downs. From 1873 to 1895, the entire Western world went through an economic slump, and then, from 1896 to 1906, there was a period of great prosperity.[58] The fact that masculine domesticity and domestic masculinity would emerge under conditions of both boom and bust was a precursor of what was to come. The modernization of fatherhood during the Machine Age also witnessed affluence (in the 1920s) and misfortune (in the 1930s); and both, in their own unique ways, fueled the reconfiguration.

The ecological factor that Marsh spoke of was suburbanization. Some scholars have argued that suburbanization made men's commute longer, and that this resulted in their being torn from their families.[59] Marsh suggests, however, that just the opposite was true; suburban living promoted family togetherness. She notes, for example, that commuting time between work and home at the turn of the century was not as long as one might think, typically under a half hour by train or trolley. Also, the architecture of the suburbs provided a setting wherein masculine domesticity (and domestic masculinity) could be played out. Family rooms, backyards, and community parks all offered spaces where fathers could interact with their families.[60]

Fathercraft and Mothercraft

At least one other factor contributed to, if not the emergence of, certainly the receptivity to, masculine domesticity and domestic masculinity at the turn of the century. That factor was the mothercraft movement. The mothercraft movement professed that mothering (child rearing, broadly defined) was an important occupation—nay, a profession—to which women should aspire and of which they should be proud. It also said that good mothering resulted not from instinct but from serious study.

What distinguished the mothercraft movement from other types of parent education was the emphasis given to protracted and methodical learning. Becoming a proficient parent, in other words, was assumed to be so difficult that it demanded not only an openness to professional advice but also a long-term commitment to formal schooling. Thus, an important consequence of the mothercraft movement was the creation of a child study industry—weekly discussion groups, annual conferences and symposia, professional lyceums and training institutes, college and university curricula, seminars and textbooks, licensing boards and a host of experts, all dedicated to instructing people in child rearing.

Placed in a historical context, the mothercraft movement can be seen as an outgrowth of the child-saving movement that had begun in the late nineteenth century. Early on, the child-saving movement had stressed moral reform, or "the manipulation of the circumstances of child life through public policy." It was during this time that "the juvenile court, the organized municipal playground, the reformatory, and the public school" were all instituted.[61] Beginning around the second decade of the twentieth century, however, the child-saving movement entered a scientific phase, stressing "the use of the human sciences and technologies to investigate children." From this point on, child study took on a decidedly technocratic hue. The mothercraft movement was part of this new phase.[62]

The term *mothercraft* was coined by Mary L. Read, who also founded the first American School of Mothercraft in 1911 (in New York City). As she described it in her book *The Mothercraft Manual,* the purpose of the school was "to work out experimentally a training course for educated women." Students spent their time "in a home atmosphere, under home conditions, using the household for their practice work, caring for resident babies and children, educating and training them in the course of the day's regime, and receiving their own training in personality and techniques as well as in theory." The school also provided "extension classes" for "young mothers, brides, and engaged young women."[63] Noting that elementary and secondary schools were beginning to offer courses in "domestic science," Read felt that it would not be long before universities began to grant "M.A. and Ph.D. degrees in mothercraft and fathercraft, as well as in philology, astronomy, history, or other more consequential branches of learning."[64]

Fathercraft? Yes. One of the ironies of the mothercraft movement was that in order to professionalize mothering it also had to acknowledge fathering. The reason was simple: If child rearing depended not on biology but on socialization, then anyone could learn how to do it—even fathers. But if anyone could learn how to do it, why should mothers see child rearing as their special profession? Maternal instinct made women naturally unique, but it also negated the need for child study. Mothercraft created "a branch of learning" that placed it alongside "more consequential" pursuits, to use Read's terminology, but it also diminished, if only to a degree, the prestige that women gained from being society's biologically chosen caregivers—and so on, back and forth.

What to do? One strategy that the leaders of the mothercraft movement used to ensure that mothers would occupy a higher professional plane was to define fathercraft as an adjunct or subsidiary activity. Consider, again, how Read approached the subject. Mothercraft, she said, was "the skillful, practical doing of all that is involved in the nourishing and training of children, in a sympathetic, happy, religious spirit"; it was "mothering . . . made intelligent and efficient and joyous." Fathercraft, on the other hand, was something else:

> What of fathercraft? Every child has two parents, equal in responsi-
> bility for his heredity and likewise for his rearing. Fathers could hardly
> be expected ordinarily to be versed in the intricacies of clothing, feed-
> ing, and bathing the baby. But why should not every man understand
> the principles of hygiene and foods as a matter of his general knowl-
> edge quite as much as for cooperation with the mother in the children's
> regime? Why should he not with equal zest make a study of growth and
> development during childhood? Even more, why should he not be inti-
> mately acquainted with child psychology and the fundamental prin-
> ciples of child training and education, that he may understand his own
> children and cooperate sympathetically in their upbringing?[65]

Fathercraft, in other words, was intended not to be an equivalent to mothercraft but its complement. Whereas mothercraft involved "doing

[it] all," fathercraft meant "cooperat[ing] with the mother." Whereas mothercraft was supposed to consume a woman's time and identity, father-craft was conceptualized as an avocation. Men, in short, were being told that they should be mothers' helpers.

What appeared on the surface, then, to be an open invitation to fathers to become partners in the child-rearing process was, from another angle, something less. Aided by the experts and in support of the experts, moth-ers would be the licensed, in-home authorities on matters pertaining to children; fathers would be the parental "cooperators," women's assistants. Mothers would have the time, and be encouraged to make the time, to attend child study classes and read child study books. Fathers, because of their jobs and because some experts seemed intent on directing their messages to women, would remain outsiders.

The fact that fathers were not being asked to share fully in child care served to reinforce the attitude that mothers should be the primary car-egivers. Yet, to look at the fathercraft movement (for in time, it became a movement of its own) only in these terms is to overlook other things that also were important. No doubt, many child study groups were adver-tised—sometimes subtly, sometimes not—as "for mothers only" clubs, so even if a father wanted to sit in on a lecture or discussion, he might think twice about it. (Why go, if you are not invited?) But it is also true that, while some in the child study industry may have attempted to relegate fathers to the hinterlands, not all fathers were eager or willing to be sent there. A number of fathers demanded to be let in—demanded access to the mothers' classes or study groups, or demanded classes and groups of their own. Mothers, too, were not always intent on excluding husbands and often were instrumental in opening up the study groups to men. (Ex-perts as well were not all of one mind on the subject.) Then, there is the matter of instinct versus socialization as the source of proper parenthood. Socialization *for* parenthood made knowledge *about* parenthood publicly available and open to discussion and debate. Thus, men who had the op-portunity, or who created the opportunity, to learn the industry's rules and maxims had the chance to become bona fide players in the child-rearing game. As for the men who did not actively participate in the fathercraft movement, they were not necessarily rendered impotent. Just because a woman happened to attend a child study group and bring home a child-rearing idea did not mean that the idea automatically was made part of the family's consensual world. A lot depended on the power struc-ture in the home ; the more patriarchal that structure, the more influence the father exerted, however uninformed about the latest child-rearing fad he may have been.[66]

AND THEN CAME THE MACHINE AGE

There is little doubt that, from end of the nineteenth to the beginning of the twentieth century, masculine domesticity (and its counterpart, domestic masculinity) "cropped up," as Marsh puts it, in a variety of places.[67] A book or article here, a slight change in recreational patterns there, provide evidence that something new was in the wind, but collectively they do not a social transformation make. Marsh, I suspect, would agree. Her main point is that historians need to pay more attention to the domestic scripts that in the late nineteenth and early twentieth century were *just beginning* to be applied to middle-class men.

The scripts changed quickly, however, once the Machine Age arrived. During the 1920s and 1930s, popular magazine articles incorporating discussions of fatherhood proliferated; child study groups for men multiplied (though they still would not be the norm). Parenting books expanded their coverage of fathers' paternal responsibilities; caring for, not simply playing with, infants was as likely as not to be among the jobs prescribed. Father's Day became an American holiday. Last but not least, mothers changed; influenced by an expanding coterie of experts and by a shifting economy, mothers became more accepting of, and more excited about, fathers' inclusion in children's affairs and their own diminished (but still significant) parental fiefdom.

Throughout all of this, both masculine domesticity and domestic masculinity had a strong effect—but not in equal measure, and not at the same time. In the 1920s, domestic masculinity—or *the father as pal*—gained center stage. This version of New Fatherhood emphasized the importance of being a "daddy"; of being a chum, a companion, a playmate, nonautocratic and willing to get down on his child's level. In the 1930s, however, masculine domesticity—in the guise of *the father as male role model*—came more to the fore, not replacing domestic masculinity but moving it to the side and maybe one square back. This version of New Fatherhood emphasized the importance of being a manly guide not only to sons but also to daughters, an active parent whose job it was to counterbalance the presumably emotionally laden and potentially destructive influence of women.[68]

As significant as masculine domesticity and domestic masculinity were during the Machine Age, at no point did these two scripts ever supplant the *father as economic provider* as the principal precept for men to follow. Nonetheless, it would be a mistake to assume that because this role was the dominant of the three, the other two were inconsequential. Just as the tint of a paint is altered with even small amounts of other shades, once masculine domesticity and domestic masculinity were added to the mixture, the color of fatherhood was forever changed.

3   Fatherhood and the Baby Doctors

> This book is intended to help mothers and fathers in taking
> care of babies.
>
> From the 1942 edition of *Infant Care,*
> published by the Children's Bureau

At what point a "modern" or "scientific" approach to child rearing filtered into the American consciousness is not entirely clear, but most historians identify Luther Emmet Holt's 1894 book *The Care and Feeding of Children: A Catechism for the Use of Mothers and Children's Nurses*[1] as the first "to distill the knowledge of child science and technology" to the general public.[2] A cofounder of the *Archives of Pediatrics* and a key figure in the creation of the American Pediatric Society, Holt was one of the most respected teachers in the field of medicine at the turn of century.[3]

Although the subtitle suggests that *The Care and Feeding of Children* was written primarily for mothers and secondarily for nurses, the reverse was actually true. "When in the fall of 1889 the Practical Training School for Nursery Maids was opened in connection with the Babies' Hospital of New York," Holt reported, "the need was soon felt for some simple manual to put into the hands of nurses. None could be found which fulfilled the requirements of simplicity, brevity, and exactness with reference to matters of infant feeding and nursery hygiene."[4] That the book might be of some use to parents seemed almost an afterthought to Holt: "This catechism is now, at the request of many friends, published with the hope that it may serve a useful purpose in other institutions where similar schools for training may be established. At the same time, it is thought that it may be of value to many mothers in the care of their own children, or a book which they [mothers, again] may safely put into the hands of the ordinary (untrained) child's nurse."[5]

How much attention did Holt give to fathers in *The Care and Feeding of Children?* None at all. Not a single reference was made to fathers anywhere in the book. The same can be said for the 1897, 1903, 1906, 1909, 1912, and 1914 editions. Indeed, the only acknowledgment that fathers received, beginning with the second edition, was where Holt dealt with the question of when children could be expected to talk. His reply: "Generally at one year a child can say 'papa' and 'mamma' or other single words."[6]

Although there were no significant modifications in the book with respect to fatherhood, there was one qualification inserted in the second edition and repeated through the seventh that is worth mentioning. In the first edition, Holt said that *The Care and Feeding of Children* was a "simple manual" that "emphasize[d] strongly the essentials." It may not have gone into "many minor details which would have increased materially the size of the book," but it still was considered fairly comprehensive.[7] For the second edition, however, Holt added the following caveat: "In the matters discussed it is the needs of the well child, not the sick one, which have been considered. The well child must in the great majority of cases be left to the care of the mother or nurse for whose guidance and assistance these pages are intended. For direction in matters of illness, however, no mother should depend upon any manual, but upon the advice of a physician."[8]

Warning readers that the book was not a cure-all might be viewed as both prudent and predictable, just what one would expect from a responsible doctor. Holt's statement, however, must be viewed in relationship to the times. In the late nineteenth century, pediatrics was not the multibillion dollar industry that it is today but a fledgling discipline in search of recognition and legitimation.[9] Thus, by telling women to turn to a physician "in matters of illness," Holt was doing more than offering sound advice, he was promoting a new field. Eventually, pediatricians would become members of the ruling elite in the child care industry, experts not only on the physical care of infants but on emotional care as well. But from the turn of the century to the beginning of World War II, they would be engaged in a battle of sorts for the right to be the master architects of America's child- rearing agenda.

And here really is where my part of the story begins. Not with families, per se, but with the medical community and its efforts to create a science of pediatric care.

THE CHILDREN'S BUREAU

The most prolific producer of scientific child-rearing advice during the early twentieth century was not, as you might expect, a huge New York publishing house but a small, by Washington standards, government agency known as the United States Children's Bureau. Established in 1912 by an act of Congress and subsumed under the Department of Labor, the Children's Bureau was mandated to "investigate and report . . . upon all matters pertaining to the welfare of children and child life among all classes of our people." [10]

From 1912 to 1929, the Children's Bureau probably did more than any other organization in the country to define the direction of child welfare work. Thereafter, its influence began to wane, as physicians and psychologists increasingly demanded and were given control of government policy pertaining to children. [11] (The Children's Bureau still exists, only now it is housed under the Department of Health and Human Services.) [12] Yet, through the good times and the bad, the Children's Bureau continued to revise and distribute its child-rearing tracts. [13]

Two individuals, Florence Kelley and Lillian Wald, generally are given credit for bringing the Children's Bureau to life. Kelley was a child-labor activist who in 1905 had proposed that a national commission for children be created and that it be charged primarily with the study of infant mortality. [14] Wald was a nurse and the founder of the Henry Street Settlement House in New York City. It was Wald who in 1906 first suggested the idea of a bureau for children to President Theodore Roosevelt. [15]

Kelley and Wald's ideas met considerable resistance at the start. Some were of the opinion that a federal agency devoted to child welfare was altogether unnecessary; that the states and not the federal government were in the best position to deal with the concerns of children. Others thought that much of what the Children's Bureau would be doing was being done already by existing agencies (e.g., the Bureau of Education and the National Child Labor Committee). Still others felt that infant mortality and other problems were "medical matters," to be handled not by the government but by the for-profit medical community, particularly physicians.

Kelley and Wald's plan was at something of an impasse, but in 1909 it got the push it needed when hundreds of delegates convened at a White House Conference on the Care of Dependent Children and voted to petition Congress "to create a federal bureau concerned with 'child-caring work' and 'the needs of children throughout the United States.'" President Roosevelt, soon to leave office, "gave [the delegates] a rousing speech and endorsed their sentiments in a special message to Congress." [16] With the president now taking a stand, Children's Bureau lobbyists picked up support from women's clubs, parent-teacher associations, trade unions, and civic groups throughout the nation.[17] The effect was not immediate. It took three more years to convince Congress to pass a bill authorizing the agency, but on 9 April 1912, President William H. Taft signed the Children's Bureau Act into law, and on 23 August 1912, the Children's Bureau began operations.

Although the Children's Bureau generally was forced to operate with limited funds (making do with minimal resources may have been part of the compromise worked out to get the bill passed), it managed to accomplish a host of reforms, largely because of the tireless efforts of its early leaders—or "Chiefs," as they were called.[18] First there was Julia Lathrop, "a political unknown on Capitol Hill," who was a graduate of Vassar College and long-time resident of Hull House in Chicago (and a close friend of Jane Addams, Hull House's founder). Lathrop served as the Chief of the Children's Bureau from 1912 to 1921.[19]

Then there was Grace Abbott. A graduate of Grand Island College and the University of Chicago (M.A. in Political Science), Abbott was active in the women's rights movement, had considerable experience in social service, and had served as the Director of the Child Labor Division of the Children's Bureau since 1917. Like her predecessor, Abbott also had been associated with Hull House. Abbott's tenure ran from 1921 to 1934.

Next there was Katherine Lenroot. Lenroot was a graduate of the University of Wisconsin and had been a Children's Bureau staff member almost from the beginning. A strong advocate for children's rights during the Depression and Second World War, Lenroot ran the Children's Bureau from 1934 to 1951.

The fact that the Children's Bureau was headed by women, and primarily staffed by women, is noteworthy on three counts. First, that a government agency would be controlled by women before the passage of the Nineteenth Amendment in 1920, giving women the right to vote, is a testimony to the strength of the women's movement in the early twentieth century.[20] On the other hand, that the agency was devoted to children's concerns underscores the social connection being made at the time between children and women in the early 1900s. Conservatives and feminists alike generally "considered the interests of women and children to be identical."[21] Third, that the Children's Bureau was led by women put the agency at a power disadvantage in government circles. Operating within the patriarchal Washington establishment, the Chief and staff of the Children's Bureau periodically were reminded—sometimes subtly, sometimes not—that they were to tread gingerly, or else they would be tread upon.[22]

Infant Care

What was the official attitude of the Children's Bureau toward fathers? One way to answer this question, as we did with respect to Luther Emmet Holt, is to look at the way men were portrayed within the pages of a publication. The question is, which publication? The bureau put out so many.

If centrality to the bureau is a guide, we would have to select *Infant Care*. Issued in 1914, *Infant Care* was not only the first child-rearing manual that the Children's Bureau published but its most popular, undergoing revisions in 1921, 1929, 1931, 1938, 1940, and 1942.[23] If research precedence is a guide, we would still choose *Infant Care*, because *Infant Care*, more than any other manual, is what scholars have relied upon when they have written about the agency's influence on child-rearing philosophy.[24] If we turn precedence around, the absence of previous investigations also would lead us to choose *Infant Care*. While there have been scholars who have talked about how fathers were depicted in the manual, no scholar to my knowledge has systematically compared the way fathers and mothers were described, nor has anyone that I know of gone to the trouble of analyzing how men were characterized in *Infant Care* from one edition to the next. This is more than a little odd. Historians of fatherhood seem to have assumed, a priori, that the most influential child-rearing manual of the early twentieth century was not worth examining. Having carried out the analysis, I would have to say I disagree. For within the first seven editions of *Infant Care* (from 1914 to 1942) may be found some of the best evidence of how the U.S. government both supported and suppressed the modernization of fatherhood.

The First Edition: 1914

The author of the first edition of *Infant Care* was Mary Mills West (or "Mrs. Max West," as the byline reads), "a graduate of the University of Minnesota . . . [and] a widowed mother of five who [had] turned to writing to support her family."[25] The ideas in the book, however, were not West's alone. Rather, as Julia Lathrop explained in the "Letter of Transmittal" to the Secretary of Labor (technically her boss), *Infant Care* was based on an "exhaustive study of the standard literature on the hygiene of infancy as well as consultations with physicians, nurses, and other specialists."[26]

The fact that the manual was based on the literature indicates the shift toward a scientific approach to child-rearing philosophy that was taking place in the child study industry. *Infant Care* was not the first manual to espouse this approach. (By most accounts, Holt's *The Care and Feeding of Children* was.) Nor was *Infant Care* the most ardent proponent of the approach; West, it seems, tried to steer a course midway between the scientific view (avowedly relying on Holt's book along the route) and "motherly common sense."[27] *Infant Care*, however, was the most widely read manual in this genre. Estimates indicate that 1.5 million copies of the first edition of *Infant Care* were distributed between 1914 and 1921, and that 17 million copies of the manual had been circulated by 1945.[28]

Note Lathrop's point that the first edition of *Infant Care* was based on "consultations with physicians, nurses, and other specialists." This statement was designed not only to lend credibility to the work, but to communicate that the Children's Bureau was not trying to step on anybody's professional toes. "There is no purpose to invade the field of the medical or nursing professions," added Lathrop, "but rather to furnish such statements regarding hygiene and normal living as every mother has a right to possess in the interest of herself and her children." Lathrop apparently had not forgotten the reservations that physicians had about the Children's Bureau when it was being debated in Congress.

Also note Lathrop's statement that *Infant Care* was designed to provide information that "every mother has a right to possess." The 1914 edition of *Infant Care*, like virtually every other child-rearing manual published at the time, was directed not to parents but to mothers (or, in Lathrop's words, "the average mother"). Here and there, the words *parent* or *parents* might be used; for example, Mary West said that "parents should make sure that [birth registration] . . . is not neglected." But when West turned her attention to the actual care of children, *mother* or *mothers* prevailed.[29]

As for fathers, they were not ignored entirely (as they were in Holt's book). When fathers were mentioned, however, the message that West conveyed was either that they should be as supportive as possible of their wives, or that they should stay out of the way: "The family, especially the husband, should realize how important it is to shield the nursing mother from *unnecessary* work and worry, and to provide her at intervals with the opportunity for rest and recreation."[30] She also said, "It is a regrettable fact that the few minutes of play that the father has when he gets home at night, which is often almost the only time he has with the child, may result in nervous disturbance of the baby and upset his regular habits." [31]

The Second Edition: 1921

The second edition of *Infant Care* was published in 1921 and was again written primarily by Mary West. In her letter of transmittal, Julia Lathrop noted that a Dr. Dorothy Reed Mendenhall had prepared the sections of the book on infant care and that an "advisory committee of pediatrists" (Dr. Howard Childs Carpenter, Dr. Julius Hess, and Dr. Richard Smith) had offered "valuable assistance." [32] (The word *pediatrist* may seem unusual, but that is what pediatricians often were called in the late nineteenth and early twentieth centuries.) [33] In contrast to her comments in the first edition, Lathrop excluded any reference to the bureau's invasion of other professions. Given the efforts by male physicians to control the Children's Bureau, it is not at all surprising that the three members of the advisory committee were all men, and that nurses had been dropped as consultants on the project.

The 1921 edition was very similar to the 1914 edition. (In subsequent revisions, the bureau acknowledged this fact.) There were, however, a few changes pertaining to fatherhood that deserve mention. One was the deletion of the sentence about fathers coming home at night, wanting to play with the baby, and upsetting the baby's "regular habits." No explanation was given as to why the sentence was cut; it simply was not there anymore. [34] Another occurred in the section on what to do if the baby was sick. The first edition minced few words on who was to be in charge if and when the baby was not well—it was to be the mother. The second edition repeated this point and, if anything, emphasized it even more: first, by beginning its section on "The Sick Baby" with the statement, "A mother should know the ordinary symptoms of disease in order to decide when it is necessary to send for a doctor" (the rationale given is that "she usually acts as nurse"); and second, by adding to the section on "The Sick Baby" a subsection boldly labeled "What a Mother Should Note." [35] Labeling the subsection resulted in the phrase being reproduced in the table of contents, thus establishing from the outset what the division of labor should be in times of illness. [36] It would seem, therefore, that the Children's Bureau was offering no more encouragement to fathers in 1921 than Holt had offered the decade before.

The Third Edition: 1929

The third edition of *Infant Care* was mailed to the Department of Labor on 4 October 1929—three weeks before the stock market crash and the onset of the Great Depression. The 1929 edition was a departure from the 1921 edition in a number of ways. First, author Mary Wells had been replaced by Dr. Martha M. Eliot, a physician who, at the time, was Director of Child Hygiene for the bureau and who, from 1951 to 1956, would serve as the bureau's Chief. Second, although Eliot probably did most, if not all, of the writing, the "advisory committee of pediatricians" (the same group of men who were cited in 1921) was given coauthor status: "This revision is the work of Dr. Martha M. Eliot . . . *and* of the bureau's advisory committee of pediatricians [my italics]."[37] Third, the 1929 edition relied heavily on behaviorism, the psychological theory of motivation that emphasizes conditioning and reinforcement schedules in habit formation (more on this last development in a moment).

That the new senior author of *Infant Care* would be a physician is hardly astonishing; nor is the fact that "the committee of pediatricians" would be given higher billing this time around. The Children's Bureau had been at odds with physicians since its inception, and it was perhaps inevitable, given the clout doctors had, that the medical establishment would prevail. The advisory medical committee that had "assisted" West in the preparation of the second edition of *Infant Care* actually had been brought in under pressure from physicians. The committee had wanted to replace West then, but was unsuccessful. It did, however, manage to have her name removed from the front cover. West, as one might expect, was hurt by the insinuation that she was not qualified to offer advice on child care. "[The committee] allows me nothing, save the ability to write simply and pleasingly," she said in a memo to Julia Lathrop. "I think there is a slight injustice in this attitude, for, after all, I had born five children, and as I am not a hopelessly feeble-minded woman I must have learned a few things for myself by that process. Also, everyone learns from others. Even doctors themselves."[38]

And now to behaviorism: What difference did it make? Behavioristic approaches to child care were the rage in America in the 1920s, being promulgated not only in professional journals and books but in the popular press as well. John Watson's scholarly treatise *Psychology from the Standpoint of a Behaviorist*, published in 1919 and revised in 1924 and 1929, was being read and debated by academicians, while his 1928 manual *Psychological Care of Infant and Child*, "dedicated [in all seriousness] to the first mother who brings up a happy child," was attracting the attention of many parents.[39] The Children's Bureau appears to have been quite taken by these events, because when we look at the 1929 edition of *Infant Care*, we see a manual thoroughly infused with behavioristic principles.[40]

The fact that behaviorism was popular in the 1920s is not the only factor that accounts for its influence on the bureau. From the first edition, *Infant Care* had pushed the idea that scheduling and habit formation were crucial to raising a happy and healthy baby. This reflected, in part, "the combination of science, efficiency, and sentiment" that characterized the women's movement during the Progressive era,[41] but it reflected something else, too. Reducing the care of the baby to "a system," as West phrased it, made considerable sense if the goal was to ensure, on the one hand, that children got basic, life-preserving care and, and on the other, that overworked mothers got a rest every once in while.[42] The rationalization and routinization of the parenting process in *Infant Care* was designed, in other words, to save lives. Behaviorism provided a scientific ideology for what the Children's Bureau had been advocating all along.

How, specifically, did the 1929 edition differ from the 1921 edition? In earlier editions, the idea that mothers should not be swayed by "superstition" but must rely on "the experts" was located around the middle of the book. In the 1929 edition, this point was made on the second page: "Sometimes a young mother has so much advice from earnest and well-meaning friends that she is bewildered. . . . The doctor should be the mother's guide, and this bulletin is intended to help *her* carry out *his* orders intelligently [my italics]." This was followed by the statement, "Baby care is a great art. It is the most important task any woman ever undertakes, and she should apply to this work the same diligence, intelligence, and sustained effort that she would give to the most exacting profession."[43]

With the exception of one small change, the same statement had appeared in the 1921 edition, but now it was in the beginning rather than in the middle of the book. This accentuated two key themes: (1) that baby care was "the woman's task," and (2) that it was a "profession." The one small change was that in the 1921 edition, the statement read, "Baby care is a great art and a great science." *And a great science.* For some reason, Abbott (and the committee) chose to delete this phrase in the 1929 edition. This would seem to suggest that the Children's Bureau had backed away from the scientific approach to child rearing. Then again, maybe it had not. Dr. Abbott et al. might have been trying to say that the *science* of child rearing was best left to the doctors, while the *art* of child rearing was the mother's purview. A mother could—indeed should—rely on science; she, however, could not pretend to be scientist herself. Thus, the "profession" of motherhood took "diligence, intelligence, and sustained effort" because the process of learning how to be a mother (from doctors) was hard work.

What about the father? What was his role? The 1921 edition of *Infant Care* had a picture of a baby on its cover. The 1929 edition replaced this picture with a drawing of a mother holding a child, which would suggest that fathers were being made even less central. The change on the cover, however, masked the changes that had occurred inside. Behaviorism, aside from providing an ideology for the Children's Bureau system of infant care, created a *larger* place for men in that system. Again, let's look at the text.

In keeping with behavioristic principles, a key feature of the 1929 edition of *Infant Care* was a series of "schedules for the baby's daily program and habit training." Because of the emphasis that behaviorism—and now *Infant Care*—gave to "absolute regularity and consistency" in the "formation of habits," the success of the system depended on the cooperation of all who came in contact with the baby.[44] If, for instance, the mother was trying to put the baby on a sleep schedule, and if this training entailed ignoring the baby when it cried, the principle of consistency dictated that the father also ignore the baby's crying. This is why, at the end of each schedule, there was the following maxim: "Parents must work together from the baby's birth to teach him good habits." Under behaviorism, in other words, fathers could still be nuisances, but they could not be ignored. *Behaviorism thus drew fathers into the family circle.* In symbolic recognition of this fact, the 1929 edition, the first to include pictures (again drawings) throughout the manual, saw fit to include a scene of a mother, daughter, *and* father looking at a baby lying in a bassinet. Other scenes appear here and there—some of babies, some of mothers taking their babies to the doctor—but the bassinet scene was the only one to include a father.

Although the father had acquired more duties in the infant care process, one rule remained unchanged: The mother still was expected to be in charge. The father thus may have become a cog in the system, but mother was the one who was supposed to set up the system and make sure that it worked. This was made all the more clear by the inclusion, for the first time, of a bibliography at the end of manual: "Selected Books of Interest to *Mothers*" [my italics].[45]

The coworker status of fathers also appears to have been limited to habit training. In matters outside the purview of behaviorism (e.g., matters pertaining to the baby's health), the father was presumed not to be a major figure. Hence, again, when the discussion turned to "The Sick Baby," it was the mother who was expected to keep track of the baby's normal skin color, bowel movements, and levels of activity, so that she could use this baseline to determine when the baby was not well; and it was the mother, too, who was expected to learn how to read a thermometer and to know what to do "before the doctor comes."

For the hundreds of thousands of parents who read *Infant Care* and took it to heart, the impact of behaviorism on the division of infant care in the home could be crucial, not simply because the father had to be included in the regimen, but also because child training now more closely resembled the corporate and manufacturing world to which men were accustomed.[46] In other words, behaviorism may have given fathers a certain amount of authority in matters pertaining to child rearing, which may have offset, to some degree at least, the segregation of men's and women's responsibilities that Watson also was promoting.[47]

The Fourth Edition: 1931

The fourth edition of *Infant Care* was published in 1931, and again was the work of Dr. Eliot and the committee of pediatricians.[48] Little was changed from the 1929 edition, but between 1931 and 1938, the fourth edition was reprinted several times (as earlier editions had been). The reprintings essentially followed the 1931 version (or 1929 version, since, as I said, the 1929 and 1931 editions were virtually identical). However, the 1935 reprinting, published a year after Katherine Lenroot took over as Chief, *was* different—but by only *one word*. The two-page bibliography that earlier was titled "Selected Books of Interest to Mothers" now was titled, "Selected Books of Interest to *Parents.*"[49] Thus, in 1935, the Children's Bureau formally acknowledged for the first time the possibility that fathers might have an interest in reading about children.

The Fifth Edition: 1938

When the fifth edition of *Infant Care* was published in 1938, it had not one but two senior authors. Dr. Ethel C. Dunham, the new Director of the Division of Research in Child Development of the Children's Bureau, was one. Dr. Marian M. Crane, who worked with Dunham, was another. The "committee of pediatricians" was said to have offered "assistance."[50]

In terms of how to care for the baby, the fifth edition basically was the same as the 1935 printing of the fourth edition. In terms of how fathers were portrayed, however, it was very different. First, the drawing of the mother, daughter, and father looking at a baby lying in a bassinet was moved from page 3 to page 1. The scene was also modified somewhat: Now the father was holding the older child and looking directly at her. In the 1929 and 1931 editions, the father was leaning down and appeared to be giving the daughter a boost so she could see the baby.

Second, two sentences were added to the introductory section. Immediately after the statement about baby care being a "great art" and a woman's "most exacting profession," there was the following: "Her husband shares the responsibility for the child's training, whether or not he helps with the child's physical care. The parents should work together from the baby's birth to teach him good habits."[51]

The expectation of cooperation from fathers was not new to this edition; it had first appeared in the 1929 edition when behaviorism was embraced. It is significant, however, that the point now was made early in the book, and that it followed on the heels of the thematic statement on what the mother's role was expected to be. Even more significant was the inclusion of the phrase, "whether or not he helps with the child's physical care." This addition would seem to indicate some acceptance on the part of the Children's Bureau that fathers could be doing more than training the baby; they could also be helping with some of the dirty work (e.g., changing diapers).

The idea that fathers not only could but *should* be involved in the physical care of the baby was given its strongest endorsement in the daily schedule for babies from one to four months old. New to the 1938 edition of *Infant Care* was the statement, "It would be wise for the father also to help with the care of the baby so that if the mother becomes ill or has to leave home for a period he can meet this emergency until help can be provided. Under these circumstances he will also be prepared to supervise the infant's care."[52]

Granted, fathers were being told to help only so they would know what to do in an emergency. Still, the fact remains that while earlier editions gave the impression that fathers might be allowed to be involved in the physical care of the baby, in the 1938 edition the Children's Bureau explicitly gave fathers the license to feed the baby or change its diaper.

The Sixth Edition: 1940

The sixth edition of *Infant Care* was published in 1940, and again primarily was the work of Drs. Dunham and Crane. In her letter of transmittal, Katherine Lenroot said that this edition "follows in the main the edition of 1938, differing chiefly in the addition of an index and in the recommendation of the larger quantities of vitamin C, which recent research has shown to be necessary."[53] With regard to fatherhood, the 1938 and 1940 editions were identical.

The Seventh Edition: 1942

The seventh edition of *Infant Care* was published in 1942. Joining Dr. Ethel Dunham and Dr. Marian M. Crane in writing the book was Dr. Dorothy Whipple of the Division of Research in Child Development of the Children's Bureau. Drs. Dunham and Crane appear to have had smaller roles this time (Dunham was credited only with writing the section on the premature baby); Dr. Whipple appeared now to be the senior author. The new director of the Division of Research in Child Development, Dr. Katherine Bain, unlike her predecessors, was not involved in the actual writing; however, it was said that the book "was done under [her] general supervision." The bureau's advisory committee of pediatricians was credited with reviewing the manuscript and offering "many helpful suggestions."[54]

Similar to previous editions, the new edition had a picture of a mother and a baby, only now the picture was a photograph, and the mother was bending down and smiling at the baby rather than holding it. Inside, the changes were much more telling. The 1942 edition of *Infant Care* shifted away from behaviorism and constituted the sincerest effort yet to include fathers in the caregiver ranks. The movement away from behaviorism was subtle but important. In the 1929 edition—following John Watson's dictum that babies should not be "loved too much"—mothers were told that if they paid too much attention to their infants, they would create demanding children. In the 1942 edition, the message was that conditioning was important (thus behaviorism was not abandoned altogether) *but also* that babies had a legitimate right to attention. Thus, in 1929, a good parent was one who did not always pick the baby up when it was crying.[55] In 1942, a good parent was one who recognized that crying was an honest form of communication.[56]

Similarly, the 1942 edition, like the 1929 edition, devoted considerable attention to the baby's daily schedule, but now the adults were not the only ones who dictated the pace; the baby had a say, too: "There are no fixed hours at which every baby should be fed. If your baby does not fit into the routine you plan for him, try to change the plan to suit his needs."[57]

What happened in the 1942 edition was that the behaviorism of the

1929 edition was being tempered with a new philosophy of child rearing, one that gave greater weight to the child's desires and developmental abilities. Thus, the baby had become something of a partner in the socialization process. One result of this shift in philosophy was an increase in the amount of work and level of responsibility required of the caregivers; each move the caregiver made could have serious developmental consequences. As historian Nancy Pottishman Weiss notes, "Now a misstep could spell both psychological mischief and cognitive harm, just as earlier mistaken care could result in severe physical illness."[58]

Accompanying the change in child-rearing philosophy was an open invitation to fathers. In a clear and demonstrative way, *Infant Care* began to talk directly to men—and it did not waste any time in the process. On the inside front cover of the book, there was now a section titled, "The Purpose of This Book," which said, "This book is intended to help mothers *and fathers* in taking care of babies [my italics]." Earlier editions had used the words "mothers and fathers" (or "fathers and mothers"), as well as "parents," but this was the first edition to say that the book itself was for both parents. Also, as if to reinforce the point, the bibliography that had been buried in the back in earlier editions was now on the inside front cover, and (following the change begun in 1935) it was titled, "Publications of Interest to Parents."[59]

Then, on the first page, the message that had been in every edition since 1921 and that had been moved to the introductory section in 1929 was repeated, with three small changes, here italicized: "*Child* care is a great art. It is an important task, *perhaps* the most important task any *parent* ever undertakes.[60] First, "child" replaced "baby." This seems to have been a stylistic change more than anything else. *Infant Care* still focused on babies. Second, the word "perhaps" was inserted. This qualifier may reflect the more significant change that followed, namely the substitution of "parent" for "woman." If it was motherhood that was being addressed, there was no "perhaps"; from the point of view of *Infant Care*, child care *was* the most important task any woman could undertake. If it was parenthood that was being addressed—that is, if fathers *and* mothers were included—then, in order to take into account that fathers often were employed in important jobs (outside the home)—child care only *may* be the most important thing they do.

Again, it was not simply the fact that the word "parent" was used here, for earlier editions had acknowledged that a new baby meant responsibilities for both father and mother. What was different about its use on the first page of the 1942 edition was that child care was being defined as "perhaps the most important task" for fathers as well as mothers. Until this time, only women's identities were presumed to be tied to parenthood. Now it was *possible* for men's identities to be tied to parenthood, too. In the hierarchy of roles that men played, fatherhood was becoming more salient. At least, this is what *Infant Care* seemed to be suggesting.

Changes in wording also denoted a shift in the bureau's attitudes toward fathers. Early on we find, "A young mother and father need the doctor's help in planning the health of their baby," and later, "Bath time, next to feeding time, is the time many mothers and babies enjoy most—and fathers, too, on Sunday morning."[61]

The most apparent indication of a change in attitude toward fathers, however, was the pictures. Prior to 1942, the only picture of a father in *Infant Care* was the drawing of the father in the bassinet scene, described previously. In the 1942 edition, however, there were three photographs of fathers, all of which portrayed the fathers *doing something* with their babies. One was a picture of a father giving a baby a bath. Another was a picture of a father with a baby on his knee; the father is showing the baby something on the ground. The third was a picture of a father holding a baby and looking at him; a caption under this picture (and under another of a mother rocking a baby) read, "Sometimes the baby needs a little extra attention."[62]

Although fathers were accorded more physical space in this edition than in any previous edition, the social space that they were given still was not large. It is ironic, for example, that earlier editions of *Infant Care,* in which fathers received less consideration, used the phrase (at least off and on) "father and mother," while this edition preferred "mother and father." Also, bathing and playing with the baby were things that mothers primarily were expected to do. And fathers? They could do this, *too.* Finally, there was the area of infant care that the physicians who wrote the manual apparently felt should not change. In the 1942 edition, as in every edition before, care of the sick baby was "the mother's responsibility." Despite all the "parents" this and "mother and father" that, the book's section on childhood illnesses held the line: "Every *mother* has the responsibility of deciding whether *her* baby is sick and whether *she* should call the doctor [my italics]."[63]

Summary

It is clear that from 1914 to 1942, the Children's Bureau not only changed its philosophy of infant care, it changed its philosophy of fatherhood as well. Behaviorism (both implied and expressed) in the 1920s served to incorporate men into the technocracy of modern infant care. A more child-autonomous philosophy in the 1930s worked to make fathers both warmer and less peripheral in the parenting process. Thus, if *Infant Care* is to be believed, the Progressive Era and the Machine Age constituted two different phases in the history of fatherhood; and within the Machine Age itself, several different subphases prevailed.

Note that I said "if." *Infant Care*, no doubt, offers some important clues for deciphering the history of fatherhood, but it still constitutes only one set of clues and only one locus of production. How do we know, for example, whether similar changes were occurring in other books or manuals or in other segments of the culture? How do we know whether changes, even if they were occurring elsewhere, were occurring at the same rate, or at the same time? The answer right now is that we do not know.

Suppose, however, we examine another group of texts—texts that, in their own unique way, were also an integral part of early-twentieth-century child-rearing lore. Suppose we look at child psychology texts. What do we see then?

THE CHILD PSYCHOLOGY MOVEMENT

Although the child science period of the child-saving movement is said to have begun in the 1910s, it was not until the late 1920s and early 1930s that the scientific study of children really came into its own. In 1925, a Committee on Child Development was established under the National Research Council, which itself was a part of the National Academy of Sciences. One of the stated purposes of the committee was to promote child science and research *over* child social welfare and direct-to-parent education. Thus, on some level, the committee was a repudiation of the moral approach to child saving of decades before.[64] In the wake of the committee's efforts came the *Child Development Abstracts and Bibliography* (in 1927); the journal *Child Development* (in 1930); the first *Handbook of Child Psychology* (in 1931); and the Society for Research in Child Development (in 1933).[65] In the eight years between the founding of the Committee on Child Development and the founding of the Society for Research in Child Development, the "scientific study of children was transformed from sporadic, local, modestly funded activities to institutionalized, nationwide, relatively well funded research."[66] In short, what had been created was a "national professional scientific subculture" devoted to the study of child psychology.[67]

Given all that was going on in the burgeoning field of child psychology, child psychology textbooks are a good way for us to learn how other "baby doctors" were viewing fathers. But we are faced again with the issue of having to decide which books to examine. My decision was to focus on the texts that had gone through multiple editions.

I chose this path for two reasons, basically. First, multiple-edition texts were the most successful, with the largest sales. (Why else would a publisher come out with a new edition?) Second, and equally important, multiple-edition texts allow us to plot continuity and change over time while controlling (at least to some extent) for the influence of both author and publisher. This is what we were doing when we looked at *Infant Care*: a multiple-edition text with the same publisher and with authors chosen by the publisher.

The point I am making here is methodological. If we were to compare textbook A published in 1930, with textbook B published in 1940, and leave it at that, we would not know whether the difference in the two books was a function of historical change or a function of the interests of the respective authors and backers. On the other hand, if we compare the second edition of a book with its earlier edition, we can be more confident that the continuity and change from one edition to the next result from societal influence.[68]

If multiple editions are any indication, the four most successful academic developmental psychology textbooks published during the Machine Age were Florence Brown Sherbon's *The Child: His Origin, Development, and Care* (1934 and 1941); John J. B. Morgan's *Child Psychology* (1931, 1934, 1942); Winifred Rand, Mary Sweeny, and E. Lee Vincent's *Growth and Development of the Young Child* (1930, 1934, 1940); and Ruth Strang's *An Introduction to Child Study* (1930 and 1938).[69]

Strang vs. Rand et al.

Proceeding chronologically and comparing the 1930 edition of *An Introduction to Child Study* with the 1930 edition of *Growth and Development of the Young Child,* we can see immediately the range of options that college professors had. Although both books made reference to fathers being involved in child rearing, Strang's *An Introduction to Child Study* was definitely more traditional than Rand et al.'s *Growth and Develop-*

ment of the Young Child. For example, Strang in 1930 wrote this regarding "Relationships with the Father" in a chapter titled, "Development During the Second Year":

> The father should have his duties and privileges in regard to the care of the baby during these first years. The duties should consist of more than paying the bills, and the privileges of more than talking to his friends about the cunning things the baby does. The father might well study one of the baby's problems, a feeding problem, for example, and assist in this phase of education whenever he has the time. . . . Singing to the baby, reading or telling him a story at bedtime is [*sic*] frequently one of the father's privileges, and furnishes a maximum of pleasant associations in a minimum of time."[70]

By way of contrast, Rand et al. in 1930 said this of the father's role in a chapter on "The Philosophy of Family Life":

> [T]he signs of the times indicate that the patriarchal type of family must be and is being greatly modified. . . . The educational advantages open to women have widened their vision and opened up many paths of work hitherto unknown to them. Woman are today in business and professions as never before. . . . Many interesting questions arise out of this modern condition of the earning woman. . . . If she is her husband's partner in carrying the financial burden may he not be her partner in some of the home duties and share with her in the care of the children? Should he not learn about baby feeding and some of the other aspects of child care as well as his wife? Is there any reason why he should not help in the care of the sick child if his wife is carrying as heavy a work program as he is?[71]

One could say that Rand et al. also presented a traditional picture, because they talked about fathers "sharing" only when their wives worked in "business and professions." However, the fact that the authors applauded the passing of the "patriarchal type of family," and made a point of referring to the husband and wife as "partners" both outside and inside the home, would suggest that their approach to fatherhood (and motherhood) was more modern than was Strang's (and certainly more modern than that of the Children's Bureau). Note, too, the fact that Rand et al. included infant care as a father's duty, whereas Strang did not have fathers becoming involved until the child's second year.

What happened when *An Introduction to Child Study* and *Growth and Development of the Young Child* were revised? A second edition of *An Introduction to Child Study* was published in 1938, with one important change. In the new edition, Strang said that fathers should not wait until the second year to become involved with their children; for example,

"Many mothers act as though the father were nothing but 'a biologic and economic necessity,' and forget that the baby is his baby as well as theirs. To love and understand infants is not an exclusive feminine characteristic, as anthropological studies have shown. The father will understand his child better if he knows him at least a little when he is very young."[72]

A second edition of *Growth and Development of the Young Child* was published in 1934, and a third edition in 1940. In these later editions, Rand et al. took what had been in the introductory chapter on "The Philosophy of Family Life" and moved it to the chapter on "The Home and Family as a Background for Growth" (which also appeared in the first edition). In terms of the authors' approach to fatherhood, the second edition was pretty much like the first. The third edition, however, was different in one important respect. In the section describing why fathers and mothers should be partners, Rand et al. inserted several passages (here highlighted in italics) that made the book even more modern, perhaps even feminist:

> Is there any reason why he should not help in the care of the sick child if his wife is carrying as heavy a work program as he is? *"H.W." (house wife) are the initials one finds on records indicating that a woman is staying at home caring for her home. If in addition to being a house wife she carries on a business or profession, is it not fair that the husband become something of an "H.H." (house husband)?* If the husband is indeed to share with his wife in the training of the children *and really function as something more than a biological father,* should he not as well as she know something about what the care and training of children mean, *irrespective of whether she is engaged in some business or not?*[73]

Morgan vs. Sherbon

John J. B. Morgan's *Child Psychology* was introduced in 1931 and revised in 1934 and 1942. This text was the only one of the four that was written by a man, and the only one that focused almost exclusively on child development, all but ignoring issues like the household division of labor. Morgan did communicate, however, who he thought should be in charge of child care by referring repeatedly to "the mother." One of the few times that fathers were discussed was in the chapter on "The Child's Adjustment to His Family." What concerned Morgan here was that sometimes a father or mother could become jealous over the devotion of the other to a child.[74] Morgan made changes from one edition to the next, but these essentially were attempts to integrate the latest studies. The third edition, published after, in his words, "child psychology [had] grown into a self-respecting and mature member of the psychology family," was noteworthy (especially to Morgan) for the attention that it gave to "developmental sequences."[75] The third edition also had more drawings than the other editions. One drawing showed a father cowering from a lightning storm while his son stood nearby. The caption for the drawing was, "Parents with unreasonable fears set a bad example for their children."[76] Morgan's decision to depict fathers as cowards is interesting, especially given that the war was on. Too bad we cannot ask him why he chose this particular drawing and caption.

The fourth and last multiple-edition child psychology book to be published during the Machine Age, and one that offered a striking contrast to Morgan's, was Florence Brown Sherbon's *The Child: His Origins, Development, and Care.* The first edition of the book was published in 1934; a second edition came out in 1941. *The Child* started out as a very traditional text, "the fruit," said Sherbon, "of some fifteen years of teaching child development and child care to women students in the University of Kansas."[77] Apart from a reference to fathers and mothers washing dishes together, and two pictures of fathers encouraging "the development of the 'top of [a baby's] body,' this was a book that assumed that mothers were solely responsible for child care.[78]

The 1941 edition, however, took a decidedly modern turn. In the preface to the second edition, Sherbon said that "two stimulating experiences with a man student in a women's class, together with the discovery that engaged and married students were sharing their texts with fiances and husbands, led her to change the word 'mother' to 'parents' in many connections and led her also to think more intensively of the family group as a constant presence and of the father as a personality to be considered."[79]

Sherbon's avowed intentions were not always realized, in that she sometimes referred to "mothers" when "parents," technically at least, would have been just as appropriate. In a discussion of what to do if the child seems sick, for example, Sherbon wrote: "The mother should note any redness, swelling, or patches of gray, white or yellow exudate on the tonsils."[80] Sherbon, like the Children's Bureau, apparently felt mothers should understand that it was their responsibility to tend to sick babies.

Conversely, there were points in the book where Sherbon did seem to be trying to expand the boundaries of responsibility for men. In a section titled "The New Role of the Father," for example, Sherbon theorized that "[a]t present the sharp lines which traditionally have demarcated the roles of father and mother in the life of the family group are fading under current revolutionary scientific and social changes." She went on to talk about the movement toward father inclusion that she had observed in the field of parent education:

> It is at last coming to the general attention among educators that the child has two parents. Here and there study groups have been organized for fathers and even for expectant fathers. . . . Here and there young men are seeking admission to college classes in child care and child development and are indicating their desire for instructions as to the functions, responsibilities, and educational philosophies involved in parenthood. . . . Young mothers and fathers are now more inclined than formerly to read the same books, talk over what they read, go together to classes and conferences, and really share parental responsibilities."[81]

To illustrate her point, Sherbon told the story of a dual-career couple who taught at a small college and who "arrange[d] their teaching schedules" so they could alternate infant care:

> From the time that the baby was three weeks old to the end of the school year, the father took care of the child during the hours when the mother was carrying on her work on the campus. The father said that he wished to do it, he enjoyed it, and he thereby 'felt that it was really half his baby.' When the infant was five months old, the mother said proudly that John could and did do everything for the baby quite as well as she, except for the one item of breast feeding. It was reported that the whole matter of the arrival and care of the baby was of great interest to the campus and that the young father lost no prestige with faculty or students."[82]

It is tempting to speculate about how many couples there may have been like this one, husband-and-wife teams pursuing careers and simultaneously trying to share child care. We should be careful, however, about making too much of a single case. If we had the opportunity to visit with and talk to Sherbon's role-sharing couple, we might find that the division of child care was not as egalitarian as the father and mother led Sherbon to believe.[83] The important thing about Sherbon's case study for our purposes, however, is not whether it was accurate but that it was *there,* in the book, serving as a role model for students to ponder. What is important, too, is that it was *not there before*—that is, it was not in the 1934 edition. Like two of the other multiple-edition books, Sherbon's *The Child* had significantly modernized its stance on the father's role.

Summary

What do these child psychology texts add to our understanding of how baby doctors treated fathers during the Machine Age? We see a shift in attitudes that mirrors the shift detected in *Infant Care,* indicating that not only did the 1920s differ from the 1930s but that the early 1930s differed from the late 1930s and early 1940s. In other words, the modernization of fatherhood, according to the evidence reviewed here, did not simply proceed apace during the Depression; it accelerated.

As to the question of how representative *Infant Care* was, it appears to be representative, as long as we are talking about both continuity and change. Most of the books modernized in some fashion. *Infant Care*, however, did not change as quickly as the child psychology textbooks, although there was one exception to this rule: John J. B. Morgan's *Child Psychology*. In contrast to the other textbooks and to *Infant Care* as well, Morgan's book made little effort to incorporate fathers.

It is interesting that the most father-inclusive texts were produced by women who were profeminist, and that the most conservative series of texts (i.e., the *Infant Care* series) was largely written under the auspices of pediatricians. What we may be seeing here is a pattern that was prevalent in the past and that persists today. Feminists have long been in the vanguard of the New Fatherhood movement. Physicians, on the other hand, have a history of supporting patriarchal norms. That the Children's Bureau changed *Infant Care* at all, with respect to fatherhood, may have had a lot to do with the fact that its chiefs were dedicated to improving the lives of women and children, issues central to feminism. That the bureau moved toward father inclusion at a comparatively slow pace, however, may say even more about the countervailing influence that the medical profession had. Something to ponder: If physicians were the only voice during the Machine Age, the modernization of fatherhood probably would not have occurred at the speed that it did.

4   Men and Infants

Suddenly you hear a cry from the nursery and then a wail.
What can be the matter? You tiptoe softly into the baby's
room. He is howling by this time at full lung power. Oh! Oh!
He is wet—good and wet—and he won't go to sleep until the
wet diaper is off and he is nice and warm and cozy in clean
dry pants. To the well-trained father this is but a simple pro-
cedure. But to the uninitiated it is a nightmare!
> Hazel Corbin, from *Getting Ready to Be a Father* (1939)

Soon after its formation, the Children's Bureau began receiving letters
from people around the country who were seeking child-rearing advice.
One of the earliest letters, and typical of the many received, was from a
Chicago parent who had read about *Infant Care* in the newspaper and
wanted suggestions to cure a five-month-old's sleeping problem: "I have
read of the book . . . and thought possibly there might be something con-
tained therein that would be of interest to me." A staff medical doctor
wrote back within the week to say that the manual was in the mail: "We
take great pleasure in sending you, under separate cover, a copy of the
bulletin *Infant Care*. On page 56 and following of this pamphlet, you will
find several paragraphs on the subject of baby's sleep, which I believe will
be of service to you. If we can be of further help please let us know." [1]

From the time of its inception to the beginning of World War II, the
Children's Bureau received approximately 400,000 pieces of mail. Most of
this correspondence was addressed directly to the bureau; some of it was
addressed to other federal agencies, including the White House, and was
then forwarded to the bureau. [2] All letters received, and copies of all letters sent in reply, are stored with tons of other historical documents at the
National Archives in Washington, DC. Anyone with the time and inclination can examine the letters and enter a world both strange and familiar—
strange in the sense that, when it came to medical expertise, the early
twentieth century was an era far removed from our own, and familiar in
the sense that the letter writers often talked about problems that just as

easily could have been written about today, so basic and universal were some of their concerns.

Accessing the letters is not easy. The correspondence between parents and the Children's Bureau is not separated physically from other agency-related materials (e.g., interoffice memos and budget reports) or organized chronologically, but is interspersed throughout the hundreds of boxes that make up the collection. The reason for this is that the Children's Bureau staff used an elaborate coding system to classify all incoming mail, and the archivists chose to follow this system when they assembled the collection.[3]

Here is how the system worked. Soon after a letter was received, someone on the Children's Bureau staff would inscribe a set of numbers at the top of the first page, which would route the letter to a particular folder or cabinet. For example, letters that dealt with allergies to foods might be coded 4-5-11-5-6. (The multiple code reflects the use of subcategories. Thus, 4-5 dealt with pediatrics, 4-5-11 dealt with pediatrics/nutrition, and so on.)[4]

Only by using the coding system as a map can one discover items that might be relevant to the study of parenthood per se. My own search through the Children's Bureau collection gave me a sense of what it must be like to be an archeologist. Sometimes I would put in an enormous amount of time and not discover anything of value (to this project, at least). At other times, after a lot of perseverance and no small bit of luck, I would unearth a real find.[5]

How valuable are the letters? For our purposes, they are extremely valuable. First, they make it possible to compare what was written in *Infant Care* with what was actually being done inside the home. Secondly, the letters reveal the family situations to which the bureau was exposed, and raise questions as to why the manuals were aimed at some individuals and not others.[6]

Who were the letter writers? Historian Molly Ladd-Taylor, an authority on the Children's Bureau, says that "[w]omen from every geographic region, social class, and educational background wrote to the bureau. . . . Most of the correspondence [however] appears to [have] come from native white women on farms and in small towns, although race and ethnicity are impossible to determine."[7] Letter writers also had to be literate (or have relatives or friends who were literate and willing to write on their behalf). But being literate did not necessarily mean that they were learned. A number of letters in the collection, while eloquent and riveting, are filled with grammatical and spelling mistakes, and document, via their content and form, the struggles of the disenfranchised and the poor.[8]

This brings us to the issue of the discrepancy between the reality communicated in the manuals and the reality communicated in the letters. Echoing the personal interests of a credentialed and professionally minded staff, *Infant Care* exhibited a distinctive middle-class bias, assuming that children had their own rooms and ignoring the impact of the Great Depression. (If one had to depend on *Infant Care* to learn about what was going on in the 1930s, one would not know there was a Depression.) The manual also tended to convey the notion that caring for an infant required little more than serious forethought, perhaps a willingness to abide by a schedule, and that family life was mostly warm, loving, and harmonious.[9] Finally, *Infant Care* paid comparatively scant attention to men or to fatherhood. Although, as we saw in the last chapter, men gradually were incorporated into later editions of the manual, fathers never achieved the parental status of mothers, and when it came to taking care of sick babies, fathers never achieved any status at all. If we look to the letters, however, we see a different picture.

"THIS TYPE OF LETTER IS BECOMING TOO FREQUENT"

On 28 February 1916, a Chicago mother, after reading an editorial on the Children's Bureau drive to "Save the Babies," decided she had had enough; she had to speak her mind. ("I cant help but sit down and write you.")[10] "I wonder how many of you Gentlemen have ever stopped to consider the cause of infant deaths and why most mothers do not nurse their babies[?]" she began, not knowing that ultimately her letter would be read not by a man but by a woman. The mother said that she often had to go without nourishment so her children would have enough to eat, and that when her son was born, five years before, the only food in the house was that which her neighbors had provided. She said that her breast milk was not always enough to feed the babies, and that, because her husband refused to support them, she often was caught between staying home with the children (and starving) or going out to look for work (and leaving the children alone).

> I nursed my baby mornings and night at night time after working all
> day then nursing my child. every drop it swallowed it would throw it
> up. at the same [time] I [was] suffering the awfull torture with my milk.
> pumping it and throwing it into the sink, while my *baby starved* and my
> husband *refused* to *provide* for us. at the end of one month my milk
> had dried up[.] there I was without the fountain nature had provided

me with to feed my child. after Christmas, the loss of my position [made me] now unable to buy food for the baby[.] I must starve and also see the rest of the children do the same. at the end of 3 months my chubby little fellow that weighed 11 lbs at birth now was just merely a skeleton.

When the mother sat down to write to the bureau, she was pregnant once more, and was horrified by the thought that the nightmare of before would recur.

> I am to become a mother again this coming month and just what I have endured I must go through again. no food for the ones I already have and nothing to nourish the coming. only *abuse* and *torture* at the hands of the man who *promised* to *provide* and *protect woman*. and no *law* to *enforce* this *promise*. . . . I love my children and willing would have as many as possible but never before have I dreaded the ordeal of child birth, as I am afraid to look upon its little face. how can it be human and a perfect child after all that I have been through this last time[?] each place I have asked for advice what to do or for to compel my husband to work and provide for me and the children, the best I receive is, (why do you live with him and have children for such a man[?] You deserve no pity.) nice advice to poor mothers. who are nothing but fools for men but to bear their children for them and then afterwards neglect them to go out to work for to buy their food. God help the poor mothers of today. the cry is Save the babies but what about the mothers who produce these babies[?] [11]

Upon receiving the letter, Julia Lathrop, then Chief of the Children's Bureau, requested, via an interoffice memo, that someone visit the woman to "see if there is some human way to help her. . . . This type of letter is becoming too frequent." [12] What exactly Lathrop meant by "this type" is not known, but if she was referring to letters in which deprivation, abuse, and victimization were dominant themes, she was perhaps more prescient than she realized. For during the Machine Age, the Children's Bureau received thousands of letters that showed a dark and terrifying side of American family life. The following are examples from among these letters.

A farmer's wife and mother of nine children from Winterville, Georgia, wrote that she was tired of having to care for children who were constantly underfoot and for a husband who did not "sympathize" with her "one bit" but only talked "rough" to her. "Should I be [de]nied of a few simple articles or money either[?]" [13]

A Southington, Connecticut, woman complained, "[The] father [of my girl and with whom I am about to have another child] is getting so mean because he can not find work so he started beating me often, so [I] got him arrested got 30 days am afraid when he comes back home will beat me more, and do not know [what] to do.[14]

A Brooklyn, New York, mother detailed the "tortured lives" she and her six-year-old daughter were forced to endure as the result of her husband's "disordered mentality." "Shortly after [my daughter] was born, upon reaching home from work in the evening, if I happened to be giving my child her feeding, he would snatch the bottle from her mouth and say 'who in the hell does she think she is, I ought to be ready to serve him with supper immediately' although he came home at indefinite times. And whether it was 4 o'clock PM or 4 AM we had to suffer, as we often do now, his thunderous demands. Kissing me, loving me, striking me, all in the same moment."[15]

A 15-year-old girl from Hillsvale, Virginia, beseeched President Roosevelt, "While every one has gone off and left me this morning I will try and write you a few lines. I can't go to school because I have to work to hard at home, but still Mother and Dad seem to think I don't do anything. I have a big brother they send him to school and buy him pretty clothes while I haven't hardly any clothes. What I do have are not pretty like other girls are. Daddy drinks very much & always is cussing me. I wonder why they can be so mean to me if I'm really their child. I used to play my guiator every spare minute I had but I didn't play to suit mother and she made me stop. Mr. Roosevelt I am so very unhappy what can I do that will make my life happy? I know you haven't time to fool with a little girl like me, but you was the only one I know to tell my story to. Well I'll stop for I have to scrub the floors & get dinner before mother gets back. Love, . . . P.S. Answer soon as possible. My parents would whip me if they knew I wrote you. I'll wait for the mail though so pleas ans."[16]

Finally, a "step-mother" from Glendale, California asked what she could do about a father-in-law whom she suspected was sexually abusing one of her husband's daughters. "[At bedtime] Grandpa goes in with D. *always,* closes the door and actually gets in bed with her and stays until she is asleep. . . . I no longer believe that he loves D., but I have come to believe that she is an obsession with him. . . . For instance, he was putting vaseline on her 'pee-pee' every night. . . . He fondles her constantly and nobody knows what goes on behind those doors, when he takes her to bed."[17]

I introduce these letters because in a discussion of New Fatherhood it is possible to lose sight of the fact that fatherhood has both a good side and a bad. (The same can be said of motherhood.)[18] Because the modernization of fatherhood was basically about making men more caring and more involved, I have focused, and will continue to focus, on the first side more than on the second. What must be kept in mind throughout, however, is that coexisting with the New Fatherhood of the Machine Age were enclaves of irresponsibility and abuse. For some children and women, fatherhood was not synonymous with hugs and kisses at all, but was a living hell.

In one of the preceding letters, a mother said that she was "willing . . . [to] have as many [children] as possible." Not everyone, it seems, was as willing as she; consequently, over the years, the Children's Bureau received numerous requests for birth control advice. These requests, generally prompted by fears that having more children would tax already meager provisions, illustrated also the gulf that existed between the reality communicated in the manuals and the reality communicated in the letters. Typical of the letters in this category was this plea from an Axtell, Kansas, mother:

> I have followed Your book on Infant Care and found it Wonderful. But I'm Comming With My largest problem. I am Mother of 2 little boys 1 yr. apart & expect to be Mother again this summer. Im only in my twenties. We Rent a farm & find it a hard row to hoe. To provide food & clothe for us all. We can not Meet expenses. My health is going down hill from hard work & Bearing babies. My husband Works hard & Worries. Also has the Asthama so bad in Winter I find Myself doing a Man's work. This is hard to be mother, wife, & especially the out side work. Now what I want to know is why can't we poor people be given Birth Control as well as Dr.'s & the Rich people that could provide & Dr. their families. We need help to prevent any more babies. . . . don't you think it better to be Parents of 3 which We are willing to work & do all we can for them, to raise & provide food for us all, then to hafto have 6 or more that would take us down into the grave & leave 6 or more for poverty to take & be Motherless.[19]

As much as the Children's Bureau staff may have sympathized with the mother's situation, it could not offer much assistance. The reason is that during the Machine Age, the U.S. government had a policy of not offering information about birth control. Thus, the Children's Bureau's official response to this letter—and to all the letters it received on birth control during this time—was both brief and deliberately unsupportive: "Your letter of January 13 is acknowledged. We are glad our publication on Infant Care has proved helpful. We have no publications on 'Birth Control.' Very truly yours, . . . "[20]

When the 1930s arrived, the Children's Bureau, as well as many other government agencies, began to receive letters from people whose family incomes had precipitously dropped. *Infant Care* may have been able to ignore the Great Depression; the average American could not. An Elk River, Minnesota, woman pleaded, "I'm going to make an appeal to you to see if I cant get some help. We have written to the Senator and he said to go to the bussness men and also wrote to the Governor but nothing has been done and the bussness men refused to give my husband some work so we wouldn't have to ask for things and the Welfare Board refused to give us what we need we have asked serval times all we can get out of them is flour and yeast and 3 of my children are sick with the whooping cough.[21] A Bronx, New York, mother confessed, "[T]his letter is written to ask charity. My husband has been out of work for several months and we have been living on the charity of neighbors. I have a new-born babe and cannot see where the next meal is coming from. Won't you please help us, or have someone help us as we are in terrible need. Naturally we cannot feed a child with no money. Hope to hear soon, my strongest hopes are going with this letter."[22] And from Brooklyn, New York, there was this: "I would appreciate it very much if it is in within your power to help me out. As you know I have two children and am about to become mother to another one. Therefore if it's possible for you to get a letter of recognition from some high authority in Washington so that my husband will be able to get some kind of work. He has tried to work for the last nine months but it has not been successful to get any work and Besides my children are not getting the proper care."[23]

During the Depression, there were some men who translated unemployment into more contact with children. Most fathers who lost their jobs during the Depression, or who suffered a loss of income, however, tended to withdraw, physically and psychologically, from family life.[24] For households with infants, a father's absence could take on special significance, because of the amount of effort that infant care required (the diapering, the feeding, the getting up in the middle of the night, etc). Without the father, there would be one less worker to share the load.

The question is, however, did men during the Machine Age really have all that much to do with infants? And if they did not, why say their contribution would be missed? The answer, briefly stated, is this: There were men during the Machine Age who contributed little in the way of infant care, but there were others who were not oblivious to their newborns' needs.

MEN WROTE, TOO

The fact that most of the letters received by the Children's Bureau were from women probably explains why scholars generally have applauded the letters for their importance in understanding motherhood rather than parenthood or family life. Nancy Pottishman Weiss, one of the first to bring the Children's Bureau collection to attention, talks of "women" using the manuals and refers to the queries as "letters from mothers" and "mothers' correspondence." [25] Likewise, Molly Ladd-Taylor, in her book *Raising a Baby the Government Way,* a study of the bureau from 1915 to 1932, chooses to focus almost exclusively on mothers in order to demonstrate, among other things, "that motherhood was hard work" and "the tremendous spirit, wit, and resourcefulness with which women raised their children." [26]

Without a doubt, the letters that women wrote to the Children's Bureau are national treasures, substantiating everything that Weiss and Ladd-Taylor say about them, and more. What is difficult to understand, however, is why women's letters—and only women's letters—have gotten literally all of the attention up to now. After all, men wrote, too. Although you would not know it from most published accounts, sprinkled throughout the collection are letters from men; letters that, as far as I know, have been essentially ignored and indicate that fathers in the early twentieth century may have been more involved with infants than most historical accounts would have us believe.[27]

Let me be clear about one thing: Men did not write to the bureau very often. (I estimate that fewer than 10 percent and possibly as little as 5 percent of the letters in the files were from fathers.) But the fact that men wrote at all is remarkable, given the degree to which fathers were disregarded in *Infant Care,* especially in the earlier editions. Of course, one could claim that the men who wrote were writing for their wives and thus were not necessarily involved with their children. And one would be right—but only to a certain point. First, even the letters in which a man explicitly said that he was writing on his wife's behalf fall under the category of father involvement, because they suggest some contact with infants, albeit indirect. Second, most of the men's letters do *not* suggest that the fathers were acting as proxies for their wives. Indeed, many of the letters, by their detail, show fathers very much engaged in the nitty gritty of parenting.

What did the men write about? I did not find any letters in which men complained about being abused by their wives or exploited by the division of labor in the home—there were no letters like the one from the Winterville, Georgia, woman who had nine children and was constantly tired from having to toil in the field and in the kitchen. Nor did I find any letters like the one from the Brooklyn, New York, mother who spoke of the "tortured lives" she and her daughter were forced to endure because of her husband's "thunderous demands." Also, when I compared the length of the men's letters with the length of the women's letters, I found that, on average, the men's letters were only about half as long, indicative of a mechanical quality not often revealed in the women's letters. Apart from these differences, however, the men seemed mostly concerned about the same kinds of issues that the women were concerned about: how to best care for their babies.

I am not trying to minimize the differences between the men's and the women's letters, for they are significant. My point simply is that if we were to rely exclusively on published accounts about the Children's Bureau, we would be led to conclude that men in the early twentieth century had next to nothing to do with babies. The files of the Children's Bureau, however, indicate that there were fathers during the Machine Age who played a larger and warmer role in caring for smaller children than they generally have been given credit for. Their story also deserves to be told.[28]

FOCAL POINT: MEN WRITING ABOUT FEEDING

Because the Children's Bureau was created, in part, to stem the tide of infant mortality, and because its manual, *Infant Care*, got by far the most attention, inside the bureau as well as out, the overwhelming majority of the letters that the Children's Bureau received dealt not with the inequity of the division of housework or with wife or child abuse but with the physical or medical aspects of taking care of babies. Parents wanted to know how to deal with a child who would not eat, or who was prone to throwing up. They asked whether the Children's Bureau approved of this or that kind of milk, this or that kind of tonic, this or that kind of sun lamp. What could be done about diarrhea, or about a baby who refused to sleep? How could a child be taught not to masturbate? What about bed wetting? Left handedness? Thumb sucking? Stuttering? Behavioral problems were also represented—stealing, lying, talking back—but these were not as prominent as questions about health.

Topping the list of parents' health concerns was feeding. Within the context of the times, this is not surprising. In the early twentieth century, thousands of infants died from having been given milk that either was low in nutrition or poisonous. The Children's Bureau, and the medical community in general, advised mothers to nurse their babies, while the milk manufacturers pushed the value of animal milk and artificial powders. It was this political climate, this war over children's and women's bodies, that framed the requests for feeding advice.[29] Whether parents were writing about milk for a one-month-old, or the proper breakfast cereal for a four-year-old, not far from their thoughts was the belief that children could die if given the wrong foods.

Because feeding was a source of considerable concern, and because it clearly is related to the question of care, I decided that focusing on the subject of feeding would be a good way to begin to get a sense of men's involvement with infants, as seen through the Children's Bureau correspondence. I thus made an effort while at the National Archives to copy as many letters as I could on matters pertaining to diet and nutrition. Here, essentially, is what I found.[30]

In 1915, a Chicago father wrote for a copy of *Infant Care,* and also asked for advice.

> We had to wean our baby and our Doctor recommended a baby food called 'Mammala' manufactured by the Ambrosia Milk Cor'n,' 120 Liberty St., N.Y.C. and he stated that it was the very best food that could be given to the baby. I enclose you their pamphlet which comes with the food. I also enclose a sample of the food, in case you have never had occasion to test it. I want you to note the claims made for this food and then to give me a fair, unbiased opinion of it. Do you think it is what is claimed? . . . P. S. When a little of this milk is forced back to the baby's mouth, by reason of overfeeding or too rapid feeding, it seems to evaporate and looks like a cheesy substance. Has this any meaning?[31]

In the same year, another father, this one from East Palestine, Ohio, wrote to say that his wife had died two months before, and that he needed information on feeding his eight-month-old baby girl. In the letter, the father talked about the formula he was using (milk plus meal), and how he regularly rubbed his child "with olive oil baths."[32] In 1916, a father from Grangeville, Idaho, wrote to ask for advice on feeding his young daughter and son:

> I have two children, girl three years and boy ten months. I have been trying for two years to find the proper foods of the different kinds suitable for my growing girl and also to begin feeding my baby as his mother cannot supply him much longer. Our ten months baby boy weighs net 23 pounds. He is not so very fat but is in good health and I want him to keep this good health. My girl is not getting the proper foods. She will eat as much as two and sometimes more soft boiled eggs for breakfast if we permit. She is very fond of chocolate or cocoa coffee. I want to know if these two foods are alright, and I want to know what are the proper foods, how to cook them and in what amounts. I want all the information you can supply on this line.[33]

After World War I, fathers' letters on feeding continued unabated and, if anything, became more detailed. In 1919, a Cresco, Pennsylvania man wrote for advice on what to give a twelve-week-old. "Please tell us whether or not milk sugar should be used or cane or whey sugar in modified milk. Tell us also whether Milk of Magnesia should be used in preference to lime water. We have had our baby on modified milk for four weeks without very good results. . . . How could we find out whether or not the breastmilk is good." And so on. Then, noting that the child had suffered from constipation, the father provided the bureau with a microscopic analysis of the baby's stool. "The stool is firm, smooth and medium yellow in color followed sometimes in the same stool by soapy-like-foamy-like, spongy stool, not particularly offensive in odor. Little white lumps are always to be seen." The letter ended with the kind of plea that helps us to understand why so many parents wrote to the Children's Bureau, and why the agency was so important to the nation as a whole. "We are stationed out in the country 7 miles from a physician and thirteen miles from real medical skill, hence our writing to you." [34]

Two months later, a Los Angeles man wrote to ask what to do about his baby girl, who drank a quart of milk a day and loved to eat dirt and sand but did not like fruit of any kind. The father said that the local doctor did not "seem to understand such a case." [35] In 1921, an Ashland, Kentucky, father of two boys—one sixteen months, the other just fourteen weeks—requested (upon the advice of his family doctor) information on artificial milk formulas. The man's wife had been forced to discontinue nursing the children because her breast milk "contain[ed] no nourishment."

> We fed [the older child] Dennos Food and while at first we had trouble in getting the right formula he soon began to pick up and now weighs about 25 pounds. [As for the younger child] We have been giving Dennos Food also but for some reason or other he is not gaining on it as did the other baby. . . . His mother has tried different strength formula both without any improvement. . . . We would like your suggestions with regard to the proper feeding of these two babies. [36]

In 1923, one of the most descriptive letters to come from a father was written by an Akron, Ohio, man who, familiar with the bureau publications ("I have your bulletin on the care of children"), wanted specific information on colic and breast feeding. Posing thirteen questions, he asked that the Children's Bureau answer each and every one in order. ("I have numbered the questions so in your reply you can simply number your answers and I will be able to tell which questions your answers refer to.") [37]

In 1935, an Attleboro, Massachusetts, man also voiced a series of concerns: "As the father of two infant children I would appreciate answers to the following questions if you have such information available." Things that were asked included the following:

> 1. Does the sucking action of infants in taking nourishment either from the mother direct or through a nipple attached to the bottle have any thing to do with the proper formation of an infants lips, jawbones, or mouth in general? 2. Does the taking of nourishment as described above have any thing to do with the general health of an infant? 3. If a method of feeding infants liquid nourishment without the use of either the mother's breast or a nipple could be devised would it be detrimental specifically to the formation of the infant's mouth or its health in general? (Infants over three months of age meant here). . . . If any or all of these questions can be answered by your department I shall pay my income taxes with gladness.[38]

And, in 1938, there came this request from a father in Howard, Rhode Island: "[A]nd if I should give The Child This Butter and The Cod Liver Oil Every Day that would be Ten Spoonfulls that the Child would be taking every day and would this be too much oil for the child to take every day. Or did you mean for to give only The Butter daily Or Only the Cod Liver oil Daily. Or did you mean for me for to give the child The both of them daily, and I kind of thought that giving one of them daily was enough."[39]

Beginning in the late 1920s and continuing through the 1930s, the question of whether goat's milk was a suitable food for infants arose. (The Children's Bureau said it was fine, but that some babies did prefer cow's milk.) A Cleveland, Ohio, father wrote, "I would very appreciate any information on pamphlets you can send me regarding Feeding of Goats Milk to a ten months old baby, weaned but not thriving and can not take Cow's milk in any form and also show other food aversions."[40] A Mio, Michigan, father said, "I understand that Goats milk is the best of feed for babies (outside of cours its mothers milk). Our baby is being fed goats milk. He is gaining every week only the baby is constipated. How can I feed goats milk and the baby not be constipated. If we dilute the milk the baby looses weight so we feed whole milk. The baby is 8 weeks old. We have no cows."[41] And, in 1938, a New Kensington, Pennsylvania, man wrote: "Herewith is 10 ¢ for your bulletin on infant care. I have been told that the most alert hospitals are now using goats' milk in their maternity wards when mothers' milk is not available. The reason being, that goats' milk is much more easily digested than cows' milk, the curd of goats' milk being soft like that of breast milk. Do you have any information on this subject, especially regarding the time required for digestion of breast, goats', and cows' milk?" [42]

Toward the end of the 1930s and at the beginning of the 1940s, attention shifted to whether canned milk and frozen foods were acceptable. In 1939, a Lander, Wyoming, man asked for the bureau's ruling on the matter: "Kindly advise whether or not you would advise the feeding of canned milk to our baby which is now 2 months and 6 days old. Would you deem it advisable to feed canned milk in place of cows whole milk? Our baby is now on cows milk. Also, please inform us what brand of canned milk is the best for infant feeding. We plan to be away from home about 2 months this summer and wondered what milk would be the best." [43] Finally, in 1940, a Scotch Plains, New Jersey, man requested, "[W]ill you please send me information regarding the value of useing quick frosted foods in feeding infants. Also the beneficial values of useing quick frosted foods today by all housewives." [44]

WERE MEN CULTURAL DOPES?

A central theme in much of the scholarship on early-twentieth-century family life is the notion that the "scientific" approach to child rearing, characteristic of the time, created a "therapeutic" culture that, by its very existence, transferred decision-making power from individual families to a host of experts. Whereas before, parents could rely on their own "instincts" or folk remedies passed down from one generation to the next, now they were expected, nay presumably compelled, to rely on people whom they did not even know, much less necessarily agree with— *strangers,* literally, who, because of their scientific credentials, had the rationally based authority to dictate child welfare policy. The child study industry, so the argument goes, had become a power-hungry monster that ate up family autonomy wherever it went and whenever it could. [45]

No doubt, the emergence of a technocratic elite has had a considerable effect on everyday life. The fact that fathers and mothers would even consider scientific discourse as potentially legitimate input to decisions on how to raise their own children is indeed noteworthy. I wonder, however, whether fatherhood scholars have mistakenly assumed that the very existence of a child-rearing elite dedicated to this or that scientific idea necessarily translates into unbridled power for that elite. The notion of a therapeutic culture conjures up images of men and women in white lab coats forcing various prescriptions down the throats of their patients. It is this very image that has prompted some researchers to talk less about a therapeutic culture than a "self-help" culture, which on the one hand is prescriptive, but on the other is not deterministic in its influence.[46] From this alternative viewpoint, people can interpret in various ways and, in the end, *choose not to follow* the advice they are given, or even seek. Says sociologist Ann Swidler,

> The reader of the Bible can find a passage to justify almost any act, and traditional wisdom usually comes in paired adages counseling opposite behaviors. A culture is not a unified system that pushes action in a consistent direction. Rather, it is more like a "tool kit" or repertoire . . . from which actors select differing pieces for constructing lines of action. . . . A realistic theory [thus] should lead us to expect not passive 'cultural dopes' . . . but rather the active, sometimes skilled users of culture whom we actually observe.[47]

Similarly, and with specific reference to child-rearing lore, sociologist Terry Strathman warns, "We must not assume too easily that parents followed 'the book' to the letter of the law—even middle class parents. . . . [R]eaders are choosers—even in a society under the sign of mass production."[48]

The issue of how much power experts actually wield figures significantly in the historical study of fatherhood and in the perceptions we have about men's contributions to their children's upbringing. In his book *Fatherhood in America,* historian Robert L. Griswold draws a distinction between the ways fathers and mothers responded to experts in the 1920s and 1930s. According to Griswold, while some mothers may have blindly followed the prescriptions that were offered, "most more than likely accepted what worked, reinterpreted or rejected what did not, and continued to try to expand their knowledge about child development, psychology, and physiology." As for fathers, they became "dependent" on the experts or their wives and revealed essentially their "ineptitude" and "frustration." Mothers during the Machine Age, in other words, are depicted as careful shoppers in the marketplace of parental ideas, while fathers are seen as cultural dopes, pawns who did only what they were told.[49]

Was this, in fact, the case? Determining the epistemological inclinations of yesterday's fathers is not easy, but a careful reading of the letters to the Children's Bureau indicates that men in the early twentieth century may have been more skeptical of scientific advice than has been suggested. True, fathers may have been frustrated by what the experts were telling them and angry at the inconsistencies in the prescriptions, but inept? I would have to say no.

Note, for example, the following: In 1919 a Walla Walla, Washington, man wrote about his and his wife's concern over the fact that his twenty-two-month-old baby daughter's urine had the strong smell of ammonia. Doctors in the area had been consulted; however—and this is the critical point—the doctors' opinion was not considered the ultimate word. "Local physicians say it is not serious, simply waste matters from albuminous food, but it is now three or four weeks since we first noticed this condition and we do not seem to be able to check it except with use of medicine." The father also reported that he and his wife had tried to adhere to the Children's Bureau dietary advice, as laid out in *Infant Care* and Luther Emmet Holt's *The Care and Feeding of Children,* but had found the advice lacking. "We have followed as closely as possible the diet prescribed in your bulletin or that of Holt's Baby Book but we could never get our baby to eat anything like the amount allowed under these diets. . . . We have your Bulletin No. 8, Series 2 on Infant Care but get no help from it on this trouble." The father then closed the letter with this word of advice to the bureau: "We shall certainly appreciate any suggestions you may be able to make for us—and if serious wire me at my expense and spare no details. However, don't scare us too much for we lost one baby (not through this trouble at all) and we aren't set for any trouble this time." [50]

In 1938, a New York City man wrote to apprise the Children's Bureau of an ongoing situation with his son; in the process he noted his own reservations about advice from the doctor:

> Ever since our baby, P., has been improving I have meant to drop in or write you that my anxieties of the time when I called on you have disappeared and we are now very happy over what appears to be a complete recovery from the mysterious intestinal infection which we discussed. He is now 3 months old and weighs 11 pounds 6 ounces. . . . You may remember that when I spoke to you I questioned the wisdom of the doctor always putting the baby back on evaporated milk when he showed signs of improving. Everytime he got on evaporated milk the symptoms of the infection returned. It was only when he permitted him to stay on the boiled fresh milk that he recovered. This may be just a coincidence. However, even me, an uninformed layman, noticed the child's reaction to evaporated milk early in the case. . . . I know that this does not accord with the reputation which evaporated milk has made for itself. But it may be worth noting for what it's worth. [51]

Some fathers opted to go public rather than register their doubts about expert advice in a personal letter. In 1939, for example, one man who had just become a father for a second time, wrote an article for *Esquire* magazine in which he criticized *Infant Care,* in particular, and the Children's

Bureau, in general, for "betraying" him and his comrades. Using humor to his advantage, the author said that he was upset over the bureau's decision to change its prescriptions on the matter of diapers.

> I am sure a great many American fathers will be shocked to learn that the three-cornered diaper, the sum of the squares of two sides of which was equal to the square of the hypotenuse, has given way utterly to a new fangled square diaper, the sums of the squares of which are equal to nothing much whatever, and which, in addition, are the very devil to pin. Nor is that the worst of it. Right at this very moment there is an insidious movement afoot, a restless stirring among the experts, to substitute for the square diaper a fancy cornucopiate variety, which is neither fish nor fowl, and which I frankly doubt will do the work. The mothers of this and succeeding generations are going to find an increasing reluctance among fathers to have any traffic with diapers, and they will have no one to blame but themselves. For, while it is possible for the man of average intelligence to learn to master the old triangular wrap in a month or two, I know by actual text that it simply does not lie within the male creature to fathom the intricacies of the square and cornucopiate types in less than a year. The fathers are going to say the hell with it, and deservedly, too.

The author proceeded to list other indignities to which he thought fathers should refuse to submit:

> There is a small group of us young fathers who gather every Saturday night in the neighborhood to discuss infant care and to try to fill an inside straight, and recently we drew up a list of a few things we bitterly resent. We resent the passing of the old-style gum-rubber panties and the substitution of oiled silk; we resent dehydrated cereals which have somewhat displaced cooked cereals; we resent the growing preference for cotton undershirts in the place of wool; we resent the fact that babies are now going on a three-meal schedule at the age of five and six months when formerly they didn't dream of drawing up their highchairs until they were at least nine months old. We resent the use of cheesecloth instead of flannelette and bird's eye cloth for diapers.[52]

Some may say that because the *Esquire* article was sarcastic, it should not be taken seriously. But to adopt such a position would be to minimize the rhetorical power that sarcasm wields (*sarcasm* etymologically means "to tear flesh"). Sarcastic people rarely communicate ineptitude (unless they practice naive sardonicism). Indeed, the best of them know how to hit people exactly where it hurts. If anyone was made to appear inept here, it was the experts.

There is more to the father-as-cultural-dope thesis than simply a one-on-one battle with child science. Griswold goes on to postulate that there was a deceptively sinister three-sided game, involving the experts and mothers in collusion against fathers. He says, for instance, that the experts helped to marginalize fathers by creating "privilege" between themselves and mothers. That is, the experts had the knowledge, aimed it at mothers, and thus made fathers "ignorant outsiders in the land of the educated."[53] The marginalization, according to Griswold, was made especially acute by mothers' greater participation in various child study groups. In the end, mothers lost power, too, though not as much as fathers did, because ultimately the collusion turned out to be an imbalanced affair, with the experts still holding sway.

Griswold does indeed make some valid points. There was a coalition of sorts between experts and mothers that did have the potential to create an "odd man out" situation. And it is true that by directing their message to mothers, experts helped to reinforce traditional divisions of labor.[54] But, again, I think that while it is significant that parents were now turning to strangers for child-rearing advice, we must be careful not to grossly overestimate the power of these strangers, whose ties to their audience were not as strong generally as the ties that the members of the audience had among themselves. (Why should a mother side with a stranger, if it meant being in conflict with the person whom she presumably loved and with whom she lived?) Nor should we minimize the fact that because expert knowledge was publicly produced and thus open to public debate, a variety of outcomes could result from contact with the therapeutic or self-help culture, not just one.

One key factor, often overlooked, for example, is the *substance* of an expert's recommendation. Consider, for example, the following letter. In 1926, a Montesano, Washington, woman requested that the Department of Agriculture mediate in a dispute between her and her husband. The Department of Agriculture, in turn, sent her request to the Children's Bureau. Her letter said,

> Please help to settle a few words that will result into a argument if kept up. This is the subject. What may a baby of 4 months eat? My husband is many years older than I and I suppose he thinks he knows more about feeding her than I. I use Mellin's Food and have started to feed her Graham crackers soaked in milk and he says that eather one should not be feed her as they are not good. All though our Dr. Book says use Mellin's Food and she is just as healthy as can be. Some one tolled him to feed her carrots, beans, soups, apple sauce, rubarb, potatoes, and gravy. I do give her a taste of the last two mentioned now and then. All so he wishes me to give her water from 6 to 8 ounces between feedings and I say that is too much for so small a baby as it is hard on their kidneys.[55]

The Children's Bureau replied that the *mother* was right about the baby's water intake, but that the *father* was right about the Mellin's Food and graham crackers, and that *both* were wrong about the vegetables. "We are sending you our booklet on Infant Care. You will see on pages 71, 72, 73, 74, and 75 the foods for your baby. We do not recommend Mellin's Food, but cow's milk, and the formulas you will find on page 75. . . . We do not advise vegetables until the sixth month, and Graham crackers not at all." [56] We see here that what an expert said could discredit a father and bestow privilege on a mother, but it also could do just the opposite. Yet another possibility, shown here as well, was that both parents could be discredited or privileged by a prescription. Again, the substance of the recommendation can be a factor.

Another variable, seemingly ignored, is that whatever an expert happened to say or write would have to be filtered through the power structure in the home. To suggest that fathers were rendered impotent on matters pertaining to child rearing because experts tended to direct their messages to mothers is to assume that the politics of the family (which favored men) had somehow disappeared or been suspended. Given the patriarchal society of the 1920s and 1930s, the availability of scientific knowledge may have meant *not* privilege for mothers but more debate and conflict between husbands and wives. (Note, for example, that in the previously cited letter, the mother told the Children's Bureau that she and her husband were bickering over what their baby should eat.) Since the advice being offered could be interpreted in any number of ways, whether the father or mother ended up on the winning side may have had less to do with who was the target of the advice and more to do with who generally wielded the power. In other words, even if the Children's Bureau responded that the mother was correct, which it did with respect to the baby's water intake, there was no guarantee that the father would permit the bureau's ruling to dictate family policy. If, for some reason, he saw the question of water intake as a challenge to his esteem, he could, if he had the power, veto the ruling. Therapeutic culture or no therapeutic culture, men still called the shots in early-twentieth-century America.

Infant Care *versus Infant Care*

The fathers' letters on feeding suggest that fathers were more involved in infant care than we would assume from reading *Infant Care*. Other letters on other topics—from both fathers and mothers—indicate the same thing. A Camden, New Jersey, father wrote to ask what to do for his eleven-month-old son who was not sleeping "as he should." In the process of explaining the situation, the father revealed not only that he was unimpressed with the advice from the doctor (supporting again the proposition that fathers could be skeptics, too) but also that it was *he* who sometimes brought the baby to the doctor. "I have had him to a Doctor and explained it to him and he said: He does very well for a modern baby. This doesn't satisfy me."[57] A mother from Philadelphia wrote to ask if it would be okay if her three-and-a-half-year-old daughter took her daily nap in the afternoon rather than in the morning. That way, she said, the child would have enough energy at the end of the day to stay up until after her father got home from work. "Her father leaves early in the morning and does not see her, and when he comes at night at 6:30 he does not see her as she goes to bed at 6 o'clock. . . . Of course I want to do the right thing for her but I also would like her to see more of her daddy as he feels badly about it."[58] The Children's Bureau replied that it was fine to alter the child's nap schedule, that "the important thing for children is that they should have an ample amount of sleep regularly and a shift of an hour or so makes very little difference so long as they get the requisite amount."[59]

A father from New York city wrote to say that his boy, four and a half years of age, often cried out in his sleep, "sometimes asking either for his mother *or for me,* keeping up this crying for five or ten minutes at a time [my italics]."[60] A Hudson, New York, mother said that when her three-and-a-half-year-old son cried during the night, "he calls either 'Mother' or 'Daddy,' " and that when *they* went in the child's room, he would make "the most outlandish demands [my italics]."[61] The Children's Bureau picked up on the fact that both parents were caring for the boy during these moments of crisis and advised, "when he next awakens at night either you or his father go to his room, ascertain if he wants to go to the toilet, and if not, tell him quietly 'This is sleeping time,' and leave him to his own devices."[62]

A father from Harrison, New York, who had listened to the Children's Bureau's radio program on a particular morning wrote that very day to say, among other things, that it was difficult to get their son to go to sleep. "[W]hen my wife *or I* try to get him to take a nap, he just seems to want to get away from the idea altogether. Although he yawns and stretches and tells us he is tired we have quite a time getting him to lie down [my italics]."[63] Finally, there was the baby girl who was "a perfect lamb at home" ("she lays and hides and coos") but a terror if taken anywhere ("she kicks and screams something awful"), which meant that the parents, who were "of very moderate means," could not go out together but had to take turns staying home with her. "Most of the time one of us stays with our four month old baby girl while the other goes," the mother wrote. "Will we have to stay home the rest of her babyhood?"[64] The Children's Bureau responded reassuringly, saying that, in time, the baby would grow accustomed to strangers.[65]

How typical were the fathers who wrote to the Children's Bureau, and the fathers described by the mothers above? A good question certainly, but one that has no simple answer. The difficulty that we run into is that there were not many studies carried out during the Machine Age that focused on men's involvement with infants. Still, more evidence is available than scholars seem to realize. When we examine this other evidence in depth, it becomes even clearer that there were a number of fathers during the Machine Age who did more than watch from the sidelines. The men who wrote to the Children's Bureau, it turns out, may not have been so unusual after all.

Let's begin with the surveys that do exist. In 1930, a White House Conference on Child Health and Protection sponsored a nationwide survey of close to three thousand families, which asked about various aspects of parental and child life. According to the study, most mothers of children between the ages of zero and five had played with their babies the day before (75.8 percent), but then so had most fathers, though not as many (65.4 percent). For children between the ages of six and eleven months, the percentage who were played with by either their mother or their father (or both) increased to 91.0 percent and 82.4 percent, respectively. If you think about it, a figure of 82.4 percent actually is quite high for a group of men who, in all likelihood, were employed full-time, and who may have come home from work just before their babies were being put down for the night.

When it came to disciplining infants, the difference between parents was sharper, but not so much as to suggest that fathers were uninvolved. For boys up to one year, the percentage who were punished by their mothers was 98.5 percent; by their fathers, 66.2 percent. For girls up to one year, the numbers were 96.4 percent and 57.4 percent, respectively.[66]

One thing to keep in mind when evaluating these findings is that they are based almost entirely on women's reports. In only about 5 percent of the cases, in fact, was a father asked a single question.[67] Investigators have long recognized that excluding men's reports in family research can pose serious measurement problems because an important reality, or set of perceptions, ends up missing. It also has been shown that while husbands and wives often will exhibit a partner-centric or credit-giving bias in marriage, idealizing their relationships in the process, they will display an egocentric or credit-taking bias when it comes to child care. What this means in concrete terms is that perceptions of father involvement generally vary according to the gender of the perceiver and that studies that exclude men tend to underestimate father involvement. Thus, the White House Conference study probably produced findings that made the division of care look more segregated or traditional than it actually was.[68]

This leads me to the second survey, one of the few to rely on men's responses (although historians of fatherhood rarely cite it.) Carried out some time between 1939 and 1941, and drawing on three hundred interviews with fathers ranging in age from twenty to seventy-nine, the study supports the picture of fatherhood presented in the Children's Bureau correspondence. It, too, has its flaws. One obvious limitation is that the men were asked to recall events that, for some, had occurred decades before. Also, the same credit-taking bias that limits the White House study also limits this study, although in this case we have to assume that the fathers tended to overestimate their involvement.

When asked how much they played with the baby, 19 percent of the fathers reported that they had played occasionally, while 59 percent reported that they had played frequently (22 percent did not answer the question). When asked how much they had "helped" with "the routine care of the baby," 35 percent said they had given little or no care, 53 percent said they had variably performed "routine activities," and 7 percent said they had given "plenty" of care (5 percent of the fathers did not answer the question).[69]

Here is how the fathers phrased their activities:

"[Did] very little except to set a good example."

"[Did] very little, consider that women's work."

"[Did] very little, had to work too much."

"[Did] very little, had too much to do on the farm."

"Did everything from changing their diapers to singing them to sleep. It was fairly frequent."

"Took care of the middle child for first two years as wife was ill, almost all the care."

"Considerable care. Changed diapers, clothed and put to bed, fed. At least did my share of it."

> "Quite a bit as my wife was ill during the first six months and I had most of the routine care."

> "Relieved wife when I had off days and weekends and did the usual night pacing when necessary."

> "Stayed with the child nights, fed him occasionally, put him to bed."

> "Walked floor at night and did the spanking."

> "Gave baths, changed diapers, walked floor, gave night bottle."

> "Changed pants, bathed, fed formula, and amused baby."

> "Minded the children when mother was busy." [70]

One interesting point that the author of the study makes is that the amount of care that fathers provided "seemed to be largely determined by the inclination of the father and the disinclination of the mother. Again and again fathers of the same occupation would be found giving children in their homes no care or much care. . . . If they enjoyed their children, they made the time for them." [71]

Surveys are not the only evidence we have that shows yesterday's fathers were more involved in infant care than has been supposed. The media often highlight the fact that fathers-to-be nowadays are likely to attend prenatal classes in order to support their wives during labor and delivery and to learn how to care for their babies when they are born—proof, it is said, of New Fatherhood. [72] We find, however, that although there may not have been many men during the Machine Age who were asked to assist at the birth (it was during the 1920s that the middle class began to embrace the idea of hospital-based deliveries and "twilight sleep"), there were some who were learning the rudiments of diaper changing, bottle feeding, and middle-of-the-night rocking. [73] In 1933, the Cleveland Child Health Association announced that it would be offering prenatal classes for men to go along with the prenatal classes for women that it had been offering since 1922. [74] When the announcement was posted, twenty-five fathers "enrolled at once," and the number "steadily increas[ed]" from there on. The classes met one evening a week for fifteen weeks. What prompted the men's classes, according to published reports, was that "so many of the questions by the mothers" were "coming from their husbands." Also, some of the mothers complained that they could not "keep their babies on a feeding schedule" because their husbands "insist[ed] that babies should be fed when they cry." (Note that these men actively worked to avoid marginal status and were successful.) Finally, it was felt that because of the Depression, fathers who were out of work often were alone with their babies, and thus "greatly in need of such knowledge." Because of the interest in the classes, efforts were made "to start similar groups in other parts of the city."[75]

The Cleveland Child Health Association program continued throughout the 1930s, though interest apparently waned in the mid-1930s because the course was considered "too lengthy and over technical." In 1939, the program was "reorganized" with cooperation from the Academy of Medicine. By 1940, there were three hundred men attending the classes each year.[76] This is not a lot compared to today's numbers, but enough to communicate more involvement than contemporary stereotypes of yesterday's fathers would lead us to believe.

In the late 1930s and early 1940s, similar types of classes for fathers were formed in other towns and cities: Flint, Michigan; New Haven, Connecticut; and New York City, among them. Flint reportedly had yearly enrollments of over five hundred.[77] New York City's course, sponsored by the Maternity Center Association of New York, included sessions where fathers experimented with a life-sized doll. The *New York Times* ran a story about the course in February of 1942 and mentioned that what the instructors called "bubbling" ("expelling air from the baby before and after a feeding by administering a pat on the back") the fathers referred to as "burping." Who would have guessed that it would be the fathers' term that would survive?[78] The New York City course also spawned what may have been the first nonhumorous manual for prospective fathers, Hazel Corbin's *Getting Ready to Be a Father.*[79] Previous books for prospective fathers—Douglas Vass Martin's *Expectant Fathers* (1930) and David Victor's *Father Doing Nicely* (1938)—were more tongue in cheek.[80] Victor's book, however, did contain a serious side, a point picked up by one physician who, in talking about the Maternity Center Association course, recommended *Father Doing Nicely* as a book that, while "written in fun contain[ed] honest advice between the lines."[81] The fact that the "fun" subsided in the late 1930s is indicative, again, of the difference between New Fatherhood in the 1920s and New Fatherhood in the 1930s. What in the 1920s was considered a joke, in the 1930s was considered serious business.[82]

BACKLASH

At the end of chapter 3, I talked about two college professors who were husband and wife and who in the late 1930s or early 1940s alternately cared for their baby while they taught their classes. It was said then that "the young father lost no prestige with faculty or students" because of his intense commitment to his child.[83] Not all fathers who took an active role in infant care during the Machine Age were able to escape recrimination, nor were the wives of these men necessarily safe either.

In 1918, in an article appearing in the *New Republic,* a mother shared the uneasiness that she and her husband felt from being a dual-career and dual-parenting couple in suburbia:

> My husband and I have a baby. It belongs to both of us. We also have jobs and a nurse. It was not long before I learned that this was wrong. In the first place the baby should belong to me. Of course my husband should help me if I needed help; should shove the baby carriage and get up at night. But under my jurisdiction should come all matters connected with the baby's digestion and training, his clothing and airing. If he gets sick it should be primarily my business, though a kindly interest on the part of his father is permissible. This is not the way we run our affairs. My husband is to have an equal share in the baby—in his welfare and bringing-up and, when he acquires any, his affections. As a matter of fact neither of us just now carries a large part of the manual labor connected with his care. We bathe him often, with equal dexterity, and give him occasional bottles. During his infrequent hours awake we hear him gurgle with equal delight. For the rest we have a nurse—Miss Smith. . . . But Miss Smith tells me of the complete aloofness of other fathers on the block and I feel sure that if Mrs. Lawrence and Mrs. Williams and Mrs. Lewis and Mrs. Beatty knew that my husband bathed the baby and changed him and gave him his bottle they would deeply disapprove. Not for these humble functions were fathers invented. [84]

Years later, when baby manuals like *Infant Care* and college textbooks like *The Child* were openly inviting fathers to become active participants in the care of the newborn, the fact that some men were doing what these publications asked, and more, did not to sit well with everyone. The medical magazine *Hygeia,* in 1942, published one man's tirade against what was euphemistically, and cynically, referred to as "the maternal father": "We have been married for fourteen years. During that time we have lived in four different communities. In each one there was a maternal father who menaced the peace and happiness of our friends by planting in the minds of otherwise contented wives and mothers the feeling that their Tom or Bill or Hugh was not properly interested in and attentive to the new, squirming baby in the basket." [85]

The author then offered this description:

> The maternal father arrives home promptly after work. If he commutes
> he has his hat on and is sprinting for the train while his fellow workers
> are straightening their desks or their accounts. He shoves through the
> crowd waiting for the train in order to get a seat or standing room near
> the door, for he can be depended on at whatever cost to himself or oth-
> ers not to lose one precious moment with his infant. On arriving home,
> he speedily sheds hat and coat, scrubs his hands with approved child
> study technic, then, clucking gently, lifts the baby from the basket and
> takes over the cares of the mother until bedtime for the small creature
> approaches, and it is tenderly laid away for the night. He bathes and
> diapers, and holds the bottle. With his mouth full of pins he coos in
> ecstasy and calls on the world to marvel at the baby's growth. In the
> meantime the adoring mother sinks into a comfortable chair to relax,
> or tiptoes out of the room—leaving father and child together in gur-
> gling bliss. [86]

What was it that was being objected to? "We have no quarrel with the
maternal father, or for that matter with the woman who refuses to accept
maternity, . . . [b]ut we protest that neither should he be glorified as rep-
resenting a standard by which others should be judged." The article went
on to blame mothers for the sad state of affairs that the American family
had gotten itself into. To this critic, at least, there was not a collusion
between experts and mothers that left out fathers; no, the sinister plot, if
there was one, was that fathers were being "unnaturally" convinced to
become more central: "The extreme need of many women today to urge
and encourage the father to assume a more maternal role seems to be
compensatory and not based on the role of the male in the development
of the race." [87]

No sooner had this point been made, however, than the principal targets of the piece were revealed. The maternal father, according to the
author, was not the creation of mothers per se but of feminists:

> Might it be possible that as a result of their emancipation there has
> arisen in the minds of many women an inability to accept sexual differ-
> ences either biologically or temperamentally, a desire to lessen the gaps
> of the past, so that they necessarily tend to interpret the role of man as
> nearly as possible as similar to that of woman? . . . However, the fact
> remains that feeding a newborn child is not as natural a function for the
> father as for the mother. . . . Why not encourage fathers to be them-
> selves and to follow a more paternal pattern? Encourage them to romp
> and play and work with their children in their own way, developing pa-

ternal bonds and deepness of affection which may be just as lasting as that which the maternal father develops by pinning on diapers or spooning out mush. To us, it seems in many ways more wholesome. . . . Might it not be better to encourage paternal fathers and leave maternity to mothers?[88]

The gender politics surrounding infant care could not be clearer. A social movement that started out small had become, in the minds of some, dangerous. If perceived threat is one measure of success, then by 1942 New Fatherhood had become a force to be reckoned with.[89]

Picture postcards were a popular means of communication at the turn of the century and are a favorite of collectors today. This card, published in the early 1900s, showed a father presumably forced to care for his child because of his wife's political activities. Note how silly he was made to appear. Humor directed at fathers was common in the early twentieth century, but it was also something that wavered. In the 1920s, men were significantly more likely than women to be depicted as incompetent by the media. In the 1930s, however, the gap between men and women converged, demonstrating along with other evidence that the modernization of fatherhood was not a linear process.

This postcard was one of a "Suffragette Series" of cards published by the Dunston-Weiler Lithograph Company in 1909. Here the father was made to appear not so much silly as saintly. And maternal. In some people's minds, the modernization of fatherhood was akin to the "madonna-ization," or feminization, of fatherhood. Interesting, too, is a comment made by the sender of the card. "Do I see you on the opposite side?" the writer asked his "Cousin Jay."

This painting of a father and son was used in an advertisement for Capitol Boilers and Radiators in *Time* magazine in 1927. The opening text of the ad read: "A great quietness reigns outdoors, broken only by the regular crunch-crunch of hurrying feet, and the crackle of crystal-laden trees swaying in the high wind. You awake slowly, lazily. Someone has already closed the window. And as the boy rushes in to have you read the 'funnies' to him, you feel the glow of benevolent heat rapidly filling the room." Whoever created this ad apparently felt that there were enough homeowners in the 1920s who would identify "warmth" with men and young children to warrant this depiction of fatherhood.

Mothers did most of the housework in the 1930s, much as they do today. But there were fathers (and sons) who washed and mopped, as this advertisement for Congoleum Gold Seal Rugs, published in the *Ladies Home Journal* in 1931, tried to convey. People who might see these activities as unmanly were sometimes told by the popular press that housework done *with* children was a good way to communicate the importance of duty and responsibility. (Courtesy of Congoleum Corporation.)

The modern versions of Father's Day and Mother's Day both have their roots in the early 1900s. But while the two holidays were established around the same time (Father's Day in 1910, Mother's Day in 1908), the rates at which they became accepted differed greatly. Mother's Day was signed into federal law in 1914, Father's Day not until 1972. Still, as popular as Mother's Day was, it was not without its critics. Shown here is a rally in New York City's Central Park in 1934 to promote the idea that Mother's Day should be changed to Parents' Day, so as not to exclude fathers. Parents' Day celebrations, held every Mother's Day from the mid-1920s to the late 1930s, were not viewed fondly by the business community, which saw more profit in two holidays. By the beginning of World War II, cultural and economic forces joined to make Father's Day an institution (though not a federal holiday), leaving the Parents' Day concept to die on the vine. (*The New York Times/* NYT Pictures.)

The effort, on the part of at least some, not to single out one parent on a given holiday is further illustrated in this 1931 Father's Day card aimed at both fathers and mothers. Observe the card's use of "Dad" without the corresponding use of "Mom." Central to the political maneuvering surrounding the modernization of fatherhood was the question of where to draw the line between fathering and mothering. Coupling "Dad" with "Mother" permitted men and women to be recognized as parents and, at the same time, differentiated. (Courtesy of Hallmark Archives, Hallmark Cards, Inc.)

During the Depression, father-child interaction often declined among both the employed and the unemployed. By contrast, the culture of fatherhood—the beliefs, norms, and values pertaining to fatherhood—continued to move forward during the 1930s and, if anything, became more modern. Most of the texts on fatherhood did not, however, acknowledge the Depression, which is one reason why this 1935 birthday card is so unique. Calling on the President to take some action, it took the risk of mixing personal celebration with public woe. (Courtesy of Hallmark Archives, Hallmark Cards, Inc.)

The modernization of fatherhood was fueled by the growing belief that child rearing was a science and that good parenting required expert advice. One of the better-known and most influential advice givers at the time was Angelo Patri (1876–1965), a New York city junior high school principal who hosted a radio show and wrote a syndicated newspaper column titled "Our Children." Patri, shown here when he was in his mid-forties and about to enter the most productive period of his life, received thousands of letters from parents throughout the country. These letters reveal ways in which the modernization of fatherhood was enacted in American homes. (Library of Congress, Angelo Patri Papers, LC-USZ62-99368.)

The modernization of fatherhood was fueled also by the technological innovations of the Machine Age. The explosive popularity of radios in the 1920s and 1930s, for example, helped to disseminate the experts' messages and create a mass culture. Radios also made it more likely that children would be directly exposed to the new child-rearing philosophies, as some experts broadcast their advice in the evening when everyone in the household might be listening. (Aristock/Atlanta.)

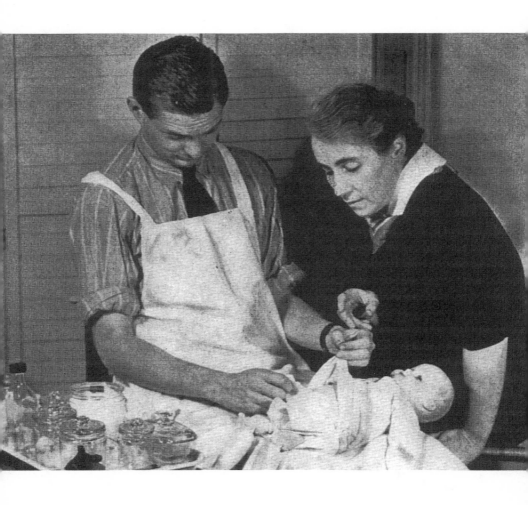

In addition to the books, magazine articles, and radio shows on fatherhood, there also were educational programs and child study groups. In the 1930s, the Maternity Center Association of New York City began to offer classes for expectant fathers. This man, watched by his instructor, was learning how to change a diaper. (From Hazel Corbin, *Getting Ready to Be a Father;* New York: Macmillan, 1939.)

Historians sometimes have characterized the nurturant fathers of the 1920s and 1930s as model-airplane-building "daddies" or poor souls lost in a maze of child-rearing lore. Little mention is made of the contact these fathers had with infants. Evidence suggests that more fathers than generally realized took an active interest in the health and well-being of their babies and also cleaned them, fed them, and put them to bed. (Aristock/Atlanta.)

Another impression we tend to have of yesterday's fathers is that they showered virtually all of their attention on sons. But even though many may have spent more time with sons than with daughters, few were oblivious to their daughters' needs. Indeed, some fathers exhibited a considerable amount of concern for their female children—especially in the 1930s, as the image of the father as male role model once again captured the public imagination. (Aristock/Atlanta.)

Fathercraft

> Heroic efforts must be made to prevent the parenthood in-
> struction crusade from becoming a woman's club enterprise.
> Ernest R. Groves, from *Social Problems of the Family*
> (1927)

The advantage of focusing on the Children's Bureau is that it was the principal government agency for the dissemination of child-rearing advice;
what it said about fatherhood had the approval of Uncle Sam (or "Aunt
Sammy," as one letter writer put it).[1] But to focus only on the Children's
Bureau would be to neglect a host of other public and private agencies
that also had an enormous impact on the modernization of fatherhood.

THE CHILD STUDY GROUP MOVEMENT

By 1932, according to one U.S. government report, child study groups,
parenting courses, and the like had been established or instigated at the
national level not only by the Children's Bureau but also by the American
Association of University Women, the American Home Economics Association, the National Congress of Parents and Teachers, the Child Study
Association of America, the Federal Board for Vocational Education, the
Cooperative Extension Service in Agriculture, and the U.S. Public Health
Service. Also, California, Iowa, New York, and Ohio had state programs;
Cleveland had a Child Training Committee; and Philadelphia had a Par-
ents' Council. Additionally, there were numerous local programs spon-
sored by universities, hospitals, churches, and private organizations.[2]

What role did fathers play in all of this? To what extent did they participate in, and contribute to, the child study group movement of the
1920s and 1930s? By some accounts, not much. One research project,
carried out in the late 1920s, examined the registration cards of 540
Minnesota residents who had enrolled in child study groups between
1 October 1926, and 15 April 1927, as well as 750 other residents who had
participated in a correspondence course. The research revealed that only
one registrant out of the entire sample was a man.[3] Another project, the

White House Conference Study discussed in the previous chapter, surveyed close to three thousand families nationwide in 1930 and found that
only 3.6 percent of white fathers and 3.2 percent of black fathers had ever
attended a child study group meeting. The figures for white mothers and
black mothers, respectively, were 28 percent and 19.1 percent. The White
House Conference Study also found the social class of the parents to be a
significant predictor of participation in child study groups. Approximately
8.3 percent of the white fathers in the "professional and semiprofessional/
managerial" classes (the top two classes in a seven-category scheme), and
about 5.1 percent of the black fathers in the "upper" class (the top class
in a two-category scheme) had attended a child study group. The figures
for white mothers and black mothers in these classes were 46.6 percent
and 24.8 percent. In the "day laborer" category (class seven), only 2.1
percent of the white fathers had attended a child study group, while in
the "lower" class (the bottom class in a two-category scheme), only 2.0
percent of the black fathers had attended a child study group. The figures
for white mothers and black mothers in these classes were 11.2 percent
and 15.1 percent.[4]

The Minnesota project and the White House Conference project have
been used to support the contention that "women dominated parent education" in the 1920s and 1930s.[5] "Dominated," however, may be too strong
a word, in that it implies that men had hardly any input. No matter what
the phrasing, I think we should be careful about using these two research
projects as barometers of the gender composition, power structure, and
group dynamics of the child study group movement.

There is, first of all, the question of methodology. One limitation of the
Minnesota project, overlooked by most, is that the registration cards used
to gather the data assumed that the registrants were women. (The cards
requested, among other items of information, "husband's occupation.")[6]
This simply may have reflected what was in fact the case, but it also may
have confounded the data collection process and ultimately masked men's
true participation rate. For example, men may have accompanied their
wives to the sessions but felt it unnecessary to fill out the cards, or they
may have read the materials for the correspondence course but not officially registered. What also is unclear from the published report is when
the study groups were scheduled. If the groups were scheduled during
the day, when most fathers were at their jobs, the low attendance of the
men is not surprising. Not every study group held its meetings in the
morning or afternoon, however.[7] What is more, reports indicate that

when child study group meetings were scheduled at times convenient for men, their participation noticeably increased.[8] Next, the educational program in Minnesota from the fall of 1925 through the spring of 1927—which includes the study's time window—was "devoted entirely to the preschool child."[9] The emphasis on the preschool child may have affected men's attendance in this particular program, because then, as now, mothers were presumed to be responsible for the young children. Finally, the fact that data collection for the Minnesota projects was carried out in the 1920s may be significant. As I have already pointed out and will demonstrate again, the culture of fatherhood in the 1920s and the culture of fatherhood in the 1930s were not identical.

Looking to the White House Conference project, one of its drawbacks, also mentioned before, is that it was based almost entirely on reports by women. This does not invalidate the data, but given the tendency of fathers and mothers to exhibit an egocentric, or credit-taking, bias when it comes to child care, there is the strong possibility that the measured level of father involvement, having been based on the perceptions of mothers, was underestimated.[10]

Apart from the methodological concerns that we might have about these two projects, we should remember that they do not represent all that was going in the child study group movement at the time. Before we draw any conclusions about men's roles in the movement, we should try to get as complete a picture as we can.

Looking beyond these two surveys, here is what I found. In 1913, a Council Bluffs, Iowa, man persuaded thirty of his male friends to come by the local school so he could tell them that they should be more involved in their children's lives, and especially in their children's educations.

> "[H]ow much do you know about your own children, much less other people's children?" he inquired of the men. "[A]nd how much do you know or care about the schools where those children's whole future lives are being shaped? As fathers we are failures, and worse than failures. Men don't *think* of themselves as fathers. They think of themselves as workers, and business men, as voters, but almost never as fathers. . . . Will you get together with me and tackle the job of learning how to be an intelligent, efficient father of children?"

The challenge that was laid down apparently touched off a spark, because, in a matter of only two years, what had started as a gathering of a few had grown to over one thousand men organized into fourteen clubs, all under the auspices of "the Federated Fathers' Clubs of Council Bluffs." The groups generally met once a month, using as their slogan, "What sort of father are you?".[11] The federation or its descendants may have exerted some effect through the 1930s.[12]

Elsewhere, in 1926, the Cleveland School of Education initiated a course for fathers to "attempt to teach them how to rear their children." "The movement," as it was called, was for the benefit of "little folks who have not yet reached school age."[13] In the late 1920s, a Dads' Club in Rutherford, New Jersey, met every other Thursday night at 8:00 P.M. in a school auditorium.[14] In the 1930s, a Fathers' Club in Elizabeth, New Jersey, was formed in connection with the local Y.M.C.A.,[15] and a Father's Organization in White Plains, New York, was created under the auspices of the Girl Scouts of America.[16] Also, there are reports that throughout the 1920s and 1930s, small coteries of men, often close friends, would arrange to take their children on weekend outings. These small get-togethers were study groups of sorts, opportunities for men to share their child-rearing strategies.[17]

In 1925, the College of Home Economics at Cornell University decided to "develop laboratory facilities with a view to putting [homemaking and child care] . . . on a more practical basis," and to target, among others, groups of fathers and mothers who might benefit from consultation with the laboratory staff and from periodic lectures. Fathers' groups apparently were also started "through the request of the fathers, after the mothers' course had been conducted." At a conference in New York city, where the Cornell lab was made public, "much interest was shown in the fathers' groups" by other parent educators, some of whom had experienced the same thing: fathers asking for their own parent training.[18]

In 1927, The United Parents' Association (UPA) of New York City claimed that at least half of its membership of 30,000–60,000 was made up of men. (The UPA president at the time was a man, and five of the eleven members of the governing board also were men.)[19] Several years later, in 1935, the UPA said that male membership had dropped, but it was "convinced" that "the tide [had] turned":

> [A] distinct trend is seen toward more participation by fathers in parent associations. One striking indication is the large number of fathers taking part in the work of parent groups connected with progressive schools, the number often equaling that of the mothers. Other evidence is to be found in the constant reiteration on all sides of the need of the most active participation by fathers, and the insistence on the part of teachers and parent educators that the child's welfare requires thorough understanding on the part of both parents of the child's whole world, especially the school.[20]

The Federal Board for Vocational Education (FBVE), founded in 1917, enrolled 105,838 adults in homemaking classes in 1932, noting that "[a]t first only women were enrolled in the parent education groups, but requests from women to bring their husbands to classes when problems of child development and family life were discussed led in some instances to enrollment of fathers as well as mothers." Apparently, some fathers took the initiative to ask for separate, fathers-only classes.[21] The Child Study Association of America also worked vigorously during the 1920s and 1930s to create child study programs for fathers. Indeed, the Child Study Association of America probably did more during the Machine Age to involve fathers in parent education than did any other organization. (I will have more to say about this group in a moment.)

In 1933, at the height of the Depression, the American Home Economics Association and the National Council on Parent Education sponsored a study of 331 families. Attendance figures were nearly three times as high for fathers and over twice as high for mothers compared to the 1930 White House Conference study. (I can offer only rough comparisons because the 1933 study combined attendance at child study groups with attendance at parent-teacher meetings.)[22] A possible explanation for the difference between the two studies is that the sample for the 1933 study was a more select group, one in which 88 percent of the fathers and 97 percent of the mothers had some college training.[23]

So, how involved were men in the early-twentieth-century child study group movement? With the additional information now in the equation, it would appear that fathers were more involved than has been suggested. Still, it is difficult to get a clear picture of what transpired. The problem may be that child study statistics can take us only so far. Let's look further—past the numbers.

FATHER-TO-FATHER BOOKS

Historians of fatherhood do not generally acknowledge that the early twentieth century witnessed an upsurge in what may be termed *father-to-father* books. (I say upsurge because father-to-father books had been in existence before.) A father-to-father book, as defined here, is one that is written by a man, probably a father himself, and directed primarily to other men who are either fathers-in-fact or fathers-to-be.[24]

In their turn-of-the-century manifestation, father-to-father books generally dealt with teaching the facts of life to daughters and sons,[25] providing advice to college-bound children,[26] or relating what it meant to be a parent of a World War I soldier.[27] By the time the Machine Age rolled around, father-to-father books more often than not focused on broader issues of child rearing, though almost always the attention was on sons rather than on daughters. Among the books published during the 1920s and 1930s were Frank H. Cheley's *The Job of Being a Dad* (1923), *Dad, Whose Boy Is Yours?* (1926), and *Fathering the Boy* (1933, an edited work); John Crawley's *Reveries of a Father* (1924); Fairfax Downey's *Father's First Two Years* (1925); Samuel S. Drury's *Fathers and Sons* (1927); T. W. Galloway's *The Father and His Boy* (1921); Edgar A. Guest's *My Job as a Father and What My Father Did for Me* (1923); Philip E. Howard's *Father and Son* (1922); Douglas Vass Martin's *Expectant Fathers* (1930); Martin Panzer's *Father Knows Better* (1940); David Victor's *Father's Doing Nicely* (1938); K. M. and E. M. Walker's *On Being a Father* (1929); and Frederic F. Van de Water's *Fathers Are Funny* (1939).[28]

Frank H. Cheley, as one can see, was the most prolific author, with three books to his credit. Cheley's influence in this genre, however, was more profound than his list of titles suggests, for Cheley also happened to be the Editor-in-Chief of a series called The Father and Son Library, which had begun publication in 1921. The purpose of the series was, in Cheley's words (in his 1933 edited book), "the practical aiding of the father in the home in providing for a boy a sound normal growth and education." Cheley said also that it was "the conviction of the editors and publishers of this Library that it will aid fathers to understand better their sons, as well as inspire sons to have a larger appreciation of their fathers, to the end that the finer type of man needed throughout the world in the coming years may be normally grown and developed in the homes of our land." [29]

By 1933, there were twenty volumes that the Father and Son Library had sponsored. Technically, these too were father-to-father books because, even though they often were written for children, the main idea still was that fathers would buy the books (and read them) to train their sons. For example, *The Boy's Own Book* (volume 2), edited by the Father and Son Library board, was advertised as "an intimate, friendly book in which, by means of quiet chats, the various outstanding features of all-around development are attractively discussed *with the boy.*" *Tools and Handicraft* (volume 5), edited by Harris W. Moore, was said to fully meet "the instinctive desire of every boy to make things" and included crafts that "center about the home itself, . . . developed so that father will find them interesting, as well as his sons." *Choosing a Life Work* (volume 16), edited by Clarence C. Robinson, was promoted as a book that "will stimu-

late every boy who reads it to desire *to make a life as well as a living* . . .
full of suggestions and wise counsel from the most successful men in
America—*their personal messages to boys.*" [30]

What the father-to-father books illustrate is that the science of fathercraft was not confined to the study group or fathers' club. If their work
schedules kept men from participating in a group or club, they still could
learn how to be modern fathers by buying and reading child-rearing
books that spoke directly (or indirectly) to them. The father-to-father
books also demonstrate that men could play, and indeed did play, a significant role in parent education during the Machine Age.

The principal message of most of the father-to-father books was, Get
involved! Philip E. Howard in *Father and Son,* for instance, maintained
that every father "must allow a large section of time in his life program
for fatherhood." As a model for other men to follow, he told of a

> father, admittedly one of the busiest men of our time, a man of world-
> wide interests, great productivity in the writing of important books, and
> away from home in public work about half his time, [who had] for years
> made it his rule to take one Sunday a month out of his crowded sched-
> ule of addresses to devote to his home, in family fellowship and family
> attendance upon the services of the Church. And on all his week-day
> home evenings, a certain time after dinner [was] carefully set apart be-
> fore he [went] to his study as the children's own time. [31]

Granted, Howard was not talking about a major commitment here. One
Sunday a month; a few minutes after dinner each day. Thus we can see
that certain Victorian concepts of fatherhood prevailed during the Machine Age. But there were other maxims in Howard's book that pointed
to a more modern version of fatherhood. Howard, for example, maintained that a father should "not leave out of his program of responsibility
the first years of his child's life," nor should a father confuse "the difference between doing things for, and living with" his boy.[32] Said Howard, "A
father learned a lesson in sharing when watching one of his small boys
busily at work with building blocks. From his armchair the man ventured
one or two off-hand architectural suggestions, whereupon the little chap
remarked wistfully, 'I like it better when you play on the floor with me.'
On the floor it was the next instant; and on the floor of the boy's unfolding
experiences, *with* the boy, not towering above him." [33]

In *My Job as a Father and What My Father Did for Me,* Edgar A. Guest
did not talk about becoming acquainted with his son when he was an infant. Rather, it is when his son, Bud, "graduated from his babyhood into
his boyhood" (at the age of 10) and "quit his mother's knee and turned to

[him] for counsel and comradeship" that his "job as a father" really began. Throughout the book, Guest tried to impress upon fathers the importance of making time for their children. In a scene that is reminiscent of some of the choices I have had to make while working on the book that you have in your hands (I happen to be the father of two boys), Guest talked about the occasions when his son would interrupt his writing: "Bud is calling me now to play marbles again. He wants his dad and he needs him. . . . Boyhood is calling to its father, and boyhood cannot wait. If I lose this opportunity to be his comrade I may lose him forever. So out I go to play marbles."[34]

As for Father and Son Library Editor-in-Chief Frank H. Cheley, he wanted fathers to be everything that Phillip E. Howard and Edgar A. Guest desired fathers to be—and more. In *Fathering the Boy,* Cheley told fathers that their jobs included not only playing with and teaching their sons (precepts spelled out in his earlier books, *The Job of Being a Dad* and *Dad, Whose Boy is Yours?*) but also designing their sons' habitats. "The boy's own room," Cheley wanted men to know, was "not merely a place to sleep or be apart" but "a place to make or break a boy." According to Cheley,

> The dominant idea of the place, . . . if it is to serve its largest purpose, must be a "place where the boys can feel the same sense of ownership that Mother feels in the kitchen and that Father feels in the garage or barn." If you are building a home, or expect to build in the future, be shrewd enough to work into your plans your finest conception of a room for boys. The mere fact that modern parents do not do this very thing accounts in no small way for the difficulties they experience in keeping their boys at home. . . . There should be good pictures that are suitable to a boy's room, among which should, by all means, be a Hoffman's "Head of Christ" and a well-framed print of Sir Galahad. Avoid the cheap-colored trash that so often finds its way into the boy's room. An exceptional magazine cover may serve for a time, but will rarely be permanent. There should be school and athletic pennants, as well as athletic equipment that is dear to the heart of the boy. Some of this, such as paddles, tennis rackets, and snowshoes, look well on the wall, while such things as bats, masks, and hiking paraphernalia should be kept in a convenient corner or cupboard. . . . The furniture should be straight-lined, substantial, and preferably of fumed oak. Under no circumstances let the boy feel that the old, worn-out, repaired stuff from the living room is good enough. This is a fatal error.[35]

The men who wrote and sponsored father-to-father books generally were middle class, if not upper middle class. (Cheley was actually serious when he said that old furniture in a boy's room was a "fatal error.") Indeed, the whole fathercraft industry was decidedly middle class, and thus not representative of all men. Some may feel that because of the industry's class bias the industry's impact on American fatherhood was minimal at best. We should be cautious, however, about dismissing the fathercraft movement on class grounds.

First, while I can understand how one might question the significance of what these men were trying to do by pointing to the small number of fathers who participated either as authors or readers, I would suggest, in response, that we look at the fathercraft industry in relative terms. No doubt there are more men taking parenting classes of one sort or another today, more men reading father-to-father books. But we should remember that today over 53 percent of mothers with children under one year of age are in the labor force, whereas in 1940 only 16 percent of married women, with or without children of any age, were employed.[36]

If we compare men's participation in parent education during the Machine Age with their participation at the present time, relative to the economic status of mothers in society, a different kind of assessment between fatherhood then and fatherhood now becomes apparent. The new comparison would force us to ask whether the change in men's participation in parent education over the course of the twentieth century has kept pace with the change in women's participation in outside work. If men's participation *has* changed more rapidly or at the same rate, then we would have to say that we are, without a doubt, in the midst of a major fatherhood revolution. On the other hand, if men's participation in parent education over the course of the twentieth century *has not* kept pace with the change in women's participation in outside work (and it has not), then we would have to say that a lot of the excitement surrounding today's New Fatherhood is overdrawn. Noteworthy, it may be; major revolution, it is not.[37]

I also think that we should be careful about using the social class variable to dismiss what took place during the Machine Age. It certainly is true that the vast majority of men who were involved in parent education programs during the Machine Age were middle class, but almost the same can be said of the men who are involved in parent education programs today. I am not arguing that men's involvement then and now are equivalent; I am contending only that if we are going to introduce the social class variable to qualify what fathers of the Machine Age were trying to do, then we must apply the same standard to contemporary fatherhood. New Fatherhood was then and still is the purview of the middle class.[38]

THE CHILD STUDY ASSOCIATION OF AMERICA

Examining scattered bits of evidence is one way to understand the fathercraft industry, but citing a father's club here, or a father-to-father book there, does not give us a handle on the people and organizations who were behind the myriad efforts to create a new brand of fatherhood during the Machine Age. To study the social construction of fatherhood—indeed, to study the social construction of anything—without paying close attention to the human agents in the construction process itself is both methodologically limiting and sociologically naive.[39]

In chapter 3, we had the advantage of being able to zero in on one particular agency—the Children's Bureau. In this chapter, we can gain a similar advantage by focusing on what arguably was "the most important child study and parent education organization" of the 1920s and 1930s: the Child Study Association of America (CSAA).[40]

The CSAA was founded in 1888 as the Society for the Study of Child Nature; it became the Federation for Child Study in 1908, and then changed again in 1924 to become the Child Study Association of America.[41] In its early days, the society essentially was a book discussion club. Members met at someone's home to talk, amidst refreshments, about how the ideas in a particular text could be used with children. Although child-rearing manuals were available at the time, the society preferred books with a philosophical (and particularly an "Enlightenment") bent. The first bibliography of the group included works such as Plato's *Republic*, Aristotle's *Ethics* and *Politics*, John Locke's *Thoughts on Education*, and Jean Jacques Rousseau's *Emile*.[42]

By the mid-1920s, CSAA-sponsored child study groups were as likely as not to be discussing modern books such as the CSAA's own *Outlines of Child Study: A Manual for Parents and Teachers*.[43] The meetings themselves, which now often enough were held in a pubic hall, had become informal opportunities for parents to get together and talk about the art and science of parenting. When I say informal, I do not mean to suggest that there was no agenda. Indeed, just the reverse was true. The CSAA prided itself on the amount of structure and "work" that was demanded from its chapters, and openly encouraged the use of speakers and information-guided discussions. (Every group had at least one designated leader.) The ideal size of a group, or "chapter," as it was called then, was between fifteen and thirty people. Meetings were held once a week or every other week.[44]

The first CSAA chapters were based in New York, with the main office being located in Manhattan. As early as 1917, however, satellite chapters could be found in Boston, Chicago, Cincinnati, Louisville, New Haven, and New Orleans. By the late 1920s, chapters or affiliated organizations had sprung up in Canada, China, Great Britain, and Japan.[45]

Although sponsoring child study groups was the organization's original goal and continued to be a central feature of its curriculum throughout its many transformations, by the time the society (or federation) had evolved into the Child Study Association of America, it had become a parent education conglomerate with a variety of interests and functions. During the 1920s and 1930s, for example, the CSAA published a periodical called *Child Study* (originally titled the *Federation for Child Study Bulletin*), penned its own child-rearing books (i.e., *Outlines of Child Study, Our Children,* and *Parents' Questions*),[46] ran a speaker's bureau (in 1925 in New York city alone there were 1,400 CSAA-sponsored lectures),[47] and endorsed (or refused to endorse) books, films, games, and comic strips.[48]

As to who was behind the CSAA, there were many who helped to make the organization what it was. Several men and women, however, were especially influential, and deserve mention.[49] First, there was Felix Adler, the father of the Ethical Culture movement, who, according to lore, was the CSAA's "inspiration." It was Adler who suggested the idea of an organization "for the purpose of studying the problems of child nature from the mental, moral and physical view points."[50] Also, it was Adler's book *The Moral Instruction of Children,* along with Locke's and Rousseau's, that provided the intellectual ferment early on.

While Adler may have helped to launch the organization, he was not the society's captain or its compass. That honor goes to the original members. At the first meeting of the society, the five mothers in attendance debated "the relative merits of being either an autonomous association or an extension of the Ethical Culture movement," and decided that being an extension of the Ethical Culture movement would be "too limiting as it would tend to exclude members of 'other religions.' " A vote was thus taken to make the society "an independent nonsectarian organization."[51] The society's first president was Mrs. Harry Hastings.[52]

Two other leaders were Bird Stein Gans and Cecile Pilpel. Gans was a member of the society from its inception, became president of both the Federation for Child Study and the Child Study Association of America, and was a strong advocate for making a place for parent education in adult education. Pilpel joined the organization in 1898 and, for a number of years, was the Director of Child Study Groups, one of the most critical positions in the organization.

Probably the most influential figure in the CSAA was Sidonie M. Gruenberg. A professor of education at Columbia University, Gruenberg had become a member of the organization in 1908 and served as the chief administrative or staff officer for a number of years. She also coauthored several books sponsored by the CSAA, including *Our Children* (1932) and *Parents' Questions* (1936 and 1947). Gruenberg chaired the White House subcommittee that issued the 1932 government report on parent education, which was discussed at the beginning of the chapter. Her husband, Benjamin C. Gruenberg, also played a significant role as the editor of the first child-rearing manual sponsored by the CSAA, *Outlines of Child Study* (1922 and 1927).

Finally, there was Lawrence K. Frank, who helped to shape the organization not so much from within as from without. Frank was in charge of child study programs for the Laura Spelman Rockefeller Memorial in 1922, and through a grant from the Memorial to the Federation for Child Study in 1923, "engineered the metamorphosis" of the federation into the incorporated Child Study Association of America. This change was more than a change in name. The federation "had a heavily middle- and upper-middle-class Jewish membership. . . . [but] was entirely secular in its approach to child study." The restructuring of the federation was intended to not only "disguise the ethnicity" of the organization's membership but also to communicate "that Jews were an integral part of national culture." Thus transformed, the federation (now the CSAA) "could disseminate its rather sophisticated curricula and publications on child study to a national constituency."[53] Lawrence K. Frank, through his influence at the Laura Spelman Rockefeller Memorial, also was instrumental in the professionalization of child science research and in the creation of the Society for Research in Child Development, discussed in chapter 3. He played a part, too, in the founding of *Parents' Magazine* in 1926, which I will talk about in chapter 6.

"EVERY FATHER A MEMBER"

We know that men played a part in the creation and nurturance of the organization, but what about membership in the study groups? Could men play a part there, too? In keeping with nineteenth-century mores, the study groups originally were open only to women. As time passed, however, men were welcomed, too. Exactly when the organization officially changed its membership policy is difficult to determine, but one piece of evidence may be used as a benchmark. The 1924–1925 "Federation for Child Study Program" (a document that outlined the organization's activities and listed the "specific subjects" chosen "as the work for the season" [November to April]) said that "any group of *mothers or students* [could] be organized into a 'chapter' for the systematic, cooperative study of problems connected with child training [my italics]."[54] One year later, however, the 1925–1926 "Child Study Association of America Program" (1924 is when the new name was adopted) said that the CSAA was made up of "groups of *mothers and fathers* working together, studying authorities and discussing their problems in the light of present-day knowledge [my italics]."[55] The same brochure also announced that chapter 80 in Webster Groves, Missouri, was planning to have two fathers' meetings, one on "The Modern College as Essential in a Liberal Preparation for Life," and another on "The Unadjusted Child" (i.e., the child with a "Superior Intellect" or "Pathological Complexes"). Thus, the organization's new identity in the mid-1920s appears to have ushered in a more modern attitude toward men. The CSAA, it could be said, had joined the New Fatherhood crusade.

Did the CSAA really wait until the mid-1920s to allow fathers to participate in its groups? Was it really as open to New Fatherhood as the 1925–1926 program suggested? The answer to both questions, paradoxically, is no. Herein lies the value of closely examining the texts of this industry giant, for what these texts allow us to see is the *interpretive process* (in colloquial terms, the wrestling with oneself and others) that child-rearing experts of the Machine Age were caught up in.[56]

The process essentially came down to this. The modernization of fatherhood meant that there would be losers as well as winners resulting from the shift in social terrain. That much was clear. What was not clear was which side of the scoreboard men and women would end up on, once the dust had settled. Hence, while there was a willingness among various child-rearing experts to work toward finding a new and higher place for men in the home, there was a general reluctance to shake things up too much, for fear that women would be displaced. After all, if men were to be considered women's parenting equals and still be able to control the marketplace, then what special skills could mothers claim to have? What, in other words, would the status of men and women be under the new system? How the CSAA dealt with these issues sheds considerable light on the mind-set of early-twentieth-century parent educators.

As I said, the 1924–1925 program reported that CSAA membership was open only to mothers or students. Yet, the 1923–1924 program indicated that one of the chapters was planning a child study group for "men and women."[57] Also, in December 1923, one month into the 1923–1924 season, an announcement was made that a whole series of father and mother conferences had been planned: "In response to an insistent demand from *pater familias,* we are organizing in addition to our day-time and evening chapters conducted for mothers alone, a series of 8 study conferences for fathers and mothers together on 'Behavior Problems in the Home,' under the leadership of Dr. Bernard Glueck, director of the Bureau of Children's Guidance [my italics]."[58]

Hence, as early as 1923, and *before* the official membership policy change in November 1925 (using the brochure test), the CSAA was directing some of its programs to men. There is evidence to indicate that even by 1920, and possibly earlier, the CSAA was thinking seriously about the roles of men in child care. While I was reviewing the CSAA documents housed at the Social Welfare History Archives at the University of Minnesota, I found a handwritten set of notes that outlined the major events in the history of the CSAA from 1888 to 1926. Under the heading for 1920, a single entry appeared: "Father's Share in the Training of Children."[59] Whether this entry referred to a lecture, a conference, or a study group meeting, I do not know. Nor can I say whether or not men were expected to participate. It, whatever "it" was, may have been *about* fathers but not *for* fathers.

In April 1925, the CSAA launched a membership drive to recruit men. (The decision to change the 1925–1926 brochure probably was made during the previous season.) The theme of the drive was "Every Father a Member," implying a major commitment to restructure the gender composition of the groups. Notice, however, how the CSAA phrased its drive:

> Let's begin at home. Of course father is concerned with the children's welfare. Does he know what Child Study is doing for you and your children? Have you "sold" him the Child Study idea? If not, why not? If he is confident of the value of our work he surely won't refuse to help us. "Every father a member." Make yours one now. Here is the coupon. Fill it out, send it now, and help us start our campaign with a 100 percent father membership. "Every father a member." Then we can begin upon our relatives, our neighbors, our friends.[60]

At first glance, the advertisement would seem to indicate that the CSAA was inviting men to become full-fledged members of the organization. But look again: "Does he know what Child Study is doing *for you* . . . ? . . . . If he is confident of the value of our work he surely won't refuse to *help us.*" Taken literally, the call to fathers was not so much an invitation to join the CSAA as it was a request for moral or financial support. Indeed, financial support seems to have been very much the motivation: "Do you know that the Child Study Association uses over $30,000 yearly to support its various activities, in addition to its appropriation from the Laura Spelman Rockefeller Memorial? Do you know that our membership roll *at present* contributes only $5,000 of that amount? In the past the deficit has been met partly by donations, partly by various entertainments. These activities have sapped the energies of our working staff and at the same time have offered only a variable and insecure revenue. We must do better than that."[61]

Also, what are we to make of the following strategy? Two years after the CSAA formally opened its doors to men, it announced that it had "initiated the use of a registration card" that, curiously enough, assumed every new member to be a mother. Each registrant, for example, was asked to give "her age, education and training, her occupation before and during marriage; similar information about her husband; number of children in her family, their age, sex, and school status."[62] You will recall that a similar kind of registration card was used in the 1926–1927 Minnesota study and probably biased its results. That any men were willing to show up for the meetings—or to stay after they had arrived—is interesting all by itself, given the disconfirming messages they were sent.[63]

Yet show up and stay they did. During the 1925–1926 season, thirty-four New York City fathers and mothers enrolled in an evening course called "Sex Education for Parents." In St. Louis, a special meeting for fathers on the topic "Habits and Personality" was so successful that "more evening gatherings" were planned. In Queens, New York, there was a lecture, again in the evening, titled "The Role of the Father in the Life of the Child." In another part of town (location not specified), "fathers and mothers" were invited to an evening presentation titled "The Adolescent in Modern Society." During the 1927–1928 season, a series of five evening conferences "for fathers and mothers" was planned, "and a special joint fee for membership was offered," which turned out to be "most successful." (Among the new members were 20 husbands of already existing members.) "The average attendance at each meeting was 175," with a "lively discussion following each lecture." Lecture topics included the following: "Discipline"; "The Use of Money"; "Self Reliance and Responsibility"; "Sex Education"; and "The Parent-Child Relationship."[64]

A SYMPOSIUM: "FATHERS AND PARENT EDUCATION"

By the early 1930s, fathers had become semipermanent fixtures in many a child study group, but the question that was being asked was whether "the experiment" was working. In an effort to address this question, the

CSAA newsletter published (in February 1932) a symposium titled "Fathers and Parent Education."[65]

The CSAA may have been at the forefront of the modernization of fatherhood, but what is striking about the comments of the various contributors to the symposium was how traditional they were. The consensus of opinion seemed to be that, regardless of whether fathers were involved in child rearing, fathers and everyone else had to remember that fathers and mothers were different. Thus, in one respect, the symposium would seem to belie the proposition that the CSAA was committed to New Fatherhood. A more reasonable conclusion, however, is that the symposium illustrated the contra-dictions (what, in chapter 1, I called "conflicts in expression") surrounding New Fatherhood. As is true today, the fact that the New Fatherhood had made its way into popular culture did not mean that the Old Fatherhood had disappeared. Understanding the modernization of fatherhood requires that we appreciate and study the fragmentation, not sweep it under the rug.[66]

As to the specifics of the symposium, Lawrence K. Frank argued that "the father's role in child nurture" was "the principal source of the children's ego-ideals and the arbiter of their security as it is concerned with position, rank, achievements and acquisitions in the social life." The mother, according to Frank, was "usually more influential in forming the child's emotional reactions and patterns of personal relationships."[67] Cecile Pilpel wanted to emphasize that to "share" did not mean to "share alike": "The real question is not how can father be taught and urged to *do* the mother job? but how can he be taught what the mother job *means?* How can he learn what is involved in child rearing—physically, educationally and emotionally—so that, instead of washing his hands of the whole thing, or assuming a critical or a disruptive attitude, he may contribute something real and positive in understanding, in sympathy and in moral support?"[68] Eduard C. Lindeman, whose contribution was titled "Bringing Father Back into the Family," also drew a hard line: "Education for fathers needs to be based on important differences between fathers and mothers." Lindeman offered in support of his position his personal observations of study group interactions:

> When fathers have organized study groups, certain experiences and rules come to the fore indicating differences between such male groups and groups consisting of women. In the first place, it has been discovered that fathers are more likely to attend study groups if they are not asked to break too many established habits. In one instance, fathers were not merely permitted but were urged to bring pipes. Since fathers

have for the most part enjoyed very little daily experience in parent-child relationships, they do not respond to an appeal to exchange experiences; on the contrary, they like to be addressed by specialists, authorities.[69]

Mr. and Mrs. Robert E. Simon began their essay on the theme of father inclusion. They noted that men's participation in fathers' study groups was "successful" and "surprisingly large," and they related the story of a mixed-gender meeting that was almost canceled due to inclement weather but was held anyway because "many fathers were sufficiently interested to come *without* their wives." The Simons also thought it important, however, to emphasize the point that while the "harmonious home requires cooperative, unselfish parents . . . biological differences and training of the man and the woman are such that each performs a definite, distinct function. Neither can completely take the place of the other." They warned, too, "Some of those who would educate the father as well as the mother in parenthood start out with the mistaken theory that the father should know as much and the same kind of detail about children as the mother. It would be very unfortunate if that were so. While there are some fathers who enjoy bathing and otherwise caring for the baby, we should make it perfectly clear to the father that we are not trying to make a mother of him, though his place in his child's development is vital and important in other ways."[70]

The Simons' last sentence may have gotten to the heart of the contradictions. The controversy over fathers' attendance at child study groups, for the CSAA at least, seemed to center on the question of what it meant to be a man, and what it meant to be a woman: gender politics again. If fathers did attend child study groups, they might learn a lot, but was there not also a chance that their masculinity would be threatened? And what about mothers? Would they feel less feminine, sitting in a room where men were licensed to talk about "the mother job" (to use Pilpel's terminology)? On the other hand, if fathers did not attend the child study groups, would their lack of education render them useless and uncooperative (dopey and ultimately marginalized) when it came to the important task of child rearing? Would closing the schoolhouse door to men give women undeserved power over men? Would this shift in the power structure breed resentment on the part of fathers or conflict between husbands and wives (hardly positive outcomes in the age of the companionate ideal)?

One variable that can help to explain the amount of attention that the CSAA gave to masculinity and femininity and its own reflexiveness on the distinctions is the reliance of its leaders on the ideas of Sigmund Freud. If a child expert embraced Freud, it is likely the expert would advance a fairly traditional view of how fathers and mothers are supposed to behave, because Freud's theories of child development were predicated on the assumption that there were essential differences between men and women, boys and girls.

While Freud may have first spoken to an American audience as early as 1909 (at Clark College, and at the behest of the psychologist G. Stanley Hall), and while his ideas may have filtered into the consciousness of American intellectuals in the 1920s, it really was not until the late 1930s and especially the 1940s and 1950s that Freud's ideas began to have an impact on the fathering and mothering discourse in the United States.[71] If we examine the texts of the Child Study Association of America, however, we see evidence of Freudianism in the 1920s, that is, before many other members of the child-rearing intelligentsia had incorporated Freudianism into their theoretical repertoire.[72] The attempt to combine Freudianism with New Fatherhood may seem contradictory, and on a certain level it is. Freudianism, however, also provided a theoretical rationale for promoting masculine domesticity or, again, the infusion of masculine traits into the domestic sphere. In the next chapter, I will show how masculine domesticity (versus domestic masculinity) increased in popularity in the 1930s, and how it contributed to the modernization of fatherhood during the Depression.

The issues raised in the 1932 symposium were not new, but had been part of the discussion surrounding the fathercraft movement from the beginning. Also, these were not issues that the CSAA leaders and other parent educators were ignorant of, or tried to dismiss. To the contrary, they wrestled with them virtually every day, and worked hard to find solutions.

For example, at an October 1925 Conference on Parenthood sponsored by the CSAA, Cecile Pilpel ruminated that men seemed especially interested in attending meetings when the topic of discussion was discipline. She wondered whether the men's "interest [was] due to the fact that the new insight and ideas in handling disciplinary problems which the mothers were acquiring were so far removed from the traditional ideas that the fathers resented them." She noted, too, that "sometimes a father is disappointed that his wife should feel it necessary to go to a group outside to get knowledge which, merely by virtue of being his wife and mother of his children, she ought to have." Pilpel went on to explain this as "an undercurrent of feeling which, when met, [could] be successfully combatted."[73]

Douglas A. Thom, a physician associated with the Harvard Medical School and author of the highly regarded 1927 book *Everyday Problems of the Everyday Child*, expressed concerns similar to Pilpel's:

> The difficulties and complexities of caring for the child are stressed so much that the father is led to believe that any contribution he might make would raise havoc with all the careful thought and premeditated ideas that the mother has been daily putting into the task of child training. Whatever he says is apt to be the wrong thing. If Johnny asks for a story, it's time for bed. If Dad brings home candy, it's a foregone conclusion that it will make him sick. If plans are made for a football game, it's too cold or rainy or something else unsuitable. Dad seems to have the faculty of always suggesting the wrong thing.[74]

Anyone who had read Thom's book—and many apparently did, because it was on almost every recommended reading list, including the CSAA's— could not help but be made aware of the pitfalls of excluding fathers from parent education. Forewarned was forearmed.[75]

Resentment and marginalization were feelings that fathers sometimes felt, to be sure, and to the extent that they were allowed to fester, they could pose serious problems inside the home. But there were key figures in the parent education movement who were aware of these feelings and who often did what they could to minimize or eliminate them. Hence, to suggest, as do some historians, that the parent education movement invariably erected barriers between fathers and mothers is not entirely correct. Granted, the possibility for paternal exclusion was there and probably was, in fact, exhibited on a number of occasions. However, what historians generally have failed to report were the routine efforts by some in the parent education movement to prevent this from happening.

GROUP DYNAMICS

Fathers were not the only ones who could be marginalized by parent educators; mothers could be, too. Again, parent educators were not oblivious to, nor necessarily eager to reinforce, boundaries between themselves and the people they were trying to help. Sidonie M. Gruenberg, for example, once told her students, "We have taken confidence away from parents. Just because the teacher has had more courses in child study, etc., we have made the parents feel that they cannot cope with the situations. [But] the parents have one tremendous asset—the child cares for them and they care more than anybody else can about the child and they have to retrieve their confidence in themselves that they are able to cope with the situation." [76]

We know what Gruenberg said to her students, because one of the documents that I came across in my efforts to uncover information about the Child Study Association of America was a nine-page, single-spaced transcript of a discussion that took place on 7 October 1931 in Gruenberg's Columbia University Course on Parent-Child Relationships (Education 251-E). What makes this transcript especially valuable is that, although the topic for the day was called the "Changed Status of Woman," much of the conversation centered on the role of fathers in child study groups. The transcript is revealing not only for what it says about Gruenberg's attitudes toward fathers but also for what it says about the interpretive process (again, the wrestling, or give and take) that was part and parcel of the parent education movement in general and the fathercraft movement in particular. [77]

It was Gruenberg herself who directed the discussion to the question of fathers when she asked the students, "Do you feel that the father's interest in his children and his participation in the family life as it relates to children is the same as the mother's? Whether you feel it should be the same or not, it is different. Where do the differences lie?"

Note that Gruenberg both asked and answered the question that she posed. She told the students that even if they felt fathers and mothers should be the same, they were not. Like the presenters at the symposium on fathers and parent education, Gruenberg had decidedly traditional views on men and women. (The symposium had taken place only six months earlier.)

The students agreed with Gruenberg's assertion that fathers and mothers were different—no surprises there. One student did mention some similarities between fathers and mothers that she had observed in the groups she had led. However, she quickly followed that observation with another, one that highlighted gender dissimilarity: "I had a group of mothers and fathers together and it gave me a chance to watch the difference in the kinds of questions they asked. The fathers of little children were apt to ask just as concrete questions as the mothers did, but even so the fathers were apt to be far sighted and look for philosophic principles and what effect they would have tomorrow." [78]

Gruenberg confirmed what the student said, and then went on to offer a history of the CSAA's experience with fathercraft. Gruenberg's points and the responses of her students are reproduced below.

Mrs. Gruenberg: Men can be more objective. Now that women have "equal rights" we can look at the differences in the sexes without feeling inferior. In the early days of the parent education movement we said the fathers must come in—it isn't just a mother's job alone. We thought they must come in on the same basis and go through the same procedures and be interested in the same things. Here in New York the fathers were at first tolerant of it—they thought of it as just another "culture" club and that their wives were interested in that instead of a Browning club. They had a very patronizing attitude. But when they began to suspect that the mother's point of view regarding the child was changing, the fathers' attitude became more defensive and they asked, "What is this you are bringing back here? My mother brought me up without belonging to a study club, and look at me. Could anything be more wonderful?" Or he said, "Who is this woman I married who has to go to study to bring up her children[?] Generations have brought up children without reading books." Then they began to see there might be something in it after all, but they said they would like to have a group of their own, not a coeducational group. That raised a problem—why men leave home—to go to a child study group! That lasted two or three years and they found it was perfectly all right for mothers to go to a child study group. Then we had a coeducational group but it did not go very well. Since then there have been only sporadic efforts to bring fathers in. At the present time there is no difficulty in getting them interested.

Question: [Posed by whom? It was not made clear.] Why didn't groups for fathers work out well?

Mrs. Gruenberg: Because the mothers were in the lead and they took it for granted that the fathers must be interested in just what they were. It was forcing the issue. While it has been said that fathers will ask these concrete questions, their interest is more academic and objective and not quite so personal and heated. Where the effort has been made to have special father groups, the content of the fathers' discussion and the sequence and the approach have been different. I think it is fair to recognize the difference. But men are just as susceptible to being swayed by one or two members of the group as women. (Instance of Lincoln School Fathers Group.)

Student: That bears out my own experience—that men have not as yet learned how to function in groups for discussion or for cultural advancement.

Mrs. Gruenberg: Women, as the only leisure class in America, have had much more experience along that line. But one point I would like to make clear is that, vrom [*sic*] our present experience, the individual father today is just as interested as the mother.[79] The means that he chooses for manifesting that interest or the method that we can offer for serving this interest, may not be the same as that which has come of the women's groups. We need to do more research to determine just what the men want—just what will serve this specific purpose. . . .

Question: Isn't the father's interest similar to the interest the wife takes in the business or professional life of the husband? It must of necessity be once removed. The father's interest will be one more of advisory nature, rather than so much participation that comes from the mother's continuous relationship with the children.

Student: In many cases, mothers assume that their interest is greater than the father's, and relegate fathers to some of the other interest[s] which do not mean so much.

Mrs. Gruenberg: I suppose that there is probably greater difference within each situation than between situations. There will be fathers who will participate more, and mothers who will participate less, but by and large under the present setup, and certainly during the early days, we must admit that the father cannot be specifically concerned in the same manner as the mother. He can be just as greatly concerned, but not in the same manner. Of course, mothers who are out of the house all day are apt to have the same objective attitude as husbands. Take the situation that came to one habit clinic. The little girl of three years was a feeding problem. The mother had to sit there and put the food into her mouth, and the moment the mother stopped talking, she stopped eating. You investigated the whole life of this family. You found there was no substantial agreement between father and mother as to how the child should be managed. . . . It is very essential that parents agree, in general, on some of the major concerns. . . .

Student: What validity is there in the view point that perhaps fathers and mothers are not the best people to take care of their children? In the long run, better trained people are more desirable.

Mrs. Gruenberg: This question arises inevitably and also in relation to sending children away to boarding school or away all day. . . . There are certainly some parents who can be replaced much better. We cannot take it for granted that because a woman has given birth to a child that she is necessarily qualified for all the aspects of its care. She may be very well qualified for certain aspects and not for others. We have introduced an element of choice for the parent. . . . The home has always utilized other people, but formerly you did not have to go out into the community to get them. There were always other adults around a home to whom you could relegate a little of the care of the child. This idea of one woman with one child and tied to that child inevitably, regardless of her desires and inclinations is a new aspect. . . . Sociologically speaking, one of the strains and stresses in modern family life is due to the fact that each individual claims the right for a complete life. That brings up to the mother whether she should have the complete care of a child. You have each member of the family striving for a personal adjustment. Being a martyr has gone out of fashion. No one admires you for it. . . . [E]ven when there are only a few children—you find the father striving for a personal adjustment. He doesn't feel that just because he is a father he has to give up his claims on life as a human being. A woman does not want to be just a mother and a wife. Then when you have a child or two or three, each with individual capacities, each individual striving within this small unit, you have quite a problem. That is a new aspect of this whole situation. No one is willing to take the whole responsibility. Can that responsibility for the family be shared or will it come back again to the mother[?] Somebody has to be there and see that somebody gives in. I cannot see the family continuing with any great satisfaction to the individual members of the family unless somebody takes that responsibility. I personally have been giving a great deal of thought to it and it seems to me it is the mother's responsibility. No matter what else she is, she is the chief executive of that little establishment. It has to be centered and she has to see to it that each one gets his rights and his needs and his desires. You cannot leave it for them just to fight it out. There are some people who feel it can be equally shared. I believe it should be shared by the father, but even under the most favorably [*sic*] situations I do not think it can be equally shared. I have come to the conclusion that women are better equipped psychologically for this. Ten or fifteen years ago I would not have said this.[80]

There is so much said here that it is hard to know what to address, and in what order. Perhaps the best thing to do is to start at the beginning of the transcript.

Gruenberg first stated that in the early days of the parent education movement, there was a concerted effort to get fathers involved so they would know that parenthood was not "just mothers' job alone." As to why it was important that fathers know this, Gruenberg pointed to the issue of women's rights, saying that as long as women were not considered equal, the implication that parenthood was solely the mothers' job made the inequality worse. Believing that by the early 1930s, women *had* achieved equality with men, Gruenberg said that women could now "look at the differences in the sexes without feeling inferior." Gruenberg, in short, felt comfortable arguing that men and women were different, not because she wanted to preserve men's prerogatives, but because she believed that society had reached a point where it would no longer automatically translate discussions of gender dimorphism into endorsements for gender stratification.

Gruenberg was not the only leader of the CSAA who thought along these lines. A similar argument had been made by Cecile Pilpel in a chapter of the CSAA's 1932 handbook for parents, *Our Children:*

> The emancipation of women which came through our acceptance of the worth of the individual for his own sake, as well as for the role which he plays in the scheme of things, has made family living still more complex. There was very naturally at first an overemphasis on freedom, an attempt to play the man's role. But now we have passed the Doll's House stage. Women of intelligence see very clearly today that it is not necessary or desirable for them to be *like* men. . . . The younger generation of women who did not have to fight for their emancipation and therefore do not have to prove their "equality" with men are working out a new family pattern, or rather are discovering that the age-old pattern is still the most satisfying, provided it is interpreted in harmony with our present-day economic and social setting.[81]

Both Gruenberg and Pilpel were naive to believe that the fight for women's rights was over. But the sociological axiom, "If people define situations as real, they are real in their consequences," makes their behavior understandable. Gruenberg and Pilpel *saw* men and women as equal yet different, and they *acted* on the basis of that perception.[82]

To return to the transcript of the class, Gruenberg next said that during the early stages of the parent education movement, men were "tolerant" of their wives' involvement because they figured it was just another "culture" club. When men noticed their wives' attitudes toward child care changing, however, they "became more defensive and they and began to ask, 'What is this you are bringing back here?' " The infusion of new child-rearing ideas into the home thus seems to have had the same effect on the marital relationship that other forms of consciousness raising have had on relationships in general. Mothers felt that they were being enlightened. Fathers felt that mothers were being led astray. Here were two definitions of the situation—two perceptions of what was moral and what was right.

Let's stop for a moment. If fathers did indeed disagree with their wives over the value of parent education, then the leaders of the parent education movement had a serious problem. Without the approval of fathers, parent educators could not be sure that women would be allowed to come to the study groups or be allowed to put into practice what they had learned. Obviously, the men had to be won over. Note, for example, in the transcript that when the three-year-old with the feeding problem was being discussed, Gruenberg said, "It is very essential that parents agree in general, on some of the major concerns." Gruenberg understood that parent education required cooperation, not marginalization. In order for it to work, men had to be incorporated somehow into the system.

Because the CSAA leaders knew they could not succeed without men's endorsement, they were anxious to know what fathers thought about child study and would often ask the mothers in the groups to report on the reaction that they were getting at home. In one set of interviews, the answers the mothers gave to the question, "What is your husband's opinion of the work done by the Child Study Group?" included the following:

> "He thinks it is very nice and helpful to mothers, also fathers, as well as to those who take interest in children. Every meeting he asks me what I learn and then we sit down and talk it over."

> "He thinks I should never miss a meeting and he is quite proud to have me explain what subjects we had or discussed. He says it gives us both new ideas."

> "He thinks it is very good and would like to attend the group himself if he had more time at home." [83]

We may now have a better understanding of why, in the mid-1920s, the CSAA decided to open its membership ranks to fathers but did not necessarily assume that the men would show up at the meetings. The CSAA seems to have wanted the men's approval more than they wanted their presence. ("Does he know what Child Study is doing *for you*. . . . If he is confident of the value of our work he surely won't refuse to *help us*.") Also operating, though it is hard to pin down the sequence, was the feeling that men needed to understand that parenthood was not the mothers' job alone. This had the effect of encouraging fathers to get involved in parent education. Gruenberg said that fathers initially balked at the idea, but eventually they came around. What the fathers wanted—what they asked for—were *their own* groups.

Groups of men requesting forums of their own created, according to Gruenberg, a new problem: men leaving home. Gruenberg may have felt—and others may have, too—that asking men to go out again after they came home from work reduced the very contact between fathers and children that the experts were trying to achieve. It was one thing for mothers to have an evening out; they were spending plenty of time with the children to begin with. Men were another story, however. The idea of men going out after work brought up the specter of the absentee father spending his time in amusement with his friends rather than at home. In the 1800s, remember, evening club life for middle-class men was a very popular pastime, but this extracurricular activity had already begun to wane by the turn of the century.[84]

Here is something else to consider, however. If the comments from the mothers about their husbands' attitudes toward parent education were indicative of how other fathers felt, then even though a father may not have attended a study group himself, he still could profit from what the mother had learned. Indeed, it turns out that sometimes the very questions the mothers were asking in the group were their husbands' questions. The CSAA staff acknowledged as much by writing in their 1936 book *Parents' Questions:* "It may perhaps seem, from the form in which the questions come, that mothers are the only questioners, and that fathers are for the most part either inarticulate or uninterested. It is true that far more questions are *voiced* by women than by men. But this does not imply any lack of fundamental interest on the part of fathers, and it is often evident that the father is really the asker for whom his wife is acting as proxy."[85] In other words, we should not assume that women necessarily used their new expertise to their personal advantage. It is also possible that women were encouraged to share their new knowledge with their husbands, and that men vicariously participated in the movement by framing some of the questions that came up at the meetings. The parent education movement thus need not have exerted a direct impact on fathers to contribute to the modernization of fatherhood. It could just as easily, and perhaps more efficiently, have changed the course of American fatherhood *via mothers.* (In Chapter 7, empirical evidence will be offered in support of this proposition.)

Let's go back to the transcript. Conversations being what they are, contra-dictions from one moment to the next are not unusual. (In fact, this transcript probably lends more coherence to Gruenberg's arguments than was actually the case. Transcriptions from tape generally, and often unintentionally, are made more sensible by the transcriber.) Thus, when we encounter the last three sentences of Gruenberg's first set of comments, we may be a bit confused. I know I am. First, she said that the CSAA "had a coeducational group but it did not go very well." Then she said, "Since then there have been only sporadic efforts to bring the fathers in." Finally she said, "At the present time there is no difficulty in getting them interested." What is the story here? Were fathers involved or not? There is no way to tell from these remarks, but maybe we can get some insight from the section of the transcript where Gruenberg said, "I suppose that there is probably a greater difference within each situation than between situations. There will be fathers who will participate more, and mothers who will participate less."

Gruenberg here has made an important point, one central to the whole argument before us. Sometimes people ask a simple question like, "Were (are) fathers involved with their children, *yes or no?*" and expect a simple answer. But a simple question does not always warrant a simple answer; at least this is the case if one believes there is a difference between what is valid and what is not. The modernization of fatherhood during the Machine Age was a very complex process. Part of that process—but only part—was the parent education movement, and part of that movement—but only part—was the fathercraft movement. On the one hand, it makes sense to talk about gender and class variations, to acknowledge that women are more likely to care for children, and that middle-class men are more likely to attend child study groups and the like. However, these kinds of comparisons obscure the enormous variation that existed (and that still exists) *within* the two genders, and *within* the various classes. Only if we ignore these variations can we be comfortable with the simple and sometimes simplistic comparisons between genders, among classes— *or among historical periods.* Thus, it is undoubtedly true that mothers are more likely to care for children, middle-class fathers are more likely to participate in fathercraft, and contemporary men are more likely to have changed a diaper. It is also true that some fathers care for children better than some mothers do, some working-class fathers put some middle-class fathers to shame with regard to parenthood, and some Machine Age fathers, were they alive today, would be ideal subjects for this month's media barrage on New Fatherhood.

In the last section of the transcript, Gruenberg focused on the question of overall parental responsibility. A student asked, "What validity is there in the view point that perhaps fathers and mothers are not the best people to take care of their children?" Given the amount of attention paid to the science of child rearing during the Machine Age, the student's question is not unusual. If being a parent has more to do with learning than instinct, then it makes sense to ask whether someone who is not a parent, but who has been dutifully trained in fathercraft or mothercraft, can do a better job of raising children. In her response, Gruenberg acknowledged the dilemma of parent care versus nonparent care; however, her coverage of the topic sets up what for her was a more pressing problem: child neglect. The Machine Age, with its modernistic ethic, was a time when individual freedom and personal choice were highly valued. ("Being a martyr has gone out of fashion.") But if "each individual claims the right for a complete life," unfettered by the demands of children (a man "doesn't feel that just because he is a father he has to give up his claims on life as a human being"; a woman "does not want to be just a mother and wife"), then who will take responsibility for others? Who, in other words, will subordinate her or his own needs to that of the child?

Gruenberg's answer: the mother. Why? Because, Gruenberg said, the mother is "better equipped psychologically" for the task. This stance was similar if not identical to the stance taken by her colleagues. But in her response, Gruenberg indicated, more so than they had, the journey she had taken to reach that end. (And it was a journey. Gruenberg said that ten or fifteen years earlier, she would have given a different answer.)

What made her change her mind? I mentioned earlier her belief that gender equality had been achieved, which meant (as she saw it) that discussions about gender differences no longer carried the same negative connotations for women as before. But putting aside for the moment whether her political instincts were right, this explanation tells us only why she would be willing to talk about the differences; it does not tell us why she thought there were differences in the first place. A close examination of the transcript, however, may offer a clue as to her reasoning.

The conversation between Gruenberg and her students shows a genuine effort to embrace the notion that men's and women's proclivities for child care are related to their respective positions in the social structure. Men are said to be more "objective," but only because they spend so much time in the outside world; and women "who are out of the house all day are apt to have the same objective attitude as their husbands." The use of the phrase "under the present setup" also implies that Gruenberg viewed the division of child care at the time as socially produced and socially reinforced. All of which would lead us to think that Gruenberg and her colleagues would take not a traditional but a feminist stance toward men's and women's child care roles.

Philosophical discussions aside, however, what the CSAA dealt with at each group meeting was a legacy of socialization that the fathers and mothers brought with them into the room. Whatever the CSAA might have wanted to say about New Fatherhood, and however they may have hoped it would be received, the reaction of the audience was something over which they had little control. Indeed, if a group leader's agenda was completely out of sync with that of the audience—something Gruenberg suggested happened early on—the leader could be faulted for having tried to force the issue, which, in turn, could mean fewer in attendance the next time around.

Gruenberg also seemed genuinely concerned about situations where no one felt the need to look out for the child's welfare. Perhaps she knew of families where the children were ignored because the adults were interested only in pursuing their own "personal adjustment." Perhaps she was prodding her students with a "what if"—as in what if "no one [was] willing to take the whole responsibility?" More than likely, her concern stemmed from a decade or so of trying to merge theory with fact. To wit: Fathercraft and mothercraft, in principle, were closely connected—outgrowths of modernization. The fathers and mothers who attended the groups, however, were less interested in abstract concepts like New Fatherhood (or New Motherhood) than in trying to convince their children to do their homework, or mind their p's and q's. Gruenberg's conclusion that the father and mother should share responsibility for child care, but that the mother should be "the chief executive" in the home—the one who makes sure that everyone in the family "gets his rights and his needs and his desires"—thus may have been based on her perception of how much value the members of the group placed on family harmony and cooperation. ("You cannot leave it for them just to fight it out.") In short, pushing a radical agenda was one thing; but experience may have told her that what parents—and students—really wanted were down-to-earth and comprehensible solutions.

It could be argued, of course, that the class discussion shows only that the New Fatherhood of the Machine Age was more traditional than not. And I would agree; it *was* traditional. The principal message here, though, in terms of understanding the modernization *process* may not be that Gruenberg and the others in the fathercraft movement were hedging their bets—saying that fathers should get involved but insisting still that women should be the primary caregivers. Rather, it is that the effort to involve fathers in the study group movement was both *conscientious and ongoing.*[86]

6   Fatherhood and the Popular Press

> "I've just counted thirty-two fathers in three blocks, pushing
> perambulators!" announced the Young Grandmother to the
> kindergartner and myself as we sauntered up Riverside Drive
> one sunny Sunday afternoon recently. "Things certainly have
> changed since I was a girl. Why, my father would no more
> have pushed a pram on a public highway than he would have
> ridden in one himself!"
>
> Grace Nies Fletcher, *Bringing Up Fathers* (1927)

Parents today generally turn to popular magazines more than they do to
books, or even television, when they are seeking guidance about child
rearing. Of those who consult magazines, most turn to *Parents' Magazine*.
(With a circulation of nearly two million, *Parents' Magazine* is the most
widely read child-rearing periodical in the world.) [1]

If we focus on the Machine Age, we see an almost identical picture.
The 1930 White House Conference Study and the 1933 American Home
Economics Association Study both reported that while parents often relied on books, child study groups, and the like for guidance, the outside
sources that they turned to the most (besides their families) were popular
periodicals. This was especially true when it came to mothers. Of the
women surveyed, 80–96 percent said that they depended on magazines
for help. The comparable figures for fathers were 40–55 percent. [2] As for
Parents' Magazine, it did not begin publication until the late 1920s. By the
early 1930s, however, it had become the leading periodical in the parent
education field. [3]

Clearly, the magazine industry, *Parents' Magazine* in particular, was a
force to be reckoned with during the Machine Age. The question for us
here, however, is, How important was this industry and this magazine to
the modernization of fatherhood?

Some would say that the popular press contributes little to our understanding of fatherhood during the Machine Age, because men were less
likely than women to read parenting magazines in the 1920s and 1930s.
(They still are less likely: *Parents' Magazine* recently reported that only 17

percent of its current readers are men.)[4] The problem with this argument, however, is that it ignores the two-step flow of communication that operated in many, if not most, homes. In the previous chapter, we discovered that whether or not a father was present at a child study group meeting may not have been as important a factor as one might think, because mothers often shared with their husbands what they had learned at the meetings. From this finding, it seems reasonable to assume that mothers often shared with their husbands what they were reading in popular magazines. (Of course, not all men were passive recipients of knowledge; 40–55 percent of the men targeted in the above studies were said to be direct consumers of magazine lore.)[5]

Consider this point as well: Even if mothers did not discuss what they had read with their husbands, their perceptions of their husbands may have been modified by what they had read. This would seem especially true among mothers who were striving to be "modern." Given that women's attitudes toward men, as fathers, have been shown to predict changes in men's involvement with children, anything that has the power to affect mothers also has the power to affect fathers, and thus cannot be ignored.[6]

FOCAL POINT: FATHERHOOD ARTICLES

The effect that popular magazines may have had on parental attitudes and actions is a question that I will address in subsequent chapters. Right now, however, I want to examine the magazine articles themselves. More specifically, I want to discuss the magazine articles that primarily were about men and their relationships with their children, hereafter referred to as the *fatherhood articles*.

Limiting myself to the fatherhood articles has its drawbacks, I know. For one thing, I cannot compare what was said about fathers in a fatherhood article with what was said about fathers in a motherhood article. (Motherhood articles would be those articles that were primarily about women and their relationship with their children.) Nor can I show how the fatherhood articles may have differed from the motherhood articles (did the fatherhood articles exhibit a special style or tone?)

If we look at the ratio of fatherhood, motherhood, and parenthood articles (the latter falling into a gender-nonspecific category), the decision to focus on fatherhood articles may seem odder still. During the first four decades of the twentieth century, the ratio of fatherhood articles was relatively stable, increasing significantly only in the 1930s. The ratio of motherhood articles, on the other hand, went up and then down, and showed movement toward father inclusion prior to the 1930s. When motherhood articles went up and down, in other words, they tended to replace or be replaced by parenthood articles. It would seem, therefore, that the history of fatherhood in popular magazines is lodged not in the fatherhood articles but in the *non*fatherhood articles.[7]

Yet it is precisely because the proportion of fatherhood articles remained for the most part unchanged that they are so interesting and worthy of study in their own right. Were these articles truly as monotonous as the ratios suggest, or do they reveal, upon closer examination, fluctuations and nuances that mirror the shifts in the motherhood and parenthood articles? Also, what about the 1930s? Why did the number and proportion of fatherhood articles increase then?

As we shall see, the fatherhood articles tap into aspects of the modernization of fatherhood that are not apparent in the historical documents reviewed so far. The articles, for one thing, suggest that at the level of popular culture, domestic masculinity grew in intensity from the turn of the century to the late 1920s, while masculine domesticity grew in intensity from the early 1930s to the beginning of World War II. (Recall from chapter 2 that domestic masculinity denotes the creation of a "softer," more playful man, i.e., the "father as pal," while masculine domesticity denotes the infusion of masculine traits into the domestic sphere, i.e., the "father as male role model.") The fatherhood articles also demonstrate that the changing ethos of fatherhood often centered on the question of men's proper place inside the home. This was so because some writers were of the opinion that the social ills of the Machine Age stemmed mainly from the lack of a strong paternal presence in children's lives. Finally, the articles offer evidence of a "culture of daddyhood"—a set of beliefs, norms, and values that accentuated the parental role for men and, ironically, marginalized them at the same time.

PARENTS' MAGAZINE: IN MEDIAS RES

Fatherhood scholars sometimes have analyzed magazine articles in the 1920s and 1930s as a monolithic unit and thus have conveyed the erroneous impression that, when it came to the culture of fatherhood, what was true for one decade was pretty much true for the next.[8] The fact is, however, that the 1920s and 1930s were very different periods both in the history of parenting magazines and (as shown in other chapters) in the history of American fatherhood in general. Not to recognize this fact is to miss a lot.

To show how and why the 1920s and 1930s differed, I shall move in a counterintuitive direction, beginning with the late 1920s and 1930s rather than the early 1920s. I do so in order to initiate my discussion with *Parents' Magazine*, which made its appearance in 1926 as *Children: A Magazine for Parents*, and which published more fatherhood articles during the Depression than all the other magazines combined. *Parents' Magazine* is the standard against which all parenting magazines before or since must be measured.

The person responsible for getting *Parents' Magazine* off the ground was George J. Hecht, a well-known businessman and social-service entrepreneur.[9] What prompted Hecht to launch the magazine is not entirely clear. Asked once how the idea came to him, Hecht said that he was inspired by a woman whom he had met on a ship returning from Europe. The woman said that she and her husband lacked parenting knowledge and skills and that, because of this, her children were a constant source of disappointment: "I have failed where every woman wants to succeed—as a mother. As parents, both of us meant well, but we didn't know how to bring up our children."[10]

On another occasion, when asked again about the magazine's roots, Hecht remarked that *Parents' Magazine* grew out of the social welfare work he had done after the war, while involved with another periodical (also his creation), *Better Times*. Reportedly while publishing *Better Times*, Hecht came to "the conclusion that the work that was the most productive and the most longlasting was work with children and work with parents in teaching them how to bring up their children."[11]

Somewhere in the middle of all of this, Hecht's sister was having trouble raising her own children. One particular cause of her frustration was that she could not decipher the child psychology books available at the time. Nor could Hecht: "I tried to read some of them just as a matter of interest and I had a great deal of difficulty reading that kind of book. I came upon the idea that a popular publication for mothers and fathers on the rearing of children was sorely needed."[12] The connection between the child psychology books and *Parents' Magazine* is noteworthy. Though financially secure, Hecht still needed start-up capital for his new venture, and in 1924 he approached the Laura Spelman Rockefeller Memorial Fund (LSRM) seeking support for the project. As the LSRM was committed to promoting scientific research on children, Hecht's request was not unusual. Two years earlier, the LSRM had provided support for the Child Study Association of America. The key figure in that transaction was Lawrence K. Frank, who, aside from serving on the CSAA board, was also one of the LSRM's program officers. By reason of his position, Frank was involved in the negotiations between Hecht and the LSRM as well.

I say "negotiations," because that it is exactly what they were. The idea of a magazine that could translate the latest scientific findings into a format that the average (middle-class) parent could understand was an intriguing one for the LSRM. Still, the fund was concerned about becoming involved in a venture that was likely to make huge profits for Hecht, and it wanted to exercise more control over the magazine than Hecht was willing to concede. Each side staked out a position, and letters and telegrams went back and forth. In the end, however, Hecht proved to be the more skillful negotiator. Hecht "outmaneuvered [the LSRM and its successor foundations] at nearly every turn and used *Parents' Magazine* as a base on which to amass a personal fortune." The scholarly impact of the LSRM and its affiliated universities proved to be minimal. In a very short period of time, *Parents' Magazine* had "acquired a life of its own that was only marginally related to the growth of scientific knowledge in child development." [13]

For whom was *Parents' Magazine* written? Both the inaugural title, *Children: The Magazine for Parents,* and the revised title, *Parents' Magazine,* suggest that Hecht's new periodical addressed both men and women. The truth of the matter is, however, that *Parents' Magazine* was primarily for mothers. This becomes obvious not only when we look at the relative number and length of articles (or passages) about motherhood, but also when we see the preponderance of advertisements intended for women. Then, as now, even if a commercial product was not biologically connected to women, it could be—and was—socially connected to women through the words that people used to describe it. In the 1930s, for example, "parents" were told in an ad that they could "reach the top" of the "profession of childrearing" by reading the *Mother's Encyclopedia,* available to new subscribers: "In so important a matter as the welfare of the next generation we preferred to give these indispensible books Free to Mothers, and Fathers, rather than sell them outright. By making them a Gift with a three-year subscription to *Parents' Magazine* we have the happy assurance that with the *Mother's Encyclopedia* as your foundation and emergency reference work . . ." and so on. Note that fathers were mentioned in the ad, but they were also slighted. This talk-to-fathers/ don't-talk-to-fathers pattern was characteristic of commercial copy during the Machine Age and appeared in the articles as well. [14]

Although *Parents' Magazine* was, in principle, a mothers' magazine, it was not oblivious to men. The cover of the first issue (October 1926) announced that the reader would find "Inside Tips for Fathers and 21 Features of Interest to Mothers." The tenth anniversary issue (October 1936) proclaimed that, among the offerings that month, "14 articles interest mothers of babies and toddlers, 17 interest mothers of preschool children, 15 interest mothers of teen-age boys and girls, 14 interest fathers." The cover also reported that *Parents' Magazine* had "more than 400,000 paid circulation."

Not every article that was said to interest fathers was a fatherhood article, per se. If, again, we focus only on the fatherhood articles, we find that from 1926 to 1942 (the latter year being the publication date of the seventh and most "modern," edition of *Infant Care*), there were seventy-five articles in *Parents' Magazine* that were primarily about men and their relationship with their children. To fully appreciate what this number means in terms of the influence that *Parents' Magazine* had, one has to understand that this constitutes 47 percent of all the fatherhood articles published in that sixteen-year period. To appreciate even more the enormous influence that *Parents' Magazine* could have on parental culture during the Machine Age, consider the fact that during the early years of the Depression (specifically 1930 to 1934), *Parents' Magazine* accounted for 59 percent of all the fatherhood articles published. (Imagine a magazine or any other media channel having that kind of a market share today.) The story of how fathers were portrayed in popular magazines during the late 1920s and throughout the 1930s thus is largely the story of how they were portrayed in a single periodical.[15] Historians of fatherhood—especially those who rely on popular magazines for data—should make it a point to acknowledge this skew.

THE RHETORIC OF THE MAGAZINE INDUSTRY

Every magazine, like every book, bears the imprint of its producers. Magazine articles, therefore, do not simply or even necessarily reflect what is happening in the larger society, but they most certainly reflect the agenda of their publishers, editors, and authors. Looking at the fatherhood articles in *Parents' Magazine,* we can begin to discern an agenda that in some ways was similar to that of the Children's Bureau and Child Study Association of America but in other ways was different. The social fabric of fatherhood during the Machine Age had many diverse threads.

What immediately stands out about *Parents' Magazine* (as viewed through the fatherhood articles) is how aggressively it promoted the following ideas: (1) Fathers should be recognized as important players in the child-rearing game and as genuine contributors to their children's well being, not simply mothers' helpers; and (2) being a good parent depends on getting a sound parenthood education (from, of course, *Parents' Magazine* and from other socializing agents deemed legitimate by the magazine's hierarchy). What also stands out is that if, for some reason, there was a conflict between these two themes, *Parents' Magazine* sided with the first over the second.

In a 1929 article, for example, titled "Every Baby Needs a Father," *Parents' Magazine* offered "Advice to a young father on how, in spite of Mother and nurse, to get acquainted with his own child." The author of the article said he based his views on his first four months as a father of a baby girl. He began as follows: "We know where woman's place is—in the home. And her place regarding the baby is well known, too: a rather hovering, roving position, encompassing all territory from the catcher's box to the far outfield and all way stations. But Man! Nobody, no book, has ever shown him where his place is when the baby enters." [16]

The father, we know now, was wrong in one respect: there *were* manuals in the 1920s that attempted to define both men's and women's "place" after the arrival of a baby. However, even if the father had known about the manuals and had read them, he would not have been appeased, because he would have seen that men typically were portrayed in the manuals as little more than "cooperators." What this father wanted most of all was a book that identified a special place for men, a privileged spot where only the male of the species could reside: "All negative assertions notwithstanding, a father yearns terribly to amalgamate himself into a definite niche in his baby's existence. The age-old trouble seems to be that nobody has taken the trouble to work out his position and give him any duties. He is only a hat-holder, an errand-runner, a catch-all and sort of unwelcome itinerant whatnot—something to lay all the baby's bad traits and features on—something to be 'taken after.' " [17]

Frustrated but not willing to give up, the father said that he deliberately "stood around, making a wretched attempt at hovering, getting in people's way—with the idea of pouncing upon some role [he] could fill, some particular thing that [he] *only* could do." Having been denied other avenues of access to his child (music, bedtime stories), he eventually "was handed" responsibility for the weekly weigh-in. No casual weigher was he, however. "I grabbed at this weighing job in a spirit little suspected by the donors of it," he announced. "I would make this a rite, an insidious process whereby I could work my way into the child's affections in spite of every belligerent agency directed against me. And how? By combining music and conversation at the same time as the weighing."

What did the father hope to accomplish by publishing his story in *Parents' Magazine*? Just this, he said: "It is mixed with feelings of great joy, and the assurance that I may be helping other ostracized fathers to find a way out (or rather in), that I write of what has happened recently. It seems that someone of the Licensed Hoverers read a piece that said a father ought to have an hour in the day with his own baby. It must have been an awful blow to them, but there it was in print. I suppose the idea was in the nature of a preventive; so baby wouldn't get him mixed up with the tradespeople and letter carrier; would know her Dad when she saw him."

Some may view such fatherhood articles as evidence that fathers were marginalized during the Machine Age. Perhaps this is so. But if we limit ourselves to this interpretation alone, we will overlook something else that is equally if not more important. Magazine articles about fathers being shunted aside—indeed all magazine articles—basically are *rhetorical forms* designed to persuade. Thus, if we read an article about fathers not being taken seriously, what we have before us is not so much a piece of news as a call to arms.[18]

The main point of the above article, in other words, is not "Oh, isn't this interesting, fathers have no special place," but "Stop excluding fathers, they *are* important." Articles such as these show not only that the parent education movement had the potential to marginalize men but also that it was willing to discipline itself if it did so. Perhaps the most interesting point to make is that the attack came not from without but from within— from *Parents' Magazine,* arguably the most powerful agent in the entire industry.

To communicate its message that fathers needed to become involved in the educational process, *Parents' Magazine* commissioned articles that portrayed fathers experiencing an epiphany of sorts when they came in contact with the educational system. One 1930 piece, for example, told the story of a father's unplanned visit to his nine-year-old son's school. What happened is that the principal at the school saw the father dropping off his son and prevailed upon the father to stay for the morning assembly. New to his child's school regimen, the father was convinced to visit his son's classroom and was given a series of minilectures by both his son and the teachers. ("Come on, Dad, let me show you the whole works.") At the end of his "lessons" and before he was about to leave, the father was said to remark to the principal: "You've taught me a great deal about new ideas in education and they sound good to me. There are a lot of us fathers who need to go to school just as I have this morning." [19]

Both this article and the one before relied on an anecdote to make a point. Writers often use anecdotes for illustrative purposes, but wrapping an argument around a *solitary* anecdote goes one important step beyond illustration in that a solitary anecdote is more likely to stereotypify.

Let's go back to the idea that the magazine articles can be seen as rhetorical forms. From a rhetorical point of view, publishers, editors, and authors are not simply reporters of what is or was. They are also claims-makers trying to motivate readers to act. Commenting on the various strategies used in the claims-making process, sociologist Joel Best tells us, "The language adopted by claims-makers is meant to be persuasive. Claimants want to convince others that their concerns about particular social conditions deserve attention, that their assessments of those conditions are correct, and that their proposals offer solutions that should be adopted as social policy." [20]

Stated simply, the people behind *Parents' Magazine* were engaged in the art and science of social control. In an effort to influence their readers, they used the same three elements that claims-makers generally employ. They relied on *data* to ground their claim; they offered a *solution* to show how the problem could be alleviated; and they employed a *warrant* to bridge the gap between the data and the solution. [21]

The data for any given magazine piece could be numerical or anecdotal, or both. The numerical data did not need to be statistical or even valid; it could consist of nothing more than the unsubstantiated statement of the first author above that "no book" existed to show fathers what they were expected to do when a baby arrived. Similarly today, we might be presented with historical "information" of this nature: "My father's generation often said, sadly, that they just didn't have a clue how to be a father. They didn't know how to hug, to be there, even to talk because their fathers never did it with them." [22] Fact? Hyperbole? It does not really matter. If the proposition has the potential to move people, and, more important, if it sells magazines, it has a good chance of making its way into print.

Anecdotal data also need not be entirely accurate. The literary—or rhetorical—license allows authors of popular magazine articles to embellish where they see fit. Thus, we honestly do not know whether the two case studies used to ground these articles happened just as they were described. We do know, however, that the two tales—combining elements of both failure and triumph—helped to grab the reader and stereotype the problem. Atrocity tales of fathers who failed as well as success stories of men who triumphed abound in the early-twentieth-century popular press as they do today. Sinners and saints, bums and heroes—they all played a part in the modernization of fatherhood.[23]

What about the second element that claims-makers employ, the solution? Both articles show someone solving a problem. The first made the father the problem solver, conveying the message that if fathers were willing to try, they could overcome the misguided intentions of the medical establishment and the "Licensed Hoverers." The second article credited the school principal with having the good sense to implore the father to stay. Here the lesson was that conscientious teachers could make a difference.

As for the third element, both articles rested on some warrant to justify their points, some ideology about how the world should be. Both were predicated on the belief that children need their fathers.

The warrants to which claims-makers subscribe are what drive rhetorical arguments. Warrants thus help to explain how data can be fudged and solutions to problems can be simplistic at best. In the case of parenting magazines, the ideology may be noble, or at least presented as such ("We are here to educate the public"), or it may be financial ("We are here to make money"). Whatever the magazine's ideology—and typically it is a combination of these two—it is this, perhaps more than anything else, that largely determines what is found between a magazine's covers.

Once the ideology of a magazine is deciphered, the content of the articles inside becomes somewhat predictable. Thus, knowing what we do about *Parents' Magazine* during the Machine Age, we should not be surprised to learn that when fathers were asked, in a 1931 article titled "Are You Fit to Be a Father?," whether they should be guided in their dealings with their children by (1) instinct, (2) what their own parents did, (3) the neighbors' customs and criticisms, or (4) a study of children, the correct answer was number 4. Neither should we be surprised, if we remember the magazine's earlier stand on fathers and infants, to learn that the correct answer to the question of when fathers should assume responsibility for training children was "from birth."[24]

"FOR FATHERS ONLY"

In its sixth year of publication, *Parents' Magazine* gave special attention to fathers by creating a column just for men. Titled "For Fathers Only," the column appeared more or less on a monthly basis from June 1932 to December 1937.[25]

The first "For Fathers' Only" article was written by the father of a new-born. It was an admonishment to men not to wait until their children were out of diapers before they got to know and enjoy them. Much is lost, the author argued, if one does not jump into child care from the very beginning. As for those who would say that caring for an infant was "effeminate" or "woman's work," the author countered, "Taking care of a young baby entails pure manual labor. If you don't believe it, send your wife away for the week-end. When she returns you'll be going around like the folks in the old kidney pill ads—all bent over with 'that pain in the back.' " [26]

The effort made by the author to allay fears that becoming involved in child care threatened a father's manhood brings to the fore the question of whether domesticity and masculinity were, as historian E. Anthony Rotundo suggests, "a contradiction in terms." [27] The answer, as I said in chapter 2, hinges on whether the ideology in question is domestic masculinity or masculine domesticity. While domestic masculinity posed identity problems for men, masculine domesticity had the potential to increase men's status in the home.

If we read the first "For Fathers Only" article carefully, we discover that masculine domesticity, more than domestic masculinity, drove the piece. Consider how the father talked about giving his baby a bath:

> [A]bout this baby's bath business. Don't consider it unless you have a sense of humor. And by all means avoid it if you have had butlers to draw your tub since you were very young. Otherwise here are the man-to-man directions: Take six-months-old baby into bathroom. Lock door to avoid mother's advice. Play one hand of strip poker with His Highness, being sure you both win—otherwise you'll have to wait until your clothes dry, for splash is his specialty. Draw shallow warm tub—the big one of course. Set the old boy right in it and watch him. He'll be tickled pink for his mother bathes him in a dinky little rubber affair. Result: grand waves. Shrieks of laughter from—yes, from a six-months-old baby—believe it or not! [28]

Observe the author's reference to "man-to-man directions," and to "lock[ing] the door to avoid mother's advice." What the baby was about to receive was a very unique and very masculine kind of bath, something that the child supposedly needed and something that only a father could provide. At least, this was the message that the author was trying to convey. This was his rhetorical point.

Caring for or being with children in a manly way was a theme that cropped up routinely in the "For Fathers Only" series. In April 1934, a father proudly described how he taught his seventeen-year-old son—

who, he said was "no mamma's boy"—to do housework: "When Bill and I do housekeeping we disdain the ways of his mother, who would put us in aprons and dust-caps. We don, more appropriately, our hunting garb, with rubber boots. We use a wax mop much as we might use a shovel in a gravel pit, and our dust-rags wave like unfurled banners of a vandal horde. We attack a cobweb stealthily but fearlessly, and drive a bit of lint from ambuscade with intrepid wariness. Occasionally, in our zeal, we break a piece of bric-a-brac but we know how to hide the traces of our crime."[29] In November 1936, another father, "a soldier by profession," bragged about how he had successfully "run" things, while his wife was away, by dividing the children's areas of responsibility along military lines: "(1) The Bulletin Board will be kept in the living room on a shelf by the big light. All children will read and initial all notices posted thereon. This will be done between the hours of 4:00 P.M. and 8:00 P.M. daily. (2) John shall be the timekeeper. He will have custody of the big alarm clock. He will set the alarm so as to get the girls up in plenty of time to get breakfast on time. When the alarm goes off he will get up and cut it off; awaken the girls; clean up his room, make his bed, awaken me; clean up my room and bathroom; make my bed; and get ready for breakfast. On school days he need not clean my room and bath and make my bed until after school. (3) Barbara shall be the cook. She will prepare the meals; order the groceries, etc.; attend to deliveries; give instructions to Joe; police the downstairs hallway, the children's bathroom, front porch, steps and walk; make her bed and take her medicine," and so on. When the mother returned she reportedly "was delighted with the way things had gone in her absence." Concluded the author: "Army orders had been good for us all."[30]

The theme of the value of having a man in the house (masculine domesticity, in short) could also be seen in the "For Fathers Only" articles that chided mothers for not allowing children to take risks. In October 1936, for example, an aviator father who had been in a crash in which his co-pilot was killed told of the dilemma he found himself in when his seventeen-year-old son expressed an interest in learning how to fly. It was not his own fears that created the dilemma, he said, but his wife's. She, more than he, was apparently afraid that the same tragedy could result again. If it were up to the father, the boy would be allowed to fly: "If one feels fear, he should strive to conquer it. If, inherently, he is not afraid of the things that we are afraid of, then I think he is just that much better off than we. But that's only the start of things. Flying brings out the best in any man."[31]

The phrase *bringing out the best in a man* uses strong words reflecting passionate ideas. After all was said and done, it came down to a vote. The father and mother "offset each other," and the boy's inclination (to fly) ultimately made the difference. (Whether the same vote would have been allowed if the son had expressed an interest in doing something that the father *dis*approved of is an interesting but unanswerable question.)[32]

On an aggregate level, *Parents' Magazine* gave more emphasis to masculine domesticity than it did to domestic masculinity, but it did publish articles occasionally that gave more weight to the latter. From what I could gather, the people who put together *Parents' Magazine* were of the opinion that some combination of both masculine domesticity and domestic masculinity (albeit not fifty-fifty) was best. For example, the second article in the "For Fathers Only" series, based on interviews with children of all ages, gave little or no consideration to the issue of whether fathers should be suitable male role models. Rather, what the children wanted more than anything else were fathers who were willing to "be there" for them. One child said he "never actually talked" to his father. Another declared that the "only time" his father noticed him "was when he was criticizing [him] for something or other." A third reported: "'My father was so strict with my brother and me that we learned to lie to him about where we went, when we got back, whom we were with, even how we spent our own money after we were wage earners. Our motto of "anything to keep family peace" led us into a maze of deceit and lies that became second nature to us, and has since made it a struggle for us to be honest in any of the relations of life.'"[33]

Actual occurrences? Maybe. But true or not, the vignettes serve the magazine's rhetorical purpose, essentially communicating that "[m]any men . . . do not know how to be real fathers. They conceive of father as an autocrat, a provider, or as an example. But few seem to look ahead and get a broad view of life that will fit them for companionship with their sons. . . . Perhaps the answer to the frequent question, 'What's wrong with modern youth?' is simply, 'It is fatherless.'"[34]

The notion that fathers should strive to be their children's companions, their pals, their chums, is what characterized the "For Fathers Only" articles that fell within the domestic masculinity domain. Domestic masculinity also meant a minimal amount of paternal authority. "Real" fathers did not boss their children around. In a 1933 piece, for example, a father shared "a thesis on fatherhood" that he had penned when he was fifteen years old. "When I become a father," he had reflected in his youth, "I want my son to feel that he is my equal, and I'll look upon him as such. . . . Probably every father resorts too often to the role of dictator."[35] In another article, a widower who had raised two daughters proclaimed, "[T]he day of the patriarch is over. . . . Today democracy rules in the home circle (except where overthrown by anarchy) and in most cases it ought to rule there. When a father forgets this, talks big and asserts himself—does he, I wonder, get anywhere?"[36]

What, exactly, were domesticated fathers supposed to *do* with their children? Pretty much what you might expect: participate in their children's games (tag, marbles, baseball); nurture an interest in a hobby; build model railroads, or boats—indeed, build anything, as long as it meant working with tools. ("Mechanical hobbies can and should be shared by fathers.")[37] Throughout all the variations was the simple but significant maxim that fathers should *play* with their children. The best fathers knew how to entertain. The best of the best were fun.[38]

Domesticated fathers also were expected to be teachers, but they were not supposed to be professorial or austere, and they certainly were not supposed to lecture. Delicately, tactfully, and with consummate skill, domesticated fathers were men who knew how to impart wisdom without making it obvious (at least to their children) that they were doing so, as in the following example.

> "Trouble, Guy?" asked the father of his son who stood quietly at the threshold of his study. "Come, boy, tell Daddy! You'll feel better when you get it out."
> "Oh Daddy. . . . It-it was awful things! Sam Hutchins told me. I told him he was a liar. And I came home. He *was* a liar, wasn't he, Daddy?"
> "Tell Daddy what Sam Hutchins said," . . .
> "He said—he said—that the worms were going to eat you up! Me! Everybody! The worms aren't going to eat us, are they, Daddy?"

> The father admitted that Sam Hutchins "had some facts. But he didn't get the real truth." He then went on to explain that people's bodies were like clothes, and that they wore out, just like clothes wore out. But bodies and clothes were only transitory; the real "you" was inside.

> "This body of yours? Is it *you*, Guy?"
> "Me? How do you mean?"
> "Is [*sic*] your skin and your hair and your fingernails and your bones really the whole of you?"
> "Nope!"
> "Where are you, then?"
> "I'm way down inside. . . . [But] what happens to me [when I take off my old body]?"
> "What happens to you when mother takes off an old, torn blouse [shirt] and washes you up and puts on a new, clean one?"
> "Why I go off and do the things I want to do."
> "Yes, Guy! Don't you suppose that we will all do that some day, when God decides we have worn our old blouses long enough?"

> "I expect so! New blouses are fun, aren't they, Daddy?"
> "Yes," said the father. "I am sure that new blouses are going to be fun."
> "Oh, Daddy! I love you so!" [39]

The nearly fifty articles in the "For Fathers Only" series were, in a way, a matched set. Most may have emphasized masculine domesticity, while others may have given greater weight to domestic masculinity, but on the whole, the articles were predictable in their message: Fathers need to focus more of their attention on their children. The last article, however, was different.

The final "For Fathers Only" article was published in December 1937. (Why the series ended was not explained.) [40] The last article was especially interesting, in that, unlike others in the series, which emphasized father involvement, its key theme was that if fathers were not careful, they might find their children robbing *too much* of their attention. Reported the author,

> One of fatherhood's chief pleasures, I anticipated before the birth of our first child, would be to rush home from business every evening for an hour's romp with the baby before bedtime. It was with considerable shock that I discovered, within a few months after the arrival of the son of whom I was so proud, that this anticipated pleasure quickly reached satiation point, by which time father was confronted with one of his first problems of parenthood: baby was monopolizing all of his leisure hours at home, with obvious detriment to both baby and father. Babies undeniably are the most fascinating creatures in the world, but when one doesn't give you an opportunity to draw a deep breath without howling for more attention, his charm begins to wear a bit thin.

The father went on to say that he had found a "cure" for his children's "father complex": *organized distraction.*

> [One] step was to hang out the "welcome" sign for all the children in the neighborhood, and our lawn has become their play headquarters, to Johnny's great delight. Frequently he is too absorbed in fascinating play to do more than hurriedly return my greeting when I arrive home in the evening. We [also] have given our son toys with which he can do things—fitted blocks, sand-box, hammer and nails, and velocipede. They have proved excellent substitutes for the acrobatic games we used to play. . . . I'm working at the part-time job of being a father with all the enthusiasm and pleasure I had anticipated but I'm no longer an unwilling, full-time slave to my son. [41]

Today's "new fathers" have been known to complain about the raised expectations that they will take a more active role in rearing their children, and they have been known, as well, to respond to the shifts in the culture of fatherhood by disengaging—by being "technically present, but functionally absent," for example.[42] Yesterday's "new fathers" apparently had many of the same feelings and could employ the same tactics. The modernization of fatherhood during the Machine Age and the culture-conduct conflicts which it inspired, we thus can see again, were having a decided effect, at least on some. The social changes were significant and, as is the case with all revolutions, there was opposition.[43]

RHETORICAL CONTOURS, 1901–1942

Parents' Magazine may have dominated the parent education market in the 1930s, but it was not the only magazine to publish articles about men and their relationship with their children. *Parents' Magazine* also did not exist prior to 1926; thus to focus on it alone would leave open the issue of what had come before. If we broaden our angle of vision beyond *Parents' Magazine* and beyond the 1930s, we learn that a number of magazines— among them *American Magazine, Good Housekeeping, Ladies Home Journal, Women's Home Companion, Saturday Evening Post, Delineator, Rotarian,* and *Hygeia*—published fatherhood articles. When these articles are added to the mixture, what is the picture of fatherhood that emerges?

To address this question, I divided the fatherhood articles from the turn of the century to the early 1940s into seven time periods: 1901–1909, 1910–1915, 1916–1921, 1922–1929, 1930–1934, 1935–1939, and 1940– 1942. These seven periods are not discrete stages, but they are not arbitrary chunks of time either. The two periods that run from 1916 to 1921 and from 1922 to 1929, for example, constitute a thematic block (how and why will be explained in a moment); 1930–1934 and 1935–1939 are synonymous, more or less, with the early and late Depression.

What does the comparative analysis indicate? First, I will report trends in domestic masculinity (the "father as pal") and masculine domesticity (the "father as male role model"), two ideologies that figured significantly in the "For Fathers Only" articles published in *Parents' Magazine.* (Also, I am going to substitute the *father as pal* for domestic masculinity and the *father as male role model* for masculine domesticity, because within the context of the analysis these phrases are more meaningful and easier on the eyes and brain. I found that when I used *domestic masculinity* and *masculine domesticity* repeatedly in sentence after sentence, I could not keep the two straight. I figured that if I could not keep them straight, the reader probably could not either.) Second, I will discuss how the emphasis given to these two ideologies correlated with three other trends: the proclivity to write about sons, the tendency to poke fun at fathers, and the inclination to use the word *dad* in the articles themselves.[44]

The Rise and Fall of Domestic Masculinity

A close reading of the fatherhood articles indicates that in the beginning of the twentieth century, the magazine industry gave considerable weight to the father as male role model and very little weight to the father as pal. Then, around 1916, and especially through the 1920s, the father as pal was given greater emphasis, and the father as male role model was, to some degree, shunted to the background. When the 1930s came around, the father as male role model was reemphasized and "scientifically" legitimated, but this also was tempered by the ethic of the father as pal from the decade before. Finally, in the early 1940s, as America's entrance into World War II approached and became a fact, the father as male role model loomed larger still.

This fluctuating pattern reflects the impact that *Parents' Magazine* had on the child-rearing industry in the 1930s. (As I said, *Parents' Magazine* was more likely to focus on masculine domesticity or the father as male role model than on domestic masculinity or the father as pal.) It also signifies the very different brand of New Fatherhood that was at work in the years from 1916 to 1929. Whatever else may be said, the fluctuating pattern shows that we should be cautious about placing too much faith in historical renderings that paint a linear picture of the growth of New Fatherhood in the early twentieth century or convey the impression that the only important difference between fatherhood in the 1920s and fatherhood in the 1930s was that during the 1930s, many men lost their jobs and were unable to fulfill the role of economic provider.

The more I read the articles, the more I came to see a fluctuating pattern—not only with respect to the father as male role model and the father as pal but also with respect to other trends. Indeed, what I found especially compelling was how the trends in the father as male role model and the father as pal correlated with these other trends.

Daughters versus Sons

The first trend is the degree to which the authors focused on *sons*. From 1901 to 1942, sons were mentioned in about 66 percent of fatherhood articles, while daughters were mentioned in about 36 percent of the fatherhood articles—nearly a two-to-one margin. This emphasis on sons parallels what we saw when we looked at the father-to-father books and the father-only study groups, and thus was not unexpected. What came as a surprise, however, is how the degree to which the authors favored sons fluctuated over the years. Look at the breakdown for the seven periods: From 1901 to 1909, sons were mentioned in about 71 percent of the fatherhood articles, while daughters were mentioned in about 57 percent of the same articles (a 1.25 son-to-daughter ratio). The same difference was observed in the 1910 to 1915 period; sons were mentioned about 63 percent of the time, daughters about 50 percent of the time (a 1.26 ratio). From 1916 to 1921, however, sons were mentioned in 100 percent of the articles, daughters in 25 percent (a 4.00 ratio—a huge increase). From 1922 to 1929, sons were mentioned in 74 percent of the articles, daughters in 21 percent (a 3.52 ratio—similar to the period before). From 1930 to 1934, sons were mentioned in 65 percent of the articles, daughters in 33 percent (a 1.97 ratio—a sharp drop). From 1935 to 1939, sons were mentioned in 62 percent of the articles, daughters in 32 percent (a 1.94 ratio—basically no change). Finally, from 1940 to 1942, sons were mentioned in 53 percent of the articles, daughters in 47 percent (a 1.13 ratio—a small drop). Thus, beginning in 1916 and continuing through 1942, the son-to-daughter ratio got larger and then shrank (the pattern at a glance: 1.25, 1.26, 4.00, 3.52, 1.97, 1.94, 1.13), which, more or less, is what happened when we looked at how the father as pal fared. In short, the degree to which the authors favored sons correlated with the degree to which they favored the father as pal.[45]

The connection I have just drawn may appear to be upside down or inside out. Common sense would suggest that it would not be the father as pal but the father as male role model that would correlate with the tendency to favor sons, but in the fatherhood articles published in the early twentieth century, the opposite was true. Why was that? I think it comes down to this. Around the turn of the century, the son-to-daughter ratio was low when the father as male role model was high and the father as pal was low because, with the accent on masculinity, fathers were expected to counteract mothers' negative influence on both sons and daughters. The son-to-daughter ratio grew larger when the father as pal increased in value because when it came to being their children's playmates, fathers were assumed to have more in common with boys. I am not suggesting that the correlation was perfect or that there were not other trends that could account for changes in the son-to-daughter ratio.

I am saying only that the father as male role model and the father as pal, as ideologies, seemed to have been associated to some extent with the amount of attention that the authors of the fatherhood articles gave to one gender versus the other.

Humor and Fatherhood

Another trend that correlated with the rise and fall of the father as pal was the tendency to poke fun at fathers. An early example of what I mean by poking fun is a 1905 piece in *Woman's Home Companion,* titled "Girls' Fathers I Have Met." In the article, the author set out to describe some of the bad but still humorous experiences one suitor claimed to have had when he picked up and dropped off his dates. Classifying fathers into four "risk categories" (good, fair, hazardous, and extrahazardous), the author suggested that the fathers were, to put it mildly, absent-minded fools:

> [D]eliver us from the Hazardous and the Extra Hazardous. They are similar in many respects. They wear long whiskers and slouch hats. The Hazardous we honestly believe sits by a convenient window on Sunday afternoon, and with a telescope discerns you from afar. He is then on the front porch when you arrive, and before you ask he tells you he "guesses" there is no one at home—and Father is right. The Extra Hazardous! He is the one who, when you say you are pleased to meet him, forgets whether it is his cue to bite you or take a fall out of you. He usually compromises by showing his teeth and grunting.[46]

This article was only one of a number of commercial media accounts to depict a father (or fathers in general) as incompetent. Indeed, it did not take me long to discover that characterizing fathers as fools was more than a recurring theme; it was a veritable industry. Magazine articles, books, cartoons, comics, postcards—all intended to be humorous and all aimed at men's inadequacies as fathers—were institutionalized forms throughout the early twentieth century. But, again, the pattern varied; and, again, the father as male role model and the father as pal seem to have exerted some influence.

Around the turn of the century, when the father as male role model was high and the father as pal was low, humor directed at fathers was low. Then, in the 1920s, when the father as pal was high and the father as male role model was low, humor directed at fathers was high. Next, in the 1930s and early 1940s, when the father as male role model regained some its strength, humor directed at fathers declined. In short, the degree to which the authors poked fun at fathers correlated with the degree to which they favored the father as pal. (I will have more to say about this in a moment.)[47]

Mothers versus Dads

A third trend was the use of the word *dad*. So often is this term used nowadays that it generally is not paid any heed. But in the early twentieth century, whether a father should be called "dad" was the subject of debate.[48]

Some pundits felt that using dad to address, or refer to, fathers "wholly lacks reverence" and was "the apotheosis of modern flippancy."[49] Others staunchly defended the term, calling it an "endearing diminutive," and a measure of paternal quality: "[D]o fathers of to-day crave reverence? Are they not prouder to be their children's 'pals' and chums? What delights a father more than to be literally his daughter's chosen cavalier. Is he not more 'Dad' than 'Father' as, laughing and joyous, they saunter along life's pleasure-ground, or go hand in hand to meet grief. God pity the lad whose father frowns away his Dadship. Such sons are poor indeed." And later: "Between young men and their youngish fathers, simpatico is far more noticeable than in former years. Former stony barriers, built by stiff-necked tradition, have been replaced by open doors, through which youths and maidens—unafraid—may enter Dad's presence at will."[50]

Observe the connection between the use of *dad* and the notion of the father as pal. Observe, too, the connection between the use of *dad* and the diminution of the father's authority. As historian John Demos notes, with *dad*—or its variation, *daddy*—"there is a note of affectionate familiarity." However, "there may also be," Demos adds, "some implicit tendency to patronize: 'dad' slides easily into 'poor dad.'"[51]

A good example of such a patronizing slide is found in a 1913 *Harper's Bazaar* article about a man who, though "kind and generous," was said to be out of touch with the times and a constant thorn in his "grown-up" daughter's side: "Father, dear man, while progressive enough in the outer world, has one rooted idea about the home, and that is that the conditions in it shall always remain the same." Among the father's crimes was that instead of quietly going to bed when suitors called, he insisted on "sitting up till all hours to close the house." Also, he apparently had developed the nasty habit of asking for dessert toward the end of dinner—"as if we hadn't had dessert each day since the beginning of the world," the daughter exclaimed. "Of course, Dad's a perfect dear . . . but . . . "[52]

"Dad"—the "perfect dear": Was it purely coincidental that the father being made fun of here was referred to as "dad" and characterized as "dear" in the same breath? I suspect not. Given the context of the article, the combination of "dad" and "dear" had the effect of communicating that the father was lovably inept.

What about the way the mother was addressed? Although she was not above her daughter's reproach ("I don't see why you haven't taught him better, Mother, in all these years"), she was never talked about in informal terms, which means that she was never referred to as "mom" (or "mamma," etc.) Was this, I wondered, a fluke? The answer I arrived at was no. Examining the fatherhood articles from 1901 to 1942, I found that mothers were hardly ever spoken of informally; almost always they were called "mother." This turned out to be true not only in cases where fathers were called "fathers," but also when they were called "dad." It was true even when fathers and mothers were talked about together. Then, it would be mother and dad, with mother *almost always first*.[53]

One might relate this finding to the fact that these were fatherhood articles, believing that in the motherhood and parenthood articles a different pattern would appear. However, in the motherhood and parenthood articles that I reviewed, the same pattern prevailed. It prevailed, too, in the child-rearing books, in the father-to-father books, and in the advice-seeking letters—in short, in every thread of data I happened to collect. Wherever I looked, fathers were more likely to be called "dads" than mothers were to be called "moms"; and when fathers and mothers were talked about together, almost always mothers would be mentioned first ("mother and father," or "mother and dad"). I also did not find a single instance where *mom* would be coupled with *father* ("mother and dad," yes; "mom and father," never).[54]

I am not saying, of course, that, in the early twentieth century, mothers were rarely referred to as "moms." We know, for example, that during World War II, when soldiers wrote to their parents, they would sometimes begin with "Dear Mom," or "Dear Mom and Dad."[55] Also, young children, in their everyday speech, sometimes called their mothers "mom" or "mamma." What I *am* saying is that in more public and ritualized accounts (magazine and newspaper articles, books, letters from parents to various child-rearing experts), mothers were significantly less likely than fathers to be talked about in informal terms.

What about trends? In the fatherhood articles, the use of *dad* (or its variation, *daddy*) fluctuated, while the use of *mom* remained at a stable low. From 1901 to 1909, *dad*, like *mom*, was hardly ever used. From 1910 to 1915, however, *dad* was used at least once in about 19 percent of the fatherhood articles. Then, from 1916 to 1921, *dad* increased in use to about 50 percent. From 1922 to 1929, it increased again to about 63 percent. In the 1930s, the pattern reversed itself. From 1930 to 1934, *dad* was used in about 44 percent of the fatherhood articles. From 1935 to 1939, the figure was about 29 percent. Finally, in the early 1940s, the pattern reversed itself again. From 1940 to 1942, *dad* was used about 40 percent of the time. In general, therefore, the degree to which the authors used the word *dad* correlated with the degree to which they favored the father as pal.[56]

If we consider all the trends together and place the rise and fall of the son-to-daughter ratio alongside both the rise and fall of fatherhood humor and the rise and fall of the use of *dad*, we see some interesting parallels: the favoring of sons over daughters, the belittling of fathers, and the use of *dad* were all correlated with one another. The correlation was not perfect. In the 1940 to 1942 period, the son-to-daughter ratio was low, while the use of *dad* was high. But, taking the early twentieth century as a whole, the association among the three was unmistakable.

Note also that in all three cases, the years 1916–1929, especially the 1920s, were high points, when the son-to-daughter ratio, fatherhood humor, and *dad* peaked. This raises the question, what was it about the World War I era and the 1920s especially that made the articles fall into line? The father as pal, as I have already said, was a crucial element; when the father as pal was emphasized, the son/humor/*dad* connection tended to be strong. But even the ideology of the father as pal, significant as it may be, is not sufficient to fully capture the complexity of this time in fatherhood history. Something much deeper was at work: the years between 1916 and 1929 marked the emergence of the culture of daddyhood.

The Culture of Daddyhood

From 1916 to 1929, fatherhood articles began to press the theme that one of the most important responsibilities that a father had toward his children was to be a playmate and pal. One article, published in 1919, told the story of a man who had become a "thief" and a "liar"—indeed a "vicious criminal"—all because his father had refused to "join" with him "in play."[57] Another article, published in 1921, offered a positive story called "Why One Father Succeeded with His Sons," saying that what made the difference was the father's willingness to be his sons' companion: "He believed in doing a great deal *with* his boys, but not too much *for* them. . . . Instead of forbidding his sons the privilege of gang life, he made himself worthy to be elected an honorary member. . . . These are [only] a few of the reasons why two boys, grown tall and straight and true, declare that they wish to be men just like their dear old Dad." [58] Recall that earlier, whether a father should be called "dad" or "daddy" was a topic of debate. Now, several years later, the matter was being considered again but was seemingly resolved.

Being a dad, and being accepted as a dad, was to reside at the pinnacle of fatherhood. "We of the United States are sometimes humblest about our noblest achievements and braggarts about less worthy ones," began one 1919 article. "We boast of our electricity, our industry, our inventions, but the greatest thing America has ever produced is the great American 'daddy.'" The article went on to draw a distinction between fatherhood and motherhood and, in the process, communicated perhaps better than anything else what the culture of daddyhood was all about:

> There is a subtle division of parental labor and parental privilege implicit in the fact that an American household calls its male head "daddy," while it calls its female head "mother." In the nature of things, mother is a generic term, belonging to every time and country, as static in its implication as it is staunch. Mother is mother all the world over, but daddy, in the American tongue, is a word instantly whimsical with individuality. Daddy, however, is a sad rogue really, walking off with all the poetry of parenthood and leaving the prose to mother. The dentist and the doctor, the teacher and the oculist are mother's affair; tonsils and adenoids are under maternal management; candy and toys and holidays are the paternal prerogatives. [59]

The prose and poetry of parenthood—the metaphor was apt. Maybe in time, the article noted, the two would be shared ("as the woman recognizes her equal rights with the man in utter, irresponsible enjoyment of children"). For now, though, men got to write the poetry, while women got to write the prose. This was the essence of the culture of daddyhood: to be a dad was to be the poet of parenthood.

What did being the poet of parenthood mean? It meant having the "prerogative" to be the candy man and the bestower of toys; it meant holidays at the park. It also meant "irresponsible enjoyment," fun without any strings attached.

Ah, but there were strings. Being the poet also meant being less important, and it could mean being irrelevant. The dentist, the doctor, the teacher, and so on—the prose side of parenthood—these were duties crucial for the survival of the child, and they belonged to mother. Candy and toys and holidays—the poetry—were the incidentals that fathers were encouraged to take on. The culture of daddyhood created a space for fathers that posed little threat to the position of mothers. It carved a niche for fathers that left the parental stratification system basically intact. Men may have been asked to "come home" (become domesticated), but they were not invited to become full partners in the child-rearing process. Playmates, yes. Helpers, if needed. But definitely not mothers, and certainly not equals. *Dad* and *mother,* in short, were more than just words in the early-twentieth-century child-rearing lexicon; they were political symbols.[60]

As political symbols, *dad* and *mother* can be seen as crucial components in what, in the sociology of gender, is called "the law of the excluded middle." Throughout the history of gender relations, there has been an ongoing effort to assign the instrumental (the prose) and the expressive (the poetry) to various people or roles, rather than to recognize that each person and each role is a mixture of the two. If we carefully consider the role of the father in the early twentieth century, for example, and ask what expectations were associated day in and day out with that role, we would come to recognize that being a father had an expressive side (e.g., being a playmate) and an instrumental side (e.g., being an economic provider), and that the difference between being a father and mother was more a difference in degree than in kind. The culture of daddyhood, exemplified in the denotation of fathers as *dads,* however, took that difference in degree—that continuum—and cut it into two discrete categories. Then, in order to make the categories seem naturally discrete, the culture of daddyhood pushed fathers to one side and mothers to the other, leaving a chasm in what was once the middle of a spectrum. Figuratively speaking, hues of gray were transposed into black and white. To be a dad in the 1920s was to be *"not* the mother."[61]

The consequences of the politics of daddyhood can be readily seen in a 1925 article titled, "Poor Dad." Why had "contemptuous jests about father" become "the mainstay of our humoristic literature?" the author wanted to know. "How many have ever stopped to consider that the abundance of such jokes indicates that a fundamental change has taken place in our social system which makes America unique and peculiar among nations? Father has slipped from his pedestal! And not a drum was heard, not a funeral note!" Throughout the world, the author continued, fathers were held in high regard; but in the United States, they were pitied. "'[P]oor father.' From being erect, dominating, and respected he has dropped to the level where he can be 'poored.' Not only can he be, but he is. He is an adjunct of the family, but not its director. He functions as a meal ticket with no voice in the distribution. His place is secondary and ancillary. When not the butt of family ridicule he is the object of benevolent and amused toleration. In his most favorable position he is 'a dear old thing, anyhow.' "[62]

As to the reason behind the American father's decline, the author wondered whether the "main cause" was "the extension of suffrage and economic opportunities to women." (Observe, again, the connection between women's and men's rights.) This possibility, he said, "opens up a field for interesting speculation": "Has man held his foremost place hitherto solely because of his denial of equal opportunities to women? And if this reversal of the status of the man in the American home is due to the increasing power and influence of women—a reversal accomplished in the startlingly short time of thirty-five years—will man be able even to hold his own? Will he not in another period of equal length be completely submerged and subordinated? And if such a process is at work, how long will it take for the nation to become thoroughly feminized?"[63]

The feminization of fatherhood is what worried the author and is what captures the essence of the politics of daddyhood in the 1920s. The father as pal meant more than making men "soft." The father as pal, at least to some, meant transforming men into women. It was the blending of masculinity and femininity that was implied and that essentially created the "contradictions" between domesticity and masculinity to which historian E. Anthony Rotundo refers in *American Manhood.*[64]

How could this meaning have arisen when the father as pal also denoted fathers interacting with sons? Why is it that when father-son contact was high (in the magazines), poking fun at fathers was also high? The answer to both questions, I propose, lies in what it means to make fathers their children's playmates—and *only* their playmates. First, we should remember that however much fathers in the early twentieth century may have played with their children, they still did not, on average, play with their children as much as mothers did. Thus, being a playmate did not really distinguish fathers from mothers as much as one might think.[65] Nor did it distinguish fathers from other people in their children's lives. Why? Because virtually anyone could play with children—and many did (including other children and, for that matter, strangers). To limit fathers to a playmate role thus made fathers dispensable. If fathers were not there to do the job (be their children's playmates), someone else could easily serve as a substitute. In social stratification terms, fathers who were relegated to a playmate role had few resources with which to advance their position. It is not surprising, therefore, that fathers in the 1920s would become the brunt of many a joke. Having less special value to contribute, men were vulnerable to attack, much the same as unskilled workers and illiterate adults in a postindustrial economy often find themselves the objects of humor—and scorn.

If the New Fatherhood of the Machine Age was synonymous with the culture of daddyhood, then the differences between fatherhood in the early and late twentieth century would be sharper. It also would be fairer to say, as some have, that the New Fatherhood of the past meant little more than the positive sanctioning of an image of the father-as-model-airplane-builder. However, the culture of daddyhood, while it did not disappear, declined during the 1930s. Less emphasis was placed on fathers as pals, more on their importance as male role models. This shift was significant because it created a special place for fathers (a place that mothers could not occupy), made both sons and daughters men's psychological responsibility, and correspondingly increased men's status in the home. The decline of the culture of daddyhood during the 1930s thus was more positive than not—at least for fathers.

One last thing, seemingly forgotten by some: The culture of daddyhood was not a behavioral form but a cognitive schemata that framed fathers and their activities in a particular way. Hence, the fact that magazine articles in the 1920s tended to characterize fathers as "daddies" (buddies, and the like) does not mean that fathers themselves were little else. Popular magazines cannot be assumed to mirror everyday life. The culture of fatherhood and the conduct of fatherhood, though related, must be kept distinct.

How fatherhood was transformed during the Machine Age also cannot be gleaned solely from commercial media accounts. We do not know whether the consumers of these accounts changed their behavior as a result of what they read (or heard). We must still establish, in other words, whether New Fatherhood on the social-meaning level correlated with New Fatherhood on the social-interactional level. It is to this question that we shall now turn.

7   "Dear Mr. Patri"

> The art of fatherhood is like all arts, long, tedious, exacting.
> Angelo Patri, "Fathers" (radio script, 1932)

On 12 February 1925, a father in Chicago sat down to write a letter to a man he had never met, a junior high school principal in New York city. The father was seeking help on a matter concerning his son: "I am the father of a thirty-month-old boy who finished learning his alphabet both capital and small letters one month ago. He also knows his figures from one to nine. I taught him his letters at the rate of three or four a week in the form of a game and it was great fun for him. I am afraid to proceed any further without expert advice."[1]

Five days later, the principal wrote back and offered a set of prescriptions for the father to follow. Among other things, he recommended that the child be exposed to music: "It need not be solemn but it should be good. And someone should sing to him." He also thought it important that the child be told stories; and he stressed the value of manual play: "Children grow through their hands as much as through their eyes and ears; I am inclined to believe they grow more that way, and faster."[2]

ANGELO PATRI

The educator who so willingly offered his time and advice was named Angelo Patri. A product of the New York City school system and a graduate of Columbia University (M.A. in Education), Patri, in addition to running a junior high school, had his own weekly radio show and syndicated newspaper column called "Our Children."[3]

In the 1920s and 1930s, radios and newspapers were more of an everyday presence in people's lives, particularly among the middle class, than both books and magazines combined. (Radio was to the 1920s and 1930s what television was to the 1950s and 1960s.) For Patri to have a regular radio show and newspaper column meant that he was being listened to or discussed almost continuously. Thus, as important as the Children's Bureau and *Parents' Magazine* were between the wars, it probably is fair to say that Patri advised more fathers and mothers on how to raise children than just about anyone else. He was a voice across America, a genuine Machine Age celebrity.[4]

The letters to and from Angelo Patri are housed at the Library of Congress and, like the letters to and from the Children's Bureau (discussed in chapter 4), the Patri documents are open to anyone who has the time and inclination to pore through them. Also, like the letters to and from the Children's Bureau, the Patri correspondence is a gold mine of information on early-twentieth-century family life—perhaps even more so.[5]

What makes the Patri correspondence so valuable, especially given our interests here, is that they provide a glimpse of how the modernization of fatherhood at the social-meaning level was playing itself out at the social-interactional level. This is not to say that the Patri documents represent all parents; most of the fathers and mothers who wrote were white and middle class.[6] However, because the fathers and mothers who wrote to Patri were most likely cognizant of, if not enamored with, New Fatherhood, what these parents had to say about their own child-rearing efforts tells us something about the connection between the large-scale social forces that contributed to the modernization of fatherhood and the daily drama of individual families caught up in the process.[7]

Many of the documents that we have reviewed so far offer insights into this connection or intersection. Several things, however, place the Patri correspondence in its own special category. First, there is the sheer volume. The Children's Bureau received hundreds of thousands of letters, but most of them were fairly brief, and only a fraction of them shed light on the social reality of fatherhood per se. The Patri collection, by comparison, contains over seven thousand letters, many of which are fairly long, and the majority of which say something, one way or the other, about men's relationships with children. The Patri collection also includes more letters from fathers (over five hundred) than does the Children's Bureau collection, which helps to flesh out the modernization of fatherhood from a man's point of view. I should add, however, that as valuable as the fathers letters are, to examine them and them alone would be a mistake. For, as we shall soon see, it is primarily the mothers' letters that show the familial conduits through which the modernization of fatherhood flowed.[8] Finally, the range of child-rearing topics covered in the Patri correspondence is broader than in the Children's Bureau correspondence. While most of the letters to the Children's Bureau dealt with the physical health of infants, most of the letters to Angelo Patri dealt with the psychological health of school-age children. The attention given to questions of self and family makes the Patri correspondence a unique repository of early-twentieth-century modernism. Indeed, I can think of no other data set that better captures the psychosocial interior of family life in the wake of America's love affair with "the Modern."[9]

PATRI ON FATHERHOOD

What did Patri have to say about fathers in his newspaper column and radio show? The first "Our Children" column devoted to fathers was dated 11 May 1925, and titled simply "Father." In the piece, Patri deplored the fact that men often were peripheral figures in the lives of their children, but he blamed mothers for "pushing" fathers to the sidelines. "It would be very much better for the whole family if father was given a daily share in the lives of the children right from the start," Patri wrote. "There is very little that mother has to do for a child that father cannot share."[10]

In August of the same year, Patri penned a column titled "Father's Turn." This time, he said he understood that fathers could do little with their children when they were young, but he commented on what they could do as children got older: "Mother does most of the training when the children are tiny. But when they begin to walk father can do more and he ought to begin." Echoing themes that we saw in the popular magazine articles, Patri also thought that, more than simply playmates, fathers should be teachers. Saturdays and Sundays especially, suggested Patri, were days when father should have a "turn at educating the children": "He takes them to the docks to see the ships lying there and tells stories about them and the men who are manning them, the goods they are carrying and the countries to which they go. He takes them to the museums and to the Zoo and the flower gardens. They must know the animals by sight and by name. They must see the flowers growing and call them by name. The big cities have wonderful opportunities for father's teachings."[11]

Patri's third column on fathers was published in October 1926 and titled "Your Father." In it he railed against mothers who tried to get their children to obey them by threatening, "You wait until your father comes home." "That's about the worst failure a mother can make of child rearing," Patri warned. "The moment she [says it] . . . she's through as a power in that child's life. . . . Beside all that, father is coming home. Home. That ought to mean something to the waiting mother and children. Something joyful. And a whole lot of joy should be on father's side."[12]

The final "Our Children" article on fatherhood (in the collection) was published in July of 1928. Titled "Father, Explain Yourself," the article combined themes that were spelled out in the two preceding columns, namely, that fathers should participate in their children's growth after the first few years and that they should be more than disciplinarians: "No matter what the temptation, don't permit yourself to be used as the executioner."[13]

As for Patri's radio show, I found only one script devoted exclusively to men and children. Broadcast on 23 October 1932, it was called simply "Fathers." Relatively long—over eighteen hundred words (the newspaper columns, by comparison, averaged a little over five hundred words)—it hammered home the value of fathers as teachers. The radio show also told fathers to stop being so authoritarian: "Why is it that some fathers behave like 'kaisers'?" Patri wanted to know. "It's a puzzle to me." He then went on to talk about the "art of fatherhood" and what a "real father" does with—and for—his children. (See this chapter's epigraph, which is a quotation from this broadcast.) Finally, he did something that was characteristic of much of his work. He offered a personal story: "How do I know [what fatherhood is all about]? I had a fine father myself. When I was very little he carried me on his shoulder and taught me to see the beauty and majesty of the sky and the meadows, the mountain and the sea. He taught me to love the beauty that was about me. He taught me to appreciate people by telling me stories. . . . Whenever I see a father and son walking out on holidays, I go back to memory and walk again with my own father. I salute these others and I keep thinking of him."[14]

The articles and script show that Patri did not ignore the subject of fatherhood. Still, if we take these texts and place them alongside all the other texts that Patri wrote, we come to realize that he was not a promoter of fathercraft, as was, say, Robert Cheley, the editor of the "Father and Son Library" (see chapter 5). In contrast to the fathercrafters, Patri saw himself more as a psychologist of childhood than a spokesperson for parenthood.

Why did Patri not write more about fatherhood? One explanation, already implied, is that, as a teacher, Patri naturally focused more on children than on adults. Another explanation, even more basic than the first, is that, although Patri seemingly wore the mantle of "father," *patri*, he was not, himself, a father.[15]

Not having children of his own did not appear to handicap Patri professionally. (He was a child-rearing industry all by himself.) But, given the fact that the personal story was central to his style of expression, his nonparent status probably dampened, at least to some degree, his desire to write about men and children. While he could tell stories about his own father and other fathers, he could not draw on his own experience as a father.

Knowing Patri's paternal status allows us to place the correspondence within the proper context. If Patri had commented repeatedly on fatherhood, one could say that men corresponded with Patri only because he prodded them to do so. (Indeed, his 1932 radio show on fathers did motivate some fathers to write.) The fact, however, that Patri did not comment often on fatherhood leaves open the question of why the fathers decided to pen their letters. The answer to the question may be as simple as it is true. Fathers sought Patri's help because they were conscientiously involved not in fathercraft but in childcraft. Like many parents before and since, these men simply were trying to raise their kids in the best way they knew how.

"I'M IN A FIX"

Because Angelo Patri was a principal and would often talk about school issues, many of the letters that he received focused on academics. Not surprisingly, homework and grades were major concerns. A father from West Windhaven, New Hampshire, for example, wanted to know whether an hour of study after school was advisable for a second-grader.[16] A North Carolina man complained that his twelve-year-old son "puts off everything that he is required to do, including his studies," and that this and other problems were "heart-breaking" to him because he had "always imagined" he and his son to be "chums."[17] A Los Angeles father told Patri that his wife had suggested he write "for in her catalogue of saints" Patri's name "shine[d] next to that of Froebel and Bertrand Russell." He went on to recount how his ten-year-old daughter's arithmetic homework was reducing her to tears, and how he had tried to help: "I sat down and began to reason it out with my daughter. Explaining the theory of numbers in a simple way." He also mentioned that he had told his daughter that her arithmetic book and teacher were "old fashioned," a comment which had gotten him into trouble with his wife, who reminded him that Patri disapproved of parents criticizing teachers in front of children.[18]

Frequently mentioned by fathers and mothers were youngsters who were disobedient, unmanageable, or spoiled. A Chicago father said, "After reading several of your articles appearing in the daily news, I have decided to ask your advice in handling a steadfast and determined boy. He is but a child, just past 4 years old. But has a tendency to have his own way in a great many things and a strong inclination to disobey the commands of his mother. In fact, he seems to rule her, instead of vice versa." The father confessed that he was not at home a lot, but that when he was around he did what he could. "Sometimes I spank him for disobeying me, and then his mother gets sore, and things are a little unpleasant. She is a real good woman but I fear she is not stern enough with the children. . . . Will you please offer a few words of advice to a well meaning Dad?"[19] A mother from Hamilton, Ohio, asked what to do about her eleven-month-old son whom her husband and live-in mother had "ruined." "He kicks and squirms when I dress him, won't lay down when I'm feeding him and has one of the worst tempers I ever saw. I think he's too small to spank (his daddy does spank him and it doesn't do a bit of good.) So I'm in a fix. How can I make him mind me and quit being so stubborn?"[20] A Brooklyn father talked about his daughter's sixteenth birthday party, which had gotten, one could say, a little out of hand. The young men who had been invited "lacked the most elementary rules of etiquette and culture," as far as the father could tell. "When refreshments were served, they began pitching sandwiches from one end of the room to the other. When the lights were dimmed for the occasion to light the candles on the birthday cake, some of them climbed the backs of the others slapping the others' heads and shouting on the top of their voices."[21]

Boys were not the only ones accused of not following the rules. Several months after the Brooklyn father had asked for advice, a California woman wanted to know "how to handle" her fifteen-year-old daughter who, besides lying and stealing, "refuses to take daily baths, to wash her hair, brush her teeth, wash her socks, use her clothing allowance for essential clothing, to keep her drawers and dresser in order, to turn off the radio when her sister tries to study, to do her household duties voluntarily, to darn her socks, to show her report cards from school, to open front door when bell rings, to answer telephone, run errands, etc." The girl also was said to be guilty of eating sweets between meals, refusing to read good books, using too much lipstick and mascara, plucking her eyebrows, wearing silk stockings to school, biting her fingernails, and deliberately doing poor work in school despite having a high I.Q.[22]

Other sets of letters focused on developmental issues. A father in Washington, DC, was "anxious to get information on the much talked of psychological test as applied to children."[23] A New York City father wanted Patri's opinion of a "daily duties chart" to organize children's activities during the summer.[24] A mother asked about left-handedness (an issue that worried many parents and educators during the Machine Age): "I have understood that, if we use our right hand the left side of the brain is developed, and if the left the right side is developed. . . . What is your opinion?"[25] A father from Auburn, Indiana, wanted to know what to do about his fifteen-year-old son who was masturbating. The father had told the boy that touching himself that way, besides wasting his energy, could lead to insanity, a threat that had little if any, effect. "What would you advise me to say or do to help him over-come this bad habit?" the man asked. "I want to be a real pal to him."[26] A Brooklyn, New York, mother wrote to learn what could be done about a child who had "developed a bad stutter" in recent weeks: "The child specialist to whom I take my children can offer no suggestions. The stuttering seems to get worse every day."[27] Finally, a Middletown, Connecticut, woman asked Patri whether a boy of eight should be allowed to play with toy guns. "Mr. Patri, will you please tell me if I should encourage this game to my boy or not. Don't you think it is too much of a rough play?" She also was troubled because her son no longer believed in Santa Claus. "Don't you think he is too small not to believe . . . ?"[28]

Letters that dealt with gender-role socialization or the meaning of masculinity and femininity (or boyhood and girlhood) were also common. A Chicago father wrote of "a delicate child" (due to bronchitis and chorea) who, the father hoped, would grow up "to be a man we shall be proud of." Did Patri think "Morgan Park Military Academy . . . would do him any good?"[29] A Chicago woman said that her husband was concerned about how they were raising their two-year-old boy. The father swore that by demanding that the child mind them, they were running the risk of creating "a 'sissy,' or a 'yes-ma'am, no-ma'am' child, with no independence of thought."[30] A man in Kellogg, Iowa, was bothered by the fact that his son walked home with his sisters after school every day and that, as a result, he was being called "a sissy" by his friends.[31] A mother from Park Ridge, Illinois, wrote to ask advice about one of her sons who liked to play with "girl's things" and who sometimes told her that it was not "his fault God didn't make him a little girl."[32]

As was the case with the Children's Bureau, Patri sometimes was asked to serve as a referee when a husband and wife disagreed. While many letters went on and on about how wonderful couples were with their children, the letters that spoke of conflict and disagreement, predictably enough, painted the most negative portraits. A mother from Cleveland, Ohio, for example, wanted Patri to tell her how to convince her husband to stop constantly teasing their two-year-old son: "If the child tells him something is so, he'll say it is not and they keep the argument up until the baby starts to scream. Then his dad says 'you are right.' Or if the child is playing, he hides some of his toys until he starts to cry. . . . My husband claims that he is making the child brighter by making him use his wits."[33] Another Cleveland parent, a father who had separated from his wife, wanted Patri to tell him how he could protect his children from a mother who beat them. "I have raised four children from a woman that hated children . . . and if I failed to give the children the necessary attention and care there would be no children to write about."[34] A mother from Bel Air, Maryland, responding to Patri's program on "the family divided," wrote to say that her four-year-old son was "healthy, active and intelligent to a high degree," but that what was happening in their home was "going to wreck his whole life."

> My husband has taught C. to curse and use the vilest language that can be heard in the streets. . . . My husband will let him say those things and refuses to let me correct him. Says I am nagging him all the time. . . . C. is terribly excitable and becomes simply wild at times. . . . He struck me the other evening with a toy train on the wrist, leaving a mark, struck my mother on the temple with a tobacco box, raising a lump. And he [the father] refused to say a word to him. . . . This must be more of a man problem than a child problem. But can't you write to me something that I can give to him to wake him up?[35]

Often, to be sure, the problems that parents wrote about could seem trivial, perhaps even silly. At the height of the Depression, one mother actually asked Patri what sterling silver pattern she should choose for her daughters, ages eight and five.[36] Some of the most powerful letters in the collection, however, were those that dealt with anything but minor issues: victimization, abuse, death. In a letter reminiscent of some of the head-lines that we see in newspapers today, a woman from Palatine, Illinois, talked of a husband who beat her and the children: "I have never told anyone of our family affairs that is why I write to you. I don't want to even get a divorce if it causes any news and besides I think likely if we do want to leave him he will kill us, so I am scared to stay & scared to leave."[37]

Another element of the letters apparent to anyone who takes the time to seriously examine the collection is the intensity of mothers' requests, compared to those of fathers. In a number of cases, mothers did not simply ask for advice; they *pleaded* for advice, so distraught were they about their perceived inability to be "good" parents. In one year alone (1927), an Atlantic City mother told Patri that she would lie awake at night praying to God to show her "the right way" to bring up her child ("I am nearly a nervous wreck, am just groping in the dark");[38] a Lakewood,

Ohio, woman talked of "what a dreadful failure" she was as both a wife and mother, and how if she "could be assured of a good kindly, firm, patient second mother for [her] babies," she would "get rid of [herself] for their sakes";[39] and "A Despondent Mother" from Natchez, Mississippi, said that she would rather see her two boys, seven and four, "dead and buried" (the boys had a habit of "teasing children and chunking people who pass in the streets") rather than let them grow up to be "convicts" ("I have got to conquer these children right now while they are at this age for if I don't they will not only make me weep but they will make me loose my mind. . . . I may have too much pride but there's nothing so ugly as a bad child").[40]

Rarely, however, did fathers tie their requests for help to their identity as fathers or as men. Rarely was their apparent need for advice explicitly linked to the survival of the "self." Thus, both the ratio of fathers' to mothers' letters and the comparative content of the letters by gender of the writer indicate that not only the physical but also psychic division of child care among the writers was fairly traditional, by which I mean mother-centered. Yesterday's fathers may have been a lot more involved than conventional wisdom would have us believe, but they still lagged far behind mothers.

CULTURE IN ACTION

Patri was in an enviable position. He had a good job (Depression-proof, in some ways, for children needed to be taught); he was financially well off (commanding hundreds of dollars in lecture fees); and he could be take solace from the fact that thousands of people across the country thought he was a child-rearing czar.[41] The accolades bestowed upon him probably account, to some degree, for the confidence that he evinced in his prescriptions. Patri genuinely believed he had the answers; he really saw himself as the fountain of truth.

The question that we need to ask, however, is, Did the fathers and mothers believe it, too? Even more important, from our point of view, Was there a difference in the degree to which fathers and mothers did or did not bow to his wisdom?

We are returning to a question that was first discussed in Chapter 4, where we asked whether the fathers and mothers who wrote to the Children's Bureau had become dependent on the agency for advice. I mentioned that in *Fatherhood in America*, historian Robert Griswold paints a relatively unflattering picture of fathers during the 1920s and 1930s. Griswold pretty much implies that the parent education movement not only made fathers look incompetent (compared to mothers), but it also made them lose confidence in their ability to raise their own children (but if they asked their wives what to do, they would be okay). The experts were a powerful group, says Griswold, part of "therapeutic culture" that eventually robbed families of the right to decide what to do about their own children. While "most" mothers were smart enough not to swallow whole what the experts were saying, "most" fathers were either gullible followers who "depended on their wives' insight" or "ignorant outsiders in the land of the educated."[42]

There is little doubt that, when it came to parent education, women were more involved than were men. How much more involved they were, however, is the subject of some debate (see earlier chapters). There also is little doubt that the therapeutic, or self-help, culture that developed in the early twentieth century transformed people's concept of child-rearing authority (expertise shifted from tradition to science). How much fathers and mothers were controlled by the parent education movement, however, is also a matter of controversy (again, see earlier chapters).

The issue here is not only theoretical, it is practical and political. For if, indeed, the parent education movement and the therapeutic, or self-help, culture of the early twentieth century ultimately marginalized men *more than it did anything else*, then the stark comparisons often drawn between fatherhood then and now would seem more valid. Why? Because the cartoon caricatures of yesterday's fathers would seem to hold true (what a bunch of dopes those fathers were). If, on the other hand, fathers as well as mothers were critical readers (broadly defined) of child-rearing lore, whatever the source, then the culture-conduct connection becomes more complex, and the actors who are part of the connection become more dimensional.[43]

So once again we ask, Did parents, and fathers in particular, become pawns of the child-rearing intelligentsia? Did they become overly dependent on child-rearing experts to tell them what to do? The evidence that we reviewed earlier, primarily the letters to the U.S. Children's Bureau, suggests that parents were not necessarily ready to relinquish parental control to the medical establishment and hence not as subservient as we sometimes might think. But what about the psychological community? Were fathers and mothers more likely to capitulate to this group?

As I mentioned before, the crucial thing to remember is that knowing that an expert's ideas are being read or listened to does not, by itself, tell us whether parents necessarily will do what that expert advises. Fathers and mothers can and do receive information about child rearing from a variety of sources, but it is difficult to determine which piece of information, if any, will sway them, because parental culture, like culture in general, contains "diverse, often conflicting symbols, rituals, stories, and guides to action." Child-rearing lore is a hodgepodge.[44]

To restate the point: There are many products on the cultural shelves, and each one is likely to be touted as the best answer to a particular need or problem. But people do not indiscriminately internalize everything on the shelves. Rather, they move selectively through a vast, and to some degree confusing, cultural storehouse, choosing what appear to them to be compatible items. (To do otherwise is to invite cognitive chaos.) The process of "making sense" of life—work life, love life, parental life—thus demands an *active* response to what is "out there." Applying this logic to child rearing, we would say that the fact that a parent writes to an expert for advice and is given what appears to be a smug prescription cannot be taken as prima facie evidence that the parent has become dependent on that expert. Left unclear is what the parent *does with* the advice: use it, excuse it, abuse it, or lose it?

All of this is not to say that culture is irrelevant or that it is perpetually fluid; my intent here is not substitute one form of determinism for another (i.e., individual determinism for cultural determinism). I acknowledge the fact that culture has a certain "objective" quality about it that channels human behavior.[45] And I do find it significant that, during the early twentieth century, the shelves pertaining to child rearing were being stocked by a child-rearing intelligentsia gaining in prominence. All I am saying is that we must not give so much weight to culture that we neglect the politics of cultural appropriation (where one selects items of culture to suit one's own self-interest) or the indeterminate nature of social life (where probability and luck play a part). I am saying, too, that when historians of fatherhood have neglected these other variables, they have tended to mistake the culture of fatherhood for the conduct of fatherhood and to present fathers in the early twentieth century as inept and more or less "out of it."

How can the Patri data help us in this regard? Since few parents wrote back to Patri to tell him what they thought of his advice, it is difficult to know what they did with it once they got it. (The same is true for the parents who wrote to the Children's Bureau.) In the few cases where parents did write back, however, fathers and mothers proved to be anything but passive recipients of Patri's wisdom.

Consider, for example, the mother from Buffalo, New York, who wrote a lengthy letter to Patri about the problems she was having with her adopted child. Listing a host of difficulties, such as, "She is very naughty when company comes to call. . . . she wets her clothes. . . . The neighbors all dislike the child and speak of her frankly as a 'pest of the neighborhood,' " the mother hoped to receive "some constructive advice" on what she should do.[46]

Patri's reply, mailed within a week, was also lengthy. Detailed or not, however, it apparently was not the kind of advice the mother was looking for, because as soon as Patri's reply arrived, the mother dashed off another letter: "Thank you more than any words can express for your kind and understanding letter of April 30 received today. I have read it over three or four times and also to my husband and talked it over with him." Saying that she agreed with Patri "in theory," she wondered, too, whether she had made herself "clear." Being even more descriptive in her second letter than she was in her first (both letters went on for pages, but the second was longer), she again was hopeful that Patri could help: "I want to solve this problem."[47]

Two days later, Patri wrote back, and his second letter was also longer than his first. Again, what he had to say was not satisfactory, because two days after Patri wrote his second letter (and four days since her second letter), the mother wrote an even longer third letter. She said she felt she was being misunderstood: "I begin to think whoever said language was given us to *conceal* thought was right, since the long letter I wrote you explaining the situation evidently did not explain at all. Perhaps I expressed myself wrongly. And will try again." Undaunted, she laid out the situation once more. As far as her husband was concerned, however, she was getting nowhere fast. "When my husband returned home from the bank tonight and read your letter, he took fire at once and said, 'It's no use trying to get helpful counsel by letter. That man has an idea you and I are a couple of cranks not fit to have the care of a child. He can't get a real understanding of the situation by letter. . . . He is unjust to us, so just drop the subject and don't write to him anymore. It wastes your time and his.' "

The mother said she disagreed with her husband's assessment and blamed herself again for her failure to be clear: "I have no time or strength or energy to waste on resenting your injustice to us, which I suppose must be my fault somehow." Besides, she said, some of Patri's suggestions had seemed useful, and she was experimenting with them to see if they might work: "In both your letters you have given me valuable ideas which I am trying out, and for which I am very grateful." (Note that she said that she was *trying them out.* The decision to use the ideas was still hers, not Patri's.)[48]

The very next day, Patri replied to the mother's letter and offered both advice and support: "I do not think you are bluebeards. I think you [are] two very conscientious people trying to do your whole duty by a child and succeeding better than you know." [49]

One letter by itself cannot test a point; it can only illustrate it. And, if we are not careful, the use of a solitary anecdote can pigeonhole and stereotype the thousands of families who sought Patri's advice. What this letter shows, however, is what other investigations have confirmed, namely, that parents do not necessarily capitulate to the will of an expert, but *construct* lines of action where what an expert says is only one of a range of cultural products from which to choose.[50] The reason this mother kept writing back is that Patri's advice did not square with what she wanted to hear. Thus, however much she and her husband may have respected Patri (and they did respect him), they refused to concede total control to him. Patri's recommendations, rather than being passively absorbed into the couple's consciousness, were filtered through the father's and mother's own cognitive framework, itself a product of both the therapeutic, or self-help, culture and the real demands of the flesh-and-blood child whom they wre trying to raise.

The notion that the child-rearing process involves both cultural influence and personal agency (the society-and-the-individual conundrum) may seem obvious, but it apparently has mystified some. "Most historians have believed that parents operate in a vacuum, automatically applying the current advice of their time on child-rearing, without distortion, to each and every child," says Linda Pollock, herself a historian.[51] Similarly, historian Jay Mechling criticizes scholars for naively assuming that parental advice is synonymous with parental behavior.[52] The lesson for historians of fatherhood appears to be clear: The connection between the culture and conduct of fatherhood should never be taken as given, but must be investigated empirically.

How should such an investigation take place? This is the real issue—and the methodological challenge. To begin with, I would say we must shift our focus from the producers of fatherhood lore to the consumers of fatherhood lore, away from the Machine Age's experts and toward the Machine Age's child rearers. It is in this regard that the letters to Angelo Patri are especially valuable, for within them are the clues to the familial agencies of change operating during the Machine Age.[53]

THE CULTURE-CONDUCT CONNECTION

We know that during the 1920s and 1930s, the culture of fatherhood was fairly traditional, but that over time it became more "modern." What we do not know, however, at least at this point, is whether the same traditional culture could be found inside the home. We also do not know to what extent the changes in the public sphere made their way into privacy of people's lives.

To try to begin to answer these questions, I subjected the fathers' and mothers' letters to a form of quantitative analysis not commonly used in historical document research. My rationale for shifting here to a quantitative mode is that my questions require me to use some reasonably reliable criteria to test the presence or absence of a connection. Also, a quantitative analysis allows me to measure the effect of one variable while controlling for the effect of other, possibly confounding, variables.

A Quantitative Analysis of the Patri Letters

After making a number of week-long visits to the Library of Congress, I managed to photocopy almost all of the roughly five hundred fathers' letters in the Patri collection and, for the sake of comparison, a sample of the mothers' letters as well. The primary criterion for copying a mother's letter was whether it provided information pertaining to the paternal role. For example, if the mother happened to mention her husband and his contact with the children, or lack thereof, it was included. Altogether, close to one thousand letters were copied and brought back for further inspection. From this pool, 131 fathers' letters and 125 mothers' letters were randomly chosen for analysis. The first step in the analysis was to code the 256 letters on a number of variables. The most important of these variables are described below.[54]

LENGTH OF LETTER

An obvious variable on which to compare the fathers' and the mothers' letters was length. I thought, for one thing, that how much effort went into writing the letter (as measured by its length) was one indication of how committed the letter writer was to the parental role: the longer the letter, the greater the commitment. This is a crude proxy, I realize, but it does have a certain intuitive logic, and it did receive empirical support. While I was at the archives, I could see that mothers tended to write longer letters, which would make sense if one assumes that mothers were more involved in child care. By going from simply glancing at the letters and seeing that some were longer than others to carefully calculating just how long each letter was, I was able to measure the degree of the difference between the fathers' and mothers' letters and, equally important, see whether the length of the letters significantly changed over time.

GENDER OF "PROBLEM CHILD"

Generally, the Patri parents wrote about one child in particular—an "identified problem child" or, simply, "problem child." More often than not, the gender of the problem child was specified in the letters, thus allowing a gender-of-child comparison between the fathers' and the mothers' letters. In the event that a letter writer asked for assistance for more than one child and one child could be determined as the primary focus of the letter, then that child was defined as the problem child. If a letter writer asked for assistance for several children (e.g., "my children"), then that person's letter was excluded from the gender-of-child comparison.

AGE OF "PROBLEM CHILD"

Generally, the parents also specified the age of the problem child. Again, only letters that focused on a single problem child were included in the statistical analysis.

NUMBER OF PARENTAL BEHAVIORS

In the course of writing to Patri, the fathers and mothers often would describe one or more discrete parental behaviors. They might say, for example, that they had read to a child, or that they had spanked a child or talked to a teacher. Because these descriptive statements could reflect knowledge of—and involvement with—children, the number of parental behaviors in each of the 256 letters was noted.

The concept of parental behavior is important, so let me try to be as clear as I can about it. Consider the following letter from a Tucson, Arizona, mother:

> I read your column in the *Citizen* every night and am very much interested in your items. I have a little girl twenty-one months old, about whom, I wish to ask your advice. She had the whooping-cough for about five months and during that time I let her have, pretty nearly always, her own way, because every time she cried it brought on a coughing fit. Now I am trying to undo all the mischief of letting her have her own way. I don't know how to go about it. People tell me to spank her, but first I want to know if there is any other way. Hoping that you will be able to help me I am writing this letter. Thanking you in advance for any advice you may give me, I remain, . . . [55]

Note that the mother said her child had the whooping-cough, and that while the child was sick, she had pretty much let her have the run of the house. Consciously not stopping a child from doing something is an example of parental behavior, because role behaviors can include acts of omission as well as acts of commission. (Someone, in other words, can care for another person by deciding *not* to do something with that person: a parent can show that he or she cares for her teenage son by not kissing him—and presumably embarrassing him—in front of his friends.)[56] Next, the mother said that other people had suggested spanking the child to stop the "mischief." This tells us that the mother had talked to others about the problem child. Talking to others—commiserating with others— about being a parent also is an example of parental behavior, and illustrates that the work parents do involves a fair amount of conversational labor.

Altogether, 1,051 parental behaviors were identified in the 256 letters. Among these were the following:

Father takes care of child from 5:45 P.M. to 7:15 A.M. and all day Sunday.

Mother does not allow daughter to take toys outside the house because neighborhood kids steal them.

Father improves his son's bow and arrows.

Mother lets child help her put dishes away.

Father educates children to love their mother, for mothers deserve to be loved.

Mother calls another mother to thank her for giving children money to go to the movies.

Father purchases diamond ring and wristwatch for daughter's graduation.

Mother tells father to stop teaching son to use slang and swear words.

Father gently leads child to a darkened room, plays with him in twilight, and then sends him in alone (to darkened room) to fetch ball.

Mother helps child with his school work.

Father pets dogs and cats in front of son to show they are harmless.

Mother meets child every day after school to walk him home.

Father gives child "severe punishing."

Mother ties child to back of porch to keep child from running away.

Father comes home at 2:00 P.M. to "mind" child while mother goes out.

Mother purchases educational books for children.

Father protests to principal that his child will not be allowed to skip a grade.

Mother watches child to ensure that he does not hurt others.

Father takes child to the dentist.

Mother dresses son after he refuses to dress himself.

Father warns child that he will spank her for throwing things at people.

Mother makes a chart and offers a prize if son eats regularly.

Father tells daughter to be more discerning in choosing her friends.

Mother reads Patri's column to children.

Parents go to hear Patri speak.[57]

THE DIVISION OF PARENTAL BEHAVIORS

After the 1,051 behaviors were identified, they were coded as to who carried them out: father only, mother only, or father and mother both. In the following excerpt, for example, a father described the trials and tribulations of being the parent of three young children, ages two, four, and six: "It seems like I've used all within my power to get them to go to sleep but failed. . . . Would you recommend hot milk? We tried that. Good bed time stories? Maybe we didn't tell them the *right* kind of stories. I work late every night and it might have some effect on them because they want to see *Daddy*. And when they do, they want to play and talk with me. It's ten or eleven o'clock before I get them to go to sleep. Please advise me as I'm nearly *exhausted*."[58]

When the father said that "we" tried hot milk and bedtime stories to get the children to go to sleep, he implied that these were behaviors that both he and his wife had tried. Thus, these two parental behaviors were coded as "both" on the variable for division of parental behavior. When he said, on the other hand, that he sometimes played with the children when he got home late at night, he implied that he was the only one who was involved. This parental behavior was coded as "father only."[59] Linking the behaviors to the father or mother or both allowed three proportions to be computed: (1) the father-only proportion, (2) the mother-only proportion, and (3) the parents-together proportion.[60]

SINGULAR POSSESSIVE/PRONOUN USE: "MY" CHILD

While I was at the National Archives looking through the advice-seeking letters sent to the U.S. Children's Bureau, I happened to come across a letter in which a mother referred to her child as "my" child but in the next sentence referred to a cow as "our" cow. It occurred to me that a letter writer's tendency to use a singular possessive or pronoun when referring to the problem child would suggest a strong *personal identification* with that child. I thus concluded that it would be worthwhile to count the number of times the letter writer used singular possessives/pronouns such as *my, me, I,* and *myself* when referring to the problem child. (In notes to myself, I would refer to the tabulations as a test of the "our" cow, "my" child hypothesis.)[61]

PLURAL POSSESSIVE/PRONOUN USE: "OUR" CHILD

If, given the opportunity, a parent used plural possessives/pronouns like *our, us, we,* and *ourselves* when referring to the problem child, then that too was recorded. The tendency to use plural possessives/pronouns when referring to the problem child would suggest a strong *collective identification* with that child. Thus, each parent had two possessive/pronoun use scores, one for the number of singular possessives/pronouns used in the letter, and another for the number of plural possessives/pronouns used. Note that one score is not the obverse of the other. This allows for the possibility that a father or mother could be low on both scores, or high on both scores.

DADDYHOOD

The fluctuation in the use of words *dad* and *daddy* in the magazine articles made me wonder whether the same pattern would be observed in the Patri correspondence. Thus, the presence or absence of these words was noted in the 256 letters.[62]

PERIOD EFFECTS

The modernization of fatherhood implies change over time. Hence to test its effect, we must determine whether any of the above variables shifted from one year to the next. To see whether this was so, the letters were grouped into three historical periods: 1925–1929, 1930–1934, and 1936–1939. (Only a few letters in the collection were written in 1935, because Patri was ill for a good part of the year.) A multivariate analysis was carried out, with "period" serving as the independent variable, and the other variables specified above serving as dependent variables. A multivariate analysis was done to assess the presence or absence of period effects while controlling for the possible confounding influence of other variables.[63]

Findings

What did the quantitative analysis yield? First, I will talk about how the fathers' and mothers' letters compared with one another—and with the larger culture. Second, I will report how the letters that were written in the 1930s differed from those written in the 1920s.

FATHER-MOTHER COMPARISONS

When the length of the letters and the number of behaviors mentioned in them are examined, the fathers were found not only to write shorter letters but also to mention fewer parental behaviors. This is not surprising. As I said, I could see this pattern at the archives.

If the length and level of detail in the letters are taken as a measure of parental commitment, then these gender differences would provide further evidence that, while modern middle-class fathers of the 1920s and 1930s may have had more contact with their children than did other men, they still were not on a par with most middle-class mothers when it came to direct child care.

There are other important differences. Regarding the division of parental behavior, fathers were most likely to cite parents-together behaviors, while mothers were most likely to cite mother-only behaviors. For the fathers, the proportion of father-only, mother-only, and parents-together behaviors was 39 percent, 13 percent, and 48 percent respectively. For the mothers, the proportion was 19 percent, 61 percent, and 20 percent. Thus, the mothers gave far greater attention to their most popular behavior (mother-only behaviors = 61 percent) than the fathers gave to theirs (parents-together behaviors = 48 percent), which means that the mothers who wrote to Patri tended, more so than the fathers, to present both a unimodal and a mother-centered picture of the division of child care. This is something I did not see at the archives. But then, unless one studies the letters carefully and calculates the various proportions, it is unlikely that someone would pick up these nuances simply by scanning the letters.

And the nuances are important. The differences in the proportion of parental behaviors mentioned by the fathers and mothers raise some interesting questions about what we really know about yesterday's fathers. The mothers' letters to Patri present a picture of the division of child care that is very traditional and very much in accord with the pictures that were presented in the mother-based surveys from the 1920s and 1930s. The fathers' letters, however, offer perceptions that were absent from the older surveys and cause us to wonder about the generalizability of those surveys. For if the mothers in the surveys were as likely as the mothers who wrote to Patri not to mention men's contribution to child care, then it is possible that the actual division of child care during the 1920s and 1930s was less traditional than is commonly thought. That is, if we assume that the mothers in the earlier surveys were more privy to their own (as opposed to their husbands') involvement with their children, and that they had a vested interest in emphasizing, if not elevating, their own contributions (in short, a vested interest in taking credit), it seems reasonable to suggest that the studies that relied exclusively on mothers' self-reports erred toward the traditional end of the division of child care continuum.

I am not suggesting, of course, that the division of child care in the 1920s and 1930s was egalitarian. There is plenty of evidence to indicate that it was not. Nor am I arguing that the fathers' letters to Patri are without bias, for the men also had reason to accentuate their own child care efforts. I am only saying that an analysis of the division of parental behaviors in the Patri letters suggests that the picture we have of yesterday's fathers, based primarily on mothers' self-reports, may not be as accurate as we sometimes think.[64]

The fathers' and mothers' use of possessives and pronouns raises similar concerns. (More subtle nuances not likely to be apparent to the "naked eye.") The analysis of the 256 letters indicates that the fathers who wrote to Patri were as likely to say "my" child as they were to say "our" child (on average, there were 4.0 singular possessives/pronouns and 4.7 plural possessives/pronouns per father letter). This would indicate that the cognitive family map of these modern middle-class fathers was relatively father- and mother-inclusive. That is, the men saw themselves *and* their wives as partners in the child-rearing process. A different family map was revealed in the mothers' letters, however. The mothers were much more likely to say "my" child as opposed to "our" child (on average, there were 7.8 singular possessives/pronouns and 3.4 plural possessives/pronouns per mother letter). This would indicate that the mothers who wrote to Patri had a strong personal identification with the problem child and would suggest also that the cognitive family map of the mothers was not as father-inclusive. Compared to the men's, the women's family universe consisted of at least two realms: the realm of personalities that made up the entire family or household, and the subrealm of personalities that included only mothers and children.

In short, it would appear that in these mothers' minds, fathers resided on the periphery of parenthood. If the same perception of fathers prevailed among women who were interviewed for the self-report studies of the 1920s and 1930s on which historians have tended to rely, then we have to ask again whether the picture of yesterday's fathers, based on these studies, is as valid as it has been made out to be.

What about the gender and age of the problem child; what do we see there? The popular literature on fatherhood during the Machine Age, with some variation, focused largely on men's relationships with their sons; thus, one would expect the Patri fathers to write more on behalf of their male children. And, indeed, this is what was found: 73 percent of the fathers' letters focused on child-rearing problems with boys. It is noteworthy, however, that about the same percentage of the mothers' letters, 71 percent, also focused on sons.

One explanation for the gender imbalance is that parents generally perceived boys as more troublesome than girls. Another explanation is that at a time when women were treated as second-class citizens, male children may have been held in higher esteem and thought to be more deserving of special, "expert" attention than were female children.

Even though most fathers and mothers wrote on behalf of their sons, close to 30 percent of the fathers' letters focused on daughters. This figure, interestingly enough, is almost identical to the percentage of the fatherhood magazine articles published between 1922 and 1939 that mentioned daughters, but it is way above the percentage of father-to-father books that centered on men's relationships with female children (hardly any, from what I could see).[65] If one were to rely solely on father-to-father books to get a sense of father-child relations during the Machine Age, one might conclude that fathers showered almost all of their attention on boys. The Patri collection, however, indicates that there were some modern fathers who were not oblivious to their daughters' needs.

Contrary to what might have been predicted, the problem child's gender had only a minimal impact on the structure of the fathers' letters. Of all the possible variables that could have been affected, only one, the number of parental behaviors in the letter, was influenced by whether the child in question was a boy or girl: fathers writing on behalf on their female children cited more parental behaviors (but not necessarily more father-only or both-parent behaviors). The problem child's gender, however, did have a major impact on the structure of the mothers' letters: the mothers who wrote on behalf of their female children wrote longer letters, cited more parental behaviors, and were more likely to use both singular and possessive pronouns/possessives when referring to their children.

These findings would seem to contradict the tendency of both the fathers and the mothers to write on behalf of their sons. The explanation may be, however, that when the parents did write about their daughters they were writing about particularly troublesome daughters (i.e, extreme cases). Some researchers have suggested that the Depression placed a special strain on parent-daughter ties.[66]

The fact that mothers writing on behalf of their daughters wrote longer and more descriptive letters and used not only more singular but also more plural pronouns or possessives suggests that the mothers had a strong personal *and* collective identification with their daughters. In other words, when contemplating their daughters as opposed to their sons, the mothers may have been more likely to think of themselves and their daughters as occupying a special (and presumably valued) "universe," and to think of themselves, their daughters, and their husbands as occupying *another* special (and presumably valued) "universe."

As for the age of the problem child, the average age of the primary child in the fathers' letters was seven, with a range from under one year to nineteen. The average age of the problem child in the mothers' letters was eight, with a range of under one year to twenty-five. We see a difference, but not a statistically significant one. The letters themselves, however, do show some interesting correlations with the child's age. In the fathers' letters, the age of the problem child had a positive effect on the length of the letters and on the use of singular possessives and pronouns. In the mothers' letters, the age of the problem child had no effect on the length of the letters or on the use of singular possessives and pronouns, but it did have a positive effect on the use of plural possessives and pronouns and a negative effect on the proportion of mother-only behaviors mentioned.

The fathers who wrote to Patri thus seem to have been more attached to their older children, both physically (in terms of time expended on their "problems") and psychically (in terms of personally "owning" them, e.g., saying "my" child). In this case, the fathers were in line with popular prescriptions. Most child-rearing experts, including Patri, preached that fathers should increase their contact with their children once the children came of age. The mothers, too, seem to have followed the expert's line. Their increased use of plural possessives and pronouns, and their decreased reference to mother-only behaviors suggests a greater willingness to incorporate their husbands in the raising of older children.

PERIOD EFFECTS

Did the fathers and mothers modernize? Here the answer is both no and yes. Contrary to a shift toward modernization, the fathers wrote shorter letters in the late 1930s than they did in the late 1920s, and they mentioned fewer behaviors in both the early and late 1930s than they did in the late 1920s. From the mothers' letters, a different pattern emerged. There was no change over time in the length of their letters or in the number of behaviors mentioned. There was a change, however, both in the mothers' possessive/pronoun use and in the attention given to various behaviors. In the late 1930s (compared to the late 1920s), mothers, when referring to the problem child, were less likely to say "my" child and more likely to report father-only behaviors.

Using the breadth and depth of the letters as measures of parental involvement, one would conclude that *the modern fathers of the 1930s were less involved with their children than were the modern fathers of the decade before.* This directly contradicts the changes that were occurring in popular culture.

The reason for the anomaly was the Great Depression. While the Depression was a positive force in the modernization of the culture of fatherhood (motivating the business community to mobilize behind Father's Day, as we will see in the next chapter), it mainly exerted a negative impact on father-child interaction. Previous studies indicate that the Depression generally reduced the amount of contact men had with their children, so these findings are not unexpected.[67] These earlier studies, however, generally did not use statistical controls, relied on mothers' self-reports, and focused on working-class or deprived families. The proposition that the Depression reduced father-child contact thus is strengthened by this analysis of the Patri letters.

What would account for a decline in fatherly involvement in a sample of men who, by all indications, were financially secure? It is important to remember that while many men did not lose their jobs in the 1930s, everyone experienced a sense of economic insecurity, and almost everyone suffered some loss of income. Evidence indicates, for example, that between 1929 and 1933, doctors and lawyers saw their incomes drop by as much as 40 percent, and skilled stenographers took cuts in pay from $40 per week to $16 per week.[68] Thus, with financial ruin an ever-present possibility and "deficit living" an everyday reality, the Depression-era fathers who wrote to Patri may have been less able or willing than their counterparts in the 1920s to interact with their children.[69]

The fact that the economy weighed heavily on these men and ultimately reduced the amount of attention they devoted to fatherhood underscores how much, under the economic provider role, men's involvement with children is tied to employment. It is not simply a question of whether a man has a job but how preoccupied he is with that job that matters. Thus, the more a man is singularly committed to being an economic provider, the less likely he is to find time for anything else, whether it be taking a weekend off or interacting with his kids.[70] The Depression not only forced a number of men to devote attention to finding a job, but it also placed considerable mental strain on the many others who were fortunate enough to have work. The consequence for children in both instances, as indicated by earlier studies as well as by the quantitative analysis of the Patri letters, was that children were dropped, figuratively speaking, from their father's "calendars." Depression-era men, in other words, whether they were unemployed or not, may have felt that they had less spare time to devote to their daughters and sons.[71]

Considering that mothers who wrote to Patri also suffered through hard economic times, why did their letters not get shorter and the behaviors they mentioned less frequent? The answer is that, unlike the fathers, they probably did not view parenthood as an extra activity—as something to do if time permits. Rather, the mothers who wrote to Patri probably saw parenthood much the same as mothers today see parenthood—as a highly salient role.[72]

It is interesting that while the length of the fathers' letters and the number of behaviors cited in the letters declined, the fathers' possessive/pronoun use did not change. If the impact of the Depression was such that the men not only interacted less with their children but cognitively distanced themselves from their children as well, one would expect that fathers would be less likely to personally identify with their children. One would expect, in other words, that they would be less likely to refer to the problem child as "my" child. However, this did not occur. The Patri letters thus suggest that the modern fathers of the 1930s may have been less involved with their children in a *physical* sense, but they were just as involved with their children in a *psychic* sense.

Were there no points of connection between the modernization of fatherhood at the institutional level and the social reality of fatherhood inside the home? Actually, there were several.

As I said before, in the late 1930s, when the culture of fatherhood was at its most modern point compared to the 1920s, the mothers were less inclined to say "my" child and more inclined to report father-only behaviors. It is possible that these changes reflect changes in the behavior of the mothers' husbands, and if that is the case, then the negative effect observed in the fathers' letters and in other studies would be contradicted. It also is possible that the mothers' decreased tendency to use singular possessives and pronouns and increased tendency to cite father-only behaviors have less to do with the behavior of the husbands than with attitudes of the mothers. Specifically, the changes in the mothers' possessive/pronoun use and behavioral citations indicates that *the mothers' outlook toward their husbands (the fathers of their children) became more modern in the late 1930s.*

The possibility of an attitudinal shift is reinforced by yet another change in the mothers' letters, not yet revealed. Comparing the 1925–1929 period with the 1936–1939 period, we find that the mothers were less likely in the late 1930s to call their husbands "dad," a change that mirrors what we found in the popular magazine articles (see chapter 6). A decrease in the use of *dad* would seem to suggest a less modern approach to fatherhood. However, as I pointed out in the discussion of popular magazines, the use of *dad,* at least during the Machine Age, denoted a more trivial and more marginalized brand of paternal activity. The decrease in the use of *dad* in mothers' letters thus is consistent with the changes toward modernization in their letters.

As for the Patri fathers, there was no change from 1925 to 1939 in the degree to which father-only behaviors were cited, nor was there, as I have already noted, a shift in pronoun use. There was, however, a shift in the men's tendency to refer to themselves as "dad," but for them the shift began in the early rather than the late 1930s. This shift suggests that *the fathers may not have been oblivious to the transformation in the culture of fatherhood surrounding them, although, as was true for the mothers, they appeared to modernize attitudinally more than behaviorally.*

In sum, the fathers' letters indicate that changes in popular culture were not being reflected in changes in father-child contact. To the contrary, the fathers' letters exhibited changes that were directly opposite to the changes in father-child interaction being proposed in popular magazine articles and books. The Depression here seems to have been a factor; it dampened the positive impact the changes in the culture of fatherhood might have had on men's involvement with children. But, contrary to what others have reported, the story of fatherhood during the 1930s does not end here, because the quantitative analysis of the fathers' and the mothers' letters also points to a connection between the changes in popular culture and the attitudes of fathers toward themselves and of mothers toward their husbands. In small but significant ways, the fathers' and mothers' letters revealed an openness to modernization. The meaningfulness of this shift should not be underestimated. As I mentioned before, studies show that women's gender-role attitudes have a positive effect on men's gendered behaviors: the more modern women's attitudes are, the more modern men's behaviors eventually become. Thus, while the Depression may have prevented men from making the behavioral changes that increasingly were expected of them, once it ended, the pressure from their wives probably remained (though World War II probably put things on hold for a while). Another thing to contemplate is that while the attitudinal changes evidenced in the Patri letters may not have translated immediately into increases in paternal involvement, they may have influenced *other* behavioral changes during the Depression, changes that also may be linked to the modernization of fatherhood. In the next chapter, we will see how.

· · · · · ·

8   "Honor Thy Father"

Father's Day is like Mother's Day, except the gift is cheaper.
Gerald F. Lieberman, quoted in
Every Day Is Father's Day (1989)

In 1931, Angelo Patri received a personal invitation to attend a Father and Son dinner in the gymnasium of the Kenilworth Church in Brooklyn. The flyer announced that the event was sponsored by Boy Scout Troop No. 75 and was scheduled for Friday, 12 June, two days before the weekend holiday: "[Y]ou know, of course, June 14th is 'Father's Day.' "[1]

There is no indication among the papers at the Library of Congress whether Patri attended the event. One thing is certain, however. If Patri did attend, he along with everyone else would have been party to an erroneously timed celebration. In 1931, Father's Day did not fall on June 14th, but on June 21st; not on the second, but on the third Sunday of the month. The group had scheduled its dinner a week too soon.[2]

The New Fatherhood ethos that motivated the Father and Son get-together and that was endorsed in the flyer ("No longer does today's boy see his father only as a dignified, bewhiskered, stern and somewhat to be feared individual. Today it's Dad!"),[3] coupled with the confusion over when Father's Day was supposed to be, captures the complexities of a social institution in the throes of change. Yes, fatherhood was transforming. No, the process was not going smoothly.

Father's Day; how important is it to the modernization of fatherhood? My sense is that it is very important. Although festivals and ceremonies paying homage to fathers do go back to ancient times ("Honor thy father," commands the Bible), today's version of Father's Day did not take shape until the early twentieth century and was not widely practiced until the late 1930s and early 1940s, when the Machine Age was just about ending and World War II had just about begun (for America, at least). The overlap between the creation of Father's Day and the development of New Fatherhood, I believe, was not accidental. With the help of Father's Day, New Fatherhood was given a stamp of approval that even a child could understand. (A gift speaks volumes.) Through Father's Day, New Fatherhood was sanctified and made generally real. Conversely, the development of New Fatherhood, beginning with the changes that had taken place prior to the Machine Age, also facilitated the acceptance of Father's Day, first in the middle class, but later also in other classes. Indeed, were it not for the legitimating work carried out by the child-rearing intelligentsia (discussed in previous chapters), Father's Day probably would never have become the holiday that Americans came to know in the late 1930s and early 1940s.

Given the close association in time between the creation of Father's Day and the development of New Fatherhood, one would assume that fatherhood researchers long ago would have set their sights on studying the holiday—how it came to pass, what it means to ordinary citizens. Scholars working in the area, however, generally have either dismissed Father's Day as nothing more than a "commercial afterthought" (to Mother's Day) or, more remarkably, ignored it altogether. Understanding the history of Father's Day may require an understanding of the history of Mother's Day, but to assume that the former is only a commercial by-product of the latter is to underestimate an event of tremendous familial importance. To overlook it entirely would be even harder to defend.[4]

The reciprocal relationship between Father's Day and New Fatherhood, with each contributing to the other, demonstrates perhaps better than anything else how cultural and economic forces, working in tandem, were responsible for the modernization of fatherhood. The gender politics at the nucleus of the metamorphosis was, as we shall see, both a politics of ideas and a politics of the purse.

FATHER'S DAY AND MOTHER'S DAY: THE OFFICIAL HISTORY

Similar to other holidays that have achieved national prominence, Father's Day and Mother's Day both have official histories, written and circulated by sanctioning bodies. In America, the leading keepers of the flame are the National Father's Day Committee and its sister organization, the National Mother's Day Committee.[5]

The official history of Father's Day is that a Mrs. John Bruce Dodd (Sonora Louise Smart Dodd) of Spokane, Washington, came up with the holiday in 1909 as a way of paying tribute to her own father, William Jackson Smart. According to the National Father's Day Committee, "Civil War veteran William Smart" was left to raise six children on "the Northwest frontier" when his wife died during childbirth. In appreciation for her father's "devotion and care," Dodd "crusaded" for a "Father's Day" that would honor not only her father but all fathers. The official history says also that Dodd "took her idea, first, to the local Ministerial Association, and to the YMCA, for help in nurturing and developing it as a local observance." Her efforts proved to be successful ("obviously," says the distributed literature), "because the first Father's Day was celebrated in Spokane in 1910."[6]

Dodd's initial choice for the date of Father's Day was her father's birthday, June 5th, which in 1910 was the first Sunday of the month. The ministers in the area, however, told Dodd that this date did not give them enough time to prepare their special sermons; thus the observance was postponed for two weeks. It is for this reason, according to lore, that Americans observe Father's Day on the third Sunday in June every year.[7]

As for Mother's Day, the official history gives primary credit to a Miss Anna M. Jarvis.[8] Anna M. Jarvis was the daughter of Anna Reeves Jarvis who, in 1868, had organized a committee in her home town of Grafton, West Virginia, to sponsor a "Mother's Friendship Day," the purpose of which was "to reunite families that had been divided during the Civil War." Anna Reeves Jarvis had hoped to expand her friendship day into an annual "memorial" day for mothers, but she died in 1905, before the remembrance could gain momentum.[9] Two years after her mother's death, Anna M. Jarvis "announced to a group of friends that she had a concept for honoring her Mother—and all American mothers—with a day designated to recognize and celebrate their many contributions to lifestyles in the United States."[10] The next year, on the second Sunday in May (the closest Sunday to the date that her mother had passed away), Anna M. Jarvis succeeded in arranging church services honoring mothers both in Grafton and in Philadelphia, where she happened to live. Thus, 1908 is the official birth year of Mother's Day, and the second Sunday in May is its official day of observance.

FATHER'S DAY AND MOTHER'S DAY: OTHER VOICES

The stories published by the National Father's Day and Mother's Day Committees convey the impression that Father's Day and Mother's Day were the brainchilds of, at most, three people—Sonora Louise Smart Dodd, Anna Reeves Jarvis, and Anna M. Jarvis. In truth, however, the idea for a Father's Day and Mother's Day sprouted almost simultaneously from several different quarters.

Consider the case of Father's Day. Evidence indicates that Sonora Louise Smart Dodd was not the first or the only person to conceive of the idea. Similar Father's Day celebrations were held in Fairmont, West Virginia, in 1908 (the year before the Father's Day Committee says that Dodd made her pitch); and in Vancouver, Washington, in 1912 (having been suggested in the *Portland Oregonian* in 1911). Jane Addams, who founded Hull House in Chicago, lent her support in 1911 to a citywide celebration ("Poor father has been left out in the cold," said Addams), but her pleas were for nought; the proposal was turned down.[11]. In 1913, U.S. Representative J. Hampton Moore, acting at the behest of Charlotte K. Kirkbride and B. Carrie Sternberg of Philadelphia, introduced a bill to Congress "for the designation of the first Sunday in June of each year as 'Father's Day.' " Kirkbride and Sternberg reportedly had "obtained a charter for Father's Day under the state of Delaware and were instrumental [the year before] in having this new day of sentimental observance celebrated in many parts of the country."[12] In 1914, a letter to the *New York Times* proposed that 20 September be designated Father's Day, while two others, in response to the first, suggested that it be the fourth Sunday in November, because of its nearness to Thanksgiving. ("This feast day could not have been made possible if it had not been for the untiring help of our forefathers," said the letter writer.)[13]

In June 1920, the Lions Club of America named Harry C. Meek "the originator of Father's Day." (Meek was a former Lions Club president.) Meek claimed to have conceived of Father's Day while visiting his boyhood home of Carrollton, Kentucky, on Mother's Day in 1915. Sonora Dodd, too, is said to have invented Father's Day while sitting in a church in 1909 listening to a Mother's Day sermon. Meek lectured on the virtues of Father's Day to various Lions Clubs and maintained that the third Sunday in June was chosen as the day of observance because it was the closest Sunday to *his* birthday, which was June 25th. Meek apparently also tried in the 1920s to persuade Presidents Warren Harding and Calvin Coolidge to mark the day with a proclamation, but both refused, saying that they did not want to commercialize the day. President Woodrow Wilson, however, did issue a proclamation of sorts in 1916, when he pressed a button in the Oval Office that unfurled a flag at the Father's Day celebration in Spokane, Washington. Coolidge, while apparently unwilling to issue a White House proclamation, did suggest in 1924 that Father's Day be observed in every state, "declaring that such an occasion would bring about a clearer relationship between fathers and their children, and also impress upon the former their obligations."[14]

The history of Mother's Day also has its twists and turns. During the

Civil War, before Anna Reeves Jarvis had proposed a Mother's Day tribute, Julia Ward Howe, the author of the "Battle Hymn of the Republic," urged that the Fourth of July be renamed Mother's Day and that the day be used to promote peace.[15] Even official founder Anna Reeves Jarvis was actively involved much earlier, and for reasons much different, than generally has been supposed. In 1858, three years prior to the beginning of the Civil War, Jarvis lobbied for "Mothers' Work Days" throughout West Virginia "to improve sanitation in the Appalachian Mountains." [16]

To what degree were the early concepts of Mother's Day comparable to what we have today? In her book *The Way We Never Were,* historian Stephanie Coontz reports that, contrary to what is officially communicated, Mother's Day "originated to celebrate the organized activities of women *outside* the home," and was not intended as a means to privately honor one's own mother. The mode, in short, was plural, not singular (*Mothers'* Day vs. *Mother's* Day). Notes Coontz, "The people who inspired Mother's Day had quite a different idea about what made mothers special. They believed that motherhood was a *political* force. They wished to celebrate mothers' social roles as community organizers, honoring women who acted on behalf of the entire future generation rather than simply putting their own children first." [17]

Seldom mentioned in the official histories is the fact that not everyone in the beginning supported the idea of a Father's Day or Mother's Day. In fact, some thought the holidays patently absurd. In 1911, for example, the 122nd Presbyterian General Assembly, which met in Atlantic City, adopted a resolution in favor of Mother's Day. When someone in the hall, however, stood up to suggest a Father's Day as well ("I approve of honoring our mothers but I think our fathers also should be remembered"), reports are that he was laughed at.[18] In 1914, a man wrote to the *New York Times* to say, tongue-in-cheek, that if there was to be a Father's Day, then there should also be a Brother's Day, a Sister's Day, a Grandpa's Day, a Grandma's Day, an Uncle's Day, a Maiden Aunty's Day, a Cousin's Day, a Baby's Day, a Household Pet Day, and a Slush Day.[19]

As for Mother's Day, it may have been generally perceived as the more legitimate of the two holidays, but it was not without its critics. On 9 May 1908, one unnamed U.S. Senator, speaking on behalf of the Y.M.C.A., formally proposed to his colleagues that the next day (Sunday) be set aside as Mother's Day. The debate that followed "brought out a number of witty sallies." In the end, the proposal "was gravely referred to the Committee on the Judiciary, where it [was] . . . permitted to sleep peacefully." The Senate had rejected the motion "[o]n the grounds that it might let down the legislative bars to special days in honor of 'sisters and the cousins and the aunts' of its members."[20] Thirty years later, long after Mother's Day had become a perennial event, someone expressed the same concerns about giving mothers a day of their own: "Just whose idea was this anyway? Why should a day so be set aside to celebrate motherhood and all the hidden yearnings and restlessness that accompany it? Why not have a Maid's Sunday, or a Washwoman's Day, or a Dime Store Clerk's Sunday" This, from a mother of three, who, one would think, would have had ample reason to support the holiday.[21]

Surprisingly—or perhaps not so surprisingly—the most ardent and organized criticism of Mother's Day came *on* Mother's Day. And it was a criticism that had little to do with "sisters and cousins and aunts" but everything to do with fathers. In the early twentieth century, it was customary for people to attend rallies on Mother's Day to express their support for the holiday. In New York City, Central Park was a popular meeting site. Beginning in the 1920s and continuing through the 1930s, however, Central Park became the site of other kinds of rallies—counter-rallies held also on Mother's Day but with the aim of renaming Mother's Day and making it Parents' Day.

The principal figure behind the Parents' Day rallies was a man by the name of Robert Spere. Besides being a philanthropist, Spere was a "children's radio entertainer" who, when performing, was known as "Uncle Robert."[22] Spere's philosophy about Parents' Day was summed up essentially in a message he delivered in 1931, announcing the annual festivities: "We should all have love for dad and mother every day, but Parents' Day on the second Sunday in May is a reminder that both parents should be loved and respected together. No home can be happy where there is division of respect and affection. . . . The name daddy sounds good to all of us, and the name mother brings joy to our hearts. My mother, my dad— when we can say this with that real affection[,] that makes you feel like giving mother a good kiss and dad a good hug."[23]

Despite valiant efforts on the part of many, from the President of the United States on down, the Parents' Day movement died in 1940, the victim of economic politics. The business community essentially had killed it. Mother's Day followed by Father's Day was too perfect a setup financially to allow something as gender-nonspecific as Parents' Day to muck things up.[24]

"IN WITNESS WHEREOF, I HAVE HEREUNTO SET MY HAND . . ."

Although neither Father's Day nor Mother's Day were immediately embraced, and while each had their opponents, when the two were given their official sendoffs (in 1910 and 1908, respectively), Mother's Day took off more like a rocket, while Father's Day took off . . . well, more like a rock.

By 1911, three years after the West Virginia and Pennsylvania celebrations, every state in the nation was observing Mother's Day.[25] Two years later, Congress voted to make Mother's Day a national holiday. In 1914, Woodrow Wilson issued a presidential proclamation "legalizing and immortalizing" the second Sunday in May for generations to come.[26]

No similar groundswell of support emerged for Father's Day. As I said, President Wilson did participate, if only from afar, in the Father's Day festivities that took place in Spokane, Washington, in 1916. Also, President Coolidge did encourage the states to organize their own Father's Day celebrations in 1924. But Coolidge (and Harding before him) did not accede to Harry Meek's request that Father's Day be made a federal holiday.

Congress also did not follow its 1913 resolution for Mother's Day with an equivalent resolution for Father's Day—at least not immediately. It was not until 1971—fifty-eight years after Mother's Day received its imprimatur—that Congress finally saw fit to pass a bill in favor of Father's Day. In response, President Richard Nixon issued, in 1972, a proclamation ("In Witness Whereof, . . .") asking everyone in the country to make the third Sunday in June "an occasion for renewal of the love and gratitude we bear to our fathers."[27]

Why Mother's Day was almost immediately embraced while Father's Day was almost universally ignored may seem paradoxical, but it appears less so if we first understand some of the maneuvering going on at the time. The situation was this: Mother's Day had three sets of allies. First, there were the religious and political conservatives who saw in Mother's Day an opportunity to remind women that their "proper" place was in the home, not in a factory or office and certainly not out in the streets protesting. Mother's Day was seen by these interested parties as a public symbol that could be used against the women's movement, which, in the early 1900s, was picking up steam. (It was in the early 1900s that suffragists were fighting, successfully, for the right to vote.) The second set of Mother's Day supporters, ironically, could be found among the very people with whom the religious and political conservatives were feuding, namely women's rights advocates. Women's groups tended to favor Mother's Day because they viewed it as an opportunity to remind the nation that women were important. The third set of supporters included physicians and nurses who worked in the field of maternal and infant health. Members of the medical community were inclined to support Mother's Day because they saw it as an advertising tool to stress how "scientific" approaches to motherhood could reduce the infant mortality rate.[28]

Three powerful groups, in many ways different, were yet united for the moment under a common cause. What tied them all together was their commitment to elevating motherhood, even if it meant, out of necessity, denigrating fatherhood. To the extent that the groups believed that raising the status of motherhood meant keeping fatherhood in a subordinate position (albeit an important subordinate position), then that was a price that had to be paid. If Father's Day were permitted to be signed into law along with Mother's Day, the special place that the pro–Mother's Day groups were trying to reserve for mothers would not be so special after all. The gender politics of the era, in other words, had the effect of casting Father's Day as a competitor to Mother's Day.[29]

In time, however, the situation would change. Over the course of the Machine Age, Father's Day would become increasingly valued, and by the beginning of World War II, it would be an institutionalized form (though not yet a certified federal holiday). Let's look at what happened.[30]

FOCAL POINT: THE NEWS

Not many studies carried out in the 1920s and 1930s mention Father's Day and Mother's Day, let alone systematically examine how they were observed.[31] Hence, without surveys and the like to provide a sense of what took place (inside the home as well as out), we are forced to rely mainly on public documents—and especially newspapers—to chart the holidays' ebb and flow.[32]

This in itself is not a methodological handicap. Historians repeatedly have put newspapers to good use, documenting oddities and trends that might otherwise go unnoticed. Sociologists have done the same, often showing how the social construction of news has shifted over the years. Still, there are drawbacks to relying on newspapers that we should acknowledge. For one thing, what is printed in a newspaper is the result of an anything-but-random selection process that generally "reflects the intentions, will, and interests of dominant interest groups." Thus, as with popular magazines, it is difficult to determine from newspapers "whether we are analyzing patterns of historical events or patterns of news reporting." Secondly, we must recognize that "[n]ewspaper reports may be accepted as data that an event did occur, but the lack of such reports may not be an indication that events did not occur."[33]

These limitations notwithstanding, I quickly discovered that while newspaper reports may not tell us everything we would like to know about a holiday, examining them closely can be quite revealing. Two examples immediately come to mind.

The first centered around World War I. Early on, I learned that the *Stars and Stripes*, the newspaper of the American Expeditionary Force (A.E.F.) in France, had orchestrated a "Dad's Christmas Victory Letter Day" in 1918. (The war had ended the month before.) The plan, as it was framed, was to encourage soldiers stationed overseas to write a Christmas letter to "Dad, Pa, Paw, Papa, Pa-pah, Pop, the Guy or whatever other household designation he sails and flails under." The postal service announced that it was doing its part by giving special attention to envelopes marked "Father's Xmas Letter" in the upper right-hand corner. (Soldiers were told that "Xmas," as opposed to "Christmas" would save ink and time and would fit better in the corner of the envelope.) Other organizations pitched in as well. The Y.M.C.A. posted signs to remind the soldiers of the campaign. The Knights of Columbus and the Salvation Army visited the front lines to spread the word. The Red Cross helped the sick and wounded with their letters.[34] Ultimately, "Dad's Christmas Victory Letter Day" was deemed a huge success (two million letters were written) and is the sort of thing that has been cited by at least one reference work as evidence that in 1918 "a Father's Day of a different kind was observed."[35]

Heart-warming and true—but a careful reading of the *Stars and Stripes* revealed that there was more to the story than this. It seems that the campaign was not unique, but was modeled after a mother's letter campaign that the *Stars and Stripes* had orchestrated for Mother's Day only a few months before.[36] Noticing this, I began to wonder why the father's letter campaign was not coordinated around Father's Day. When I looked at the May and June issues from 1918, I could find no coverage of Father's Day, nor could I find any mention of a June Father's Day in any of the columns announcing the Christmas campaign.

I concluded that the 1918 A.E.F. Father's Day was indeed "of a different kind," having no connection whatsoever to the observance that Sonora Dodd (and others) were lobbying for back in the states. The absence of a Father's Day tie-in to the *Stars and Stripes* campaign also suggested that Father's Day was not yet an institutionalized form in 1918, which was important for me to know because I was interested in comparing the popularity of Father's Day at the beginning of the Machine Age with its popularity at the end. The *Stars and Stripes* campaign, in other words, provided a baseline from which to work.

The second example is that in reviewing early-twentieth-century issues of the *Chicago Defender*, a black, middle-class weekly (Saturday), I was struck by how many references during the 1920s and 1930s there were to Mother's Day and how few there were to Father's Day. The *Chicago Defender* typically would include in its May issues a number of articles (and poems) "in honor of" Mother's Day as well as reports of this or that club or assembly feting mothers on "their day." Articles about fathers, though few and far between, appeared also, but in none of the issues that I examined did the *Chicago Defender* sponsor an article explicitly on the subject of Father's Day.[37]

I did come across a poem, "To Dad," published on 27 June 1942 (the fourth Saturday of the month), but no mention was made of whether its publication had anything to do with Father's Day.[38] If the poem had been published the previous Saturday, which was the day before Father's Day, the tie-in to Father's Day would have been more clear. The *Chicago Defender* did publish an ode to parenthood on the day before Father's Day, but it was an ode to *mothers*. (It was titled "A Mother's Prayer.")[39]

These patterns led me to wonder whether the disregard for Father's Day seen in the *Chicago Defender* was repeated in other middle-class newspapers. That is, were other newspapers as likely as the *Chicago Defender* to ignore Father's Day? The answer is no. Or at least it is no with respect to one newspaper: the *New York Times*. Unlike the *Defender*, the *Times* devoted a fair amount of space to Father's Day during the Machine Age. Not only that, but in keeping with the changes reported in other chapters—changes showing differences in the social institution of fatherhood between the 1920s and 1930s—the *Times* quadrupled its coverage of Father's Day between 1920 and 1929 and between 1930 and 1939, from 15 articles to 60. (By comparison, the *Times* increased its coverage of Mother's Day by only two and a half times, from 55 articles to 142.) The difference between the *Defender's* coverage and the *Times's* coverage of Father's Day prompted me to hypothesize that the modernization of fatherhood during the Machine Age was more common among the white middle class than among the black middle class.[40]

If we plan to use newspapers, ideally we would look at newspapers from around the country, perhaps around the world, so that we could measure geographic, ethnic, and class variations. I decided, however, to focus exclusively on the *New York Times's* coverage of Father's Day and Mother's Day, because of my interest in focusing on the most important people and events surrounding the growth of the holidays. The fact that the *New York Times* was published in New York City also contributed to my decision. New York was the center of both the Father's Day and Mother's Day movements. Actually, if you think about it, New York was the center of the modernization of fatherhood itself. The Child Study Association of

America was based in New York City. So was *Parents' Magazine*. And so was Angelo Patri.[41]

We have seen how the 1930s figured significantly in the changes in the *Infant Care* manuals of the Children's Bureau and in the growth of the fathercraft crusade. We have seen, too, how popular magazines took a decidedly modern turn during the Depression, and how the Patri correspondence followed suit. Now, through an analysis of the *New York Times* from 1915, the year after Mother's Day became a federal holiday, to 1942, when the first national "Outstanding Father of the Year" was named, we shall see how Father's Day blazed a similar trail.

THE DANDELION YEARS, 1915–1931

Between 1915 and 1923, the *New York Times* did not publish a single article on Father's Day, while it published twenty-eight articles on Mother's Day. The fact that Father's Day was not covered at all during this period does not mean that Americans totally ignored the holiday (again, the lack of a report does not necessarily indicate that an event did not occur), but it does make one wonder how strong the Father's Day movement was during this time, if it could not grab the attention of a newspaper that prided itself on monitoring trends. (The Parents' Day rally held in New York's Central Park on Mother's Day in 1923 was, however, written up.)

In 1924, after ignoring Father's Day for close to ten years, the *Times* did find something newsworthy about the day. On the third Sunday in June, it ran a front page notice that announced: "Today will be observed in some parts of the country Father's Day." Immediately following a brief history of the holiday (1910, Spokane) and a mention of the "support" the holiday had gotten from "neckwear and slipper manufacturers," was the following report: "The official flower of the day is the dandelion, which was selected originally by the members of the Martin W. Callener Bible Class of Wilkinsburg, Pa. They picked the dandelion because the more it is trampled on the better it grows."[42] Whether the dandelion was supposed to be a metaphor for how strong fathers were, or a testament to how much fathers were picked on in the 1920s was not made clear. (Recall that the 1920s, compared to the 1930s, were when fathers were more likely to be depicted as incompetent in popular magazines. The dandelion, put-down or not, was in keeping with the "culture of daddyhood" that characterized the times.)[43]

The fact that the Bible Class would select an "official flower" for Father's Day may seem strange (why not an animal?), but flowers of one kind or another had long been associated with both Father's Day and Mother's Day. In the early twentieth century, it became customary on Father's Day for people to wear red roses if their fathers were alive, white if they were dead; and on Mother's Day, pink carnations if their mothers were alive, white if they were dead.[44]

In 1925, the *Times* reported that the tobacco industry mistakenly printed cards proclaiming the second rather than the third Sunday in June as Father's Day, causing confusion among shoppers and fear among shop owners.[45] In 1926, in an article titled, "National Father's Day Project Has Languished Twenty Years," the question was raised as to whether "it was father's natural modesty which caused the plan to fail."[46] In 1927 and 1928, this hypothesis was informally tested with a series of in-the-street interviews in which men were asked what they thought about Father's Day. "I think it's a lot of bunk," said one father. "I think it's a lot of hooey," replied another. "Father's Day makes me sick," added a third. "Someone is trying to work those 'Lindy' [Charles Lindbergh, the aviator] ties off on us," cracked a fourth.[47] These were hardly ringing endorsements. Still, the men knew enough about Father's Day to render an opinion. Father's Day thus may not have been a full-blown federal holiday in the late 1920s, but it was a cultural object.[48]

Cultural phenomenon or not, Father's Day was no more popular the next year than it was the last. "Two hundred thousand placards" had been placed in cigar stores "to persuade sons and daughters and mothers to give dad a jar of smoking tobacco, a pipe, cigars, cigarettes, a lighter, a tobacco pouch or almost anything so long as the cash register [was] enabled to chime in praise of Father's Day." Merchants did agree that in 1929 the holiday had "accelerated sales mildly," but florists reported also that they had so many surplus blossoms on hand that they had to give many away. ("The United Florists' Trades diplomatically blamed the hot weather.")[49]

Two years later, in 1931, the *Times* covered Father's Day but had nothing better to report than that the dandelion was the official flower for Father's Day (again the Wilkinsburg, Pennsylvania Bible Class was given the credit, only this time it was called the Martin W. Callender— not Callener—Bible Class). Sales figures were said to be "somewhat accelerated."[50]

THE COMMERCIALIZATION OF HONOR, 1932–1942

The official founder of Mother's Day, Anna M. Jarvis, spent much of her life trying to root out any venture connected with Mother's Day that, in her opinion, smacked of commercial gain. Once, for example, she attended the Associated Retail Confectioners convention and got into an argument with some of the delegates over how much money candy-store owners were making from "her" day. She was asked to leave the hall. On another occasion, she interrupted a Philadelphia meeting of the American War Mothers and accused them of profiteering from Mother's Day carnations. She was arrested (and later acquitted).[51]

In contrast to Jarvis, the official founder of Father's Day, Sonora Dodd, did not seem to mind one iota that people might be trying to use Father's Day for commercial gain. Indeed, in 1910, at the Spokane, Washington, celebration, Dodd expressly asked store owners to display gifts. "After all," she remarked, "why should the greatest giver of gifts not be on the receiving end at least once a year?" Merchants, not surprisingly, were happy to comply with Dodd's request and spent the week beforehand carefully arranging their window displays. One store owner created what may have been the first Father's Day poster, a portrait of George Washington with the caption, "Remember Father."[52]

The different attitudes that Anna M. Jarvis and Sonora Louise Smart Dodd had toward the commercialization of their respective days was a microcosm of what was being played out in the community at large. This, at least, is the impression that one gets from the *New York Times*. When articles on Father's Day and Mother's Day are placed into one of two categories—primarily commercial or primarily noncommercial (with the former being articles on advertising campaigns, holiday sales, and the like, and the latter being articles on the history of the day, its cultural value, and so on)—the differences between Father's Day and Mother's Day are striking. For the first four decades of the twentieth century, fewer than 4 percent of the 218 Mother's Day articles in the *Times* were commercial in content. During that same period, 63 percent of the 81 Father's Day articles in the *Times* focused on the business side of things. What is interesting, too, is the huge commercial jump that the Father's Day articles took during the 1930s. Again, between 1920 and 1929 and between 1930 and 1939, the number of Father's Day articles increased from 15 to 60; the number of Mother's Day articles, from 55 to 142. But while the percentage of Mother's Day articles centering on money and profit *decreased* from 9 percent to 2 percent, the percentage of Father's Day articles centering on money and profit *increased* from 53 percent to 72 percent.[53]

Why, when it came to Father's Day, was there more attention to the commercial factor in the 1930s than in the 1920s? One reason is that the commercialization of Father's Day—the commercialization of honor, if you will—was more organized and deliberate in the 1930s. Throughout the 1920s, the promotion of Father's Day was generally a scattered affair, with individual industries and stores doing whatever they could to drum up support (often unsuccessfully). Then, in the 1930s, the business community took a different tack. Its members decided to pool their resources and work together. What the *Times* devoted a considerable amount of space to in the 1930s—what became news (at least in the financial pages)—was the backstage work to make Father's Day an economic success.

Here is a year-by-year account of what transpired. In 1932, the *Times* reported that "a group of business men and advertising men headed by . . . [the] president of the Retail Clothiers' and Furnishing Association of New York, Inc." had chosen a slogan, "Show Dad You Remember," around which to frame their Father's Day campaign: "Some 200,000 window-display cards and about 150,000 window streamers have been prepared to advertise the day of recognition for the male parent. About 500,000 boxes to contain gifts for father and around 1,500,000 labels to go on the boxes and other receptacles have also been printed. Greeting cards for the day number around 1,000,000."[54]

In 1934, there was an article reporting that "the Associated Men's Wear Retailers" had met at a Manhattan hotel on at least two occasions to plan an "organized promotion," and that they had developed, in the end, "a set of promotional materials, including cut-outs and gummed posters" to distribute "to all units." Rather than just push neckties, as it had done the year before, the association chose a broader theme: "Give Dad Something to Wear." The best window display was awarded a prize.[55]

In 1935, the Associated Men's Wear Retailers met at "the Advertising Club" to plan its Father's Day strategy, and it decided, based on past successes, to expand the "scope of the promotion." The president of the association told the reporters present of his belief that, in time, the Association's efforts would be on a "national scale." The clothiers also decided to "broaden their campaign for funds and to appeal to stores as well as manufacturers for contributions to carry on the promotional work" of the Association: "Retailers throughout the city will be asked to contribute $5 each, although each will receive a set of posters regardless of whether he contributes." Again, the theme, "Give Dad Something to Wear," was used. Sales for Father's Day in 1935 were brisk. Noted the *Times*: "[T]here are reports indicative of an increase in the purchase volume of the usual gift article. Tobacconists, especially, tell of better sales in the choicer smokes."[56]

When retailers were asked in 1935 about the promotion, some replied that "they [were] not making any extraordinary efforts to publicize the day in a commercial way." This was a lie or, at best, an evasion, for that year we see not only a broadening of the strategy used by the Associated Men's Wear Retailers, but also the creation of an organization that at first got little attention from the press but soon would do more than any other group to put Father's Day on the map. I am talking about the National Council for the Promotion of Father's Day (also known, at various times, as the National Father's Day Committee, the Father's Day Committee, and the Father's Day Council).

The man behind the National Council for the Promotion of Father's Day was an advertising executive named Alvin Austin. Were it not for him, "there may never have been a Father's Day Movement." Or so the Father's Day Council alleged, in a book which it published on the occasion of the seventy-fifth anniversary of Father's Day (using 1910 as the founding date). The council went on to say: "Alvin's concept was to develop Father's Day, a then fledgling event, into a National Holiday, through public affairs programming, the focus of a marketing thrust, based on a civic-oriented campaign." As to how the council itself got started, Maddy Austin, Alvin Austin's widow, recalled it this way: "There were thirty to thirty-five of us at that first meeting. . . . important men, leaders of industry, men of some perception and vision, who were willing to give their time and money for a unique non-profit community concept."[57]

Note that the council was referred to as both "civic-minded" and "non-profit." The genius that Alvin Austin brought to the concept of promoting Father's Day was the public downplaying of commercial gain. "[Austin] saw that commercializing the event would be self-defeating. And so, from the very beginning, Father's Day was divorced from any commercial association that would have distorted the community-family significance of Father's Day." The council, for example, had a policy of not explicitly endorsing products, and it was careful about not writing advertising copy that gave even the appearance of a conflict of interest.[58]

Appearances aside, however, while the council may have been nonpecuniary in principle, it was anything but that in practice. From the very beginning, the council was financially supported by contributions from the business community. From the very beginning, its executive board was composed of business leaders. Alvin Austin, for one, was associated with the advertising firm Austin and Rossiter, which in 1936 handled the council's "promotional campaign."[59]

What would Austin say when he was asked about the financial interests of the council? Maddy Austin recalled her husband's response: "We were often questioned about the 'commercial' aspect of Father's day, but Alvin's answer was always logical and reserved. He just pointed to the flood of gift-giving for Christmas, the pattern of which was originally set nearly 2,000 years ago by the Magi, who brought gifts for the Christ child. Then, he pointed to the proclivity of Americans to give of themselves, and of material things for every 'occasion.' "[60]

The connection with Christmas was meant to be rhetorically powerful, and it was. Several years ago, I interviewed the current Executive Director of the Father's Day Council and asked him to explain what the Council did. He replied, "To be crass, we do for Father's Day what the Church does for Christmas." The council's job, in other words, was to *sanctify* Father's Day.[61]

The strategy can be stated as follows. If the council could promote Father's Day for what would seem to be the holiest of reasons, that is, if it could promote Father's Day in such a way as not to be accused of simply trying to make money, then it could effectively orchestrate a "second Christmas" for the business community. (Business leaders sometimes used this very phrase when they contemplated the profits that Father's Day could bring.)[62] If, on the other hand, the council could not appear to divorce itself from commercialism, then Father's Day would be seen as a money-making ploy, and the American public, feeling that it was being "taken," would refuse to participate. The key to the success of Father's Day was to make the commercialization of honor appear noncommercial.[63]

The strategy made a lot of sense. Think of how Christmas works; not the religious part, the money part. The fact that Christmas is such a boon to business has as much, if not more, to do with the sanctification that the various churches bestow upon the day (cultural endorsement) as it has to do with Wall Street's advertising campaign (economic push). And the fact that toys sell so well in December is a function of both the credence given to the notion that Christmas is for children and the ingenuity and wealth that the toy industry displays in its television commercials and newspaper ads. Thus, it is *culture combined with economics* that generally explains why people are willing to buy some commodities and not others, or why citizens are willing to acknowledge one holiday and not the next.

The creation of the National Council for the Promotion of Father's Day did not automatically eliminate the for-profit organizations already in existence. It did not take long, however, for the council to move into the position of being "the church." The advantages of having a formal sanctifying body soon became clear to others besides Austin. (Incidentally, an interesting point about Austin's group is that it preceded the creation of a similar organization to promote Mother's Day by six years. In this instance at least, Mother's Day was a "commercial afterthought" to Father's Day.)[64]

In 1936, the Associated Men's Wear Retailers opted to finance their promotion by publishing a "souvenir journal" that "carr[ied] $5,000 worth of advertising, the proceeds of which [were] used for publicity purposes for Father's Day." About 60 percent of the book was comprised of "reading matter," and inserted in each was a "colored poster suitable for window display."[65] What the "reading matter" entailed is not known. My guess is that it contained the same kind of reading matter that the council circulates today, namely, nostalgic pieces on the history of Father's Day and "hard news" accounts of the importance of fatherhood to children and to the country as a whole. The 1936 season also saw an increase in Father's Day ads. Reported the *Times*: "Newspaper advertising in connection with Father's Day next Sunday is running more than double that for the week prior to the event last year, a check-up yesterday showed. In addition to retailers increasing the size of their copy on merchandise for father, a number of manufacturers took space in newspapers for the first time to promote their products."[66] The promotions worked—at least for some. Haberdashers, tobacconists, and sporting goods dealers "enjoyed a cheery Sunday because of a minor trade boom preliminary to the day." Florists, on the other hand, whose sales did not significantly increase, "went about their business phlegmatically" and looked forward to next year's Mother's Day, which unfortunately for them was "still almost eleven months" away.[67] The heavy promotions seem also to have had an effect on religious leaders. (Religious leaders, similarly, had played a big part in the sanctification of Mother's Day in the early twentieth century.) One pastor "deprecated the 'commercialization' of the idea of Father's Day, *yet* welcomed 'the fact that the church had taken it up as one of the things we ought to emphasize in these days in family life, which is threatened by modern conditions of living [my italics].' He said also, 'the day should bring us back to a recognition of the Fatherhood of God.' "[68]

In 1937, the "volume of national and local newspaper advertising devoted to Father's Day . . . doubled . . . and was the largest on record."[69] The ads, however, had a paradoxical effect. Sales were up, but men's wear retailers, who had done more than any other group (at least up to then) to promote Father's Day, found their own profits dampened by the competition from other products.[70] Unless men's wear retailers could figure out a way to increase the overall volume of gifts, their share of the profits from Father's Day would continue to be disappointing. The *Times* suggested, too, that the holiday might be ailing: "In spite of valiant efforts to observe Father's Day throughout the nation yesterday, a sample canvass indicated that the observance was spotty. Only one in six fathers reported that the day had any special significance in his home. Many fathers were remembered with socks, ties, suspenders, pipes and other gifts, but others were unaware of Father's Day until reminded by apologetic members of their families." [71]

As for the National Council for the Promotion of Father's Day, it had changed its name to the Father's Day Committee, a move that may have been carried out to camouflage the group's commercial motives. Hidden or not, however, there is no mistaking the group's intentions in the letter that it sent to Angelo Patri on 19 May:

> Realizing that you probably prepare your feature articles some time in advance, we thought it might be advisable to get in touch with you in advance to tell you that Father's Day falls this year on Sunday, June 20th. As the outstanding child guidance counsellor, we thought you might say a few words on Father's Day, advising children how to present their little gifts or remembrances, and how fathers are to receive them. Another angle might be how to teach the child to reverence the father, and yet not feel bashful about presenting a small gift. Also, would you state whether the mother should encourage the child to save up its pennies for the Father's Day gift paying for it out of its own allowance, or should give the child the money outright. There are many little Father and Child points which many families are ignorant of, and which you could elucidate and describe in your space. We would appreciate some mention of Father's Day in your columns to remind your readers to remember their Dads. [72]

What the Father's Day Committee thought of as "in advance" and what Patri thought of as "in advance" apparently were two different things. Patri wrote back to say that he had already written and mailed his articles "covering the time up to and after" Father's Day. [73] Poor planning had cost the committee an opportunity to reach millions.

Less than optimal results in 1937 may have been the business community's wake-up call, impressing upon it the importance of working not only in unison but also with precision. Something evidently got it going, because in 1938 we see an all-out effort to make Father's Day a national observance. "For the first time in many years," the *Times* reported, "both manufacturers and retailers are taking seriously promotion of Father's Day. . . . The aim of making the day 'a second Christmas,' as far as gifts for the country's fathers are concerned, is taking hold in the industry, and the promotion this year will be on a nation-wide basis." [74] One month later, there was this: "Decision to push promotions for Father's Day, June 19, on the widest national scale since that day was inaugurated was reached yesterday at a preliminary meeting held at the office of the National Retail Dry Goods Association. It is intended, it was said following the meeting, 'to make Father's Day as important an event in the 1938 calendar as the annual Mother's Day.' " [75] And two weeks after that, the following appeared: "With fresh support promised from a number of sources, plans for participation in the merchandising campaign for Father's Day on June 19 were rounded out yesterday at a meeting attended by nearly 100 representatives of retailers and manufacturing industries." [76]

In close association with these efforts, Alvin Austin announced that the Father's Day Committee would "act as a central clearing house for the raising of funds necessary for the proper promotion" of Father's Day. Reported the *Times*, "The need for a central body such as the council arose, he explained, because the national Father's Day committee was not a business organization, but an honorary one which could have no part in raising or disbursing moneys. Up to the present, he said, individual groups and individuals had worked either independently or with some degree of concerted action, but through no formal, single body." [77]

The massive promotion was a rousing success. On the morning of Father's Day, 1938, the *Times* reported, "Upon the fathers of America there shower today neckties, shirts, socks, pipes, tobacco, golf clubs and other gifts, sentimental greeting cards and the family's best wishes. Shop counters did a brisk business last week as mothers, sons and daughters bought remembrances for Father's Day—the third Sunday in June. . . . In the last two years, . . . Father's Day, according to the merchants, has finally become established." [78]

The reference to "mothers, sons and daughters" buying remembrances deserves some comment. Up to now, I have left it to the reader to assume that wives and children were the ones who showered—or did not shower—men with Father's Day gifts. If sales were up, then it was these people, more than fathers, who were instrumental in making Father's Day "established." The likely truth, however, is that there was one household member more than any other who was instrumental to the process. That person was the mother. Children may have been prompted by their teachers to draw pictures or create crafts for their fathers. Some may even have saved up their "pennies" to spring for a gift. There is little doubt, however, that the mothers of America did the bulk of the shopping for Father's Day. They were the ones to whom the advertisers were making their pitch. [79]

Whether mothers could be convinced to "honor" their husbands with gifts, and whether they could be convinced to initiate and supervise the purchases that their children made (e.g., take them to the store, help them to pick something suitable) rested on more than the ability of advertisers to persuade. Even though the business community can create organizations like the Father's Day Council to sell a product or idea, it usually cannot independently manufacture consumer desire. Almost always, it must have help from other groups. When it came to pushing Father's Day on the public, the business community received valuable assistance, though not necessarily with intention, from the child-rearing intelligentsia, which since the turn of the century, but especially since the beginning of the 1930s, had been promoting the ideology of New Fatherhood with as much energy as it could muster. As significant as the Father's Day Committee was to the sanctification of Father's Day—trying to do for Father's Day what the church did for Christmas—its efforts, when you think about it, actually paled in comparison to the sanctification of fatherhood that the child-rearing intelligentsia had been fostering for years and that, according to evidence presented in the previous chapter, was apparently beginning to have an effect on the gender-role orientations of middle-class mothers—*in the 1930s.*[80]

This is not to say that the Father's Day movement was only on the receiving end, for it too played an independent role. Specifically, the Father's Day movement was able to fuel the modernization of fatherhood in ways that the fathercraft movement could not. With the resources of the business community behind it, the promoters behind Father's Day were able to spread the ideology of New Fatherhood beyond the middle class and beyond the world of adults. Father's Day, I would hypothesize, was the ritual that embodied America's New Fatherhood. Through the ceremony of giving and receiving Father's Day gifts, families could "do" or "enact" the modernization of fatherhood. And again, *the 1930s* were the key.[81]

There is one other way in which the creation of Father's Day may represent a synthesis of culture and economics. In order to see it, one must have an appreciation for how the Depression and World War II could have worked to the promoters' advantage. If you read the *Times,* you will see that one of the reasons why the business community was working so hard to turn Father's Day into a national honor was that it believed Father's Day offered some security from the Depression. The Depression may have ended up being more than an incentive, however. Whether the business community recognized it or not, the Depression also seemed to make the work of the Father's Day Council easier, in that it redefined the commercialization of Father's Day as an *honorable* endeavor. By the mid to late 1930s, Americans had long grown tired of financial insecurity. They wanted the economy to grow; they wanted business to succeed. Thus, what may have looked like crass commercialism on the eve of the Depression could very well have come to be seen as healthy capitalism in the midst of the Depression.

World War II also played a part in the creation of Father's Day. Glancing at Europe, Americans could see that an unhealthy economy could be fatal to a country. Although the United States did not enter the war until December 1941, talk about the country's role in the conflict was commonplace in the late 1930s. Hence, it is not surprising to learn that business leaders would use a forum on the Father's Day movement as an opportunity to speak out against international oppression. At the 1938 meeting of the one hundred representatives of retailers and manufacturing industries, for example, Saul Cohn, president of the National Retail Dry Goods Association and head of the City Stores Company, commended "the expanded movement to promote Father's Day," and said that it was "vital that business unite to accomplish in any sound way the accelerated movement of goods and an expansion of purchasing power." If business failed to do so, said Cohn, "dictatorships [would] thrive."[82]

The prospect of war also gave the promoters of Father's Day something that they could use to tug at the heartstrings of women and children. War allowed Father's Day to be tied to soldiering—and to dying. The Nazi threat made Father's Day a singular and well-deserved honor, the least that a nation could do for its defenders.[83]

By 1939, the Father's Day Committee and its allies in the business community had managed to convince growing numbers of public officials and private organizations to throw their support behind Father's Day. The governors of New York, Minnesota, New Mexico, New Jersey, Florida, Wyoming, Maryland, Virginia, Utah, Kentucky, Michigan, Ohio, and Texas reportedly gave their approval. So had the boards of the Rotary, Kiwanis, Lions, Exchange, and other men's organizations. Advertising was strong. One hundred thousand Father's Day posters were printed and distributed, and more than ninety newspapers around the country had promised to publish the Father's Day promotion advertisements that had won the national competition sponsored by the committee. Sales were up, 20 percent higher than they had been in 1938.[84] On Father's Day, there was a rally in honor of fathers at the New York World's Fair. "A crowd of 10,000 persons gathered . . . in the Court of Peace . . . with the completion of a contest to select the typical father in the metropolitan area. Entertainment was supplied by stars of stage, screen and radio."[85]

In 1940, the World's Fair was the scene of not just one but a variety of formal and informal celebrations in conjunction with Father's Day, and Alvin Austin and his Father's Day Council continued to garner support. (Governors in almost every state had issued proclamations. Many had done so at Austin's request.)[86] On the Wednesday preceding Father's Day, the *Times* reported, "Advertising of Father's Day gifts by retailers . . . reached a new record, . . . as men's specialty stores, chains, department stores and others placed substantial ads in newspapers. Linage so far this month was estimated as at least 30 per cent greater than a year ago, and with big promotions due tomorrow and Friday, this spread may be widened. It has been the aim of those promoting the commercial activities of Father's Day to make the event second in importance only to Christmas as a gift-buying period, and this year the plan appears to be succeeding."[87] And on the Monday after Father's Day, the following appeared: "Father's Day messages went by all means of communication and included telegraph messages relayed in song by telephone. The Western Union reported that the number of messages wired to fathers this year exceeded by 10 per cent the number sent last year. The Postal Telegraph Cable Company announced 'a general increase' in the number of greetings telegraphed to father, including 'singing messages.' "[88]

In 1941, Father's Day sales were 22 percent higher than they were in 1940, and in 1942 there was yet another 20-percent jump.[89] Financially speaking, the Father's Day movement was the strongest it had ever been. The years 1941 and 1942 were also a time when Father's Day was most immediately and most deliberately tied to the war effort. The 1941 slogan chosen by the Father's Day Committee was "Salute Dad the American Way." The 1942 slogan was "Father—The Defender of the Home."[90]

In 1941, New York's main Father's Day celebration had a military theme: "New York's fathers celebrated their day in a somber mood yesterday in exercises on the mall in Central Park as they heard their sons pledged to fight in defense of the nation. Five thousand persons attended the ceremonies, sponsored by five posts of the New York county American legion. 'The fathers in the American legion are the ones who fought in the last war,' Alvin S. Mela, county commander, declared. 'Now they are the fathers being honored here today and we are proud to offer our sons for the supreme sacrifice again.' "[91] In 1942, New York Mayor Fiorello La-Guardia's Father's Day proclamation echoed a similar message: "In the name of the people of my city, I give praise to the fathers who are conscientiously fulfilling the demands made necessary by the conflict in which we are engaged for survival and, for their inspirational leadership in guiding their children through these chaotic days and instilling in them a spirit of strength and courage which assures us of ultimate victory and the continuance of our cherished American way of life." [92]

Also in 1942, the Father's Day Committee introduced a new promotional strategy, the naming of "The Outstanding Father of the Year." The recipient of the award and the first to hold the national title was General Douglas MacArthur. The general was chosen, said the committee, because of his "inspiring and heroic leadership in helping to make the world safe for democratic family life and human freedom." [93] MacArthur could not personally accept the award. He was in Melbourne, Australia, after having been rescued three months earlier from Corregidor in the Phillipine Islands, which had been encircled by the Japanese. He did, however, wire a reply:

> Nothing has touched me more deeply than the act of the National Father's Day Committee. By profession I am a soldier and take pride in that fact, but I am prouder, infinitely prouder, to be a father. A soldier destroys in order to build; the father only builds, never destroys. The one has the potentialities of death; the other embodies creation and life. And, while the hordes of death are mighty, the battalions of life are mightier still. It is my hope that my son, when I am gone, will remember me not from the battle but in the home repeating with him our simple daily prayer, "Our Father Who art in heaven." [94]

War and fatherhood, fatherhood and God; the legitimation of the father-child bond could not be stronger. Although the hostilities eventually would take men out of the home, at this particular juncture, the concept of the father as economic provider, pal, and male role model all rolled into one was soaring. Father's Day, I would hypothesize, was the collective ritual that helped to pull it all together. Father's Day was the symbol that fused New Fatherhood into America's consciousness—and conscience.

9   Conclusion

> Mommy, where do Daddies come from?
>
> Jim Borgman (cartoon caption, 1994)

When people think of a "baby book," they tend to think of Dr. Benjamin Spock's *Baby and Child Care,* first issued in 1946, probably because of its omnipresence. (It has sold over 40 million copies.) [1] When people think of the changes that American fatherhood has undergone, they also may focus on *Baby and Child Care,* but for reasons that are less clear. As an example, the *New York Times* and *Time* magazine recently pointed to *Baby and Child Care* and the revisions it has undergone as evidence for the late-twentieth-century arrival of "The New Father." [2]

There is nothing wrong really with talking about how Spock modified his book from one edition to the next, how in 1946 he mentioned that fathers should change diapers and get up for 2 A.M. feedings—but only "occasionally" and "when the mother is still pretty tired"—and how thirty years later he said that fathers and mothers should work together "in the spirit of an equal partnership." [3] The problem occurs when *Baby and Child Care* is used as a metaphor for the major changes in twentieth-century fatherhood. No book, however popular, can legitimately carry this load. And what about American fatherhood prior to the 1940s? Are we to assume that nothing of consequence happened before Spock's book came along?

My goal, stated from the beginning, has been to write not a comprehensive chronicle of fatherhood but an explicit historical analysis, concentrating on a specific period of time and on a particular social process occurring within that time. [4] Mine is the story of how American fatherhood was reshaped and welded during the 1920s and 1930s into the modernized form that we see idolized today; a tale of how New Fatherhood emerged in the midst of the Machine Age to reanimate, at the cultural level if nowhere else, the father-child relationship.

Here, in a nutshell, is what I found. Infant care manuals became more father-inclusive from the turn of the century to the beginning of World War II. While the manuals did continue to talk more to women than to men and were reluctant to acknowledge fathers when it came to the matter of sick babies, it still is clear that the books drifted away from a mothers-should-do-it-all philosophy as the years went on. When the Great Depression hit, the modernization of fatherhood, as exhibited in the manuals, did more than proceed unabated, it accelerated, lending credence to the proposition that the New Fatherhood of the 1930s was a more modern type than what had come before. With these early-twentieth-century manuals on the table, the tendency to rely on Spock's *Baby and Child Care* to document how much twentieth-century fatherhood has changed becomes all the more questionable, since in a number of respects, the 1946 edition of Spock's book was a step *backward* from the modernization of fatherhood that had occurred in previous manuals.[5]

The early twentieth century also witnessed the emergence of the "scientific" approach to child rearing. As mother-affirming as this approach was designed to be, it appears also to have had a paradoxical effect on the expectations surrounding parenthood. By making child care a learned activity, child care experts elevated their own prestige and also bestowed a sense of accomplishment upon those women who happened to become the most ardent students of the experts' lore. At the same time, however, shifting child care from an innate to a learned activity meant the rudiments of "good" parenthood were now available for public consumption. Some fathers, to be sure, were excluded from the discourse and felt marginalized as a result. Other fathers, however, used the parent education movement to justify their own expertise. After all, men could read the books, too. Equally important, but not generally recognized by historians of fatherhood, is the fact that whatever a mother may have claimed she had learned about child rearing was not necessarily accepted as dogma but was subject to debate inside the home. Men had a power advantage then, as they do now, and thus it may have made little difference to the outcome of child-rearing discussions that the mother was presumably the more informed. What the scientific approach to child rearing did, in other words, was to place the parenting process more squarely within the politics of the family.

While some early-twentieth-century child-rearing philosophies drew sharp distinctions on the basis of gender, other philosophies blurred the boundaries between fatherhood and motherhood, stressing unanimity and cooperation. Behaviorism is a good example of the latter. In order for behavioristic principles to have the desired effect, child training had to be consistent across care givers. Thus, even though mothers may have been primarily responsible for creating the utilitarian systems that behaviorism encouraged, fathers still had to be persuaded to abide by the systems that had been set up.

Also, some early-twentieth-century child-rearing philosophies were more compatible with men's than with women's socially derived view of the world, and thus more likely to draw men into child-rearing work. Again, behaviorism is a good example. The idea of creating a child care arrangement where rewards and punishments were foremost probably sat rather well with men who were used to being in offices and factories that operated pretty much according to the same rules. Interesting, in this regard, is the evidence indicating that mothers were not always happy with behaviorism's "do not hug, let your baby cry" approach.[6] Consider the scenario where the wife says, "Let's go with this strategy," while the husband says, "No, let's go with that." Who won in these situations may have had little to do with who was the expert's proxy.

When the reality portrayed in the infant care manuals was compared with the reality that existed inside the home, the inconsistency was apparent. An analysis of the letters written to the Children's Bureau, coupled with a review of the studies that reported on father involvement in infant care, suggested a higher level of father involvement than was indicated either in the manuals or by most historical accounts. Thus, it seems wrong to imply that fathers during the Machine Age were little more than playmates to their children or to claim that few men, if any, participated in the heavier demands of child care work. I am not saying that there were no men who fit this mold. Many, perhaps most, probably did. The simple point is that these men did not represent all men.

The solution, as I see it, is to acknowledge the *variety* of fathering styles in the past. Thus, instead of being satisfied with caricatures of yesterday's fathers, cartoonlike descriptions that depict men's relationship with children in the narrowest of terms (weekend buddies or playful buffoons), we would do well to broaden our perspective to allow for the fact that there *were* men in the past who cared for children—changing diapers and getting up in the middle of the night. How many men performed these tasks regularly is hard to know. (I would estimate that the figures are higher than most historical accounts indicate, but still lower than the figures for today.) Still, the absence of a clear-cut profile cannot, and should not, be used as a license to grossly misrepresent those who came before.

The letters written to the Children's Bureau as well as the letters written to Angelo Patri indicate that fathers as well as mothers could be discriminating shoppers in the world of child-rearing ideas. This is not to say that the child-rearing experts of the early twentieth century were a weak influence or that the therapeutic, or self-help, culture developing then was of little consequence. We have to be careful, however, about assuming that because a child-rearing expert proposes a course of action, fathers and mothers naturally will follow. Child-rearing prescriptions, like cultural prescriptions in general, do not determine what parents do; rather, the prescriptions operate more like a set of social products or commodities from which fathers and mothers may choose. And what they happen to choose or not choose cannot be determined solely by the popularity of a book or magazine or television program. Equally, if not more, important is the question of what they perceive *benefits them*. Politics, again, is crucial. Thus, a workaholic father may choose a prescription that provides an excuse *not* to be intimately involved with his children. At least then, he can feel better about his detachment. Or a father who has recently divorced and lost custody of his children may choose a prescription that minimizes or denigrates a mother's value in the household (e.g., the mother as "viper").[7] He would find it easier then to fight his ex-wife tooth and nail. There is, in short, no simple isomorphy between the culture and conduct of parenthood but a complex social psychological and political dialectic that historically minded scholars would do well to consider more carefully.

As others have noted, one of the distinguishing characteristics of parent education in the early twentieth century was the proliferation of child study groups. Most of these groups were made up of mothers; in many cases, there was not a father to be found. To believe, however, that fathers were insignificant players in the child study group movement is to gloss over social patterns of real importance. For one thing, women-only groups were not always oblivious to the concerns of fathers. Not uncommonly, husbands would pass on to their wives the questions for discussion in the groups. Frequently, too, the women who went to the meetings would talk about how they should relay to their husbands what they had learned. Hence, a give-and-take between fathers and mothers existed that child study group head counts fail to measure and that scholars up to now have opted to overlook.

Second, although it is generally not reported, there were child study groups that did include both fathers and mothers, and others that were made up of entirely of men. In some instances, the creation of these groups was instigated by mothers and experts, suggesting that the science of child rearing did not always drive a wedge between husbands and wives, as sometimes has been suggested. In other instances, it was the men themselves who took the lead, showing that yesterday's fathers were not always the befuddled bystanders they have been made out to be. Noteworthy, too, is the fact that the groups were not limited to fathers with school-age children. Expectant-father classes and fathers-of-newborns groups, while not as widespread as they are today, were not as uncommon as we may think.

Father-to-father books—books that were written by men who were probably fathers themselves and that were directed primarily to other men who are either fathers-in-fact or fathers-to-be—also have received scant attention from scholars. This neglect has been unfortunate. Such books are important because they were addressed to men and they allowed the messages of the child study group movement to be communicated in men's absence. Thus, men who wanted to be modern fathers did not have to attend a child study group; they could buy a book that spoke to them and take its message home. (By contrast, most infant care manuals, up until the 1930s at least, were clearly aimed at women.) Granted the father-to-father books, and the whole child study industry for that matter, were the purview of the middle-class; still, this should not lead us to dismiss them out of hand. If we look at the father-to-father books and child study industry of today, we see pretty much the same middle-class bias.

Popular magazines of the Machine Age also ardently tried to convince fathers to get more involved with their children. *Parents' Magazine,* founded in 1926, hammered home this theme more than any other, especially in its "For Fathers Only" series, which ran from 1932 to 1937, but it was not alone in this regard. Looking at the magazine articles as rhetorical forms, we uncovered some interesting trends. Most notably, the degree to which the articles emphasized domestic masculinity (or the "father as pal" ideology) correlated with the degree to which the articles (1) favored sons, (2) poked fun at fathers, and (3) used the word *dad.* The son/humor/*dad* connection not only showed variation and fluctuation where others have postulated a straight line, but it also pointed to the emergence between 1916 and 1929 of a "culture of daddyhood"—an ideology that, on a manifest level, was pro-father but that, on a deeper level, may have been anything but. The culture of daddyhood cast fathers as warm and friendly, but it also framed them as peripheral and less consequential: men were depicted as playmates, nothing more. "We want daddies!," proclaimed a *Good Housekeeping* article in 1930.[8] What a "daddy" was, however, was basically a father "who manages, somehow, to live his life with [his son], take him places, have hours of real companionship at home and jolly little holidaying abroad." No mention was made of the more serious side of child care—the prose as opposed to the poetry of parenthood. One way to look at it is that the culture of daddyhood was patriarchal fatherhood with a happy face.

It is important to keep in mind that the culture of daddyhood did not necessarily coincide with what fathers were *doing*. The evidence gathered shows that, for some, being a father meant more than simply being a companion to one's son; it meant also having a close enough relationship with one's daughter to care about her problems (remember the Patri letters), and it also meant being involved in parental "dirty work." The culture of daddyhood, however, did provide a cognitive schema or framework through which men's contribution to child care could be deciphered. Thus, when the culture of daddyhood was strong, men's contributions to child care were less likely to be acknowledged. In a significant way, the culture of daddyhood helped to shape people's *memories* of fatherhood.

We can now perhaps understand how historians of fatherhood who disproportionately focus on the magazine articles of the 1920s when writing about early-twentieth-century New Fatherhood run the risk of making at least two mistakes. First, they may erroneously assume that the articles of the 1920s represent the range of attitudes that existed during the Machine Age. Second, they may be drawn into the culture of daddyhood themselves and fail to look beyond the rhetoric to the evidence that shows more variety in the division of child care than the culture of daddyhood allows. (The culture of daddyhood hence continues to shape our memories of fatherhood.)

On a theoretical plane, the culture of daddyhood accentuates the role of language and communication in the social construction of parenthood. The fact that, during the Machine Age, fathers were far more likely to be called "dads" than mothers were to be called "moms," and that the phrase *mother and dad* was a lot more common than *dad and mother* or *mom and father*, both reflected and directed how fathers and mothers were perceived. If words are the medium through which society is made real and ultimately reified, that is, made "thinglike," then the use of *dad* in the absence of *mom*, one may conclude, contributed to the parental stratification system that existed then and that persists today. The historical making and remaking of the American "daddy," through symbolic interaction, is a phenomenon deserving serious scholarly attention.

The modernization of fatherhood—as a transformational process— was clearly operative at the level of popular culture during the Machine Age. If we examine the content, for example, of child-rearing books or magazines from the end of World War I to the beginning of World War II, we see evidence of changes in New Fatherhood from one year to the next. The question is, however, Was this process also going on inside the home? Did fathers and mothers also change in the interim? Focusing on the letters to Angelo Patri gave me an opportunity to address this question. What I found was compelling: The letters suggest that the Depression of the 1930s had a countervailing effect on the modernization of fatherhood inside the home. Contrary to what one would expect if cultural prescriptions were being directly translated into paternal action, the slumbering economy reduced men's involvement with their children. This dampening process might lead one to believe that the modernization of fatherhood was chimerical. This was not, however, all that the Patri correspondence revealed. The letters also show that between 1925 and 1939, the parents who wrote to Patri became more modern in their *outlook.* For example, during the 1930s, both fathers and mothers were less likely to use the word *dad* in their letters, indicating a shift away from the culture of daddyhood. Mothers, too, were less likely to speak of their children using singular pronouns or possessives (e.g., "my" child as opposed to "our" child) and were more likely as well to cite instances where their husbands interacted with their children one-on-one—trends which reflect a bent toward a father-inclusive attitude.

It would appear, then, that the modernization of fatherhood had at least two routes through which it could make its way into the home: one was through the father; the second was through the mother. The second route is especially significant because we know that women often modernize their attitudes about gender distinctions before men do, and we know also that women's gender attitudes can have an effect on men's gender behaviors. Hence, even if a father never attended a class on New Fatherhood or never read *Parents' Magazine,* if his wife participated in any of these activities and was moved by the messages she had received, the chances are good that he would be exposed to New Fatherhood and probably asked to take up the cause.

Then there is Father's Day. Why this holiday has gotten so little attention from historians is a puzzle to me. Apart from the fact that the story behind Father's Day is interesting in itself, there is the analytical point that the creation of Father's Day probably was instrumental to the modernization of fatherhood. Succinctly stated, Father's Day was a fascinating bit of theatrics produced by commercial interests, directed by mothers (who socialized the family into the proper thing to do on the holiday), and played out by fathers and children (who in enacting the day discovered what being a "good" father meant). Father's Day thus permits us to view, from a different vantage point, how the modernization of fatherhood manifested itself in everyday life.

If we look at where the holiday was in 1910 when, officially speaking, it was first observed, and at where it was in 1942, having passed through the Machine Age, we see yet another sign of both the durability and the elasticity of New Fatherhood. Finding a place for fathers that did not devalue mothers was, for many, the key. Mother's Day had been created in the early twentieth century in part to show that women were special. Father's Day seemed to dilute that assertion; hence, it received little support at first. By the late 1930s and early 1940s, however, New Fatherhood had taken a definite turn toward emphasizing the importance of male role models, which elevated men's status but not entirely at women's expense.[9] By the late 1930s and early 1940s, the business community also had managed to create the National Council for the Promotion of Father's Day, which gave the holiday the advertising resources needed to make it profitable.

Interesting here is the fact that when the father as male role model grew in popularity in the late 1930s and early 1940s, the honor accorded men increased. A general rule may be that when the goal of an individual or group is to highlight men's value to the community, the father as male role model is likely to be emphasized. (The father as pal does not seem to work as well, because of the extent to which it trivializes men's contributions.) The rhetoric of today's men's rights groups would seem to support this axiom, in that for many of these groups, the father as male role model is a rallying call.

Let me repeat that it has not been my intent to glorify fatherhood or to cast the 1920s and 1930s as some kind of Golden Age. What I have tried to do is encourage a reexamination of some of the assumptions held about yesterday's fathers, assumptions which I think distort both what we know about the past and what we perceive of the present. The belief, for example, that it is only in recent years that fathers have given any thought to the meaning of fatherhood, much less spent any serious time with their children, creates a surreal world where almost anything fathers do in the way of child care is prized. Thus, being helpful is more than what fathers did before, and being there at all, in the case of, say, divorced fathers, is still impressive, if only to fathers themselves, because of our sense of how little yesterday's fathers bothered with their kids. Even the reverse argument, "fathers are worse now than before," tends to be flawed because it is often based on comparisons with the television fathers of the 1950s, as if the history of fatherhood began with the sitcom. Lost in the "let's return to yesteryear" nostalgia is a true appreciation for the twists and turns that have marked fatherhood through the years.[10]

Finally, I offer this: My father used to say that people should do things scientifically, by which he meant "sitting down." (He had a wonderful sense of humor.) What he was trying to tell me, I surmised, is that if people are committed to doing something well, they should plan to stay for a while and give the task the attention it deserves. I did a lot of sitting down to complete this project, and the going was not always easy. I learned a lot, though, and feel good about having had the opportunity to "hear" and now share the voices of the men and women who "spoke" to me. I strongly recommend that fatherhood scholars do some serious sitting down in the years ahead in order to develop *histories* of *fatherhoods* that are empirically valid and ultimately usable (it is time to return to the plural).[11] Anything less, we have to realize, is a disservice not only to the fathers and mothers of before, but to the men and women and children of today.

Acknowledgments

"Have you finished it yet?" That was the question that Brian and Adam, my two sons, wanted answered. Along with, "When are you going to be done? You have been writing that book *forever!*" Well, it hasn't exactly been "forever," though it may have seemed so, but it has been a number of years since I started the project, and I have accrued a number of debts. First, and most importantly, to Brian and Adam. I'm finally done, guys, and I'm sorry it has taken me so long. Sorry, because there have been too many evenings and weekends when I should have been out there with you rather than holed up in my den or office slumped over my computer.

My mother, too, would ask when I planned to finish. She passed away, unfortunately, before she could see the book in its final form, but she did review some early drafts and did offer comments. What I valued and now miss the most, however, was her confidence and heartfelt anticipation. My father, sadly enough, did not get an opportunity to read any part of this work; he died about the time I started collecting data. I have to admit it's been difficult to write about fatherhood and not have him around to share ideas with, especially since he, I now realize, was so much a product of the Machine Age. From the beginning, however, I have felt his warm presence by my side.

This project was funded by a grant from the National Science Foundation ("A Social History of Fatherhood in America, 1918–1941") and was supported as well as by two research initiation grants from Georgia State University. Phyllis Moen was the sociology project director at the National Science Foundation when my proposal was funded. Her faith in the study was a real boost and is very much appreciated. Kirk Elifson, the former chair of the Department of Sociology at Georgia State, helped me to combine a teaching leave from the GSU Research Office with a previously scheduled quarter off, thus giving me a six-month period to work intensively on the book.

Early on, when the project was just a concept, and a vague concept at that, I received sound advice and constructive feedback from Mitch Allen, Rob Palkovitz, Robert Pickett, Paul Rosenblatt, Joyce Seltzer, Charles Strickland, and Alexis Walker. Mitch, I should add, has always seemed to be there for me and has followed the book's progress (or lack thereof) with mild amusement.

The Georgia State University Interlibrary Loan staff—Jane Hobson, Margie Patterson, and Matt Stinson—proved eager and willing to search for items that I could not find on my own. Marie Mulligan (who is also my mother-in-law) served, for a short time, as my own personal reference librarian, tracking down information on the history of Father's Day and Mother's Day. David Klassen was my guide to the Child Study Association of America Papers at the University of Minnesota. Jerry Hess, Rod Ross, Aloha South, and Catherine Tumber helped me navigate through the materials at the National Archives. Without Aloha South's guidance, I never would have been able to make sense of the Children's Bureau Collection. I especially appreciate her willingness to take me up to the stacks to pick out what I needed. Fred Bauman and Mary Wolfskill were my principal contacts at the Library of Congress, where the Angelo Patri collection is stored. Both were gracious hosts. I want to thank also the family of Angelo Patri, and especially Frank Merolla, for making the collection available to the public. I treasure the visit we had in New York, where I had the opportunity to view Angelo Patri's guest book and to hear a recording of his voice.

Colleagues who read various sections of the manuscript include Phillip Davis, William Doherty, Denise Donnelly, Paula Dressel, Charles Jaret, Stephen Marks, and Donald Reitzes. Bill Doherty deserves special recognition for reading the whole manuscript not once but twice and for cheering me on toward the end. I am also grateful for his wise counsel and sympathetic support. He is a dear friend. Don Reitzes, too, played a significant role. Don and I worked together on the quantitative analysis of the Patri letters, and we wrote two articles together based on that analysis. Don has been a close friend as well for a long time and has always offered encouragement when I needed it most.

Graduate students contributed immeasurably to the success of this project. Pam Priddy Daniels was the first. She hunted down many of the magazine and newspaper articles and made copies of the documents that I brought back from my trips to the archives. Ronald Jay Werner-Wilson filled the role of project manager and set up the computer files. He was terrific. Betty Anne Simons Gordon came on board about the time that Ron was getting ready to leave. Betty Anne's attention to detail and good common sense were tremendous assets at a number of points. Stacey Scoggins and Laurie Tezza had the laborious task of checking the quality of the computer transcriptions. Laurie also proofread an early draft of the manuscript. Laurie's eye for grammar and form was superb. Other graduate students who provided help along the way include Cathryn Brubaker, Jaimie Carboy, Ann Clark, Margaret Hughes, and Michelle McLoughlin. Jaimie and Margaret were indispensible in the home stretch. Four undergraduate students who played significant roles were Sonya Alston, Barbara DuVall, Kimberly Hayes, and Linda Mosby. Their job was to type the letters and articles onto disk.

Toward the end, the dean asked me to take on major administrative responsibilities that prevented me from finishing the book sooner. Selma Poage, the Sociology Department's business manager, deserves a great deal of credit for helping me get through the morass. And then at the very end, as luck would have it, my computer started to act up. I turned to the College of Arts and Sciences' computer consultant, Andrea Georgalis, who immediately found a replacement, one that was faster. What a difference that made.

At the University of Chicago Press, I have been fortunate to have outstanding support. My editor, Doug Mitchell, saw the value of the book when it was just a prospectus and graciously and skillfully shepherded the manuscript through the various evaluations. (Let me thank, too, the anonymous reviewers for the Press, who offered the most detailed comments that I received.) Matt Howard, Doug's assistant, proficiently guided the book through the production process. Others on the team include Beverley Becker, Marty Hertzel, Martin White, and last but not least Margaret Mahan and Nicholas Murray, who did a great job of copyediting.

And then there was Maureen Mulligan LaRossa. I cannot adequately express the many things that Maur did to make this book a reality. When I couldn't decide how to frame the study, she was there to offer advice. When I had a bad day of writing, she was there to comfort me. ("You'll do better tomorrow.") When all sorts of barriers seemed to stand in the way of completing the work, she helped me to figure out how to remove or go around them. Time and again, she provided the intellectual and emotional nurturance I needed. Time and again, her strength made the difference. Thanks "Kid." We did it again.

Ralph LaRossa

Notes

Prologue: 1932

1. "[Mayor Jimmy] Walker Enlivens Parents' Day Fete," *New York Times*, 16 May 1932, p. 17.

2. Mr. and Mrs. Robert E. Simon, "Pulling Together," *Child Study* 9 (February 1932), pp. 165–66.

3. Charles P. Pelham, "Confessions of a Newborn Father," *Parents' Magazine*, June 1932, pp. 6, 43.

4. "Fathers" (Radio Script), Box 40, 23 October 1932, Angelo Patri Papers, Library of Congress.

5. J.R.B. (male) to Angelo Patri, Box 21, 25 October 1932, Angelo Patri Papers, Library of Congress.

6. F.B. (male) to Angelo Patri, Box 21, 5 October 1932, Angelo Patri Papers, Library of Congress. I say the young man was "an avid listener" because his letter said he listened "every evening" and had been doing so for "a whole year."

7. *Infant Care* (Washington, DC: U.S. Department of Labor, Children's Bureau, 1932).

8. M.T. (male) to Children's Bureau, Box 368, 22 August 1932, Children's Bureau Papers, National Archives.

9. N.C. (female) to Children's Bureau, Box 368, 9 November 1932, Children's Bureau Papers, National Archives.

Chapter 1: The Modernization of Fatherhood

1. For Americans, World War I ended on 11 November 1918 (Armistice Day, now known as Veterans Day), while World War II began on 7 December 1941, following the attack on Pearl Harbor. Some readers may wonder why the interwar period, rather than the nineteenth century, with its industrial revolution, is called the "Machine Age." There was a machine ethos that defined the years between the wars, and the phrase "Machine Age" was not uncommon at the time. In a brochure describing a Machine Age exhibition that toured the United States in the late 1980s, the period was described as follows:

> Between World War I and World War II America witnessed the prosperity and Prohibition of the 1930s and the Depression of the 1930s. It was a period of contradictions and ironies, of hopes and fears. Through it all, the machine was a pervasive and defining factor. Although the initial advances in American technology took place during the Industrial Revolution in the nineteenth century, it was not until after World War I that the rapid growth of technology with its sophisticated machinery be-

came diffused throughout American life. New sources of power, new communications, new forms of transportation, and new technologies in the home created what seemed to some an age dominated by the machine. In fact, the term "Machine Age" was coined and widely used during this time. (*The Machine Age in America, 1918–1941*, 1 December 1987 to 14 February 1988, High Museum of Art, Atlanta. Exhibit produced and sponsored by the Brooklyn Museum.)

Also noteworthy is the fact that the *New York Times Index* began using "Machine Age" as an entry in 1927 and that *The Reader's Guide to Periodical Literature* followed suit in 1929. One of the most comprehensive statements about the Machine Age is the book that accompanied the exhibition (and that, in an endnote, identified the dates when the *Times* and *Reader's Guide* began using the term): see Richard Guy Wilson, Dianne H. Pilgrim, and Dickran Tashjian, *The Machine Age in America, 1918–1941* (New York: Harry N. Abrams, 1986). See also Reyner Banham, *Theory and Design in the First Machine Age* (London: Architectural Press, 1960, reprinted as a second edition by the MIT Press, 1980); Sean Dennis Cashman, *America in the Twenties and Thirties: The Olympian Age of Franklin Delano Roosevelt* (New York: New York University Press, 1989); Floyd Dell, *Love in the Machine Age: A Psychological Study of the Transition from Patriarchal Society* (New York: Holt, Rinehart and Winston, 1930; reprinted by Octagon Books, a Division of Farrar, Straus and Girous, 1973); Edward A. Filene, *Successful Living in This Machine Age* (New York: Simon and Schuster, 1932); John M. Jordan, *Machine-Age Ideology: Social Engineering and American Liberalism, 1911–1939* (Chapel Hill: University of North Carolina Press, 1994); Dora Russell, *The Religion of the Machine Age* (London: Routledge & Kegan Paul, 1983); Gilman M. Ostander, *American Civilization in the First Machine Age: 1890–1940* (New York: Harper & Row, 1970); Terry Smith, *Making the Modern: Industry, Art, and Design in America* (Chicago: University of Chicago Press, 1993); Warren Susman, "Introduction," in *Culture and Commitment, 1929–1945*, ed. Warren Susman (New York: Braziller, 1973). I do not want to give the impression that the term "Machine Age" can *only* be applied to the early twentieth century; for a recent exception, see James J. Farley, *Making Arms in the Machine Age: Philadelphia's Frankford Arsenal, 1816–1870* (University Park, PA: Pennsylvania State University Press, 1994). Nor do I mean to imply that the Machine Age abruptly began with the end of the World War I or with the onset of the twentieth century; clearly its roots are deep. But it does seem clear that the use of the term to refer to the period between the wars has considerable precedence and, more important, substantive and theoretical value. As we shall see, the technological revolution that marked the twenties and thirties had a profound effect on people's lives.

2. The phrase "war to end all wars" is from Edward M. Coffman, *The War to End All Wars: The American Military Experience in World War I* (New York: Oxford University Press, 1968). The significance of the 1920s and 1930s in the modern history of gender relations has been widely noted. See, for example, Peter Filene, *Him/Her/Self: Sex Roles in Modern America*, 2d ed. (Baltimore: Johns Hopkins University Press, 1986), in which he argues that "[i]n the history of American sex roles, the 1920s marked the beginning of modernity" (p. 115). See also Dorothy M. Brown, *Setting a Course: American Women in the 1920s*. (Bos-

ton: Twayne Publishers, a Division of G. K. Hall, 1987); Susan Ware, *Holding Their Own: American Women in the 1930s.* (Boston: Twayne Publishers, a Division of G. K. Hall, 1982). Finally, the use of the singular—*fatherhood* and *father*—may seem inappropriate. Is there actually *a* twentieth-century fatherhood, or *a* twentieth-century father? The answer, of course, is no. But there is an icon of fatherhood—a cultural stereotype that defines an ideal father—that has a certain singularity; and it this icon to which I refer here. I will have more to say about the singular-vs.-plural issue in chapter 2.

3. The configuration I am talking about primarily is *cultural.* Demographically, of course, there are significant differences between American fatherhood in the early twentieth century and American fatherhood in the late twentieth century. To put things in the proper historical perspective, here is how the U.S. Census Bureau pictured the average American father in 1941, as reported by the *New York Times:*

> Age: 44. The odds are 9 to 1 that he is married living with his wife and has one to two children living at home. The rest of the fathers are mostly widowers and a very small sprinkling of divorced males. The chances are 3 to 2 that he will live in a city of 2,500 or more. The odds are 8 to 1 that he has a job in private or non-emergency work. If he works in an industrial establishment his yearly wage is about $1,100 to $1,200 a year. Figures are not completed on white-collar workers and professional workers. It is 9 to 1 he is white and 3 to 2 he is a native American whose parents were born here. He spends about $1,200 a year [his entire annual income?] for family purchases in retail stores; he worries over a $480 annual tax bill. About 2,250,000 fathers each year have the thrill of childbirth in the home, about 25,000 of which involve twins, 274 triplets and 2 quadruplets. One father in the United States has twenty-seven children. Father's Day should replenish his wardrobe, the statisticians believe. ("Census Characterizes the Average Father as 32,000,000 have their Day in Nation," *New York Times,* 15 June 1941, p. 31)

4. Among the essays and books which discuss the various aspects of the history of fatherhood are these: Leonard Benson, *Fatherhood: A Sociological Perspective* (New York: Random House, 1968); Mary Frances Berry, *The Politics of Parenthood: Child Care, Women's Rights, and the Myth of the Good Mother* (New York: Viking, 1993); Mark Carnes, *Secret Ritual and Manhood in Victorian America* (New Haven: Yale University Press, 1989), especially pp. 93–127; Mark Carnes and Clyde Griffen, eds., *Meanings for Manhood: Constructions of Masculinity in Victorian America* (Chicago: University of Chicago Press, 1990); Scott Coltrane, *Family Man: Fatherhood, Housework, and Gender Equity* (New York: Oxford University Press, 1996), especially chapter 2; John Demos, "The Changing Faces of Fatherhood: A New Exploration in Family History," in *Father and Child: Developmental and Clinical Perspectives,* ed. Stanley Cath, Alan Gurwitt, and John M. Ross (Boston: Little, Brown, 1982), pp. 425–45; Filene, *Him/Her/Self;* Stephen M. Frank, " 'Rendering Aid and Comfort': Images of Fatherhood in the Letters of Civil War Soldiers from Massachusetts and Michigan," *Journal of Social History* 26 (Fall 1992), pp. 5–31; Frank F. Furstenberg Jr., "Good Dads—Bad Dads: Two Faces of Fatherhood," in *The Changing American Family and Public Policy,* ed. Andrew J. Cherlin (Washington, DC: Urban Institute Press, 1988), pp. 193–

218; Robert L. Griswold, *Fatherhood in America: A History* (New York: Basic Books, 1993); Michael Kimmel, *Manhood in America: A Cultural History* (New York: Free Press, 1996); Michael E. Lamb, "Introduction: The Emergent American Father," in *The Father's Role: Cross-Cultural Perspectives,* ed. Michael E. Lamb (Hillsdale, NJ: Lawrence Erlbaum, 1987), pp. 3–25; Charlie Lewis, *Becoming a Father* (Milton Keynes, England: Open University Press, 1986); Charlie Lewis and Margaret O'Brien, eds., *Reassessing Fatherhood: New Observations on Fathers and the Modern Family* (London: Sage Publications, 1987); J. M. Mogey, "A Century of Declining Paternal Authority," *Marriage and Family Living* 19 (August 1957), pp. 234–39; John Nash, "Historical and Social Changes in the Perception of the Role of the Father," in *The Role of the Father in Child Development,* ed. Michael E. Lamb (New York: John Wiley & Sons), pp. 65–87; Ross D. Parke and Peter N. Stearns, "Fathers and Child Rearing," in *Children in Time and Place: Developmental and Historical Insights,* ed. Glen H. Elder Jr., John Modell, and Ross D. Parke (Cambridge: Cambridge University Press, 1993); E. Anthony Rotundo, "American Fatherhood: A Historical Perspective," *American Behavioral Scientist* 29 (September/October 1985), pp. 7–25; E. Anthony Rotundo, *American Manhood: Transformations in Masculinity from the Revolution to the Mod-Era* (New York: Basic Books, 1993); Joseph H. Pleck, "American Fathering in Historical Perspective," in *Changing Men: New Directions on Men and Masculin-* ed. Michael S. Kimmel (Newbury Park, CA: Sage, 1987), pp. 83–97; Peter N. Stearns, *Be a Man! Males in Modern Society* (New York: Holmes & Meier, 1979); Peter N. Stearns, "Fatherhood in Historical Perspective: The Role of Social Change," in *Fatherhood and Families in Cultural Context,* ed. Frederick W. Bozett and Shirley M. H. Hanson (New York: Springer, 1991)

5. David Blankenhorn, *Fatherless America: Confronting Our Most Urgent Social Problem* (New York: Basic Books, 1995), pp. 12–13.

6. For uses of the term *usable past,* see Michael Kammen, *Mystic Chords of Memory: The Transformation of Tradition in American Culture* (New York: Knopf, 1991), p. 6; Warren I. Susman, *Culture as History: The Transformation of American Society in the Twentieth Century* (New York: Pantheon, 1984), p. 7.

7. Gerda Lerner, *The Creation of Feminist Consciousness: From the Middle Ages to Eighteen-seventy* (New York: Oxford University Press, 1993), pp. 12, 166.

8. John Demos, "The Changing Faces of Fatherhood," p. 425.

9. One of the first books to question assumptions about fatherhood in the past was Charlie Lewis's *Becoming a Father.* Moving beyond the paternal role, for discussions that show yesterday's men more modern than one might think, see Michael S. Kimmel, "The Contemporary 'Crisis' of Masculinity in Historical Perspective," in *The Making of Masculinities: The New Men's Studies,* ed. Harry Brod (Boston: Allen and Unwin, 1987), pp. 121–53; Michael S. Kimmel and Thomas E. Mosmiller, eds., *Against the Tide: Pro-Feminist Men in the United States, 1776–1990* (Boston: Beacon Press, 1992).

10. Lerner, *The Creation of Feminist Consciousness,* p. 12.

11. The first statement was reported in Susan Harte, "Fathers and Sons," *Atlanta Journal and Constitution,* 21 June 1987, p. 6G. The second is the opening for Jonathan W. Gould and Robert E. Gunther, *Reinventing Fatherhood* (Blue Ridge Summit, PA: TAB Books, a Division of McGraw-Hill, 1993), p. vii.

12. The phrase *reinvent the wheel* in terms of an absence of a usable past is Lerner's. See Lerner, *The Creation of Feminist Consciousness*, p. 19.

13. See Bo Emerson, "Daddy Discovers It's Not Easy Being Mom, But the Job Has Some Rewards," *Atlanta Journal and Constitution*, 14 September 1993, p. B-1. For examples of similar essays during the Machine Age, see Bruce Barton, "My Awful Day of Motherhood," *Women's Home Companion*, June 1931, pp. 9–10, 150; Wakelee R. Smith, "Father's Day At Home," *Parents' Magazine*, March 1942, pp. 29, 81, 82.

14. For a discussion of the role of men's excuses and justifications in the social construction of gendered divisions of child care, see Ralph LaRossa and Maureen Mulligan LaRossa, *Transition to Parenthood: How Infants Change Families* (Beverly Hills, CA: Sage, 1981); For an example of a similar discussion during the early twentieth century, see Mary Ware Dennett, "The Right of a Child to Two Parents," *Century Magazine* (May 1915), pp. 104–8.

15. Two recent books that present both sides of the debate ("Just how involved are fathers today?") are Jane C. Hood, ed., *Men, Work, and Family* (Newbury Park, CA: Sage, 1993), and Kathleen Gerson, *No Man's Land: Men's Changing Commitments to Family and Work* (New York: Basic Books, 1993). Joseph Pleck conscientiously advances the position that men's involvement with children has changed in recent years. See, for example, his chapter in *Men, Work, and Family:* "Are 'Family Supportive' Employer Policies Relevant to Men?" I tend, as Kathleen Gerson notes in *No Man's Land* (p. 302), to be more pessimistic about the level of contemporary men's involvement with children. See Ralph LaRossa, "Fatherhood and Social Change," *Family Relations* 37 (October 1988), pp. 451–57. From what I can see from the most recent evidence, focusing on the last five years or so, there is more reason for optimism than before. See, for example, "Where's Papa? Fathers' Role in Child Care," *Population Trends and Public Policy Report No. 20* (Washington, DC: Population Reference Bureau, September 1993) Still, the changes, while statistically significant, remain small, and qualitative studies (those that explore the dynamics of the division of child care in depth) tend to paint less rosy pictures. See, for example, Martha McMahon, *Engendering Motherhood: Identity and Self-Transformation in Women's Lives* (New York: Guilford, 1995). Right now, I am more cautiously optimistic than pessimistic. On the matter of how New Fatherhood can thwart social change, sociologist Kathryn Keller in her book *Mothers and Work in Popular American Magazines* (Westport, CT: Greenwood Press, 1994) gets the process right, I think, when she says, "The magazines now justify a man's role by calling him a 'New Father,' the man who shares in housework and child care. The image of the 'New Father' may give hope to working women who have never met the man except in print, but this image stymies any serious analysis of the equality of domestic work between working parents. The husband may not 'share' work, but he is busy being a 'New Father'—and therefore women are told not to complain too much" (p. 162).

16. On the connection between historical accounts and power, see Joyce Appleby, Lynn Hunt, and Margaret Jacob, *Telling the Truth about History* (New York: W. W. Norton, 1994). For a general discussion of the politics of constructing social discontinuities, see Eviatar Zerubavel, *The Fine Line: Making Distinctions in Everyday Life* (New York: Free Press, 1991; reprinted by the University of

Chicago Press, 1993). For a discussion of these issues in the context of fatherhood and family relationships, see Ralph LaRossa, "Stories and Relationships," *Journal of Social and Personal Relationships* 12 (November 1995), pp. 553–58.

17. One of the harshest critics of Parents' Day was Anna M. Jarvis, the official founder of Mother's Day. See Leigh Eric Schmidt, *Consumer Rites: The Buying and Selling of American Holidays* (Princeton, NJ: Princeton University Press, 1995), p. 269.

18. Mr. and Mrs. Robert E. Simon, "Pulling Together," *Child Study* 9 (February 1932), p. 165.

19. Here is how the section titled, "The Sick Baby: What a Mother Should Note," began: "When the baby is well the mother should observe the normal position of his body, his normal activity and wakefulness, the expressions of his face, the color of his skin, also the color of his tongue and the condition and temperature of his skin, so that signs of discomfort, pain, unusual drowsiness, or irritability can be noticed quickly. . . . The mother should learn to read a clinical thermometer" (*Infant Care* (Washington, DC: U.S. Department of Labor, Children's Bureau, 1929). The 1932 imprint of *Infant Care* essentially was the same as the 1929 (fourth) edition.

20. See Susman, *Culture as History*, 1984, pp. 154, 188; also Kammen, *Mystic Chords of Memory*, pp. 302–4.

21. Richard Guy Wilson, "America and the Machine Age," in *The Machine Age in America, 1918–1941*, ed. Richard Guy Wilson, Dianne H. Pilgrim, and Dickran Tashjian (New York: Harry N. Abrams, in association with the Brooklyn Museum, 1986), p. 23. For other references on the Machine Age and for a further discussion of why the term is an appropriate one to denote the period between the two world wars, see note 2.

22. For a discussion of events and discoveries that took place during the Machine Age, see Frederick Lewis Allen, *Only Yesterday and Since Yesterday: A Popular History of the '20s and '30s* (New York: Bonanza/Crown, 1986); Cashman *America in the Twenties and Thirties;* Ruth Schwartz Cowan, *More Work for Mother: The Ironies of Household Technology from the Open Hearth to the Microwave* (New York: Basic Books, 1983); Claude S. Fischer and Glenn R. Carroll, "Telephone and Automobile Diffusion in the United States, 1902–1937," *American Journal of Sociology* 93 (March 1988), pp. 1153–78; Bernard Grun, *The Timetables of History* (New York: Simon and Schuster, Touchstone Edition, 1982); Paul Johnson, *Modern Times: The World from the Twenties to the Nineties,* rev. ed. (New York: HarperCollins, 1991); David E. Nye, *Electrifying America: Social Meaning of a New Technology* (Cambridge, MA: MIT Press, 1991); Wilson et al., *The Machine Age in America, 1918–1941.*

23. See Norman F. Cantor, *Twentieth-Century Culture: Modernism to Deconstruction* (New York: Peter Lang, 1988), p. 1. Richard Guy Wilson, in *The Machine Age in America, 1918–1941,* says that "[t]he machine in all its manifestations . . . became the fundamental fact of modernism" (p. 23). I don't think Wilson means to suggest, nor do I, that there was a simple relationship between the Machine Age and Modernism. As Terry Smith notes in *Making the Modern: Industry, Art, and Design in America* (Chicago: University of Chicago Press, 1993), p. 7, "There is . . . no simple, deterministic equation between entities such as the Machine Age

and Modernism." Still, "Broadly speaking, a new imagery of modernity evolved during the massive shift from entrepreneurial to monopoly capitalism which began in most industrial countries in the 1880s and came to dominate the social order by the 1920s."

24. Wilson et al., *The Machine Age in America, 1918–1941*, p. 339.

25. For a discussion of America's concept of progress, see Michael Kammen, *Mystic Chords of Memory*. Henry Ford was quoted in the *New York Times*, 20 May 1919, as reported in Terry Smith, *Making the Modern*, p. 4. Smith's text includes a second sentence also attributed to Ford: "We want to live in the present and the only history that is worth a tinker's damn is the history we make today."

26. Ernest W. Burgess, "The Family as a Unity of Interacting Personalities," *The Family* 7 (March 1926), pp. 3–9.

27. See Pauline Boss, William J. Doherty, Ralph LaRossa, Walter R. Schumm, and Suzanne K. Steinmetz, *Sourcebook of Family Theories and Methods: A Contextual Approach* (New York: Plenum, 1993), especially chapters 1 and 6.

28. See Cantor, *Twentieth-Century Culture*, p. 38.

29. Elements of companionate marriage can be found 100 years earlier, but the phrase *companionate marriage* seems to have been coined and was more likely to be used in the 1920s. See Steven Mintz and Susan Kellogg, *Domestic Revolutions: A Social History of American Family Life* (New York: Free Press, 1988), pp. 114–15.

30. Charlie Lewis, in *Becoming a Father,* says that "the view that men are starting to become involved in family life . . . is as old and perhaps as prominent as the notion of patriarchy" (p. 5). I think this is true in the sense that it is tied to the politics of self and other (see note 16). I suspect, however, that this view, like all perceptions, is shaped by sociohistorical forces and that there would be some periods when the view would be more prominent than in others. The 1920s and 1930s, under the influence of modernism, was such a period. The 1980s and 1990s, under the influence of postmodernism, appears to be another.

31. On the history of *Parents' Magazine*, see Steven Schlossman, "The Perils of Popularization: The Founding of *Parents' Magazine*," in *History and Research in Child Development*, ed. Alice Boardman Smuts and John W. Hagen (Monographs of the Society for Research in Child Development, vol. 50, nos. 4–5, serial no. 211, 1985).

32. *Infant Care* (Washington, DC: U.S. Department of Labor, Children's Bureau, 1929). As I said before, the 1932 imprint of *Infant Care* essentially was the same as the 1929 (fourth) edition.

33. See Berry, *The Politics of Parenthood*, p. 92; Carl Degler, *At Odds: Women and the Family in America from the Revolution to the Present* (New York: Oxford University Press, 1980), pp. 49, 82–83; Filene, *Him/Her/Self*, p. xiv; Maxine L. Margolis, *Mothers and Such: Views of American Women and Why They Changed* (Berkeley, CA: University of California Press, 1984), p. 9; Rotundo, *American Manhood*, p. 296; Viviana A. Zelizer, *Pricing the Priceless Child: The Changing Social Values of Children* (New York: Basic Books, 1985), p. 6.

34. The history of the "good provider" role is described by Jessie Bernard, "The Good Provider Role: Its Rise and Fall," *American Psychologist* 36 (January 1981), pp. 1–12. In *Middletown in Transition: A Study in Cultural Conflicts* (New York:

Harcourt, Brace, 1937), Robert S. Lynd and Helen Merrell Lynd report that "[The father in the mid-1930s] may have been narrowing his role in the home as a parent, leaving child rearing more and more to his wife" (p. 177). And in *Children of the Great Depression: Social Change in Life Experience* (Chicago: University of Chicago Press, 1974), Glen H. Elder Jr. says that fathers withdrew both socially and emotionally from family life (p. 105). Other works which describe the negative impact of the Depression on fatherhood include Robert C. Angell, *The Family Encounters the Depression* (New York: Charles Scribner's Sons, 1936); E. Wight Bakke, *Citizens without Work: A Study of the Effects of Unemployment upon the Workers' Social Relations and Practices* (New Haven, CT: Yale University Press, 1940); Barbara Salzmann Boxer, "The American Father and the Great Depression" (Ph.D. diss., Bryn Mawr College, 1976); Ruth Cavan and Katherine H. Ranck, *The Family and the Depression: A Study of Over One Hundred Chicago Families* (Chicago: University of Chicago Press, 1938); Demos, "The Changing Faces of Fatherhood," pp. 425–45; Filene, *Him/Her/Self;* Griswold, *Fatherhood in America;* Mirra Komarovsky, *The Unemployed Man and His Family: The Effect of Unemployment upon the Status of the Man in Fifty-Nine Families* (New York: Dryden Press, 1940); Mintz and Kellogg, *Domestic Revolutions;* Winona L. Morgan, *The Family Meets the Depression: A Study of a Group of Highly Selected Families* (Minneapolis: University of Minnesota Press, 1939; reprinted by Greenwood Press, 1972); Rotundo, "American Fatherhood," pp. 7–25; Winifred D. Wandersee, *Women's Work and Family Values, 1920–1940* (Cambridge, MA: Harvard University Press, 1981).

35. The *culture of fatherhood* and *conduct of fatherhood* are terms that I first employed in "Fatherhood and Social Change," *Family Relations* 37 (October 1988), pp. 451–57.

36. Articles addressed to *both* fathers and mothers also increased in the 1930s. For another study of how the popular press has depicted fathers, see Maxine P. Atkinson and Stephen P. Blackwelder, "Fathering in the Twentieth Century," *Journal of Marriage and the Family* 55 (November 1993), pp. 975–86.

37. See note 34.

38. See Ralph LaRossa and Donald C. Reitzes, "Continuity and Change in Middle-Class Fatherhood, 1925–1939: The Culture-Conduct Connection," *Journal of Marriage and the Family* 55 (May 1993), pp. 455–68.

39. The best example of this was Lewis Terman and Catherine Cox Miles's Masculinity-Femininity (or M-F) Test, first described in their book *Sex and Personality* (New York: McGraw-Hill, 1936). For a critical discussion of the M-F Test, see Kimmel, *Manhood in America,* and Joseph Pleck, *The Myth of Masculinity* (Cambridge, MA: MIT Press, 1981).

40. Mintz and Kellogg, *Domestic Revolutions,* pp. 138–39.

41. See James A. Doyle, *The Male Experience,* 3d ed. (Madison, Wisconsin: Brown and Benchmark, 1995); Clyde W. Franklin II, *Men and Society* (Chicago: Nelson-Hall, 1988); Kimmel, *Manhood in America;* Michael S. Kimmel and Michael A. Messner, eds., *Men's Lives,* 2d ed. (New York: Macmillan, 1992); Rotundo, *American Manhood.* For discussions of how motherhood also is a product of people's collective imagination, see Evelyn Nakano Glenn, Grace Chang, and Linda Rennie Forcey, eds., *Mothering: Ideology, Experience, and Agency* (New

York: Routledge, 1994); Margolis, *Mothers and Such;* Shari L. Thurer, *The Myths of Motherhood: How Culture Reinvents the Good Mother* (New York: Houghton Mifflin, 1994);

42. Eviatar Zerubavel, *The Fine Line.*

43. Ibid., p. 21.

44. Some would argue that the distinction between fatherhood and mother-hood is also blurred at the biological level. See Suzanne J. Kessler and Wendy McKenna, *Gender: An Ethnomethodological Approach* (New York: John Wiley & Sons, 1978).

45. I am indebted to Gayle Rubin's approach here: "[F]rom the standpoint of nature, men and women are closer to each other than either is to anything else—for instance, mountains, kangaroos, or coconut palms . . . the idea that men and women are two mutually exclusive categories must arise out of something other than a non-existent 'natural' opposition. Far from being the expression of natural differences, exclusive gender identity is the suppression of natural similarities." See Gayle Rubin, "The Traffic in Women: Notes on the Political Economy of Sex," in *Toward an Anthropology of Women,* ed. R. Reiter (New York: Monthly Review Press, 1975), as cited in Myra Marx Ferree and Beth B. Hess, "Introduction," in *Analyzing Gender: A Handbook of Social Science Research,* eds. Beth B. Hess and Myra Marx Ferree (Newbury Park, CA: Sage, 1987).

46. See Zerubavel, *The Fine Line,* p. 46; also Kessler and McKenna, *Gender,* pp. 161–67.

47. See LaRossa and LaRossa, *Transition to Parenthood.*

48. According to the *Oxford English Dictionary,* the origin of the word *dad* is not known, "but the forms *dada, tata,* meaning 'father,' originating in infantile or childish speech, occur independently in many languages." The earliest example of literary usage reported in the *OED* is in Shakespeare, *The Life and Death of King John,* act II, scene i, line 466: "Zounds! I was never so bethump'd with words, Since I first call'd my brother's father dad."

49. Robert Griswold in *Fatherhood in America* contends that "[u]ntil the re-birth of feminism in the 1960s, American fatherhood existed in what amounted to a political vacuum" (p. 5), and goes on to say, "Today [in contrast to prior times], fatherhood has become politicized; its terms are contested, its significance fragmented, its meaning unstable" (p. 9). While it is true that the late-twentieth-century feminist movement has been a major political force in the social re-construction of twentieth-century fatherhood and that the social meaning of fa-therhood in the 1990s has caught the attention of many diverse groups, we must be careful not to trivialize and thus misrepresent the political struggles that have come before. To say, as Griswold does, that fatherhood prior to the 1960s "existed in what amounted to a political vacuum" or that only in recent years has fatherhood "become politicized" glosses over the conscientious and ongoing efforts of some in the early twentieth century to restructure the father-child relationship, and disregards the machinations of others who wanted to maintain the status quo. Push and resistance, resistance and push—herein lies the political history of American fatherhood. Theoretically speaking, reserving the words *political* and *politics* for what is happening to fatherhood now—and only now—also conveys the impression that politics is operative in some historical periods but not others.

Politics is present in all human affairs, however, and thus operates throughout history.

50. See Boxer, "The American Father and the Great Depression," especially chapter 2; Griswold, *Fatherhood in America*, p. 145; Komarovsky, *The Unemployed Man and His Family*; Wandersee, *Women's Work and Family Values*, pp. 107–12.

Chapter 2: The Historical Roots of Standard North American Fatherhood

1. "[W]hat's past is prologue." Shakespeare, *The Tempest*, act II, scene i, line 261. This line also graces the entrance to the National Archives in Washington, DC.

2. See John Demos, "The Changing Faces of Fatherhood: A New Exploration in Family History," in *Father and Child: Developmental and Clinical Perspectives*, ed. Stanley Cath, Alan Gurwitt, and John M. Ross (Boston: Little, Brown, 1982), pp. 425–45; Robert L. Griswold, *Fatherhood in America: A History* (New York: Basic Books, 1993).

3. Dorothy E. Smith, "The Standard North American Family: SNAF as an Ideological Code," *Journal of Family Issues* 14 (March 1993), p. 52.

4. For an early formulation of SNAF, see George P. Murdock, *Social Structure* (New York: Macmillan, 1949).

5. Randall Collins and Scott Coltrane, *Sociology of Marriage and the Family: Gender, Love, and Property*, 4th ed. (Chicago: Nelson-Hall, 1995), p. 105.

6. David Blankenhorn, for example, uses SNAF as an ideal in *Fatherless America: Confronting Our Most Urgent Social Problem* (New York: Basic Books, 1995).

7. The phrase "SNAF governed" is from Smith, "The Standard North American Family."

8. Ibid., p. 51.

9. Ibid., pp. 54–55.

10. Another way to think of SNAF is to conceptualize it as an element in the social construction of reality, where *reality* refers not to truth, as in real versus unreal, but to knowledge, broadly defined. Although the social construction of reality is an ongoing human accomplishment, realities of one sort or another can, in time, *appear* to have a nonhuman (ontological) quality about them. When this happens, the reality in question has become reified (thinglike). Reification is central to the politics of parenthood, because if a group has the power to get *its* conception of fatherhood and motherhood accepted as *the* conception, the power of the group increases even more. In the vernacular of the social construction of reality, SNAF is a definition of human conduct created and sustained (and sometimes reified) by authorized agents in a politically organized society. For the classic statement on the social construction of reality, see Peter L. Berger and Thomas Luckmann, *The Social Construction of Reality: A Treatise in the Sociology of Knowledge* (Garden City, NY: Doubleday/Anchor, 1966). Richard Quinney, in *The Social Reality of Crime* (Boston: Little, Brown, 1970), p. 15, defines crime as "a definition of human conduct that is created by authorized agents in a politically organized society." The definition of SNAF that I offer above is an application of Quinney's definition.

11. What follows, in short, is not a comprehensive overview of every strain of fatherhood from the past to the present but a history of the development of "Standard North American Fatherhood" prior to the Machine Age. Even within this strain, it would be more appropriate to speak in the plural—"fatherhoods" as opposed to "fatherhood" (for there are variations within it, as well)—but, following grammatical convention, I have opted for the singular form.

12. This is a point made by a number of historians of fatherhood. For two of the earliest statements on the matter, however, see Demos, "The Changing Faces of Fatherhood"; E. Anthony Rotundo, "American Fatherhood: A Historical Perspective," *American Behavioral Scientist* 29 (September/October 1985), pp. 7–25.

13. Marvin Zahniser, *Charles Cotesworth Pinckney* (Chapel Hill, NC: University of North Carolina Press, 1967), pp. 10–11, as cited in Mary Frances Berry, *The Politics of Parenthood: Child Care, Women's Rights, and the Myth of the Good Mother* (New York: Viking, 1993), p. 47.

14. Demos, "The Changing Faces of Fatherhood."

15. The phrase "patriarchal fatherhood" is from Rotundo, "American Fatherhood."

16. Panos D. Bardis, "Family Forms and Variations Historically Considered," in *Handbook of Marriage and the Family*, ed. Harold T. Christensen (Chicago: Rand McNally, 1964), p. 425.

17. Ibid., p. 436.

18. Leonard Benson, *Fatherhood: A Sociological Perspective* (New York: Random House, 1968); Peter N. Stearns, *Be a Man! Males in Modern Society* (New York: Holmes & Meier, 1979); Peter N. Stearns, "Fatherhood in Historical Perspective: The Role of Social Change," in *Fatherhood and Families in Cultural Context*, ed. Frederick W. Bozett and Shirley M. H. Hanson (New York: Springer, 1991).

19. Rotundo, "American Fatherhood"; Stearns, "Fatherhood in Historical Perspective."

20. The notion that both ideology and resources are important factors in determining the power structure in families is axiomatic in sociology. For a review of family power theories, see Maximiliane Szinovacz, "Family Power," in *Handbook of Marriage and the Family*, ed. Marvin B. Sussman and Susan K. Steinmetz (New York: Plenum, 1987), pp. 651–93.

21. Mark Carnes, *Secret Ritual and Manhood in Victorian America* (New Haven: Yale University Press, 1989), p. 108.

22. Elizabeth H. Pleck, "Two Worlds in One: Work and Family," *Journal of Social History* 10 (Winter 1976), pp. 178–95.

23. For a discussion of the process of modernization as an outgrowth of the Enlightenment and the Industrial Revolution, see "Modernization and Industrialization," in *The New Encylopaedia Britannica*, 15th ed., vol. 24 (Chicago: University of Chicago Press, 1992), pp. 280–91.

24. Steven Mintz and Susan Kellogg, *Domestic Revolutions: A Social History of American Family Life* (New York: Free Press, 1988), p. 47.

25. Griswold, *Fatherhood in America*, pp. 11–12.

26. Carnes, *Secret Ritual and Manhood in Victorian America*, p. 110.

27. John Demos notes, "The wrenching apart of work and home-life is one

of the great themes in social history. And for fathers, in particular, the consequences can hardly be overestimated. Certain key elements of premodern fatherhood disappeared (e.g., *father as teacher, father as moral overseer, father as companion*), while others were profoundly transformed (*father as counselor, father as model*). . . . Now, for the first time, the central activity of fatherhood was sited outside one's immediate household. Now, being fully a father meant being separated from one's children for a considerable part of each working day." See Demos, "The Changing Faces of Fatherhood," pp. 433–34.

28. Griswold, *Fatherhood in America*, p. 30; also Robert L. Griswold, *Family and Divorce in California, 1850–1890* (Albany, NY: State University of New York Press, 1982).

29. Demos, "The Changing Faces of Fatherhood," p. 428.

30. Mintz and Kellogg, *Domestic Revolutions*, p. 59; also Berry, *The Politics of Parenthood*, p. 55; E. Anthony Rotundo, *American Manhood: Transformations in Masculinity from the Revolution to the Modern Era* (New York: Basic Books, 1993), p. 28.

31. Berry, *The Politics of Parenthood*, p. 49; Griswold, *Fatherhood in America*, p. 12; Mintz and Kellogg, *Domestic Revolutions*, p. 45–49; Mary P. Ryan, *Cradle of the Middle Class: The Family in Oneida County, New York, 1790–1865* (New York: Cambridge University Press, 1981), p. 190.

32. Maxine L. Margolis, *Mothers and Such: Views of American Women and Why They Changed* (Berkeley, CA: University of California Press, 1984).

33. These magazines included *The Ladies' Magazine* (founded in 1828); *Lady's Book* (founded in 1830); *Harper's Bazar* (founded in 1867, changed to *Harper's Bazaar* in 1929); *The Home* (founded in 1874, and renamed *Ladies' Home Companion* in 1886), *The Ladies Home Journal* (founded in 1883), and *Good Housekeeping* (founded in 1885). For a history of the magazine industry, see John Tebbel and Mary Ellen Zuckerman, *The Magazine in America, 1741–1990* (New York: Oxford University Press, 1991).

34. Barbara Welter, "The Cult of True Womanhood: 1820–1860," *American Quarterly* (Summer 1966), p. 151. The phrase "moral entrepreneurs" is from Howard Becker, *Outsiders: Studies in the Sociology of Deviance* (New York: Free Press, 1963).

35. Berry, *The Politics of Parenthood;* Margolis, *Mothers and Such;* Stearns, "Fatherhood in Historical Perspective."

36. Degler, *At Odds*, p. 77.

37. For a discussion of the diversity of nineteenth-century culture in the context of masculinity and fatherhood, see Mark C. Carnes and Clyde Griffen, eds., *Meanings for Manhood: Constructions of Masculinity in Victorian America* (Chicago: University of Chicago Press, 1990), pp. 6, 183 ff.; also Rotundo, *American Manhood*.

38. Stephen M. Frank, "'Rendering Aid and Comfort': Images of Fatherhood in the Letters of Civil War Soldiers from Massachusetts and Michigan," *Journal of Social History* 26 (Fall 1992), p. 6.

39. Berry, *The Politics of Parenthood*, p. 59.

40. Ryan, *Cradle of the Middle Class*, pp. 198–210; also Ruth Schwartz Cowan, *More Work for Mother: The Ironies of Household Technology from the Open*

Hearth to the Microwave (New York: Basic Books, 1883); Susan Strasser, *Never Done: A History of American Housework* (New York: Pantheon, 1982).

41. Pleck, "Two Worlds in One," p. 181; see also Nancy Grey Osterud, *Bonds of Community: The Lives of Farm Women in Nineteenth-Century New York* (Ithaca, NY: Cornell University Press, 1991).

42. Degler, *At Odds;* Demos, "The Changing Faces of Fatherhood"; Rotundo, "American Fatherhood" 1982.

43. Frank, "'Rendering Aid and Comfort,'" p. 17.

44. Paula L. Dressel and Ann Clark, "A Critical Look at Family Care," *Journal of Marriage and the Family* 52 (August 1990), pp. 769–82.

45. The crux of the matter, as I see it, is this: Research shows that an ideology of separate spheres *gained in strength* in the late eighteenth and early nineteenth centuries. That is to say, there is sufficient evidence to support the contention that there was a set of beliefs and values—a *culture*—that encouraged people to visualize a public world which men inhabited and a private world where women dwelt. To what extent this culture squared with the conduct of fathers and mothers, it is hard to say, for there is so much that we do not know about parent-child interaction in this era. (No one was doing any national surveys.) We should not be too quick to accept the characterizations offered in books and magazines, because there is a good chance that the authors of these works, in their eagerness to promote True Womanhood, may have minimized how much fathers actually interacted with children. The distortion need not have been intentional. Having accepted the belief that fathers were uninvolved, the authors' ability to recall instances of father involvement may have been impaired. Some documents and letters indicate that gender separation existed in both image and action among the urban middle class, so we do know that the ideology was not simply a figment of the publishing industry's imagination. Thus, it probably is fair to say that many urban middle-class families knew about and, to some degree, subscribed to the ideology of separate spheres. Working-class families also may have known about the ideology—that is, they may have known it existed "out there" in American culture—but they were not necessarily in an economic position to put the ideology into practice, even if they wanted to.

As for the argument that child care includes financial support as well as custodial and emotional support, there is little doubt that parents who work long and hard in factories, shops, and offices generally do so on behalf of their children and thus do not deserve to be called noncaring fathers and mothers. Still, there is a difference, certainly to the children if to no one else, between economic care and face-to-face nurturance. While American fathers in the nineteenth century no doubt cared *about* (i.e., loved) their children enough to toil on their behalf, they generally did not care *for* (i.e., attend to) their children as much as fathers before them did. In other words, as a result of the spatial separation of paid work and family work, whatever the cause, fathers did begin to become less of a physical *and psychological* presence in the home, by which I mean to say that not only did they interact less with their children but they also were probably less on their children's minds. An excellent critique of the separate-spheres argument may be found in Linda K. Kerber, "Separate Spheres, Female Worlds, Woman's Place: The Rhetoric of Women's History," *Journal of American History* 75 (1988), pp. 9–39. A briefer, more dated, but still helpful discussion may be found in Strasser, *Never Done,* pp. 314–15.

46. Demos, "The Changing Faces of Fatherhood," p. 442; Rotundo, "American Fatherhood," pp. 13–14. The idea of a "living" or "family" wage—a wage sufficient to support a man and his dependents—was first proposed toward the end of the nineteenth and the beginning of the twentieth centuries. Intended to lend dignity to both male breadwinning and True Womanhood, it was embraced by men and women alike. It also was endorsed by the religious and political elite. Pope Leo XIII's 1891 encyclical "On the Conditions of Labor" was one of the first public documents to broach the idea; and President Woodrow Wilson in 1917 suggested it as a guiding principle in determining the wages for companies involved in industrial production for the First World War. See Eli Zaretsky, "The Place of the Family in the Origins of the Welfare State," in *Rethinking the Family: Some Feminist Questions,* ed. Barrie Thorne with Marilyn Yalom (New York: Longman, 1982), pp. 216–17.

47. In their book, *The Second Shift: Working Parents and the Revolution at Home* (New York: Viking, 1989), Arlie Hochschild and Anne Machung use the phrase "the second shift" to refer to the family work that employed women generally end up having to do when they get home at the end of the day. I may be distorting their meaning here, applying it to what men were increasingly being expected to do during the Progressive era, but I think the parallels are worth noting.

48. Margaret Marsh, "Suburban Men and Masculine Domesticity, 1870–1915," in *Meanings for Manhood: Constructions of Masculinity in Victorian America,* ed. Mark C. Carnes and Clyde Griffen (Chicago: University of Chicago Press, 1990). An earlier version of this chapter was published in *American Quarterly* 40 (June 1988), pp. 165–86. See also Margaret Marsh, *Suburban Lives* (New Brunswick, NJ: Rutgers University Press, 1990).

49. Bernarr Macfadden, *Manhood and Marriage* (1916), p. 81, as cited in Marsh, "Suburban Men and Masculine Domesticity," p. 123. All of the information in this paragraph is from Marsh.

50. Rotundo, *American Manhood,* p. 263; italics deleted.

51. Marsh, "Suburban Men and Masculine Domesticity," p. 122.

52. The essay is by Clyde Griffen: "Reconstructing Masculinity from the Evangelical Revival to the Waning Progressivism: A Speculative Synthesis," in *Meanings for Manhood: Constructions of Masculinity in Victorian America,* ed. Mark C. Carnes and Clyde Griffen (Chicago: University of Chicago Press, 1990). Griffen refers to Marsh and clearly uses her thoughts as a springboard for his own, but does not reveal why he chooses to invert Marsh's term. One possibility is that Griffen's essay focuses on masculinity, and specifically on different kinds of masculinity. Thus, for him, it is masculinity, not domesticity, that was being modified. Marsh, on the other hand, may have been more concerned about domesticity and its modifications.

53. Carnes, *Secret Ritual and Manhood in Victorian America;* Marsh, "Suburban Men and Masculine Domesticity," p. 116; Richard Sennett, *Families Against the City: Middle Class Homes of Industrial Chicago, 1872–1890* (Cambridge, MA: Harvard University Press, 1970), p. 47.

54. Mintz and Kellogg, *Domestic Revolutions*, p. 46.

55. Carnes, *Secret Ritual and Manhood in Victorian America*, p. 206; Degler, *At Odds*, pp. 3–25; Griswold, *Family and Divorce in California*, pp. 4–17; Marsh, "Suburban Men and Masculine Domesticity," pp. 245–46; Mintz and Kellogg, *Domestic Revolutions*, pp. 107–31; Rotundo, *American Manhood*, pp. 163–64.

56. Griffen, "Reconstructing Masculinity," p. 197.

57. Some controversy actually has arisen among historians over exactly when the companionate family in general became a significant part of the American social fabric. On one side, there are those who argue that the companionate family had become a reality by the mid-1800s (see Degler, *At Odds;* Griswold, *Family and Divorce in California*). On the other are those who contend that the companionate family did not become a part of American society until the late 1800s or early 1900s (see Carnes, *Secret Ritual and Manhood in Victorian America*, p. 206; Marsh "Suburban Men and Masculine Domesticity," p. 246; Mintz and Kellogg, *Domestic Revolutions*, pp. 107–31). Periodization is always tricky, but the bulk of the evidence seems to support the second view. This is especially true, if the distinction between culture and conduct is not ignored (see Rotundo, *American Manhood*, pp. 163–64). As an ideal, the companionate family may have begun to take root earlier; but, as a middle-class practice, it probably was not adopted on anything approximating a wide scale until later.

58. Cantor, *Twentieth-Century Culture*, pp. 23, 25.

59. See Demos, "The Changing Faces of Fatherhood," p. 442; Stearns, *Be a Man!*, p. 107

60. Marsh, "Suburban Men and Masculine Domesticity," pp. 123–126.

61. Industrialization and urbanization brought prosperity to many, no doubt, but in the aftermath came also a general sense of unease, even fear. Overcrowding, poverty, delinquency, inadequate health care—these were not new problems, of course. But never before had so many people been affected, or so it seemed. Of utmost concern to many were the children. How were they faring through all of this? Could they be spared the negative consequences of industrialization and urbanization? Some thought the situation hopeless. Civilization, they were convinced, was at its end. Others, however, were less pessimistic. Good old American ingenuity, these individuals thought, could put things right; children could be saved, *if* the country was willing to turn the problems over to the experts. The child-saving movement was instrumental to the development of masculine domesticity and domestic masculinity because it made the fate of children a social problem. Men, who otherwise might not think much about family issues, but who prided themselves on being society's troubleshooters, got drawn into the movement of trying to save the children. Not just their own children; everybody's children. Thus, not surprisingly, the first fatherhood clubs were not small groups of men trying to figure out how to relate to their own sons and daughters; they were large groups of men trying to improve the public schools or public parks—in short, the community. This is not to say that the child-saving movement did not focus men's attention on their own children, because it did. People were being told that industrialization and urbanization had created a dangerous world. Unless fathers, along with mothers, were vigilant, the bad things that were happening

to other parents' children (as reported in the newspaper), could easily happen to theirs. As is often the case, external threats to a group reinforced internal solidarity.

62. Needless to say, child scientists were around before the 1910s, and moral reformers continued to plug away afterwards, but "the intellectual and ideological emphases of each period were distinct" enough to think of them as separate. See Hamilton Cravens, "Child Saving in the Age of Professionalism," in *American Childhood: A Research Guide and Historical Handbook*, ed. Joseph M. Hawes and N. Ray Hiner (Westport, CT: Greenwood Press, 1985), pp. 417–18.) The mothercraft movement was based, in part, on the belief that relying on maternal instinct to raise children was not only unscientific but also dangerous: "Four hundred thousand children under five die in one year in the United States. Of that number it is roughly estimated that two hundred thousand, that is, one-half, die of preventable diseases. Who might have prevented them? . . . Accidental infection may be to blame sometimes, or poverty, or a stupid nurse, or a careless doctor. But there is one cause more blamable and more alarming than all these others—often concealed behind these others—and that is the fact that a large majority of our mothers do not know the ABC of scientific motherhood. The mothers of thousands of these babies who die are those who might have prevented the deaths." See Sarah Comstock, "Mothercraft: A New Profession for Women," *Good Housekeeping*, December 1914, pp. 672–78.

63. Mary L. Read, *The Mothercraft Manual* (Boston: Little, Brown, 1916), p. xii.

64. Ibid., p. 8.

65. Ibid., pp. 5–6

66. It is imperative to keep in mind that, as active as women were in the gender politics surrounding the fathercraft and mothercraft movements, they still were operating within rules that had been largely created by men. Mary L. Read and the others who were involved in the early-twentieth-century fathercraft and mothercraft movement did make a concerted effort to protect a mother's place in the parental stratification system, to be sure, but it was not a question of women hogging power and wanting more. Motherhood was the only domain where men had allowed women to have some *semblance* of control. If women lost their rights and privileges here, what would they have left? To what social position(s) could they tie their identities then? Semblance of control or not, however, the fact that the fathercraft and mothercraft movements were made real through fathering and mothering discourses also meant that the power structure between husbands and wives and between men and women in general would figure significantly in the social construction of parenthood. Communication, whether outside the family or in, always occurs in a political context.

67. Marsh, "Suburban Men and Masculine Domesticity," p. 126.

68. The notion here that there was a cultural expectation that fathers should be responsible for counterbalancing the emotionally laden and potentially destructive influence of women is nicely described in Stephanie A. Shields and Beth A. Koster, "Emotional Stereotyping of Parents in Child-Rearing Manuals, 1915–1980," *Social Psychology Quarterly* 52 (1989), pp. 44–55.

Chapter 3: Fatherhood and the Baby Doctors

1. Luther Emmet Holt, *The Care and Feeding of Children: A Catechism for the Use of Mothers and Children's Nurses* (New York: D. Appleton and Company, 1894).

2. Hamilton Cravens, "Child-Saving in the Age of Professionalism," in *American Childhood: A Research Guide and Historical Handbook*, ed. Joseph M. Hawes and N. Ray Hiner (Westport, CT: Greenwood Press, 1985), p. 417.

3. When *The Care and Feeding of Children* was published, Holt was Professor of Diseases of Children in the New York Polyclinic as well as Attending Physician to the Babies' Hospital and the Nursery and Child's Hospital in New York City. He would soon become a professor at the College of Physicians and Surgeons of Columbia University.

4. Holt, *The Care and Feeding of Children*, p. 3.

5. Ibid., pp. 3–4. Because *The Care and Feeding of Children* was written for nurses, one might be inclined to believe that the book was aimed exclusively at the upper classes; however, in the late nineteenth century, domestic servants were much more common than they are today—and also less expensive to employ. After carefully studying the history of household labor, Susan Strasser found that "[i]n 1870, the first year the United States census listed occupations for women of all ages and races, one woman listed herself as a domestic servant for every 8.4 families in the population. Most prevalent in urban areas (where people had more money to spend), in the South (where many black women would work for low wages), and in places with large immigrant populations, domestic service embodied one possible solution—but by no means a universal one—to the care of nineteenth-century housekeeping." Susan Strasser, *Never Done: A History of American Housework* (New York: Pantheon, 1982), p. 163.

As the opportunity for factory work expanded in the early twentieth century, the number of young women choosing domestic nursing declined, which in turn increased the amount of child care not only for mothers but for others in the home as well. With less outside help, there were fewer caregivers available to carry the parenting load, and thus greater pressure on all members of the family—fathers, brothers, and sisters—to pitch in when needed. A very different pattern occurred with respect to housework, where the absence of servants meant more toil for women, and perhaps only women. The fact is, though, housework and childwork are not the same thing. Simply stated, dishes do not scream to be cleaned; but babies do. See Ruth Schwartz Cowan, *More Work for Mother: The Ironies of Household Technology form the Open Hearth to the Microwave* (New York: Basic Books, 1983), pp 119–26; also Cowan, "Two Washes in the Morning and a Bridge Party at Night: The American Housewife between the Wars," *Women's Studies* 3 (1976), pp. 147–72.

6. Holt, *The Care and Feeding of Children*, 2d ed. (New York: D. Appleton and Company, 1897), p. 23.

7. Holt, *The Care and Feeding of Children*, 1894, preface to the first edition.

8. Holt, *The Care and Feeding of Children*, 1897, preface to the second edition.

9. While doctors had always treated children as well as adults, and while American medical schools, at least since the 1840s, had taught courses on children's

diseases, it was not until the late 1800s that pediatrics became a distinct medical specialty in the United States. See Cravens, "Child-Saving in the Age of Professionalism," p. 417; see also Dorothy Pawluch, "Transitions in Pediatrics: A Segmental Analysis," *Social Problems* 30 (April 1983), pp. 449–65.

10. The Children's Bureau was charged especially with investigating "infant mortality, the birth rate, orphanage [*sic*], juvenile courts, desertion, dangerous occupations, accidents and diseases of children, employment, [and] legislation affecting children in several States and Territories. U.S. *Statutes at Large* 37, pt. 1 (1912), pp. 79–80, as reported in Jacqueline K. Parker and Edward M. Carpenter, "Julia Lathrop and the Children's Bureau: The Emergence of an Institution," *Social Service Review* 55 (March 1981), pp. 60–77. For historical accounts on the origin and structure of the Children's Bureau, see Molly Ladd-Taylor, *Raising a Baby the Government Way: Mothers' Letters to the Children's Bureau, 1915–1932* (New Brunswick, NJ: Rutgers University Press, 1986), pp. 1–46; Theda Skocpol, *Protecting Soldiers and Mothers: The Political Origins of Social Policy in the United States* (Cambridge, MA: Harvard University Press, 1992), pp. 480–524; Nancy Pottishman Weiss, "Save the Children: A History of the Children's Bureau, 1903–1918" (Ph.D. diss., University of California at Los Angeles, 1974). The size of the Children's Bureau staff in 1912 was 14 or 15. By 1915, the staff had grown to between 70 and 76. See Parker and Carpenter, "Julia Lathrop and the Children's Bureau; also Skocpol, *Protecting Soldiers and Mothers*, p. 481, each of whom offer different figures, though 15 is also the number that Katherine Lenroot, Bureau Chief, 1934–1951, offered (in Katherine Lenroot, "A Link Between the Children's Bureau and Parents," manuscript, date unknown, Box 139, Children's Bureau Papers, National Archives). By 1937, the staff had grown to 230, "including permanent and temporary employees both in Washington and elsewhere." The point made then was that "the staff of the Bureau has never been a large one. It has been the practice to keep a minimum permanent staff and employ certain staff members on a temporary basis for the limited period of a specific study." *The Children's Bureau: Yesterday, Today, and Tomorrow* (Washington, DC: U.S. Department of Labor, Children's Bureau, 1937), p. 13.

11. Ladd-Taylor, *Raising a Baby the Government Way.*

12. Edward Zigler and Susan Muenchow, "A Room of Their Own: A Proposal to Renovate the Children's Bureau," *American Psychologist* 40 (August 1985), pp. 953–59.

13. By the 1960s, some of the more important children's programs (e.g., Maternal and Child Health) had been transferred from the Children's Bureau to other agencies. "Overtaken by an increasingly complex government, the changing needs of families and children, turf battles, and the reorganization of the Department of Health, Education, and Welfare, the Children's Bureau [to the disappointment of some] lost power, funds, and status within the executive branch" (Zigler and Muenchow, "A Room of Their Own," p. 954). Also, America's war against infant mortality, of course, was not being waged solely in the United States. For a discussion of Canadian efforts along the same lines, see Katherine Arnup, *Education for Motherhood: Advice for Mothers in Twentieth-Century Canada* (Toronto: University of Toronto Press, 1994).

14. In Kelley's words, "If lobsters or young salmon become scarce or are in

danger of perishing, the United States Fish Commission takes active steps in the matter. But infant mortality continues excessive [*sic*]; yet no one organ of the national government is interested in the matter sufficiently even to gather, collate and publish consecutive information about this social phenomenon." Kelley 1905, as cited in Kristine Siefert, "An Exemplar of Primary Prevention in Social Work: The Sheppard-Towner Act of 1921," *Social Work in Health Care* 9 (Fall 1993), p. 88.

15. *The Children's Bureau: Yesterday, Today, and Tomorrow,* p. 1.

16. Parker and Carpenter, "Julia Lathrop and the Children's Bureau, p. 60.

17. Ladd-Taylor, *Raising a Baby the Government Way,* p. 7.

18. The original appropriation for the Children's Bureau was $25,640. In 1915, Congress increased the budget to $164,640 (see Skocpol, *Protecting Soldiers and Mothers,* p. 481). A lot of money, to be sure; but not a lot when you think about what the Children's Bureau was being asked to do. Was the Children's Bureau successful in its mission? It is difficult, if not impossible, to sort out the contribution that it made. It is noteworthy, however, that deaths of children in the United States during the first twelve months of life declined from 100 per 1,000 live births in 1915 to 39 per 1,000 live births in 1945. See "Inter-Agency Committee on Background Materials," 1948, p. 238, Information Files Box 50, Children's Bureau Papers, National Archives.

19. Lathrop's background in social service and her commitment to the "sociological" rather than the medical aspects of child welfare were instrumental in establishing the Children's Bureau mission as a fact-finding and social service agency. In testimony before Congress, she assured wary Senators, "We are not, in this inquiry, going into distinctly medical matters, but into social and industrial and economic surroundings of the families, including the hygienic surroundings of the child in the community in which it is born." *Hearings on the Legislative, Executive, Judicial Appropriations Bill,* 62nd Congress, 2nd session, 14 December 1912, as cited in Parker and Carpenter, "Julia Lathrop and the Children's Bureau," p. 76.

20. Ladd-Taylor, *Raising a Baby the Government Way,* p. 13.

21. Female reformers "wanted to expand women's rights but did not dream that women could find fulfillment outside of motherhood." Female employment also was couched in terms of motherhood: "As nurses, social workers, and physicians, women professionals fulfilled their maternal obligation to society by engaging in interesting and socially recognized (paid) work outside the home." Ibid., p. 12.

22. The first male Chief of the Children's Bureau was appointed in 1968. See Zigler and Muenchow, "A Room of Their Own," p. 957.

23. These are the dates of the revisions during the Machine Age. *Infant Care* continued to be widely circulated after World War II and is still in print. The principal focus of *Infant Care* was the care of children from the first few weeks "to the close of the second year." Technically speaking, *Infant Care* was the first child-rearing manual that the Children's Bureau published. It was not, however, the first manual for parents that the Bureau published. That distinction goes to *Prenatal Care* (1913). The focus of *Prenatal Care,* as the title suggests, was the medical aspects of pregnancy and childbirth. The very first pamphlet that the Children's Bureau issued was not a child-rearing or a parents' manual at all, but a research report addressed to government agencies and organizations that relied upon vital

statistics. It was titled "Birth Registration: An Aid in Protecting the Lives and Rights of Children." A companion volume to *Infant Care* was *Child Care,* issued in 1918 and later retitled *Your Child from One to Six.*

24. See, for example, Michael Gordon, "Infant Care Revisited," *Journal of Marriage and the Family* 30 (November 1968), pp. 578–83; Ladd-Taylor, *Raising a Baby the Government Way;* Maxine L. Margolis, *Mothers and Such: Views of American Women and Why They Changed* (Berkeley, CA: University of California Press, 1984); Nancy Pottishman Weiss, "Mother, the Invention of Necessity: Dr. Benjamin Spock's *Baby and Child Care,*" *American Quarterly* 29 (Winter 1977); Martha Wolfenstein, "Trends in Infant Care," *American Journal of Orthopsychiatry* 23 (January 1953), pp. 120–30.

25. Ladd-Taylor, *Raising a Baby the Government Way,* p. 11. Mary Mills West had also been the author of *Prenatal Care.*

26. *Infant Care* (Washington, DC: U.S. Department of Labor, Children's Bureau, 1914), p. 7. The "Letter of Transmittal" was reprinted in the manual as a matter of course, at least for editions published during the Machine Age.

27. Ladd-Taylor, *Raising a Baby the Government Way,* pp. 33–34.

28. Ibid., p. 2. The 17 million figure comes from Ruth Crawford to Mr. Fitzgerald, Box 139, 21 August 1945, Children's Bureau Papers, National Archives. Thus, *Infant Care* probably did more than any other manual in early-twentieth-century America to disseminate a "scientific" child-rearing approach to the general public. Its publication by the U.S. Department of Labor gave it an air of legitimacy that neither Holt's book nor any other book, for that matter, could claim. *Infant Care* was the word *ex cathedra*—the bible on "raising a baby *the government way*" (to borrow the title of Ladd-Taylor's 1986 book). On a related topic, the late comedian Jimmy Durante had a favorite punch line that some will remember: "Everybody wants to get into the act." Well, if Durante had decided to dedicate his time to studying early-twentieth-century child-rearing manuals rather than becoming one of the most popular comics of his era, he probably would be the least surprised to learn that between the time that Holt wrote *The Care and Feeding of Children* and the time that West wrote *Infant Care,* the inimitable "bachelor," "curmudgeon," and early-twentieth-century superstar newspaperman and magazine editor H. L. Mencken wrote *What You Ought to Know about Your Baby: A Textbook for Mothers on the Care and Feeding of Babies* (in 1910). As the preface to a recent reprint of the book aptly notes, "If one were challenged to list the most unlikely authors of a baby book, H. L. Mencken should soon appear, perhaps just following W. C. Fields." Mencken's hand in the book until recently was not widely known because *What You Ought to Know about Your Baby* was released with Leonard Keene Hirshberg, B.A., M.D. as the only author—"in order to enhance its credibility with mothers." What the Mencken story illustrates is how, in some circles, the "science" of infant care was a very serious—and potentially profitable—game. Well-written manuals "authored" by doctors were considered a winning combination. (The factual information in the book, interestingly enough, was based almost entirely on Holt's *The Care and Feeding of Children.*) Needless to say, even Mencken could not compete with the federal government. *Infant Care* would eventually find its way into millions of homes; *What You Ought to Know about Your Baby* sold in the tens of thousands of copies (hard figures are

unavailable), though it did go through several printings and continued to be reissued by the publisher until 1923. See Howard Markel, M.D., and Frank A. Oski, M.D., *The H. L. Mencken Baby Book: Comprising the Contents of H. L. Mencken's "What You Ought to Know about Your Baby" with Commentaries* (Philadelphia, PA: Hanley & Belfus, 1990).

29. For example: "A healthy baby should be bathed every day. During the first two weeks these and all matters pertaining to the care of the baby are usually under the doctor's or nurse's supervision. When the *mother* takes charge of the baby she will find it convenient, usually, to give the bath before the midmorning feeding and after the bowels have moved [my italics]." See *Infant Care* (1914), p. 26.

30. Ibid., pp. 34–35; italics in original.

31. Ibid., pp. 59–60.

32. *Infant Care* (1921) p. 9.

33. "Around 1875, doctors first began referring to the study and treatment of the diseases of children as *pediatry* or *pedology*. The terms were derived from the Greek word *pais, paidos,* meaning "child." Doctors who treated children were called *pediatrists*. These terms persisted until the early twentieth century, when they were replaced with *pediatrics* and *pediatrician*. See Pawluch, "Transitions in Pediatrics," p. 451.

34. *Infant Care* (1921), p. 37.

35. Ibid., p. 79.

36. Ibid., p. 6.

37. *Infant Care* (1929) p. v.

38. Letter to Julia Lathrop, cited in Weiss, "Mother, the Invention of Necessity," p. 530. Understanding how physicians succeeded in taking control of *Infant Care* in 1929 requires some understanding of the events surrounding the Sheppard-Towner Maternity and Infancy Protection Act of 1921. The Sheppard-Towner Act created "the first federal program to provide grants to states to develop preventive health services for mothers and children." To many in the social service community, it was "an exemplar of primary prevention"; the act, indeed, was instrumental in "substantially reducing infant mortality and morbidity." See Siefert, "An Exemplar of Primary Prevention in Social Work, p. 87. The Sheppard-Towner Act, however, was opposed from the start and eventually undone by political conservatives, anti-suffragists, and, most important, the American Medical Association, which saw the bill as "socialized medicine." Not everyone in the medical profession was against Sheppard-Towner. The Pediatric Section of the AMA endorsed it; so did the Medical Woman's National Association. But their support was not sufficient to offset the AMA's influence on Capitol Hill, and in 1929 the Sheppard-Towner Act was repealed.

The fight over the act served to fuel the negative sentiment of physicians toward the Children's Bureau, and the death of the program spelled the triumph of the medical perspective over the social reform approach of the Bureau's founders. By the late 1920s, "consult a physician" was the most common recommendation made by the bureau staff to the parents who wrote them and "doctor knows best" was one of the main messages that the 1929 edition of *Infant Care* conveyed. Ladd-Taylor, *Raising a Baby the Government Way*, pp. 23–32. For other sources on the

Sheppard-Towner Maternity and Infancy Protection Act, see Barbara M. Rothman, *Woman's Proper Place: A History of Changing Ideals and Practices* (New York: Basic Books, 1978), pp. 136–53; and Skocpol, *Protecting Soldiers and Mothers*, pp. 480–524.

39. John B. Watson, *Psychology from the Standpoint of a Behaviorist* (Philadelphia: J. B. Lippincott, 1919); John B. Watson, *Psychological Care of Infant and Child* (New York: W. W. Norton, 1928).

40. There is some disagreement over just how influential behaviorism was in the 1920s and 1930s. In her book *The Damned and the Beautiful: American Youth in the 1920s* (New York: Oxford University Press, 1977), Paula Fass argues that "Watson left his stamp on many American homes, but his ideas were sparingly incorporated into the family literature of the late twenties and thirties. He could not reverse the emphasis on affection that was the dominant note among family experts" (pp. 106–7). Drawing on Fass, Robert L. Griswold in *Fatherhood in America: A History* (New York: Basic Books, 1993) also says Watson's work was a "minority stream" approach to child rearing in the 1920s; that the "more dominant stream stressed affection, love, tenderness, and understanding within the family" (pp. 301–2). In contrast to these views, Weiss in "Mother, the Invention of Necessity," says that "[w]ith the advent of behaviorism in the 1920s and its hegemony in child rearing literature through the 1930s, the care of children began to lose the political affect and concern for maternal well-being that marked Progressive texts. John B. Watson, psychology's *enfant terrible,* wrote popular articles on child rearing for *Collier's* and *Harper's.* His behavioristic psychology, and particularly ideas from *Psychological Care of Infant and Child* (1928), were swiftly incorporated into child rearing advice of the late twenties and thirties" (pp. 529–30). Similarly, Terry Strathman in "From the Quotidian to the Utopian: Child-Rearing Literature in America, 1926–1946," *Berkeley Journal of Sociology* 49 (1984), pp. 1–34, argues that "[i]n the mid-twenties child-rearing specialists had advocated the rigid training and feeding schedules associated with the behaviorist approach of Dr. John Watson" (p. 1). It may be too strong to say that Watson's ideas were *the* most influential canon of the 1920s and 1930s, as Weiss suggests, but something is overlooked, too, if Watson's notions are relegated to a "minority" role. Without a doubt, Watson's ideas about child rearing were incorporated into *Infant Care,* which, as Maxine L. Margolis points out in *Mothers and Such,* "guaranteed them a large audience" (p. 52). Ben Harris may have said it best in his article "'Give Me a Dozen Healthy Infants . . . ': John B. Watson's Popular Advice on Childrearing, Women, and the Family," in *In the Shadow of the Past: Psychology Portrays the Sexes,* ed. Miriam Lewin (New York: Columbia University Press, 1984):

> To the general public, Watson became known in the 1920s through his lecturing, his many articles in magazines such as *Harper's* and *McCall's,* and through books such as his best-selling *Psychological Care of Infant and Child.* In these popular forums, Watson's message was both unorthodox in content and dramatic in style; it is best exemplified by his often repeated story of how he experimentally induced a severe animal phobia in a young infant named "Albert." The cumulative effect of such stories, of Watson's public exposure, and of the controversy surrounding his theories was significant. It was such that by the end of the decade, mil-

lions had heard about the new behavioristic view of childrearing, marriage, and family life. Regardless of whether the public completely believed these popularized concepts of Watson, his writings were soon required reading for the middle classes—rivaling psychoanalysis as the popular psychology of the moment. (p. 127)

See also Ben Harris, "What Ever Happened to Little Albert, *American Psychologist* 34 (1979), pp. 151–60.

41. Ladd-Taylor, *Raising a Baby the Government Way,* p. 34.
42. Weiss, "Mother, the Invention of Necessity," p. 525.
43. *Infant Care* (1929), p. 2.
44. Ibid., p. 54.
45. Ibid., p. 121.
46. Strathman, "From the Quotidian to the Utopian," p. 19.
47. I am not ignoring the fact that the science of child rearing, as exemplified by behaviorism, had a tendency to reify gender stereotypes, and that to some extent it was a conservative influence in the social construction of gender. See Clyde Griffen, "Reconstructing Masculinity from the Evangelical Revival to the Waning of Progressivism," in *Meanings for Manhood: Constructions of Masculinity in Victorian America,* ed. Mark C. Carnes and Clyde Griffen (Chicago: University of Chicago Press, 1990), p. 201; also Griswold, *Fatherhood in America,* pp. 89, 116–17. I am simply pointing out that the same scientific ideology could support a more father-inclusive outcome, one in which fathers and mothers cooperated in the care of their infants, albeit with mothers still the care managers. It is interesting in this regard that scholars who tend to paint a relatively pessimistic (men were hardly involved) view of fatherhood during the Machine Age tend also to neglect or downplay both infant care manuals as well as the division of infant care itself. Ironically, however, while these are the texts and behaviors over which mothers seem to have had the most influence, they are also revealing, especially if examined in detail, for the extent to which they show that culture and conduct were not always in sync. More on this asynchrony appears in the next chapter.
48. *Infant Care* (1931).
49. *Infant Care* (1931; 1935 printing), p. 128.
50. *Infant Care* (1938), p. ii.
51. Ibid., p. 2.
52. Ibid., pp. 6–7.
53. *Infant Care* (1940), p. ii.
54. *Infant Care* (1942), p. vii.
55. *Infant Care* (1929), pp. 53–54.
56. *Infant Care* (1942), p. 56.
57. Ibid., p. 61.
58. Weiss, "Mother, the Invention of Necessity," pp. 35–36.
59. *Infant Care* (1942), inside front cover.
60. Ibid., p. 1
61. Ibid., pp. 2, 32.
62. Ibid., pp. 33, 42, 43.
63. Ibid., p. 125.
64. Alice Boardman Smuts, "History and Research in Child Development," in

History and Research in Child Development, ed. Alice Boardman Smuts and John W. Hagen (Monograph of the Society for Research in Child Development, vol. 50, nos. 4–5, serial number 211, 1985), p. 112. See also chapter 2, note 62.

65. Leroy Ashby, "Partial Promises and Semi-Visible Youths: The Depression and World War II," in *American Childhood: A Research Guide and Historical Handbook,* ed. Joseph M. Hawes and N. Ray Hiner (Westport, CT: Greenwood Press), p. 502.

66. Smuts, "History and Research in Child Development," p. 124; also Harriet Rheingold, "The First Twenty-Five Years of the Society for Research in Child Development," in *History and Research in Child Development,* ed. Smuts and Hagen, pp. 126–40.

67. Cravens, "Child-Saving in the Age of Professionalism," p. 449.

68. Of course, unless we know *all* the decisions that went into retaining or altering a passage in a book and know, too, the editors and reviewers employed from one edition to the next, we never can be sure what accounts for continuity and change in a multiple-edition work.

69. Florence Brown Sherbon, *The Child: His Origin, Development, and Care* (New York: McGraw-Hill, 1934 and 1941); John J. B. Morgan, *Child Psychology* (New York: Richard R. Smith, 1931, 1934, and 1942); Winifred Rand, Mary Sweeny, and E. Lee Vincent, *Growth and Development of the Young Child* (Philadelphia: W. B. Saunders, 1930, 1934, and 1940); Ruth Strang, *An Introduction to Child Study* (New York: Macmillan, 1930 and 1938). Some of the these textbooks were revised *after* 1942. A fourth edition of *Growth and Development of the Young Child,* for example, came out in 1946. But these later editions, which fall too far out of the Machine Age, will not be discussed here.

70. Strang, *An Introduction to Child Study* (1930), pp. 112–13.

71. Rand et al., *Growth and Development of the Young Child* (1930), pp. 23, 25, 27. One sentence edited out of this excerpt is interesting for its feminist overtones: "The 'women who work' (a phrase which amusingly is used in such a way that it excludes the woman at home—as if she did not work!) [*sic*] are found not only among those women who are compelled to work in order to feed hungry mouths, but are found also in other classes."

72. Strang, *An Introduction to Child Study* (1938), p. 79.

73. Rand et al., *Growth and Development of the Young Child* (1940) p. 364.

74. Morgan, *Child Psychology* (1931), p. 73; (1934), p. 79; (1942), p. 506.

75. Morgan, *Child Psychology* (1942), pp. vii–viii.

76. Ibid., p. 196.

77. Sherbon, *The Child* (1934), p. vii.

78. Ibid., pp. 274, 376.

79. Sherbon, *The Child* (1941), p. ix.

80. Ibid., p. 706.

81. Ibid., pp. 8–9.

82. Ibid., pp. 10–11.

83. When I first read Sherbon's case study, I was struck by how similar it was to a case study that Maureen Mulligan LaRossa and I had written years ago. In our case study, just as in Sherbon's, a college professor rotated the care of his newborn son with his wife, also a college professor. He would take the morning shift while

she taught her classes; she would reciprocate by taking the afternoon shift while he taught his classes. In-depth interviews with the couple revealed a more traditional arrangement than was immediately apparent. See Ralph LaRossa and Maureen Mulligan LaRossa, *Transition to Parenthood: How Infants Change Families* (Beverly Hills, CA: Sage, 1981), in particular chapter 8, "Sharon and Stuart."

Chapter 4: Men and Infants

1. A.H.D. to Children's Bureau, Box 26, 17 February 1915, Children's Bureau Papers, National Archives. I said that a parent wrote this letter, because only initials were given by the writer.

2. Nancy Pottishman Weiss estimates that the bureau sometimes received as many as 125,00 letters in a year. Nancy Pottishman Weiss, "Mother, the Invention of Necessity: Dr. Benjamin Spock's *Baby and Child Care*," *American Quarterly* 29 (Winter 1977), pp. 519–46. My estimate of 400,000 over a number of years is based on my examining the card file that the Children's Bureau kept. (Each letter received, for at least some period of time, was recorded on its own card and then alphabetically arranged under the last name of the letter writer. If someone wrote to the bureau again, that fact would be noted by the additional entries on the card.) What I saw were forty drawers of cards, but some of the cards in the drawers may have reflected letters written after the Machine Age. My scan suggested that there were about 11,000 cards per drawer.

3. The Children's Bureau received volumes of mail, including products sent by manufacturers hoping to get the agency's endorsement (which the Children's Bureau refused to give). Every item received, it seems, was retained and is now part of the collection. One of the more interesting artifacts was a metal thumb cage that was designed to be affixed to a baby's thumb to prevent thumb sucking. (Try chewing a mouthful of paper clips.)

4. See *Preliminary Inventory of the Records of the Children's Bureau* [PIRCB], Record Group 102. (Washington, DC: National Archives and Records Administration, 1976), p. 11. I say that the correspondence related to allergies to foods "might" be coded 4-5-11-5-6 because the staff changed its coding scheme every now and then. Thus, letters on allergies to food prior to World War I could be coded one way, and letters on the same subject written during the Depression could be coded another way. Researchers planning to examine the Children's Bureau collection should familiarize themselves with the historical writings on the agency, in particular Molly Ladd-Taylor, *Raising a Baby the Government Way: Mothers' Letters to the Children's Bureau* (New Brunswick, NJ: Rutgers University Press, 1986) and Weiss, "Mother, the Invention of Necessity." Also I recommend looking through not only the printed finding aid in the manuscript reading room— the PIRCB, cited above—but also the mimeographed finding aids (of which there are several) in the archivists' offices. The PIRCB, I learned, is not sufficient to decipher the codes for all time periods.

5. The archivists at the National Archives were a tremendous help, but one person, in particular, helped me navigate through the Children's Bureau's files: Aloha South. Not only did she teach me the ins and outs of the coding system, but, on several occasions, she escorted me through the stacks (a closed area) to allow me to see whether my request for a particular box would turn up anything of value.

6. See Ladd-Taylor, *Raising a Baby the Government Way,* and Weiss, "Mother, the Invention of Necessity."

7. Ladd-Taylor, *Raising a Baby the Government Way,* pp. 2, 3. Ladd-Taylor also notes that "the Bureau's cumbersome filing system makes impractical a quantitative analysis of the region, education, or ethnicity of the correspondents" (p. 3).

8. Even among the very poor, total illiteracy was very uncommon. See Weiss, "Mother, the Invention of Necessity," p. 522.

9. Says Ladd-Taylor in *Raising a Baby the Government Way,* "The Children's Bureau letters show a striking contrast between the composed middle-class mother portrayed in the pamphlets and real women, who experienced a range and depth of emotions. Although the bulletins instructed new mothers to remain calm and happy, actual mothers were often overwhelmed by their combined household and child rearing responsibilities" (p. 42).

10. The mother, herself, wrote "cant" rather than "can't." The handwriting in the letters to the Children's Bureau is not always easy to decipher, and the spelling and grammar are sometimes poor. I have tried my best, here and throughout, to provide verbatim transcripts, so that the reader will have a sense of the immediacy and context that I had when I first read the letters. Periodically, I have taken the liberty of inserting a bracketed word or punctuation, if I thought that doing so would better communicate the letter writer's intent.

11. H.B. (Female) to Children's Bureau, Box 25, 28 February 1916, Children's Bureau Papers, National Archives.

12. Julia Lathrop to Doctor Hamilton, Box 25, 2 March 1916, Children's Bureau Papers, National Archives.

13. H.B.R. (female) to Children's Bureau, Box 25, 14 June 1920, Children's Bureau Papers, National Archives.

14. A.B. (female) to Children's Bureau, Box 368, September 1932, Children's Bureau Papers, National Archives.

15. F.K.M. (female) to Children's Bureau, Box 519, 20 November 1934, Children's Bureau Papers, National Archives.

16. H.W. (female) to President Franklin D. Roosevelt, Box 702, 8 October 1938, Children's Bureau Papers, National Archives.

17. F.B.J. (female) to Children's Bureau, Box 702, 11 January 1939, Children's Bureau Papers, National Archives.

18. For a recent discussion on this distinction and its importance for understanding contemporary fatherhood, see Frank F. Furstenberg Jr., "Good Dads— Bad Dads: Two Faces of Fatherhood," in *The Changing American Family and Public Policy,* ed. Andrew J. Cherlin (Washington, DC: Urban Institute Press, 1988); also E. Anthony Rotundo, "American Fatherhood: A Historical Perspective," *American Behavioral Scientist* 29 (September/October 1985), pp. 7–25.

19. E.S. (female) to Children's Bureau, Box 269, 13 January 1928, Children's Bureau Papers, National Archives.

20. Viola Anderson, Children's Bureau, to E.S., Box 269, 21 January 1928, Children's Bureau Papers, National Archives.

21. G.M. (female) to Children's Bureau, Box 368, 3 November 1931, Children's Bureau Papers, National Archives.

22. R.H. (female) to Children's Bureau, Box 368, 20 June 1932, Children's Bureau Papers, National Archives.

23. M.W. (female) to Children's Bureau, Box 368, 27 June 1932, Children's Bureau Papers, National Archives.

24. Robert C. Angell found that for some fathers during the Depression a decrease in family income made them closer to their children. Robert C. Angell, *The Family Encounters the Depression* (New York: Charles Scribner's Sons, 1936), p. 91. Most studies indicate, however, that unemployment or income loss during the Depression had either no effect or a negative effect on father involvement. See chapter 1, note 34.

25. Weiss, "Mother, the Invention of Necessity," p. 523.

26. Ladd-Taylor, *Raising a Baby the Government Way*, p. 4.

27. Ladd-Taylor does include one letter from a father in *Raising a Baby the Government Way* (p. 196), but does not attach any significance to it. Weiss makes no mention of fathers in "Mother, the Invention of Necessity." Others who discuss the letters to the Children's Bureau letters as letters from mothers *only* include Nancy Cott, *The Grounding of Modern Feminism* (New Haven: Yale University Press, 1987), p. 168; Joseph M. Hawes and N. Ray Hiner, "Introduction," in *American Childhood: A Research Guide and Historical Handbook*, ed. Joseph M. Hawes and N. Ray Hiner (Westport, CT: Greenwood Press, 1985), pp. 9–10. Even the Children's Bureau talked as if the letters it received were only from women: "Mothers in all walks of life write to the Bureau to tell the staff how useful the booklet *[Infant Care]* has been to them." Katherine Lenroot, "A Link Between the Children's Bureau and Parents," Box 62, date unknown, Children's Bureau Papers, National Archives.

28. I do not know whether scholars who have combed through the Children's Bureau collection happened across the letters that I am about to review. I do think, however, that it is possible for someone to read a letter and interpret it in a variety of ways, perhaps not even remember it. In *The Structure of Scientific Revolutions* (Chicago: University of Chicago Press, 1962), Thomas Kuhn talks about how scientists interpret facts within existing paradigms and how those paradigms can prevent one from perceiving things. I believe I ran across something along these lines in the Children's Bureau correspondence. In the late 1930s, the Children's Bureau had written to the airlines to ask about the "special services" they provided to "mothers travelling with youngsters." An executive from Eastern Airlines replied to say that

> Eastern Airlines Flight Stewards are instructed to do whatever is possible to assist mothers with infants. When requested, they carry an extra thermos bottle containing hot water, this to facilitate warming the baby's bottle in case the infant must be fed while en route. Most mothers are well prepared for such en route feeding of their youngsters, therefore no special equipment is needed aboard the plane. Although no bassinettes are regularly provided for infant passengers, the Flight-Steward does what he can to make the infants comfortable by arranging pillows as a bed, which works out satisfactorily, as, usually, the babies sleep soundly throughout the flight.

Then, to illustrate his point, the executive attached a memo from a flight steward who described "his special service to a baby." The "special service" that the male attendant provided is that he changed the diaper of a baby who was in the company of his father and grandfather. Here is how the attendant described the scene:

> I recently had the honor of carrying our youngest passenger of the season on the DC-3 midnight express to Miami. This six-weeks-old baby was being taken by his father and grandfather to rejoin his mother who was convalescing from an operation down there. It wasn't long after the take-off when baby began to miss the nurse who had been taking care of him since birth. When nurse failed to respond to his first plaintive whimper, his babyship opened his lungs and brought forth a little louder hollering which presently developed into a vociferous protest. I tried every means of pacification which I could devise. I even gave him my watch to play with. But baby only squalled louder and kept the other unfortunate passengers awake. Then I decided to play both ends against the middle and supplied the other passengers with cotton to stuff their ears. This didn't help much either. Finally, a vague suspicion assailed me. Could it be—? I made a hurried survey. O Dear! O Dear! Yes, it was! Father, grandfather and I went into consultation, their knowledge of diaper technique was minus nil. Well, something had to be done. I made a momentous decision. Grimly spreading a blanket on the floor in the rear of the cabin, I took a deep breath and went to work. Baby promptly stopped crying, and, what's more, even smiled his gratitude! The operation was a complete success. Our little passenger drifted into peaceful slumber till the end of the trip, while your correspondent crossed his fingers, took two aspirins and subsided in the corner. (T.C. at Eastern Airlines to the Children's Bureau, with attachment from T.P.C at Eastern Airlines, Box 200, 27 May 1938, Children's Bureau Papers, National Archives.)

Three things struck me about this file. The first is that the father and grandfather did not change the diaper themselves, thus lending credence to the proposition that fathers of six-week old babies could remain uninformed about the rudiments of diapering, especially if they were able to employ a nurse. The second is that the person who did change the diaper and who sized up the problem almost immediately was a man. Where did he gain such knowledge? Did the situation—the midnight express over which he was responsible for the passengers' amenities—demand that he acquire such knowledge? The third and, to me at least, most significant point was the total disregard both in the airline executive's letter and in the Children's Bureau reply that this was a case study that had little, if anything, to do with mothers; it was a story about *men*. Why, I asked myself, were men not in the picture? Which led me to wonder: Were fathers not "in the picture" for the Children's Bureau staff? Could the parenting paradigm (in a Kuhnian sense) of the Children's Bureau account for why it waited so long to incorporate fathers in *Infant Care*? And as a corollary to that, Are yesterday's fathers "in the picture" for today's fathers—or historians?

29. See Nancy Pottishman Weiss, "The Mother-Child Dyad Revisited: Perceptions of Mothers and Children in Twentieth-Century Child-Rearing Manuals," *Journal of Social Issues* 34, no. 2 (1978), pp. 29–45.

30. I managed to copy sixty-two letters, fifty-one of which were written by men. This is not the percentage of men's letters in this category. I deliberately over-

sampled the men's letters. Also, the point is not that these fifty-one men were interested enough in their baby's feeding habits to write to the Children's Bureau. The question is, do these men represent the proverbial "tip of the iceberg?" For every man who cared enough to write, how many other men who cared as much if not more did not take pen in hand?

31. L.M.G. (male) to Children's Bureau, Box 27, 29 May 1915, Children's Bureau Papers, National Archives.

32. C.O. (male) to Children's Bureau, Box 26, 5 May 1915, Children's Bureau Papers, National Archives.

33. C.H. (male) to Children's Bureau, Box 27, 25 April 1916, Children's Bureau Papers, National Archives.

34. C.E.W. (male) to Children's Bureau, Box 27, 11 April 1919, Children's Bureau Papers, National Archives.

35. H.P. (male) to Children's Bureau, Box 30, 29 June 1919, Children's Bureau Papers, National Archives.

36. E.M.W. (male) to Children's Bureau, Box 188, 17 December 1921, Children's Bureau Papers, National Archives.

37. W.R.D. (male) to Children's Bureau, Box 187, 11 October 1923, Children's Bureau Papers, National Archives.

38. J.D.M. (male) to Children's Bureau, Box 500, 29 January 1935, Children's Bureau Papers, National Archives.

39. E.G. (male) to Children's Bureau, Box 675, 1938, Children's Bureau Papers, National Archives.

40. E.L.P. (male) to Children's Bureau, Box 271, 11 February 1927, Children's Bureau Papers, National Archives.

41. R.C.M. (male) to Children's Bureau, Box 500, 7 July 1936, Children's Bureau Papers, National Archives.

42. P.W.N. (male) to Children's Bureau, Box 675, 28 August 1938, Children's Bureau Papers, National Archives.

43. R.E.B. (male) to Children's Bureau, Box 675, 24 May 1939, Children's Bureau Papers, National Archives.

44. H.E.P. (male) to Children's Bureau, Box 676, 3 December 1940, Children's Bureau Papers, National Archives.

45. Sociologist Max Weber was one of the first to talk about the growth of "expert" (or legal-rational) power in industrialized societies. See Max Weber, *The Theory of Social and Economic Organization* (New York: Free Press, 1947). This is a translation of part 1 of Weber's *Wirtschaft and Gesellschaft* (published posthumously in 1922). Historian Christopher Lasch offered perhaps the most well-known and detailed analysis of the encroachment of the therapeutic culture on family life. See Christopher Lasch, *Haven in a Heartless World: The Family Besieged* (New York: Basic Books, 1977). See also Barbara Ehrenreich and Deidre English, *For Her Own Good: 150 Years of Experts' Advice to Women* (Garden City, NY: Anchor/Doubleday, 1978).

46. See, for example, Wendy Simonds, *Women and Self-Help Culture: Reading between the Lines* (New Brunswick, NJ: Rutgers University Press, 1992).

47. Ann Swidler, "Culture in Action: Symbols and Strategies," *American Sociological Review* 51 (April 1986), p. 277. For a discussion of the pitfalls associated

with viewing humans as "cultural dopes," see Harold Garfinkel, *Studies in Ethno-methodology* (Englewood Cliffs, NJ: Prentice Hall, 1967; Randall Stokes and John P. Hewitt, "Aligning Actions," *American Sociological Review* 41 (October 1976), pp. 838–49.

48. Terry Strathman, "From the Quotidian to the Utopian: Child-Rearing Literature in America, 1926–1946," *Berkeley Journal of Sociology* 29 (1984), p. 18. Earlier in the same article, Strathman notes that the child-rearing advice examined was "fragmentary and incoherent" and that this forced parents to have to decide what was useful and what was not: "If we examine again our sources of advice it will become apparent why parents—and especially parents from lower socio-economic classes—were left to make pragmatic 'pick-and-choose' decisions" (p. 17). Janice Radway also warns that one can take the reader-as-passive-consumer argument beyond what may be deemed reasonable theoretical limits: "[T]he consumption analogy is dangerous when it is carried too far, as it is when it is employed to characterize the actual process of text comprehension itself. To do so is to petrify the human act of signification, to ignore the fact that comprehension is actually a process of making meaning, a process of sign production where the reader actively attributes significance to signifiers on the basis of previously learned cultural codes." See Janice A. Radway, *Reading the Romance: Women, Patriarchy, and Popular Literature* (Chapel Hill, NC: University of North Carolina Press, 1984), pp. 6–7.

49. Robert L. Griswold, *Fatherhood in America: A History* (New York: Basic Books, 1993), pp. 129, 121. What is telling is Griswold's decision to omit fathers when he discusses the ability of some parents to use what works, and reinterpret and reject what does not.

50. W.G.C. (male) to Children's Bureau, Box 27, 20 February 1919, Children's Bureau Papers, National Archives.

51. J.H.C. (male) to Children' Bureau, Box 675, 4 August 1938, Children's Bureau Papers, National Archives.

52. Doug Welch, "We've Been Betrayed," *Esquire*, April 1939, pp. 65, 134.

53. Griswold, *Fatherhood in America*, p. 128.

54. In previous publications, I too have acknowledged the fact that child-rearing lore generally is aimed at mothers and that this has the potential effect of defining child rearing as women's work. See Ralph LaRossa, *Becoming a Parent* (Beverly Hills, CA: Sage, 1986), p. 15. See also Ralph LaRossa and Maureen Mulligan LaRossa, *Transition to Parenthood: How Infants Change Families* (Beverly Hills, CA: Sage, 1981), p. 57. But what was also conveyed, especially in *Transition to Parenthood*, is that this definition of the situation is not fixed but is an ongoing accomplishment, subject to the same political machinations that generally characterize the culture-conduct connection.

55. H.M. (female) to the U.S. Dept. of Agriculture, Box 271, 12 August 1926, Children's Bureau Papers, National Archives.

56. Alice M. Flood (Children's Bureau) to H.M., Box 271, 24 August 1926, Children's Bureau Papers, National Archives.

57. A.W.D. (male) to Children's Bureau, Box 28, 8 February 1917, Children's Bureau Papers, National Archives.

58. R.H. (female) to Children's Bureau, Box 29, 13 August 1920, Children's Bureau Papers, National Archives.

59. Dr. Anna E. Rude (Children's Bureau) to R.H., Box 29, 18 August 1920, Children's Bureau Papers, National Archives.

60. M.L.B. (male) to Children's Bureau, Box 501, 19 February 1935, Children's Bureau Papers, National Archives.

61. K.M. (female) to Children's Bureau, Box 501, 4 November 1933, Children's Bureau Papers, National Archives.

62. Dr. Ella Oppenheimer (Children's Bureau) to K.M., Box 501, 28 November 1933, Children's Bureau Papers, National Archives.

63. W.Q. (male) to Children's Bureau, Box 501, 13 March 1934, Children's Bureau Papers, National Archives.

64. E.P. (female) to Children's Bureau, Box 134, 11 June 1942, Children's Bureau Papers, National Archives.

65. Marian M. Crane (Children's Bureau) to E.P., Box 134, 23 June 1942, Children's Bureau Papers, National Archives.

66. White House Conference on Child Health and Protection, *The Young Child in the Home: A Survey of Three Thousand Families,* John Anderson, Chair (New York: D. Appleton-Century, 1936; reprinted by the Arno Press and the *New York Times,* 1972), pp. 108, 212.

67. White House Conference on Child Health and Protection, *The Young Child in the Home,* p. 344.

68. See Ralph LaRossa and Donald C. Reitzes, "Gendered Perceptions of Father Involvement in Early-Twentieth-Century America, *Journal of Marriage and the Family* 57 (February 1995), pp. 223–29. For two classic statements on gendered perceptions, see Jessie Bernard, *The Future of Marriage* (New York: World, 1972); and Constantina Safilios-Rothschild, "Family Sociology or Wives' Family Sociology? A Cross-Cultural Examination of Decision-Making," *Journal of Marriage and the Family* 31 (May 1969), pp. 290–301. For a discussion of the credit-taking bias in perceptions of the child care, see F. Deutsch, J.L. Lozy, and S. Saxon, "Taking Credit: Couples' Reports of Contributions to Child Care," *Journal of Family Issues* 14 (1993), pp. 421–37.

69. L. Pearl Gardner, "A Survey of the Attitudes and Activities of Fathers," *Journal of Genetic Psychology* 63 (1943), pp. 15–53. (This article is said to have been "received in the Editorial Office on October 16, 1941.")

70. Ibid., pp. 34–35.

71. Ibid., pp. 35–36.

72. See Nancy R. Gibbs, "Bringing Up Father," *Time,* 28 June 1993, pp. 53–61.

73. There is both anthropological and historical data to show that fathers have *not always* been excluded from the birthing room. See K. E. Paige and J. M. Paige, "The Politics of Birth Practices: A Strategic Analysis," *American Sociological Review* 38 (December 1973), pp. 663–76; J. J. Suitor, "Husbands' Participation in Childbirth: A Nineteenth-Century Phenomenon," *Journal of Family History* 6 (Fall 1981), pp. 278–93.

74. Eldred V. Thiehoff, "Classes for Expectant Fathers," *American Journal on Public Health* 23 (1933), pp. 1200–1201.

75. Robert W. Jacobs, "For Fathers Only," *Parents' Magazine,* January 1934, p. 6.

76. M. M. Powell, "I'm Prepared," *Hygeia* 18 (September 1940), pp. 835–36.

77. Ibid.

78. "School for Fathers," *New York Times Magazine,* 15 February 1942, p. 25.

79. Hazel Corbin, *Getting Ready to Be a Father* (New York: Macmillan, 1939).

80. Douglas Vass Martin Jr., *Expectant Fathers: Their Care and Treatment* (St. Louis: DeVass Publishing Co., 1930); David Victor, *Father's Doing Nicely: The Expectant Father's Handbook* (New York: Bobbs-Merrill, 1938).

81. Dr. Josephine Kenyon, "Father Handles Baby," *Good Housekeeping,* October 1940, p. 155.

82. Humor at father's expense was less likely in the 1930s than in the 1920s. See, for example, Ralph LaRossa, et al., "The Fluctuating Image of the Twentieth-Century American Father," *Journal of Marriage and the Family* 53 (November 1991), pp. 987–97. I will talk about the rhetorical functions of humor in the context of fatherhood in chapter 6.

83. Florence Brown Sherbon, *The Child: His Origin, Development, and Care* (New York: McGraw-Hill, 1941), pp. 10–11.

84. Mary Evans, "The Business of Being a Mother," *New Republic,* 15 June 1918, pp. 203–5. The reason that this fairly modern piece appeared in the *New Republic* versus, say, *Good Housekeeping,* may have had a lot to do with the fact that the *New Republic,* founded in 1914, was, as Arthur Schlesinger Jr. put it, a product of the Enlightenment and of Progressivism. See John Tebbel and Mary Ellen Zuckerman, *The Magazine in America: 1741–1990* (New York: Oxford University Press, 1991), p. 123.

85. "The Menace of the Maternal Father," *Hygeia* 20 (June 1942), pp. 468–70.

86. Ibid., p. 468.

87. Ibid., p. 469.

88. Ibid.

89. For an extensive discussion of the kind of backlash that can emerge in gender politics, see Susan Faludi, *Backlash: The Undeclared War against American Women* (New York: Crown, 1991).

Chapter 5: Fathercraft

1. "Dear Aunt Sammy. Have you a booklet which will help in feeding my baby—ten months old?" A.M.W. (female) to Children's Bureau, Box 388, date unknown but cataloged in files for 1929–1932, Children's Bureau Papers, National Archives.

2. White House Conference on Child Health and Protection, *Parent Education: Types, Content, and Method,* Sidonie M. Gruenberg, Chair (New York: Century Company, 1932).

3. John E. Anderson, "The Clientele of a Parental Education Program," *School and Society* 26 (6 August 1927), pp. 178–84.

4. White House Conference on Child Health and Protection, *The Young Child in the Home: A Survey of Three Thousand American Families,* John E. Anderson, Chair (New York: D. Appleton-Century Company, 1936; reprinted by the Arno Press and the *New York Times,* 1972). See table 35 (p. 81) and table 221 (p. 290). The 3.6 percent of white fathers and 3.2 percent of black fathers, and 28 percent

of white mothers and 19.1 percent of black mothers were computed by adding the percentage for attendance at child study group only plus the percentage for attendance at child study group and parent-teacher association meeting. The social-class figures were computed by calculating the actual numbers for the white fathers and mothers and black fathers and mothers and then creating a percentage from those numbers. For example, in table 35, of the 526 fathers in the top two classes (265 + 261), approximately 44 ([265 × 6.0 percent] + [265 × 4.2 percent] + [261 × 6.5 percent] + [261 × 0.4 percent]) had attended a child study group only or a child study group and a parent teacher conference.

5. Robert L. Griswold, *Fatherhood in America: A History* (New York: Basic Books, 1993), p. 129.

6. Anderson, "The Clientele of a Parental Education Program," p. 179. In *Parent Education: A Survey of the Minnesota Program* (Minneapolis: University of Minnesota Press, 1939; reprinted by the Greenwood Press, 1975), Edith A. Davis and Esther McGinnis reproduce a late-1930s' registration card that clearly targeted women (p. 104). For example, the card asked, in addition to "husband's occupation": "In the following spaces state exact type of work done by yourself (homemaker, stenographer, housekeeper, clerk in office, etc.) and by your husband (doctor, merchant, travelling-salesman, store-salesman, plumber, laborer, etc.)."

7. According to Davis and McGinnis, *Parent Education,* p. 127, 9.2 percent of the meetings were in the morning, 44.4 percent in early afternoon, 15.3 percent in late afternoon, 10.9 percent in early evening, and 20.3 percent in late evening.

8. Leroy E. Bowman, "Making a Parent of Father," *Parents' Magazine,* November 1935, p. 13; Worth Tuttle, "Your Child's School Needs You," *Parents' Magazine,* October 1934, pp. 15, 60, 61.

9. Davis and McGinnis, *Parent Education,* p. 119.

10. See chapter 4, note 68.

11. Rheta Childe Dorr, "Putting It Up to Fathers," *Good Housekeeping,* May 1915, pp. 497–502.

12. In 1939, *Scholastic* magazine reported the results of its essay contest in which "the younger generation" was asked to write on "The Kind of Parent I Hope to Be." Nearly all the boys who submitted letters said that "rearing children [was] as much the father's job as it [was] the mother's and that they hoped to play a very important part in the lives of their sons and daughters." Second prize went to Frederic Beck, a student at Council Bluff, Iowa, High School. He wrote about the "extreme methods frequently employed by well-meaning but misunderstanding parents" (e.g., "constant nagging") and said that when he "add[ed] the title 'Father' to [his] name" he hoped to "steer clear" of these pitfalls. George Lawton, "The Kind of Parent I Hope to Be," *Scholastic,* November 1939, pp. 3–4.

13. "A School for Fathers," *Educational Review* 71 (April 1926), pp. 184–85.

14. C.B. (male) to Angelo Patri, Box 12, 29 November 1929, Angelo Patri Papers, Library of Congress.

15. L.B. (male) to Angelo Patri, Box 22, 3 January 1933, Angelo Patri Papers, Library of Congress.

16. Phyllis Jackson, "Good Fathers Get Together," *Parents' Magazine,* February 1936, pp. 47, 62.

17. Ethel Shreffler Heebink, "For Fathers Only," *Parents' Magazine,* October

1934, pp. 12, 78. Robert Henry Miller, "For Fathers Only," *Parents' Magazine,* December 1936, p. 40.

18. Nellie L. Perkins, Ph.D., "The New Child Training Laboratories at Cornell," in Child Study Association of America Conference on Parental Education, Bronxville, NY, October 1925. Child Study Association of America Papers, Box 45, Folder 478, Social Welfare History Archives, University of Minnesota. The Child Study Association of America (soon to be discussed), made up of a number of chapters, also found that fathers would ask for their own groups.

19. Grace Nies Fletcher, "Bringing Up Fathers," *Ladies Home Journal,* September 1927, pp. 35, 199, 201, 202.

20. Leroy Bowman, "Making a Parent of Father," *Parents' Magazine,* November 1935, p. 13. Another author argued, "[N]o one knows better than do teachers and principal that when they have interested fathers as well as mothers they have 100 percent cooperation, which helps to make better pupils, better schools, a better educational system, and eventually better-equipped men and women." Ken Tuttle, "Fathers Go to School," *Parents' Magazine,* April 1939, p. 11.

21. White House Conference on Child Health and Protection, *Parent Education: Types, Content, Method,* Sidonie M. Gruenberg, Chair (New York: The Century Company, 1932), p. 89.

22. Winona L. Morgan, *The Family Meets the Depression: A Study of a Group of Highly Selected Families* (Minneapolis: University of Minnesota Press, 1939; reprinted by Greenwood Press, 1972), p. 51.

23. Data collection also was dissimilar in the two surveys. Although both relied on mothers' reports, the first was based on in-home interviews, while the second was based on mailed questionnaires. The children in the two studies also were not the same age; the AHEA survey had more school-age children.

24. Father-to-father books harken back to the pre–nineteenth century child-rearing manuals that were written *by* men and addressed primarily *to* men (see chapter 2). Recent examples of father-to-father books include Robert Bly, *Iron John: A Book about Men* (Reading, MA: Addison-Wesley, 1990); John Boswell and Ron Barrett *How to Dad* (New York: Dell, 1990); H. Jackson Brown Jr. *Life's Little Instruction Book* (Nashville, TN: Rutledge Hill Press, 1991); Michael Burkett, *The Dad Zone* (New York: Simon and Schuster, 1993). Bill Cosby, *Fatherhood* (New York: Berkley, 1986); Jonathan W. Gould and Robert E. Gunther, *Reinventing Fatherhood* (Blue Ridge Summit, PA: TAB Books, 1993); B. McCoy, *Father's Day: Notes from a New Dad in the Real World* (New York: Times Books, 1995); Kyle Pruett *The Nurturing Father: Journey toward the Complete Man* (New York: Warner Books, 1987).

25. Winfield S. Hall, *Chums: A Story for Boys* (Chicago: American Medical Association, 1913); Winfield S. Hall, *John's Vacation: A Story for Boys* (Chicago: American Medical Association, 1913); Winfield S. Hall, *The Doctor's Daughter: A Story for Girls* (Chicago: American Medical Association, 1913). Each was defined as a "sex education pamphlet issued by the Bureau on Health and Public Instruction of the American Medical Association."

26. Edward Sanford Martin, *Atlantic Readings Number 5: A Father to His Freshman Son* and *A Father to His Graduate Girl* (Boston: Atlantic Monthly Press,

1918); John D. Swain, *A Father to His Son: A Letter to an Undergraduate upon His Entering College* (New Haven: Yale Publishing Association, 1912).

27. W. J. Dawson, *The Father of a Soldier* (New York: John Lane, 1918).

28. Frank H. Cheley, *The Job of Being a Dad* (Boston: W. A. Wilde, 1923); Frank H. Cheley, *Dad, Whose Boy Is Yours?* (Boston: W. A. Wilde, 1926); Frank H. Cheley, ed., *Fathering the Boy* (New York: University Society, 1933); John Crawley, *Reveries of a Father* (New York: D. Appleton and Company, 1924); Fairfax Downey, *Father's First Two Years* (New York: Minton, Balch, and Company, 1925); Samuel S. Drury, *Fathers and Sons* (New York: George H. Doran, 1927); T. W. Galloway, *The Father and His Boy: The Place of Sex in Manhood Making* (New York: Association Press, 1921); Edgar A. Guest, *My Job as a Father and What My Father Did for Me* (Chicago: Reilly and Lee, 1923); Philip E. Howard, *Father and Son: An Intimate Study* (Philadelphia: Sunday School Times Company, 1922); Douglas Vass Martin, *Expectant Fathers: Their Care and Treatment* (St. Louis: DeVass, 1930); Martin Panzer, *Father Knows Better* (New York: House of Moreau, Young, 1940); David Victor, *Father's Doing Nicely: The Expectant Father's Handbook* (Indianapolis, IN: Bobbs-Merrill, 1938); K. M. and E. M. Walker, *On Being a Father* (New York: W. W. Norton, 1929); Frederic F. Van de Water, *Fathers Are Funny* (New York: Doubleday, 1939). The subtitle of *The Father and His Boy* suggests that it was exclusively a sex-education book. The contents, however, show a broader range of issues than sex. *Expectant Fathers* and *Father's Doing Nicely* were written for fathers-to-be. Both were briefly discussed in the previous chapter. So was Hazel Corbin, *Getting Ready to Be a Father* (New York: Macmillan, 1939), which also was targeted to men about to become fathers. Corbin's book might qualify as a father-to-father book, but it is not listed with the others because I was not sure whether "Hazel" referred to a woman or a man.

29. Cheley, *Fathering the Boy,* pp. xiii, xxviii.

30. Each volume was described in Cheley, *Fathering the Boy,* pp. xiv, xvi–xvii, xxiii (italics in originals). It perhaps is worth mentioning the kind of men who were throwing their support behind the Father and Son Library. Named among the editorial board (and shown in photographs) in *Fathering the Boy* were Arthur Capper, United States Senator from Kansas; G. Clyde Fisher, Ph.D, Associate Curator of the American Museum of Natural History in New York; and George J. Fisher, M.D., Deputy Chief Scout Executive for the Boy Scouts of America. The Father and Son Library obviously was no fly-by-night operation.

31. Howard, *Father and Son,* p. 11.

32. Ibid., pp. 22, 29 (italics in original).

33. Ibid., p. 30.

34. Guest, *My Job as a Father and What My Father Did for Me,* pp. 7, 34–35.

35. Cheley, *Fathering the Boy,* pp. 42, 43, 44.

36. Randall Collins and Scott Coltrane, *Sociology of Marriage and the Family: Gender, Love, and Property,* 3d ed. (Chicago: Nelson Hall, 1991), pp. 357–58; Edward L. Kain, *The Myth of Family Decline: Understanding Families in a World of Rapid Social Change* (Lexington, MA: Lexington Books, 1990), p. 89. The Census department began collecting data on *employed mothers* in 1976, and it found then that 31 percent of the women ages eighteen to forty-four who had a child in

the previous year were in the labor force. In the 1980, the figure was 38 percent, and in 1990, it was 53 percent (see Collins and Coltrane, *Sociology of Marriage and the Family,* pp. 357–58). Needless to say, these are aggregate statistics and do not communicate racial and class variations. The percentages for low-income black mothers, for example, are higher.

37. If we apply the same criteria to assess the New Fatherhood of the early 1900s, we would have to focus on the labor force participation rates of *married women* because, as I said (in the previous endnote), the Census department did not begin collecting data on *employed mothers* until 1976: In 1900, the labor force participation rate of married women was 4.6 percent. In 1910, it was 10.7 percent (a figure that, due to the way the census was conducted that year, is not comparable to other census data). In 1920, at the beginning of the Machine Age, it was 9.0 percent. In 1930, at the beginning of the Depression, it was 11.7 percent, and in 1940, it was 15.6 percent. See Kain, *The Myth of Family Decline,* p. 89. If we compare the 1920 rate of 9.0 percent with the 1940 rate of 15.6 percent, we see a 73-percent increase. If we look at the change in New Fatherhood from 1920 to 1940—a change that is not as easy to operationalize but that can be documented nonetheless, I think we see an equally if not more impressive rate of change.

38. Ralph LaRossa, "Fatherhood and Social Change," *Family Relations* 37 (October 1988), pp. 451–57. On the other hand, one could point to the fact that the number of men who qualify as middle class is higher today than during the Machine Age and that the impact of New Fatherhood is more profound. That would still leave the question, What percentage of middle-class men, then and now, embrace(d) New Fatherhood? For a discussion of how New Fatherhood has become a badge of the middle class, see Griswold, *Fatherhood in America,* pp. 252–54.

39. See Peter L. Berger and Thomas Luckmann, *The Social Construction of Reality: A Treatise in the Sociology of Knowledge* (New York: Doubleday/Anchor, 1966).

40. Historian Hamilton Cravens is the one who characterizes the Child Study Association of America in these terms. See Hamilton Cravens, "Child-Saving in the Age of Professionalism, 1915–1930, in *American Childhood: A Research Guide and Historical Handbook,* ed. Joseph M. Hawes and N. Ray Hiner (Westport, CT: Greenwood Press, 1985), pp. 415–88 (the point is made on p. 475). I would agree with Cravens's assessment. The Child Study Association of America *was* a powerful force during the Machine Age.

41. *An Inventory of the Papers of the Child Study Association of America,* prepared by William K. Wallach, 1974, pp. 1–2. Child Study Association of America Papers, Social Welfare History Archives, University of Minnesota.

42. *Society for the Study of Child Nature, Chapter I, Summary of the Work for the Years 1896–1906* (New York, 1907), pp. 5–6. Box 1, Folder 1. Child Study Association of America Papers, Social Welfare History Archives, University of Minnesota.

43. Benjamin G. Gruenberg, ed., *Outlines of Child Study: A Manual for Parents and Teachers* (New York: Macmillan, 1925; revised in 1927).

44. *Federation for Child Study Program, 1924–1925,* p. 6; also *Child Study Association of America, Inc., Annual Program, 1925–1926.* Box 1, Folders 2 and

8, Child Study Association of America Papers, Social Welfare History Archives, University of Minnesota.

45. "A History of the Child Study Association of America: Its Growth and Activities," 1928. Box 25, Folder 255. Child Study Association of America Papers, Social Welfare History Archives, University of Minnesota.

46. Gruenberg, *Outlines of Child Study;* Dorothy Canfield Fisher and Sidonie Matsner Gruenberg, *Our Children: A Handbook for Parents* (New York: Viking, 1932); Staff Members of the Child Study Association of America, *Parents' Questions* (New York: Harper and Brothers, 1936).

47. *Child Study Association of America Conference on Parental Education,* October 1925, p. 172. Box 45, Folder 478. Child Study Association of America Papers, Social Welfare History Archives, University of Minnesota.

48. "A History of the Child Study Association of America." Box 25, Folder 255. Child Study Association of America Papers, Social Welfare History Archives, University of Minnesota.

49. The people listed here were crucial to the organization but they were by no means the only people who had an impact. In 1928, for example, there were 23 persons on the Board of Directors, another 23 who made up the Advisory Board, and 21 staff people (Child Study Association of America, Selected List of Books for Parents and Teachers, 1928.) And, of course, there were the thousands who participated in the study groups and lectures.

50. *Society for the Study of Child Nature,* p. 5.

51. *An Inventory of the Papers of the Child Study Association of America,* p. 1.

52. *Society for the Study of Child Nature,* p. 5. Sidonie Gruenberg says in *Parent Education,* p. 76, that three mothers started the organization. "A History of the Child Study Association of America," p. 1, in the Child Study Association of America Papers, says five.

53. Hamilton Cravens, "Child-Saving in the Age of Professionalism." The reference to Frank is on p. 444. See also "A History of the Child Study Association of America."

54. "Federation for Child Study Program, 1924–1925" (New York: Federation for Child Study), p. 6.

55. "Child Study Association of America, Inc., Annual Program, 1925–1926" (New York: Child Study Association of America), p. 5.

56. Herbert Blumer, in *Symbolic Interactionism: Perspective and Method* (Englewood Cliffs, NJ: Prentice-Hall, 1969), talks about the three axioms in symbolic interactionist theory: (1) human beings act toward things on the basis of the meanings that the things have for them; (2) meanings arise in the process of interaction between people; and (3) meanings are handled and modified through an interpretive process. It is this last process to which I am referring.

57. "Federation for Child Study Program, 1923–1924" (New York: Federation for Child Study), p. 11.

58. "Thirty-Five Years of Child Study," *Federation for Child Study Bulletin* 1 (December 1923), p. 3.

59. Untitled handwritten document chronicling the history of the Child Study Association of America from 1888 to 1926, Box 25, Folder 255, Child Study

Association of America Papers, Social Welfare History Archives, University of Minnesota.

60. "Will You Help?—We Need New Members," *Child Study* 2 (April 1925), p. 7.

61. Ibid. The categories of membership included: "Donors, $100.00 or more. Sustaining, $50.00. Supporting, $25.00. Active, $10.00. Professional social workers and teachers, $2.00 or more."

62. "A Summary of Activities During the Year, 1927–1928," p. 1, Box 25, Folder 255, Child Study Association of America Papers, Social Welfare History Archives, University of Minnesota.

63. The word *disconfirming* is being used here as it is in communication theory: "[W]hile *rejection* amounts to the message, 'You are wrong,' *disconfirmation* says in effect 'You do not exist' " (my italics). See Paul Watzlawick, Janet Helmick Beavin, and Don D. Jackson, *Pragmatics of Human Communication: A Study of Interaction Patterns, Pathologies, and Paradoxes* (New York: W. W. Norton, 1967), p. 86. The fact that the registration cards were phrased as if to assume that men would never become members said to men not "You *cannot* be here" but rather "You *are not* here."

64. "Child Study for Fathers," *Child Study* 3 (March 1926), p. 8. "A Summary of Activities," pp. 3–4. In talking about the group on sex education, I emphasize the 1925–1926 season because at a Conference in October 1925, one month before the beginning of the 1925–1926 season, Sidonie M. Gruenberg reported, "We have mixed groups of fathers and mothers studying sex education and the biological foundations of childhood." See "Child Study Association of America Conference on Parental Education, Bronxville, New York, October 1925, p. 170, Box 45, Folder 478, Child Study Association of America Papers, Social Welfare History Archives, University of Minnesota. Since Gruenberg was speaking in the past tense, I am assuming that she may have been indicating that the father and mother groups were ongoing, and that the 1925–1926 course may not have been the first, or the only one. The lecture titled "The Adolescent in Modern Society" also was reported by Gruenberg, p. 173.

65. *Child Study* 9 (February 1932), pp. 159–68. The symposium itself took place in April, 1931.

66. Examining child-rearing literature published between 1926 and 1946, Terry Strathman noted the "fragmentary and incoherent nature of the advice": "I have unavoidably presented a more condensed and wholistic view of theory and technique than was readily available even to regular readers. It was actually only through great and attentive effort that the contours of the theories became visible through the clutter of techniques." See Terry Strathman, "From the Quotidian to the Utopian: Child-Rearing Literature in America, 1926–1946," *Berkeley Journal of Sociology* 29 (1984), p. 17.

67. *Child Study* 9, p. 164.

68. Ibid, pp. 168, 181.

69. Ibid, p. 161.

70. Ibid, p. 166, italics in original; p. 165.

71. Cravens, "Child Saving in the Age of Professionalism," p. 425, gives the 1909 date for Freud's visit. G. Stanley Hall was a towering figure in the child study

field at the turn of the century. The first person to receive an American Ph.D. in psychology (in 1878), Hall was instrumental in the formation of the American Psychological Association and was the founder of *The American Journal of Psychology* (in 1887). He also established a department of pedagogy at Clark University (where he eventually became President) and launched a journal devoted to publishing studies of children, called *The Pedagogical Seminary* (in 1891). Hall gained much of his reputation as a child scientist from the surveys of children, parents, and teachers which he planned and supervised during the latter part of the nineteenth century. The results from these surveys were widely distributed among parent educators, and "stimulated the development of child-study clubs, associations, and circles across the nation." See Charles E. Strickland and Charles Burgess, *Health, Growth, and Heredity: G. Stanley Hall on Natural Education* (New York: Columbia University Teachers College Press, 1965), p. 14. Some consider Hall the founder of the child study movement. See Maxine L. Margolis, *Mothers and Such: Views of American Women and Why They Changed* (Berkeley, CA: University of California Press, 1984), p. 46.

72. For example, in *A Selected List of Books for Parents and Teachers* (New York: Child Study Association of America, 1928), wherein one will find items "selected and compiled by the Parents' Bibliography Committee of the Child Study Association of America," the following works appear: J. C. Flugel, *The Psychoanalytic Study of the Family* (London: International Psycho-analytical Press, 1921); Edwin B. Holt, *The Freudian Wish* (New York: Henry Holt & Co., 1915); H. Crichton Miller, *The New Psychology of the Parent* ("An introduction to the theories of psychoanalysis interpreted in terms of practical application, helpful to parents"; New York: Thomas Seltzer, 1923); and F. S. Van Teslaar, *An Introduction to Psychoanalysis* ("A collection of articles by 'the founders and pioneers of psychoanalysis,' forming an excellent introduction to the various schools of thought in this field showing their value in social, political and educational work"; New York: Modern Library, 1924). Also, in a syllabus on "family relationships" prepared by Anna W. M. Wolf (one-time editor of the "study group department" for *Child Study* and one of the coeditors of *Parents' Questions*) and filed under 1929–1930, there are references to "unconscious motivations," "the pleasure principle," "the mechanism of rationalization," and (under the heading of "The Role of the Father in the Life of his Children) "father's detachment—asset or liability" plus the question, "Are men more adventurous and roving than women?" See Anna W. M. Wolf, "Family Relationships," Box 25, Folder 257, Child Study Association of America Papers, Social Welfare History Archives, University of Minnesota.

73. "Child Study Association of America Conference on Parental Education," p. 78. Another parent educator, Kate S. North of the Department of Home Economics Education at the University of Oklahoma happened to be in the room when Pilpel made these remarks and reported that "in her groups the father's attitude was, on the whole, one of inquiry. If any element of resentment was present it was not apparent." Ibid.

74. Douglas A. Thom, *Everyday Problems of the Everyday Child* (New York: D. Appleton and Company, 1927), pp. 48–49.

75. The Child Study Association of America included Thom's book under "Child Study" in *A Selected List of Books for Parents and Teachers* (1928 and 1931

editions), "selected and compiled by the Parents' Bibliography Committee" of the CSAA., p. 8 (1928), p. 9 (1931). The National Council on Parent Education listed it under "General References: Child Development, Mental Growth, Guidance, and Parent Education" in "Books for Parent Education Groups," University of Virginia Extension, May 1934, vol. 11, no. 13. The Children's Bureau included it among the "Selected Books of Interest to Mothers" in the 1929 edition of *Infant Care.* And Angelo Patri, one of the foremost child-rearing experts during the Machine Age (and the subject of chapter 7) often recommended it to the parents who wrote to him for advice.

76. Transcript of discussion on 7 October 1931 in "Ed. 251-E. Parent-Child Relationships, Mrs. Sidonie M. Gruenberg," p. 9, Box 33, Folder 338, Child Study Association of America Papers, Social Welfare History Archives, University of Minnesota. ("Mrs." is at the top of the first page, and used to refer to Gruenberg throughout the transcript.)

77. That there would be a transcript of one of Gruenberg's classes is not all that surprising. The CSAA believed in keeping copious records of its meetings. "We keep a record of discussions carried on at the meetings, so that we can share with other parents the helpful ideas which are talked over in each group." See "Come Join Us" (1928), Box 41, Folder 435, Child Study Association of America Papers, Social Welfare History Archives, University of Minnesota. If Gruenberg felt that the discussion in the class might be worth sharing with others, she may have given someone the job of class recorder.

78. Transcript of discussion in Ed. 251-E, p. 5.

79. The typed transcript originally said, "the independent father today is just as interested as the mother." Someone, perhaps Gruenberg, crossed out "independent" and wrote in "individual" (p. 6).

80. Transcript of discussion in Ed. 251-E, pp. 6–9.

81. Dorothy Canfield Fisher and Sidonie Matsner Gruenberg, eds., *Our Children: A Handbook for Parents* (New York: Viking, 1932), pp. 323–24.

82. "If people define situations as real, they are real in their consequences" is known, in sociology, as the Thomas axiom and was fashioned coincidentally during the Machine Age. See W. I. Thomas and D. S. Thomas, *The Child in America: Behavior Problems and Programs* (New York: Knopf, 1928).

83. These comments were made by black mothers and were included in the following report: Margaret J. Quilliard, Director of Field Work, "Statements Made by Members of the Three Child Study Groups at the Close of the Sessions," Box 41, Folder 443, Child Study Association of America Papers, Social Welfare History Archives, University of Minnesota. Under the title was the following statement: "All of these mothers were members of the Negro race." The report was not dated. The study groups for blacks, like the groups for whites, generally targeted the middle class. In a memo from Quilliard to Cecile Pilpel, dated 29 May 1930, Quilliard referred to the black parents as "fairly well educated" and "constantly 'taking courses' " and thus "like to be addressed as intelligent adults." Box 40, Folder 419, Child Study Association of America Papers, Social Welfare History Archives, University of Minnesota. In another report on study groups for black parents, also written by Quilliard and also undated, there were these statements, made by husbands and transmitted to the group leaders through the mothers in attendance:

"He thinks that the work is very instructive to the parents." "He thinks it a very good idea to have a Child Study Group, for both mother and child are accomplishing good by it. The mother learns to control her temper and the child learns to obey quicker, when you don't get excited and ask him in a nice way." "He is glad his wife belongs. She has learned a lot from the educated people." "He thinks it wonderful. It has made him think altogether differently on the subject, as the 'modern' treatment of the child question is new to him." "He thinks it is a very good thing, only it is quite hard at first to work out these new ideas. We sometimes find ourselves doing things the old way. But I am sure it will be easy when we get working these new ideas together." See "Statements Relative to Study Groups Led by Miss Margaret J. Quilliard," Box 41, Folder 443, Child Study Association of America Papers, Social Welfare History Archives, University of Minnesota.

84. Mark Carnes, *Secret Ritual and Manhood in Victorian America* (New Haven: Yale University Press, 1989).

85. Staff Members of the Child Study Association of America (Gruenberg, Pilpel, Frank, Wolf, Franklin, Brickner, and Goodkind), *Parents' Questions* (New York: Harper and Brothers, 1936), p. x.

86. Thus, I am not inclined to agree with the statement made by Robert Griswold that "[t]he call for fatherly involvement in the family was not matched by any sustained effort [during the 1920s and 1930s] to bring fathers into the modern world of child rearing." See Griswold, *Fatherhood in America*, p. 128. My sense is that the CSAA exhibited sustained effort to get fathers involved and that other organizations and individuals (introduced in other chapters) did, too.

Chapter 6: Fatherhood and the Popular Press

1. *The Four Faces of the American Family* (New York: *Parents' Magazine*, 1990), p. 27. This is a study of families with children conducted by Yankelovich Clancy Shulman for *Parents' Magazine*.

2. Winona L. Morgan, *The Family Meets the Depression: A Study of a Group of Highly Selected Families* (Minneapolis: University of Minnesota Press, 1939; reprinted by Greenwood Press, 1972). Morgan presents a table (p. 51) wherein she compares the percentages reported in the White House Conference Study and in the American Home Economics Study, but her figures for the WHC Study are higher than they should be. The mistake seems to lie in her misreading of table 32 in the WHC Study, which reports on both magazine and newspaper articles. If only magazine articles are taken into account, the WHC figures for fathers and mothers, respectively, are not 47.7 percent and 88.2 percent, as Morgan reports, but 40.9 percent and 80.3 percent.

John Tebbel and Mary Ellen Zuckerman note in their book *The Magazine in America, 1741–1990* (New York: Oxford University Press, 1991) the importance of popular magazines in American society: "[F]rom 1891 to the end of the Great War [World War I], magazines enjoyed a time when they were not rivaled by radio, motion pictures, or television. They were the only national communications medium, and their audience was unlimited. But primarily, they were the voice of the vast middle class" (p. 77). As for what happened once radio arrived in the 1920s, they say, "Radio seized the public imagination in the twenties as nothing had before and, by bringing country and city together through network broadcasting, created huge national audiences. For magazines, this was serious competition indeed. But they still retained the prime advantage of portability and the possibility of re-reading as often as desired" (p. 157).

3. While many popular magazines floundered during the Depression, *Parents' Magazine* thrived. See Steven Schlossman, "Perils of Popularization: The Founding of *Parents' Magazine,*" in *History and Research in Child Development,* ed. Alice Boardman Smuts and John W. Hagen (Monograph of the Society for Research in Child Development, vol. 50, nos. 4–5, serial number 211, 1985), p. 66. Also see Nancy F. Cott, *The Grounding of Modern Feminism* (New Haven, CT: Yale University Press), p. 170.

4. *Parents' Magazine,* "*Parents' Magazine* Demographic Profile" (1991).

5. Peter Filene acknowledges the two-step flow of communication when it comes to magazines in one of his comments about how a magazine article targeted for women could ultimately affect men: "In 1947 there were few fathers among the audience of *Parents' Magazine,* . . . but there were many mothers who would quote it to them." See Peter Filene, *Him/Her/Self: Sex Roles in Modern America,* 2d ed. (Baltimore, MD: Johns Hopkins University Press, 1986), p. 172.

6. See Rosalind C. Barnett and Grace K. Baruch, "Determinants of Fathers' Participation in Family Work," *Journal of Marriage and the Family* 49 (February 1987), pp. 29–40.

7. See Maxine P. Atkinson and Stephen P. Blackwelder "Fathering in the Twentieth Century," *Journal of Marriage* 55 (November 1993), pp. 975–86.

8. Atkinson and Blackwelder, in "Fathering in the Twentieth Century" periodically collapse the 1920s and 1930s in their analysis of popular magazine articles on fatherhood. Robert L. Griswold in *Fatherhood in America* (New York: Basic Books, 1993) sometimes uncritically uses a magazine article published in the 1920s to talk about the culture of fatherhood from 1920 to 1940.

9. See Schlossman, "Perils of Popularization"; also Terry Strathman, "From the Quotidian to the Utopian: Child-Rearing Literature in America, 1926–1946," *Berkeley Journal of Sociology* 29 (1984), pp. 1–34. If you look at how the magazine was titled in the 1930s, you will see *Parents' Magazine,* with the addition of the possessive. Today, however, if you look at the cover, you will see *Parents* in bold print with the word *Magazine* invisible. Thus, technically, it is no longer *Parents' Magazine* but *Parents.* I have decided to use the former spelling throughout (even when referring to the present day) for the sake of consistency, and because it is more in keeping with the spelling used during the Machine Age.

10. Cited in Schlossman, "Perils of Popularization," p. 71.

11. Cited in Schlossman, "Perils of Popularization," p. 71.

12. Ibid.

13. Schlossman, "Perils of Popularization," p. 77. Another factor behind the founding of *Parents' Magazine,* not to be ignored, was the confluence of Hecht's civic-mindedness and his keen business sense. Hecht's philosophy was that anything that did not "render a useful educational service" *and* "have the prospect of being profitable" was not a worthwhile endeavor; see Schlossman, "Perils of Popularization," p. 67. That is, while Hecht's and the LSRM's commitment to social welfare was admirable, it alone was not sufficient to start the magazine. What also

was needed was an informed grasp of what would sell coupled with an ability to bring together the resources, financial and otherwise, to get the venture off the ground.

14. This advertisement appeared in the January 1936 issue, p. 64. This was not, however, the only time the advertisement was run. Today, women continue to be the main advertising targets for *Parents' Magazine*. In the promotional materials that *Parents' Magazine* sends to advertisers, much is made of the fact that the people who buy the most cosmetics, the most skin care products, the most polishers and cleansers, and the most food (women) are the most avid readers. See *The Four Faces of the American Family*.

15. The percentages that I give here are based on magazine articles that were categorized by the *Readers' Guide to Periodical Literature (RGPL)* as falling under the heading of "father," or "fathers," or "fatherhood." This sample of articles may not constitute every fatherhood article published, because there probably were some articles on fatherhood that were not correctly classified by the *RGPL*. (For a discussion of the pros and cons of using the *RGPL*, see Stuart W. Showalter, "Sampling from the *Readers' Guide*," *Journalism Quarterly* 55 [1978], pp. 346–48.) I think, however, the numbers provide a fairly accurate picture of *Parents' Magazine's* influence. To be specific, my counts showed that only one of the thirteen (8 percent) of the *RGPL* fatherhood articles published between 1926 and 1929 was published in *Parents' Magazine*. By contrast, 37 of 63 (59 percent), 25 of 60 (42 percent), and 12 of 23 (52 percent)—published between 1930 and 1934, 1935 and 1939, and 1940 and 1942, respectively—were published in *Parents' Magazine*.

16. Harry Irving Shumway, "Every Baby Needs a Father," *Parents' Magazine*, December 1929, pp. 29, 30, 91, 92. Quotations in the next three paragraphs of text are from this article.

17. The father recounted an episode that he found particularly galling: "In the beginning I was supposed to be the wind-remover. The doctor told me about this. 'After the baby's feeding—sounds like cattle, this—he may be troubled by wind. You hold him up and pat his back until the wind escapes. But put him down again as soon as the wind is gone. Don't jiggle him up and down, hoping for more wind. Don't hug him—or do anything natural. Put him down and go away.'"

18. On the rhetorical dimensions of the popular press, see Joel Best, *Threatened Children: Rhetoric and Concern about Child-Victims* (Chicago: University of Chicago Press, 1990); John M. Johnson, "Horror Stories and the Construction of Child Abuse," in *Images of Issues*, ed. Joel Best (New York: Aldine de Gruyter, 1989), pp. 5–19; Craig Reinarman, "The Social Construction of Drug Scares," in *Constructions of Deviance: Social Power, Context, and Interaction*, ed. Patricia A. Adler and Peter Adler (Belmont, CA: Wadsworth, 1994), pp. 92–104. The rhetorical dimensions of the popular press underscore the media's role as "moral entrepreneur." On the significance of moral entrepreneurs in the social construction of deviance, see Howard Becker, *Outsiders: Studies in the Sociology of Deviance* (New York: Free Press, 1963), pp. 147–63.

19. Burton P. Fowler, "Father Goes to School," *Parents' Magazine*, March 1930, pp. 22, 54, 55.

20. See Best, *Threatened Children*, p. 17.

21. Stephen Edelston Toulmin, *The Uses of Argument* (Cambridge: Cambridge University Press, 1958); Best, *Threatened Children*, pp. 24–25.

22. Nancy Evans, "Editor's Letter," *Family Life*, May/June 1994, p. 11. The May/June issue featured "a special report" on "the new dad." Among the items included were "13 Non-Boring Things for Dads to Do with Their Kids" and "Dad Time: A Timeline of Great Moments in American Fatherhood." The latter listed the following "moments" for the early twentieth century: "1901—Theodore Roosevelt, father of six, is sworn in as president; . . . 1909—Mrs. Sonora Louise Smart Dodd conceives of a Father's Day; . . . 1917—Father E. J. Flanagan establishes . . . Boys Town; 1924—Little Orphan Annie makes her first appearance, accompanied by Daddy Warbucks; . . . 1930—Dagwood Bumstead debuts in *Blondie,* and embodies the '30s and '40s archetype of the harried, put-upon pop who wants nothing more from his family than time to indulge in a sandwich and a nap; 1935—The First *Addams Family* appears in the *New Yorker;* . . . 1942—*Bambi* frightens kids with an austere dad who never appears until Bambi's mom is killed . . ."

23. The phrase "atrocity tales" is borrowed from Best, *Threatened Children,* p. 28.

24. William E. Blatz, "Are You Fit to Be a Father?," *Parents' Magazine,* June 1931, pp. 33, 58, 65.

25. "So many fathers read this magazine that we believe they deserve a special department edited by a father. All other fathers are invited to submit contributions to that editor." *Parents' Magazine,* June 1932, p. 6.

26. Charles P. Pelham, "Confessions of a Newborn Father," *Parents' Magazine,* June 1932, pp. 6, 43.

27. E. Anthony Rotundo, *American Manhood: Transformations in Masculinity from the Revolution to the Modern Era* (New York: Basic Books, 1993), p. 263.

28. Pelham, "Confessions of a Newborn Father," 1932.

29. H. W. McIntire, "For Fathers Only," *Parents' Magazine,* April 1934, p. 52.

30. James A. Drake, "For Fathers Only," *Parents' Magazine,* November 1936, p. 14.

31. Lieut. M. F. Eddy, U.S.N. RET, "For Fathers Only," *Parents' Magazine,* October 1936, pp. 71–72.

32. Still another "For Fathers Only" article that stressed the importance of a masculine voice in family affairs was published in October 1937:

> I have never thought it wise for one parent to countermand the order of another—or of a maid, or of anyone given charge of a child—once that superior has spoken. . . . Yet there have been times when I have been sorely tempted to forget my scruples about a split in the parental high command. And those times have been when I have heard a mother, a maid or any female given temporary authority over a child, take him vehemently to task for something as harmless as sitting atop a tower of piled boxes and gently rocking now this way, now that. Or balancing, like a tight-rope walker, on the fence in the backyard. Or hanging from the steps to the back porch and letting himself drop from progressively higher steps. I stress 'a mother, a maid or any female given temporary authority,' because women, in particular, are guilty of such action. . . . Short-sighted, unsympathetic females! Can't they see, first of all, that

love of danger and dangerous situations is dear above all other things to the masculine heart? So dear that men, at their majority and beyond it, will leave home, family, friends and even dog for the death-lurking jungle; for precarious mountain heights; for the bounding main or, today, the cloud-tufted sky. So dear that in its name they will even brave a strange and distant city for a job and a future. . . . And there's the rub. For in not permitting the child to balance itself on the piled boxes, to walk the fence, to jump from the back porch, he grows into boyhood and manhood poorly equipped for the fight. He becomes over-cautious, timid, pigeon-livered. Thus are the Caspar Milquetoasts created, and thus are the clerical, bookkeeperish, yes-mr-jones, no-mr-jones, certainly-mr-jones jobs kept filled. For the man who succeeds is not necessarily the man who takes chances—for sometimes bravery is no more than cowardice in panic—but the man who, practiced in facing danger and confident in the knowledge thus gained, takes *reasonable* chances.

See W. J. Weir, "For Fathers Only," *Parents' Magazine,* October 1937, p. 14.

33. Mary Elisabeth Overholt, "For Fathers Only," *Parents' Magazine,* July 1932, pp. 4, 39.

34. Ibid.

35. Frank Clay Cross, "For Fathers Only," *Parents' Magazine,* April 1933, pp. 10, 11, 53.

36. Frederick Hall, "For Fathers Only," *Parents' Magazine,* September 1936, p. 92.

37. Raymond Francis Yates, "For Fathers Only," *Parents' Magazine,* October 1932, pp. 8, 61.

38. Not every "For Fathers Only" article published in *Parents' Magazine* endorsed the principle that fathers should be pals. There was at least one that took an opposite point of view:

We can share the absorbing interests of our children. We can set aside our work. We can participate in their play. But is that being a pal? Are not pals equals? Must there not be a similarity of interests as well as equality of power between pals? Can fathers really be pals with their children? . . . There is a relation between the father and children which may hold for each of them something even better than palship. It is a relation which acknowledges the differences between them. Each recognizes certain superiorities in the other and each accepts in a spirit of friendly charity certain deficiencies. Such a relation between a father and his children is based on a foundation of mutual consideration. Kindness and modesty are the materials out of which real understanding is built. Sincerity and affection closely cement this structure. I have often had a youngster hurl himself into my arms from a height, or swing himself to my grasp, at the imminent peril of his life, because he had confidence in me, a confidence that he would never repose in a pal. I was recognized as something reliable, trustworthy and staunch. He knew I was there to be depended upon. This is not palship; it is something more.

See James Peter Warbasse, "For Fathers Only," *Parents' Magazine,* August 1936, p. 74.

39. Jane Crow Maxfield, "For Fathers Only," *Parents' Magazine,* May 1933, pp. 6, 44, 45.

40. *Parents' Magazine* did continue to publish fatherhood articles, and in later years, it introduced a series called "About Fathers."

41. Benjamin Carroll, "For Fathers Only," *Parents' Magazine,* December 1937, pp. 71–72. The previous article in the series echoed a similar theme: "I have two sons of my own and they are all the world to me. I hope to raise them in the best manner possible, and I hope to give them as many opportunities as my purse can afford. I want them to have the fun that boyhood requires. But I swear that I will not give them my all. I am going to hold something back for myself. Not money. Rather, I mean those intangible riches that are worth more to me than all the gold I could ever accumulate: leisure time of my own." See Anonymous, "For Fathers Only," *Parents' Magazine,* November 1937, p. 12.

42. Ralph LaRossa, "Fatherhood and Social Change," *Family Relations* 37 (October 1988), pp. 451–57.

43. The final two "For Fathers Only" articles bring to mind the 1942 piece in *Hygeia* on "The Menace of the Maternal Father," reviewed at the end of chapter 4. Call it "resistance," call it "backlash"—the politics was the same.

44. The analysis that follows is not based on all the fatherhood articles classified by the *Reader's Guide to Periodical Literature* (by my count, 222 articles or thereabouts). Rather it is based on a *theoretical sample* of articles from this group ($N =$ 149, or 67 percent of the initial set). For a discussion of theoretical sampling, see Barney G. Glaser and Anselm L. Strauss, *The Discovery of Grounded Theory* (Chicago: Aldine, 1967); also Anselm L. Strauss, *Qualitative Analysis for Social Scientists* (New York: Cambridge University Press, 1987). I read every article and then chose for the theoretical sample those articles that provided the most robust understanding of fatherhood during the Machine Age. If I came across two articles that pretty much said the same thing, I chose for inclusion in the theoretical sample the article that said it best or said it in the most interesting way. Another way to look at the process is that if I came across an article from the same time period that pretty much repeated what other articles in that period were saying, I would not include it (unless, again, it made the point more interestingly than the others). This theoretical sample of articles was then typed onto disk, so that I could use a computer to run a variety of word searches (e.g., for the mention of daughters vs. sons).

As to the question of whether the theoretical sample deviates significantly from the larger sample, I would note simply that articles published in *Parents' Magazine* are overrepresented. Altogether, 66 of the 75 fatherhood articles published in *Parents' Magazine* from 1926 to 1942 ultimately ended up in the theoretical sample. This is a higher percentage of articles than would have been included, had I carried out a simple random sample. For this reason, I sometimes controlled for the influence of *Parents' Magazine* articles by comparing the patterns observed in the theoretical sample with patterns observed in a *Parents' Magazine* subsample. In the text, I will note where this comparison proved to be important.

45. To determine which articles mentioned sons or daughters, I ran a word search for *son* and another for *daughter.* (An article, of course, could mention both sons and daughters.) The number of articles found for each period determined the percentages. For example, the percentage for son in the 1901–1909 period

was 71 percent (10 of 14). The *son* percentage divided by the *daughter* percentage produced the ratio for that period: 1.25.

Period	Son		Daughter		Ratio	N
1901–1909	71%	(10)	57%	(8)	1.25	14
1910–1915	63%	(10)	50%	(8)	1.26	16
1916–1921	100%	(8)	25%	(2)	4.00	8
1922–1929	74%	(14)	21%	(4)	3.52	19
1930–1934	65%	(28)	33%	(14)	1.97	43
1935–1939	62%	(21)	32%	(11)	1.94	34
1940–1942	53%	(8)	47%	(7)	1.13	15
Overall	66%	(99)	36%	(54)	1.83	149

A rival hypothesis for the larger son-to-daughter (s/d) ratio in the 1916–1921 period is the impact of World War I. There were four articles published during this period that focused on men's special ties to their war-torn sons. But even if these articles are excluded from this period, the s/d ratio remains the same (4.00). This occurs not only because of the number of articles during this period that stressed domestic masculinity, but also because one of the four articles included a discussion, although brief, on daughters and the war.

46. Henry J. Leahy, "Girls' Fathers I Have Met," *Women's Home Companion,* October 1905, p. 11.

47. If we look at cartoons—and specifically, single-paneled cartoons published in the *Saturday Evening Post* from 1924 to 1944, we see that in the 1920s, fathers were significantly more likely than mothers to be depicted as incompetent. In the 1930s and especially the 1940s, however, fathers were no more likely than mothers to be depicted in such a way. Thus, the same 1920s-to-1930s shift that we see in the fatherhood articles and in virtually every other data set also can be seen in the *Saturday Evening Post,* a fairly conservative magazine. The more evidence that is brought to bear, the more it becomes clear that the culture of fatherhood in the 1930s was different. See Ralph LaRossa, Betty Anne Gordon, Ronald Jay Wilson, Annette Bairan, and Charles Jaret, "The Fluctuating Image of the Twentieth-Century American Father," *Journal of Marriage and the Family* 53 (November 1991), pp. 987–97.

48. As I mentioned in chapter 1, according to the *Oxford English Dictionary,* the origin of the word *dad* is not known, "but the forms *dada, tata,* meaning 'father,' originating in infantile or childish speech, occur independently in many languages." Whatever its origins, *dad*—as a form of address and designation—was central to the modernization of fatherhood, especially in the 1920s. As I will show, in its own inimitable way, it denoted the *social space* that the modern father was supposed to occupy.

49. Minna Thomas Antrim, "His Dadship," *Lippincott's Magazine* 89 (May 1912), pp. 743–44. Antrim was citing another individual's comments about the use of *dad,* someone whom she referred to as "Mr. Carper."

50. Ibid. Now, however, readers were being given Minna Thomas Antrim's own point of view. Antrim continued: "'Humph!' [say the critics] . . . 'Why not say

Mom?' Some *do* say 'Mom'; also *some* say 'Pop.' To the understanding ear, 'Dad'
is the sweet-sounding countersign between a man and his loving child, or brood,
not a flippant word born of disrespect. . . . Reverence is not more dead than Honor.
Filial has vanquished Filial Fear, hence presto 'Dad.'" Published the following
year was another ode to the distinction between *dad* and *pop*, as well as *father, pa*,
and *papa:*

> If he's wealthy and prominent and you stand in awe of him, call him
> 'Father.' If he sits in his shirt-sleeves and suspenders at ball games and
> picnics, call him 'Pop.' If he tills the land or teaches Sunday School, call
> him 'Pa.' If he wheels the baby carriage and carries bundles meekly, call
> him 'Papa,' with the accent on the first syllable. If he belongs to a literary
> circle and writes cultured papers, or if he is a reformer in politics and
> forgets to vote, call him 'Papa,' with the accent on the last syllable. If,
> however, he makes a pal of you when you're good, and is wise to let you
> pull the wool over his loving eyes when you're not; if, moreover, you're
> sure no other fellow you know has quite so fine a father, you may call
> him 'Dad,' but not otherwise.

This is attributed to H. C. Chatfield-Taylor in Wallace Rice and Frances Rice,
compilers, *To My Dad* (New York: Barse and Hopkins, 1913).

51. John Demos. "The Changing Faces of Fatherhood: A New Exploration in
Family History," in *Father and Child: Developmental and Clinical Perspectives,*
ed. Stanley Cath, Alan Gurwitt, and John M. Ross (Boston: Little, Brown, 1982),
p. 443. See also Filene, *Him/Her/Self,* pp. 144, 146, 173 on "poor dad." The association between power and form of address is well known. Most adults understand
that calling someone "Mr." President, or "Dr." Menninger, or "Sir" Lancelot is to
show deference. But "Mother?" What could this term possibly signify? Maybe
nothing. Maybe a lot. A former slave in the American south recalled that she was
once whipped because she happened to say, "My mother sent me" to her "missis."
"We were not allowed to call our mammies 'mother,'" she reported. "It made it
come too near the way of white folks." See Steven Mintz and Susan Kellogg, *Domestic Revolutions: A Social History of American Family Life* (New York: Free
Press, 1988), p. 71.

52. Mary Stewart Cutting, "Educating Father," *Harper's Bazar,* May 1913,
pp. 214, 238.

53. Among the 149 fatherhood articles entered onto disk, only one used the
word *mom:* "One of the very nicest valentines we saw this year—and you will
remember that there were millions of them in the stores—was addressed to 'Mom
and Pop.' The sender evidently chose it because it symbolized the oneness in her
affections, and in a very practical way, too, of her parents. To her, they are a team
pulling together, one as responsible as the other." See William Frederick Bigelow,
"Mothers' and Fathers' Day," *Good Housekeeping,* May 1941, p. 4. By contrast, 55
fatherhood articles employed the word *dad* or its variation, *daddy.*

54. One of the most interesting and most poignant instances of *dad* versus
mother was a letter, reprinted in the *New York Times,* that a dying father wrote to
his son. His instructions were that the letter was not to be read until after he was
gone. "Dearest boy of mine," the letter began. "Your mother is now your daddy as
well as your mother. Daddy has been taken away to see Sissie Ann, and some day

you will come to see both of us. Daddy is proud of his boy, and knows that he will be good to his mother and take care of her always. Each year until you are big you will get a letter from your daddy on your birthday, and then you will get your last letter when you are married. Be good, and God bless my Kathryn and Dick, and remember always that mother comes first. A big kiss and good-bye." "Dies, Leaving Message, Son Will Get Letters," *New York Times,* 3 April 1926, p. 17.

55. "World War II: Personal Accounts—Pearl Harbor to V-J Day." Traveling Exhibition of the National Archives, displayed at the Museum of the Jimmy Carter Library, Atlanta, Georgia, 1994.

56. Here are the figures for the use of *dad* and *mom* in the fatherhood articles typed onto disk:

Period	Dad		Mom		N
1901–1909	7%	(1)	0%	(0)	14
1910–1915	19%	(3)	0%	(0)	16
1916–1921	50%	(4)	0%	(0)	8
1922–1929	63%	(12)	0%	(0)	19
1930–1934	44%	(19)	0%	(0)	43
1935–1939	29%	(10)	0%	(0)	34
1940–1942	40%	(6)	7%	(1)	15
Overall	37%	(55)	<1%	(1)	149

This is one analysis where *Parents' Magazine* could have proved to be a factor. If we look only at the articles published in *Parents' Magazine,* we see a replication of the above table:

Period	Dad		Mom		N
1930–1934	41%	(14)	0%	(0)	34
1935–1939	32%	(7)	0%	(0)	22
1940–1942	44%	(4)	0%	(0)	9
Overall	38%	(25)	0%	(0)	65

On the other hand, if we look at the articles *not* published in *Parents' Magazine,* we see the following:

Period	Dad		Mom		N
1930–1934	56%	(5)	0%	(0)	9
1935–1939	25%	(3)	0%	(0)	12
1940–1942	33%	(2)	<1%	(1)	6
Overall	37%	(10)	<1%	(1)	27

The most obvious difference is the higher percentage of *dad* in the early 1930s, showing that *Parents' Magazine* made the move away from *dad* earlier. Still, there is a decline in the use of *dad* in the 1930s, and the pattern for the late 1930s is replicated all around. This supports again the thesis that not only were the 1920s and 1930s different with respect to the culture of fatherhood, but that the early 1930s and late 1930s were different as well.

Finally, it is interesting to note that five of the six articles in the 1940–42 period that used *dad* were authored by men. This was an exception to the rule. Generally, the term would be used more in articles written by women. This may reflect a third-person effect, where it is more common for a woman to refer to men as "dads" than it is for men to refer to themselves as "dads." In advice-seeking letters that were written to Angelo Patri (who will be discussed in chapter 7), mothers who wrote were more likely than fathers who wrote to use *dad*.

57. Frederick Strothman, "Will Fathers Never Learn?," *Parents' Magazine,* April 1919, pp. 109, 11, 113–14.

58. Frank Cheley, "Why One Father Succeeded with His Sons," *Good Housekeeping,* February 1921, p. 48.

59. Anonymous, "The Greatest American Invention," *The Outlook* (July 1919), pp. 463–464.

60. Not every article published between 1916 and 1921 was intent on pushing the virtues of daddyhood. The articles that did not, however, were different for a very special reason: their focus was the war. The longest, by far, of the fatherhood articles to talk about the First World War was a piece in which a man spoke about the insights and feelings that he had gained after he visited his son who was stationed in France. "Here is American fatherhood personified," he suggested:

> Of Motherhood and its relation to war much has been said—and every true man echoes every word of it. . . . But the men of America, those beyond the fighting age, what hopes and apprehensions battle in their breasts these days? What of the fathers whom our boys have left behind? . . . In two million homes at this hour of the evening two million men stand, their workworn hands clutched tight, their hearts reaching out to those boys beyond the seas, or soon to go beyond. And in every heart the same questions: *"How does he look?" "Is he well?" "Is he happy?" "Is he safe?" "Does he want for anything?"* . . . War has sounded new depths in the hearts of us fathers of America. It has drawn us close to our sons. It has given us a knowledge of them and a reverence for them which years of peace never could have brought. We shall come out of this war worthier fathers of nobler and manlier sons. And we shall understand why it was that, when Jesus Christ sought to convey to the world the quality of God's love, He could express it only with the single word—Father.

See John R. Mott, "When I Saw My Boy in France," *American Magazine,* October 1918, pp. 7–8. If there is any event that has the power to throw a wrench in the culture of daddyhood and enhance men's traditionally held prestige and prerequisites, it would be an international conflict. See Janet Saltzman Chafetz, *Gender Equity: An Integrated Theory of Stability and Change* (Newbury Park, CA: Sage, 1990), pp. 119–21. But World War I did not seem to have much of an effect, along these lines. (World War II was another story, as we will see in chapter 8.) One possible explanation is that the First World War was too short to register much of an impact, just over a year in terms of the United States' involvement. Another is that the culture of daddyhood was too strong at this point to be deterred. Whatever the case, the general direction that the fatherhood articles were taking in the late teens and early twenties was not appreciably affected by the hostilities in Europe.

61. The "law of the excluded middle" is nicely described in Eviatar Zerubavel, *The Fine Line: Making Distinctions in Everyday Life* (New York: Free Press; reprinted by the University of Chicago Press, 1991), p. 46. For a discussion of the instrumental and expressive aspects of fatherhood and motherhood, see Alice Rossi, "Transition to Parenthood," *Journal of Marriage and the Family* 30 (February 1968), pp.26–39. A recent and humorous example of how fatherhood can be separated cognitively from motherhood was the television show *Dinosaurs*, in which the baby dinosaur would refer to the father as "Not the Mamma."

62. See Merle Farmer Murphy, "Poor Dad," the *Independent*, 31 January 1925, pp. 127–29.

63. Ibid. As "evidence" for his point, the author cited what he claimed to have observed on the day before Christmas: All the department stores were virtually empty, save for the counters that sold men's furnishings. Here there was bedlam because countless numbers of wives and children, as he saw it, did not realize until the last minute that they had failed to get father a gift: "'What have we got for father?' 'We have actually forgotten father!'" Another article, also published in 1925, said that fathers generally were perceived as "dubs." By the end of the piece, the author, a father himself, opined that the label was not entirely fair: "Yes, fathers are undoubtedly comic characters to their own and other people's progeny. They were funny to me too, until I became a dub father. Now it is harder for me to appreciate the joke. Or perhaps, after all, there isn't any." See Frederic F. Van de Water, "Confessions of a Dub Father," *Ladies Home Journal*, May 1925, pp. 25, 97, 98.

64. Rotundo, *American Manhood*. One article published in 1915, on the eve of the emergence of the culture of daddyhood, referred to the blending of masculine and feminine in the world of fatherhood as "padonna and child." The modernization of fatherhood under the culture of daddyhood thus had the potential to become the *madonna-ization* of fatherhood. See Mare Ware Dennett, "The Right of a Child to Two Parents," *Century Magazine*, May 1915, pp. 104–8.

65. The same proportions prevail today. Mothers play with children more than fathers play with children, but a greater proportion of men's child care time is taken up with play. For a discussion of this phenomenon from a variety of viewpoints, see Jane C. Hood, ed., *Men, Work, and Family* (Newbury Park, CA: Sage, 1993).

Chapter 7: "Dear Mr. Patri"

1. D.J.O. (male) to Angelo Patri, Box 2, 12 February 1925, Angelo Patri Papers, Library of Congress.

2. Angelo Patri to D.J.O., Box 2, 17 February 1925, Angelo Patri Papers, Library of Congress.

3. Angelo Patri was born in the Salerno province of Italy on 24 November 1876. He and his parents emigrated to the United States when he was five. He graduated from Columbia in 1904 and became a principal in 1908. While at Columbia, Patri studied under John Dewey, one of the founders of progressive education (learn-

ing by doing). Patri may have been the first native of Italy to become a public school principal in the United States. He died on 13 September 1965. See "Patri, Angelo," *Dictionary of American Biography—Supplement Seven, 1961–1965,* ed. John A. Garratz (New York: Charles Scribner's Sons, 1981), p. 600; "Patri, Angelo," *Current Biography, 1940,* ed. Maxine Block (New York: H. W. Wilson, 1940), p. 633; "Angelo Patri, Educator, Dead; Pioneered Liberal Teaching," *New York Times,* 14 September 1965.

4. Angelo Patri first became nationally known by writing books. He started with children's stories (had a very successful series on Pinocchio). Then he penned his autobiography, *A School Master of the Great City* (1917). Finally, Patri moved on to produce a number of how-to manuals on education and child rearing, including *The School That Everyone Wants* (1922); *Child Training, School and Home* (1925); *Problems of Childhood* (1926); *What Have You Got to Give* (1926); *The Questioning Child* (1930); *Parent's Daily Counselor* (1940); *Your Children in War Time* (1943); and *To Help Your Child Grow Up* (1948). Patri also wrote freelance articles, and was on the editorial board of both *Parents' Magazine* and *Child Study,* the newsletter of the Child Study Association of America. Patri was marketed to his listeners and readers as "The Children's Friend." People looked at him that way, too. Said one father, "We all know that you are the best friend that any child ever had." L.S. (male) to Angelo Patri, Box 25, 1 December 1933, Angelo Patri Papers, Library of Congress. Patri's guest book, kept at JHS 45, indicates that he received visitors from the four corners of the globe. Children would write to him not only tell him how much they liked him but also to ask for his autograph or photograph. See A.H. (male) to Angelo Patri, Box 17, 19 May 1932; W.B.S. (male) to Angelo Patri, Box 17, 25 May 1932; N.K. (female) to Angelo Patri, Box 18, date unknown, 1932, Angelo Patri Papers, Library of Congress. In 1936, a father of a three-year-old daughter asked Patri for a photograph so that he would have "a memento of Angelo Patri" to give his child when she was older. J.W.B. (male) to Angelo Patri, Box 31, date unknown, 1936, Angelo Patri Papers, Library of Congress.

5. Because Patri's column was syndicated (to one hundred U.S. newspapers at one point—see "Died. Angelo Patri," *Time,* 24 September 1965)—Patri would get letters from around the country. Most of the letters in the collection were from New York, Massachusetts, Illinois, Ohio, Michigan, New Jersey, and California. Hardly any letters were from the south. People wrote to Patri because he asked them to. At the end of his show and column, he would invite queries on child rearing and said that he would personally reply to the mail he received. A newspaper clipping that was included with a letter sent to Patri in 1931 stated, "Mr. Patri will give personal attention to inquiries from parents and school teachers on the care and development of children. Write him in care of this paper, enclosing stamped, addressed envelope for reply." Attachment to G.G.M. (male) to Angelo Patri, Box 16, 21 June 1931, Angelo Patri Papers, Library of Congress. In 1930, Patri estimated that he was receiving about forty letters a month from the public. By 1934, Patri claimed that he was receiving as many as five thousand letters each month. Most of his correspondence is from the early 1930s, coinciding with the

time that his radio program was on the air. About 20 percent of the letter writers in the early 1930s mentioned that they had listened to his program.

How many letters Patri received overall is difficult to know because only those letters to which Patri replied were placed in the collection. Numbers of unanswered letters thus may have been destroyed. In 1935, for example, Patri was very sick, and only a handful of letters from that year are housed at the Library of Congress. When I discovered the Angelo Patri Papers (by searching through the *National Union Catalog of Manuscript Collections*), I thought I might be able to use the number of letters that fathers wrote each year as a crude measure of father involvement over time. Once I realized, however, that there was no way to tell how many letters were thrown away, I abandoned this strategy.

Just so the reader will know, the boxes in the collection that have the most letters from fathers center on the years, 1932, 1933, and 1934. How Patri managed to reply to so many letters on top of his other professional responsibilities is a testament to Patri's skill and to the depth of his heart. He may also have been aided, as was Dr. Benjamin Spock when he wrote the first edition of *Baby and Child Care,* by his wife. Patri was married to the former Dorothy Caterson, who worked for the New York school system for thirty years and who was an assistant principal herself for fifteen years. Whether she helped her husband respond to parents, I do not know. Patri's descendants suggested to me that Mrs. Patri may have typed the letters. In a few cases, in addition to the typed letter, there is, scribbled on the letter that Patri received, Patri's handwritten reply. The handwritten text and the typed text generally were identical, suggesting that if Mrs. Patri did type the letters, she did not edit them. Future scholars may want to carefully examine the text of Patri's replies to see if there are significant differences in syntax and form. It is possible, especially when Patri was very ill or busy, that Mrs. Patri was responsible for some of the replies. At this point, a determination cannot be made.

6. People who wrote to Patri generally did not volunteer direct information about their education, income, and occupation. Nor did they generally give indirect information that could be used to infer their socioeconomic status; such as whether they lived in a house or apartment, or whether they owned a car. However, the content of the letters, quality of the stationary, penmanship, spelling, and grammar all point to a middle-class clientele. I am not suggesting that everyone who wrote was middle class. Some writers apparently had trouble making ends meet, and others wrote that the Depression had "gotten" or "oppressed" them. But for every one who fell into this category, there was at least one other who wrote about private camps and colleges, or summer homes on the lake.

7. The late sociologist C. Wright Mills would have said that the letters allow us to see the connection between history and biography, the very core of "the sociological imagination." See C. Wright Mills, *The Sociological Imagination* (London: Oxford University Press, 1959).

8. The vast majority of the letters in the Patri collection were from fathers and mothers of school-age daughters and sons. Grandparents, aunts, uncles, and teachers also wrote but not often. Children, too; as I said, young boys and girls sometimes wrote to Patri asking for his autograph or photograph. More commonly,

however, when they wrote, they were lamenting about their peers or their parents. In 1937, for example, a teenager told Patri about how people were constantly finding fault with her—that her skirts were too short, her walk was not graceful enough, her hair was old fashioned. "I am so discouraged," she said. "Please tell me what to try next? My Dad won't even speak to me unless necessary, he dislikes me so." H.S.B. (female) to Angelo Patri, Box 33, 28 May 1937, Angelo Patri Papers, Library of Congress.

One interesting aspect of the children's letters is that every now and then the children would tell Patri that they regularly listened to his radio show, which was generally broadcast in the evening. This brought to mind the fact that in the early days of radio, it was not uncommon for middle-and upper-class families to assemble in the living room, be busy with their own activities (father and mother with the newspaper, children with their homework), and listen to the radio en masse. If Patri's program was on the air, it would mean that both parents and children were being exposed to his teachings. Today, most parent education programs are scheduled during the day, not during prime time. Thus, it is rare for children, with or without their parents, to view or hear lessons on child rearing. Significant, too, is the fact that fathers and mothers would listen to Patri while seated in the same room. How often nowadays do fathers and mothers jointly watch or listen to a program on raising kids? We thus see that the Machine Age had some unique features that encouraged not only close but also egalitarian ties between one generation and the next.

9. Not every letter to Patri focused on a particular child-rearing issue. Some letters fell under the heading of business correspondence. Patri was occasionally asked to speak at a PTA meeting or study group. For example, in 1936, Patri's presence was requested at the "Angelo Patri Child Study Group" of Berwyn, Illinois. L.J.B. (male) to Angelo Patri, Box 31, 8 March 1936, Angelo Patri Papers, Library of Congress. In other instances, Patri was asked to evaluate a commercial product: What child rearing books would Patri recommend? Is an encyclopedia a good idea? What did Patri think of *Parents' Magazine?* Most of the time, however, people would write to Patri to ask for his help in solving what they perceived to be a "difficult" or "serious" or "troubling" family problem.

10. "Father" ("Our Children" column), Box 44, 11 May 1925, Angelo Patri Papers, Library of Congress.

11. "Father's Turn" ("Our Children" column), Box 44, 17 August 1925, Angelo Patri Papers, Library of Congress.

12. "Your Father" ("Our Children" column), Box 45, 24 October 1926, Angelo Patri Papers, Library of Congress.

13. "Father, Explain Yourself" ("Our Children" column), Box 46, 2 July 1928, Angelo Patri Papers, Library of Congress.

14. "Fathers" (Radio Script), Box 40, 23 October 1932, Angelo Patri Papers, Library of Congress.

15. It is hard, at least for me, not to pronounce Patri's name as "Pa-TREE" which would make it sound like the Latin pronunciation for father—*in nomine Patris* (in the name of the Father). Patri's heirs, however, informed me that the first syllable rhymes with "cat" or "hat," i.e., "PAT-tree."

16. E.G. (male) to Angelo Patri, Box 3, 21 August 1925, Angelo Patri Papers, Library of Congress.

17. C.P.M. (male) to Angelo Patri, Box 30, 6 February 1936, Angelo Patri Papers, Library of Congress.

18. B.S.T. (male) to Angelo Patri, Box 24, 26 April 1933, Angelo Patri Papers, Library of Congress.

19. T.G. (male) to Angelo Patri, Box 3, 11 May 1925, Angelo Patri Papers, Library of Congress.

20. L.V.W. (female) to Angelo Patri, Box 5, 4 February 1927, Angelo Patri Papers, Library of Congress.

21. J.B. (male) to Angelo Patri, Box 34, 6 March 1938, Angelo Patri Papers, Library of Congress.

22. W.P.B. (female) to Angelo Patri, Box 34, 2 May 1938, Angelo Patri Papers, Library of Congress.

23. I.M.C. (male) to Angelo Patri, Box 3, 18 March 1925, Angelo Patri Papers, Library of Congress.

24. A.R. (male) to Angelo Patri, Box 32, 18 May 1937, Angelo Patri Papers, Library of Congress.

25. L.P.M. (female) to Angelo Patri, Box 4, 21 October 1926, Angelo Patri Papers, Library of Congress.

26. M.R.B. (male) to Angelo Patri, Box 32, 29 September 1936, Angelo Patri Papers, Library of Congress.

27. G.D.H. (female) to Angelo Patri, Box 17, date unknown, 1932, Angelo Patri Papers, Library of Congress.

28. C.C. (female) to Angelo Patri, Box 31, 10 March 1936, Angelo Patri Papers, Library of Congress.

29. W.H.G. (male) to Angelo Patri, Box 3, 17 December 1925, Angelo Patri Papers, Library of Congress.

30. M.E.L. (female) to Angelo Patri, Box 5, 5 October 1927, Angelo Patri Papers, Library of Congress.

31. M.I.S. (male) to Angelo Patri, Box 7, 29 September 1928, Angelo Patri Papers, Library of Congress. For a history of the term, *sissy*, see Michael Kimmel, *Manhood in America: A Cultural History* (New York: Free Press, 1996), p. 100; E. Anthony Rotundo, *American Manhood: Transformations in Masculinity from the Revolution to the Modern Era* (New York: Basic, 1993), p. 273.

32. K.W. (female) to Angelo Patri, Box 29, 5 June 1934, Angelo Patri Papers, Library of Congress.

33. M.H.H. (female) to Angelo Patri, Box 5, 26 November 1926, Angelo Patri Papers, Library of Congress.

34. J.H.R. (male) to Angelo Patri, Box 8, 15 December 1928, Angelo Patri Papers, Library of Congress.

35. M.M.B. (female) to Angelo Patri, Box 29, 28 April 1934, Angelo Patri Papers, Library of Congress.

36. E.Z.E. (female) to Angelo Patri, Box 19, 26 July 1932, Angelo Patri Papers, Library of Congress. Patri seemed miffed that he would receive such a request. "I'm an educator—not a silver expert," he said. He also politely advised the

mother "not [to] choose one of the modernistic patterns," and he recommended two stores. Angelo Patri to E.Z.E., Box 19, 2 August 1932, Angelo Patri Papers, Library of Congress. Keep in mind that Patri's column and radio show were not public services, but commercial ventures. Patri thus was not likely to tell too many parents what he honestly thought of their requests.

37. D.W. (female) to Angelo Patri, Box 31, 28 February 1936, Angelo Patri Papers, Library of Congress.

38. Y.S.H. (female) to Angelo Patri, Box 5, 15 March 1927, Angelo Patri Papers, Library of Congress.

39. G.W.B. (female) to Angelo Patri, Box 5, 21 April 1927, Angelo Patri Papers, Library of Congress.

40. D.S.R. (female) to Angelo Patri, Box 5, 27 April 1927, Angelo Patri Papers, Library of Congress.

41. It is obvious from the number of letters Patri received that he had a great following. It is also clear from the content of the letters that parents respected him. Accompanying a mother's letter about a child who stuttered, for example, was this message from her husband: "We, my wife and I, are *No. 1* rooters for your broadcast and column. I can think of *no* reason to subscribe to the *Brooklyn Daily Eagle* except to read your column—and incidentally I have just sent them a letter stating just that. I have also sent a letter to Cream of Wheat telling them of the High regard the people of the U.S. have for you." (Cream of Wheat was one of Patri's sponsors.) G.D.H. (male) to Angelo Patri, Box 17, date unknown, 1932, Angelo Patri Papers, Library of Congress. Another letter writer reported: "Your daily article in the newspaper has been such an inspiration to our group of women that we have named our club the "Angelo Patri Child Study Group." L.J.B. (female) to Angelo Patri, Box 31, 8 March 1936, Angelo Patri Papers, Library of Congress.

Not everyone, however, was enamored with everything that Patri had to say. In 1930, a priest took exception to Patri's suggestion that there were mothers in the world who might like to deal with their "boy-crazy" daughters by forcing them to live in a convent. Said the priest to Patri: "One is painfully surprised at the necessity of reminding one of Mr. Patri's intelligence and presumably wide information (and one bearing such a patronymic) that people are not 'shut up' in convents." R.F.H. (male) to Angelo Patri, Box 13, 10 January 1930, Angelo Patri Papers, Library Congress. Patri, himself a Catholic, replied that he "had not the slightest intention of making a reflection upon either the sisters or the convents." Angelo Patri to R.F.H., Box 13, 21 January 1930, Angelo Patri Papers, Library of Congress.

Here is another example showing that Patri could be faulted; one that shows, too, the push toward father inclusion during the Machine Age. In 1934, a man wrote to criticize Patri for writing an article titled "Father's Daughter." "Why should it be 'Father's Daughter' or 'Mother's Daughter' when it really should be 'Parents' Daughter.'? It should not be a question of the father or mother gaining the confidence of the daughter or son, but it should be a co-operation of the parents themselves so that there is no favoritism to begin with." H.S.R. (male) to Angelo Patri, Box 28, 5 April 1934, Angelo Patri Papers, Library of Congress.

Replied Patri: "I am afraid I must have expressed myself awkwardly if you got the impression that I believed in a division of responsibility in a matter of rearing children. My idea about it is that team work is essential. That every effort should be made to avoid teaching the child to pick one parent against the other and so free himself of both." Angelo Patri to H.S.R., Box 28, 10 April 1934, Angelo Patri Papers, Library of Congress.

42. Robert L. Griswold, *Fatherhood in America: A History.* (New York: Basic, 1993), pp. 128, 129.

43. Robert Griswold also draws on the Angelo Patri collection and uses it to convey the impression that fathers in the 1920s and 1930s were inept. He writes, "These fathers—many of whom were highly educated professionals or business-men—often requested advice about the simplest issues." Then, after listing some of the questions that the fathers asked, he says, "From one perspective, these questions seem fatuous, simpleminded, and hardly worthy of the attention of a nationally syndicated child rearing expert" (Griswold, *Fatherhood in America*, 1993, pp. 121, 122). Given that fathers are singled out here, one would have to assume that Griswold saw differences between the fathers' and mothers' letters, yet he makes no mention of the mothers' letters in his text. To characterize the fathers' letters as "simpleminded" without comparing them (on a number of dimensions) to the mothers' letters is not methodologically sound. Griswold also cites only about seventy letters from fathers out of the more than five hundred that are in the collection; moreover, he disproportionately samples from the fathers' letters that were written in 1920s. (Relevant here is the fact that the vast majority of the fathers' letters in the collection were written between 1925 and 1939, with the high points being 1932, 1933, and 1934. The picture is curvilinear. See endnote 5.)

Griswold's oversampling of the 1920s may account some for his tendency to characterize the Patri fathers as inept. When I systematically compared the fathers' and mothers' letters, in terms of the kinds of child-rearing problems the parents wrote about, I discovered that generally the fathers and mothers wrote about the same kinds of problems. When I focused on the 1920s, however, I saw that the fathers were less likely than the mothers to write about control or disciplinary matters. This difference between the fathers' and mothers' letters in the 1920s could be connected to the culture of daddyhood that was particulary strong in the 1920s when popular magazines were more likely to be pushing a more playful father (see chapter 6). Underscored again are the risks associated with disproportionately focusing on the 1920s to understand the modernization of fatherhood.

44. Ann Swidler, "Culture in Action," *American Sociological Review* 51 (April 1986), p. 277; see also, for example, Terry Strathman, "From the Quotidian to the Utopian: Child-Rearing Literature in America, 1926–1946," *Berkeley Journal of Sociology* 29 (1984), pp. 17–18. I will not present the full theoretical discussion on the sociology of culture here. The reader can review the section titled, "Were Men Cultural Dopes?" in chapter 4.

45. On culture as an "objectivated reality," see Peter L. Berger and Thomas Luckmann, *The Social Construction of Reality: A Treatise in the Sociology of Knowledge* (Garden City, NY: Doubleday/Anchor, 1966).

46. M.T. (female) to Angelo Patri, Box 3, 26 April 1925, Angelo Patri Papers, Library of Congress.

47. M.T. (female) to Angelo Patri, Box 3, 2 May 1925, Angelo Patri Papers, Library of Congress.

48. M.T. (female) to Angelo Patri, Box 3, 6 May 1925, Angelo Patri Papers, Library of Congress.

49. Angelo Patri to M.T., Box 3, 7 May 1925, Angelo Patri Papers, Library of Congress.

50. See Carol J. Boggs, "Train Up a Parent: A Review of the Research in Child-Rearing Literature," *Child Study Journal* 10 (1981), pp. 261–84; Strathman, "From the Quotidian to the Utopian," pp. 1–34.

51. Pollock also comments on the role that children play: "Children . . . are far from passive creatures; they make demands on their parents and parents are forced to operate within the context of these demands." See Linda A. Pollock, *Forgotten Children: Parent-Child Relations from 1500 to 1900* (Cambridge: Cambridge University Press, 1983), p. 270.

52. Jay Mechling, "Advice to Historians on Advice to Mothers," *Journal of Social History* 9 (Fall 1975), pp. 44–63. See also Boggs, "Train Up a Parent, pp. 261–84.

53. I am drawing here on sociologist Emily Blumenfeld's phrasing: "Most studies of childrearing literature have purported to document historical changes in childrearing. But in the final analysis, documentation of historical changes calls forth conceptions of agencies of change. Hence, we would suggest a shift in emphasis from source to audience is required for a historical study of childrearing. A shift away from an uncritical evaluation of 'expertise' is called for." See Emily R. Blumenfeld, "Childrearing Literature as an Object of Content Analysis," *Journal of Applied Communication Research* 4 (November 1976), p. 85.

54. Portions of the quantitative analysis appeared in Ralph LaRossa and Donald C. Reitzes, "Continuity and Change in Middle-Class Fatherhood, 1925–1939: The Culture-Conduct Connection," *Journal of Marriage and the Family* 55 (May 1993), pp. 455–68; and Ralph LaRossa and Donald C. Reitzes, "Gendered Perceptions of Father Involvement in Early-Twentieth-Century America," *Journal of Marriage and the Family* 57 (February 1995), pp. 223–29.

55. A.W. (female) to Angelo Patri, Box 6, 21 July 1928, Angelo Patri Papers, Library of Congress.

56. For a discussion of how family care is broader than generally is thought, see Paula L. Dressel and Ann Clark, "A Critical Look at Family Care," *Journal of Marriage and the Family* 52 (August 1990), pp. 769–82.

57. One can see from the list that the operational definition of parental behavior employed was intended to be expansive enough to include one-on-one interaction with a child, termed *engagement,* being available should the child call, termed *accessibility,* and being accountable for the child's welfare, termed *responsibility.* This trifold typology of parental behavior, to my knowledge, was suggested first by psychologist Michael E. Lamb. See, for example, Michael E. Lamb "Introduction: The Emergent American Father," in *The Father's Role: Cross-Cultural Perspectives,* ed. Michael E. Lamb (Hillsdale, NJ: Lawrence Erlbaum, 1987), specifically pp. 7–11.

58. V.P. (male) to Angelo Patri, Box 5, 28 November 1927, Angelo Patri Papers, Library of Congress.

59. Behaviors that fathers and mothers carried out jointly were not distinguished from those that they did alternately, for there generally was too little information to differentiate between the two situations. Also, some behaviors included other people (e.g., mother and grandmother together with a child); in these instances, the primary parent received credit for carrying out the behavior. In only one case could a person not be assigned to a behavior; it was coded, "don't know."

60. The parents-together proportion, for example, is the number of behaviors in the letter carried out jointly or alternately, divided by the total number of behaviors in the letter.

61. Rules of grammar also were taken into account. For example, if a parent said, "I drove my child to school," the "I" would not be counted as evidence of personal identification with the child because, it was assumed, only one person can drive a car.

62. Recall, for example, that the father of three who was discussed earlier wrote, "I work late every night and it might have some effect on them because they want to see *Daddy.* And when they do they want to play and talk with me." V. P. (male) to Angelo Patri, Box 5, 28 November 1927, Angelo Patri Papers, Library of Congress. And here is a letter from a thirteen-year-old girl that illustrates the use of *mother* and *dad* in the same sentence: "My mother and dad are pretty swell in most ways, but they just make a baby out of me." L.E. (female) to Angelo Patri, Box 34, date unknown, 1938, Angelo Patri Papers, Library of Congress. (This second letter did not make it into the sample of 256.)

63. A multivariate (three or more variables) analysis is best understood as a counterpoint to a bivariate (two variable) analysis. The idea behind a multivariate analysis is to examine the relationship between two variables, while holding constant the influence of one or more other variables. The variables that were controlled in the analysis include, gender and age of the problem child, kind of child-rearing problem being written about, and average number of syllables per word (to control for social class). The two kinds of multivariate analysis that I employed were multiple regression and logistical regression. The former was used when the dependent variable was a continuous variable (e.g., letter length); the latter was used when the dependent variable was a discrete, dichotomous variable (e.g., the presence or absence of *dad* or *daddy*). Due to the size of the sample, the cutting point for statistical significance was set at the .10 error level, meaning that all relationships with at least a 90 percent probability of being valid are reported. For a more extensive discussion of the variables and statistical procedures used, see LaRossa and Reitzes, "Continuity and Change in Middle-Class Fatherhood, 1925–1939," pp. 455–68, and LaRossa and Reitzes, "Gendered Perceptions of Father Involvement," pp. 223–29.

64. See also chapter 4, note 68. To further examine the division of parental behaviors, another analysis was done in which, instead of the letter being the unit of analysis ($N = 256$), the behavior became the unit of analysis ($N = 1,051$). Shifting the unit of analysis permitted a multivariate test to see whether the differences in the division of parental behaviors between the fathers and mothers would remain after the following five variables were controlled:

population, syllables, gender of child, age of child, and length of letter. The differences remained, increasing confidence in the relative effect of *gender* on perceptions of parental involvement.

Also, further coding, which categorized each behavior as a custodial behavior, an inside-the-house behavior, a child-present behavior, a socialization behavior, or a negative-sanction behavior, showed that the differences between the fathers' and mothers' letters on the division of parental behaviors were strongest when the behavior in question was custodial or a negative sanction. Mothers tended to credit themselves on the custodial behaviors and discredit themselves on negative sanctions. Fathers credited themselves on the custodial behaviors, but did not accentuate their own use of negative sanctions. The mothers, in other words, were found again to present a very traditional picture, not unlike the picture presented in the mother-based surveys from the 1920s and 1930s. See LaRossa and Reitzes, "Gendered Perceptions of Father Involvement."

65. For the figures on the fatherhood articles, see chapter 6. Father-to-father books are discussed in chapter 5.

66. See Glen H. Elder Jr., Tri Van Nguyen, and Avshalom Caspi, "Linking Family Hardship to Children's Lives," *Child Development* 56 (1985), pp. 361–75.

67. On the negative impact of the Depression, see note 34 in chapter 1.

68. Steven Mintz and Susan Kellogg, *Domestic Revolutions: A Social History of American Family Life* (New York: Free Press, 1988), p. 139.

69. For a discussion of "deficit living" during the Depression, see Winifred D. Wandersee, *Women's Work and Family Values, 1920–1940* (Cambridge, MA: Harvard University Press), pp. 27–54.

70. On the relationship between the structure of one's commitments and the perceived scarcity of one's time, see Stephen Marks, "Multiple Roles and Role Strain: Some Notes on Human Energy, Time and Commitment." *American Sociological Review* 42 (December 1977), pp. 921–36; also Ralph LaRossa, "The Transition to Parenthood and the Social Reality of Time," *Journal of Marriage and the Family* 45 (August 1983), pp. 579–89.

71. Of course the pattern could have been the reverse. Fathers who were out of work or concerned about their work could have elevated their father involvement (seeing their children as islands in the storm), and there is anecdotal evidence to suggest that some fathers did, in fact, take this course. See Robert C. Angell, *The Family Encounters the Depression* (New York: Charles Scribner's Sons, 1936). Most of the evidence, however, as I said before, indicates that the Depression reduced father-child contact.

72. A "salient" role is one that frequently is invoked and that generates the highest levels of commitment. See Peter J. Burke and Donald C. Reitzes, "An Identity Theory Approach to Commitment," *Social Psychology Quarterly* 54 (1991), pp. 239–51.

Chapter 8: "Honor Thy Father"

1. Flyer accompanying G.G.M. (male) to Angelo Patri, Box 16, 21 June 1931, Angelo Patri Papers, Library of Congress.

2. The scheduling may have been deliberate, but I suspect it was not. From the turn of the century to the beginning of the Depression, the appropriate date for

Father's Day was the subject of some confusion and, at times, debate. In 1925, for example, tobacconists launched an advertising campaign affirming that Father's Day was the second Sunday in June (14 June that year). A number of groups, including the Boy Scouts and the American Legion, objected, however, citing the fact that the second Sunday in June in 1925 was Flag Day. Tobacconists apologized for their mistake and went on record in support of what has become the standard date throughout the United States, the third Sunday in June. The fact that the Father-and-Son dinner in 1931 was sponsored by the Boy Scouts, which only a few years before had argued against the second Sunday in June, leads me to believe that the timing of the 1931 event was a mistake. See "Wrong Guess Caused Father's Day Mix-Up," *New York Times*, 5 June 1925, p. 3.

3. Ibid.

4. Peter Filene's characterization of Father's Day is typical of how historians have approached the subject: "Father's Day had begun merely as an afterthought—a commercial afterthought—to the moralistic proclamation of Mother's Day." See Peter Filene, *Him/Her/Self: Sex Roles in Modern America*, 2d ed. (Baltimore: Johns Hopkins University Press, 1986), p. 172. Robert Griswold chooses not to discuss Father's Day at all in *Fatherhood in America: A History* (New York: Basic Books, 1993), though the publisher did release the book on Father's Day. Leigh Eric Schmidt in *Consumer Rites: The Buying and Selling of American Holidays* (Princeton, NJ: Princeton University Press, 1995) offers what may be the first scholarly treatment of Father's Day (in a chapter titled "Mother's Day Bouquet"). I say "scholarly" treatment, because histories of Father's Day and Mother's Day have appeared in holiday encyclopedias; for example: Jane M. Hatch, *The American Book of Days*, 3d ed. (New York: H. W. Wilson, 1978), pp. 574–75; Maymie R. Krythe, *All About American Holidays* (New York: Harper & Row, 1962), pp. 157–61; Robert J. Meyers, *Celebrations: The Complete Book of Holidays* (New York: Doubleday, 1972), pp. 184–87. Like most others, Schmidt contends that Father's Day essentially was a commercial "spin-off" of Mother's Day. My own position on the matter is slightly different. While I agree that the business community had a lot to do with making Father's Day a national holiday, and will demonstrate as much in the pages that follow, I also think that the institutionalization of Father's Day in the 1930s was closely tied to the modernization of fatherhood in the 1930s. Thus, there is a connection to the social reconstruction of fatherhood in early-twentieth-century America that seems to have escaped even the most thoughtful observers.

5. Both Committees (a.k.a. Councils) operate out of the same office in New York City.

6. *Father's Day: 75th Anniversary Commemorative* (New York: Father's Day Committee, 1985), p. 4

7. Hatch, *The American Book of Days*, pp. 574–75; Krythe, *All About American Holidays*, pp. 157–61; Meyers, *Celebrations*, pp. 184–87.

8. "News for National Mother's Day Committee" (New York: National Mother's Day Committee, 1986); "Tenth Anniversary Outstanding Mother Awards" (New York: National Mother's Day Committee, 1988); "Mother's Day Press Kit" (New York: National Mother's Day Committee, 1994). A press kit for Father's Day also is prepared each year.

9. Hatch, *The American Book of Days*, p. 439.

10. "News for National Mother's Day Committee," p. 1.

11. Hatch, *The American Book of Days*; Krythe, *All About American Holidays*; Meyers, *Celebrations*.

12. "Father to Have His Day," *New York Times*, 3 October 1913, p. 1.

13. "Justice" (pseudonym?) to the Editor, *New York Times*, 11 June 1914, p. 10; Jack Cattell to the Editor, *New York Times*, 14 June 1914, p. II-14; Jack Cattel to the Editor, *New York Times*. 23 June 1914, p. 10. The second and third letters, as one can see, were written by the same person. The quotation ("This feast day . . . .") is in the third letter.

14. Krythe, *All About American Holidays*; Meyers, *Celebrations*. The quotation is from Krythe, p. 159. The *New York Times* was aware of the difficulties associated with trying to piece together a history of Father's Day. In 1932, there appeared the following: "Father's Day, though brief, has a long if somewhat vague and misty history. Credit for the idea is hard to place with any accuracy. Legend has it that a Mrs. John Bruce Dodd got the inspiration out in Spokane or Seattle—the records are not clear on that point—about twenty or twenty-six years ago. Harry C. Meek of the Uptown Lions Club in Chicago is understood to have let the idea get around that he was back of the movement. It seems, according to some sources, that it just came to him out of a clear blue sky one day in June, 1920. The records show that he got President Coolidge to endorse it at least twice." See "Fathers to Receive Honors Tomorrow," *New York Times*, 18 June 1932, p. 3.

15. Hatch, *The American Book of Days*, p. 439.

16. Stephanie Coontz, *The Way We Never Were: American Families and the Nostalgia Trip* (New York: Basic Books, 1992), p. 152.

17. Ibid.; italics in original. Although the original plan may have been more community oriented, a shift from the plural to the singular already had begun by the late nineteenth century. In 1887, Kentucky teacher Mary Towles Sasseen organized the first of what would become an annual musical program to honor the mothers of her students, and in 1893, she published a pamphlet that described her classroom experiences. Up until her death in 1916, Sasseen had traveled throughout the country urging other teachers to follow her lead. In 1904, Frank E. Herring, a professor at the University of Notre Dame, gave an address to his men's club, the Fraternal Order of Eagles, in which he put forth the idea that mothers should be honored on a special day each year. See Hatch, *The American Book of Days*, p. 439. In 1925, the American War Mothers concluded that the Notre Dame professor was "the inspiration for the present Mother's Day," (in this piece, Herring was spelled Hering). See "The Father of Mother's Day," *New York Times*, 9 May 1934, p. 18. Anna M. Jarvis quickly followed in 1907 with her idea for a family-oriented Mother's Day observance.

18. "Would Bar Liquor from State Dinners . . . Plea for a Fathers' [*sic*] Day," *New York Times*, 28 May 1911, p. 9.

19. "More Justice" (pseudonym?) to the Editor, *New York Times*, 14 June 1914, p. II-14.

20. "Against Mothers' [*sic*] Day," *New York Times*, 10 May 1908, p. II-7.

21. Helen K. Line to the Editor, *The Christian Century*, 18 May 1938, p. 628.

22. "To Mark Parents' Day," *New York Times*, 19 April 1931, p. II-4.

23. "Sets Parents' Day for City's Children: Uncle Robert to Lead Annual Tribute, May 10, on Central Park Mall," *New York Times,* 15 March 1931, p. II-6. In time, Uncle Robert would make "A Kiss for Mother—A Hug for Dad" the event's motto, which, by its nomenclature (mother vs. dad) may have had the unintended effect of emphasizing the differences between men and women (see chapter 6).

24. In 1939, when Spere decided to step down as the principal spokesperson for Parents' Day, he asked *Parents' Magazine* publisher George Hecht to pick up the cause. This would seem to have been a good choice. Hecht had written an editorial in support of Parents' Day ten years before: "Can this second Sunday in May become a day that all of us will be eager to observe? We believe it can and that this would best be accomplished by giving the day a broader significance. On this day it is parenthood which should be honored—not mother alone, but mother and father together for their joint share in home-making and child-rearing. . . . A Parents' Day would foster in children a proper recognition and appreciation of the unselfish devotion and self-sacrifice of both mothers and fathers." See George J. Hecht, "Why Not Parents' Day?," *Parents' Magazine,* May 1929, p. 16. In 1940, there was no Parents' Day rally in Central Park that I know of. Then, in 1941, it was announced that Hecht had become the chair of the "National Committee on the Observance of Mother's Day." "Mother's Day Is Promoted," *New York Times,* 2 March 1941, p. 41. Hecht's shift in allegiance effectively spelled the end of the Parents' Day movement.

25. Hatch, *The American Book of Days.*

26. Donald M. Scott and Bernard Wishy, eds., *America's Families: A Documentary History* (New York: Harper & Row, 1982), p. 466.

27. *Father's Day 75th Anniversary Commemorative,* p. 29.

28. "Suffragists to Storm Ohio: Mass Meetings All Over State on Mother's Day Next Friday," *New York Times,* 6 May 1912, p. 1; "Mothers Praised in Many Churches," *New York Times,* 12 May 1913, p. 9; "City Pays Homage to Mothers' Ideals . . . Maternity Care Stressed," *New York Times,* 11 May 1931, p. 3. See also Schmidt, *Consumer Rites,* p. 255.

29. The official history of Mother's Day tends to cast community leaders as the midwives. Ministers, for example, were given credit only for transmitting Jarvis's vision to their congregations (see *Father's Day 75th Anniversary Commemorative,* p. 4). The fact of the matter is, however, the religious, medical, and political elite, along with the business community, played a more significant role.

30. When I say that Father's Day was an "institutionalized form" by the early 1940s, I do not mean to suggest that it had anywhere near the kind of support it has today. I am saying simply that it had become a full-fledged national event. Even so, in 1944, when the American Library Association published *Anniversaries and Holidays,* ed. Mary E. Hazeltine, under the listing for Father's Day, there was this: "Father's Day is a newcomer to the list of special days, although its observance was growing independently under several parts of the country for a number of years. . . . The first celebration . . . was held in Spokane in June, 1910, but its definite place in the calendar is so recent, that there is little celebration material to enter in this record. All rejoice that the day is now observed in keeping with the honor and dignity of fatherhood." By "celebration material" was meant poems, speeches, sermons, prayers, party suggestions, and books. Among the items listed

was J. A. Rogers', *Parties and Programs for Parents' Days . . . Mother's Day, All-Family Days* (National Recreation Association, 1939): "A useful book, in the modern spirit, suggesting suitable ways of celebrating parents' days and conducting mother-daughter and father-son banquets. Complete with plans for entertainment, decorations, and menus, with a helpful bibliography of entertainment material" (p. 99).

31. One notable exception is Robert Lynd and Helen Merrell Lynd's study of "Middletown" (actually Muncie, Indiana) carried out in 1924 and 1925. According to the Lynds, the people of Muncie annually celebrated Father's Day and Mother's Day. Given that Muncie "[had] many features common to a wide group of communities," one might be tempted to conclude that both holidays were in full swing in America by the mid-1920s. The truth, however, is that while Muncie may have shared many characteristics with many other small cities, when it came to celebrations, it may have been in a league of its own. The Lynds reveal that, in addition to observing Father's Day and Mother's Day, the people of Muncie also celebrated Father and Son Week, Mother and Daughter Week, Child Health Week, Boys' Week, Thrift Week, Savings Day, Home Sewing Week, and many other occasions, including Non-Spit Week. See Robert Lynd and Helen Merrell Lynd, *Middletown: A Study in American Culture* (New York: Harcourt and Brace, 1929), p. 491.

32. Schmidt, in *Consumer Rites*, notes that while he was able to draw on the Anna Jarvis papers at West Virginia University for his history of Mother's Day, there were no personal papers of Sonora Dodd which could be used to help construct a history of Father's Day, "so one has to rely almost entirely on newspaper accounts" (p. 353). Though he was speaking specifically about gathering information about Dodd, the same thing can be said about gathering information about Father's Day in general.

33. Roberto Franzosi, "The Press as a Source of Socio-Historical Data: Issues in the Methodology of Data Collection from Newspapers," *Historical Methods* 20 (Winter 1987), pp. 5–16.

34. "Father's Christmas Letter Plan Gives Every Soldier Chance to Write and Get Answer from His First C.O.," *Stars and Stripes*, 15 November 1918, p. 1.

35. Hatch, *The American Book of Days*, p. 575.

36. "Sunday, May 12, is Mother's Day. Let the A.E.F. celebrate it by having every soldier, young and old, high and low, write home to his mother on that day." See "'Mother's Letter' Plan Gives Every Man in A.E.F. Special Opportunity for Observing Mother's Day," *Stars and Stripes*, 3 May 1918, p. 1.

37. It is possible that articles on Father's Day may have been published in issues that I did not examine. I have little reason to believe, however, that even if these issues did include articles on Father's Day, they would include so many articles as to undermine the proposition that the *Chicago Defender* gave considerably less attention to Father's Day than it did to Mother's Day.

38. Wilfon Copering, "To Dad," *Chicago Defender*, 27 June 1942, editorial page.

39. Lucinda Allen, "A Mother's Prayer," *Chicago Defender*, 20 June 1942, editorial page.

40. How the modernization of fatherhood in the early twentieth century played

itself out in the black community, as well as in other minority communities, is beyond the scope of this work. Clearly, however, this is an issue that deserves serious study. When I began, I had hoped to locate more information about the modernization of fatherhood beyond the white middle class but did not find as much as I would have liked. One of the reasons that I searched through the *Chicago Defender* is that I thought I might find a child-rearing column similar to Angelo Patri's and could then track down a collection of advice-seeking letters from black fathers and mothers. Alas, while there was considerable attention given to child-rearing concerns in the *Chicago Defender*, there was no column that might generate the storehouse of letters that Patri's column was able to generate. This does not mean, of course, that there are no advice-seeking letters from black fathers and mothers in the early twentieth century to be found. I just found no evidence of anywhere I happened to look.

41. For a discussion of the role that New York City played in the 1920s in the creation of both American popular culture and the world's popular culture, see Ann Douglas, *Terrible Honesty: Mongrel Manhattan in the 1920s* (New York: Farrar, Straus, and Giroux, 1995).

42. "This Is Called 'Father's Day'; Official Flower Dandelion," *New York Times,* 15 June 1924, p. 1.

43. Schmidt says, in *Consumer Rites,* that the hand-picked dandelion once had been proposed as a Mother's Day flower with the intent being to "purify the holiday by removing the blot of lucre and profit" (p. 272). But "when the same suggestion was made in connection with Father's Day, it was simply a joke."

44. The tradition seems to have its roots in Mother's Day rather than Father's Day. In 1908, at the "first" Mother's Day celebration, Anna M. Jarvis distributed carnations to each mother in attendance. See Hatch, *The American Book of Days,* p. 439. In 1913, on the second Sunday in May, "President Wilson, Cabinet Officers, members of Congress, and thousands of Washingtonians wore white carnations" to signify their allegiance to the holiday. See "Observe Mothers' Day. White Flowers are Worn by President Wilson and the Cabinet," *New York Times,* 12 May 1913, p. 9. As for the rose being the official flower for Father's Day, according to the *Times* in 1925, "The significance of the red rose as father's distinguishing emblem [had] not yet been thought out." See "Father's Day Brings Rush on Cigar Stores; Longest Day Dedicated to Glorifying Dad," *New York Times,* 22 June 1925, p. 2. For a detailed discussion of the role of the floral industry in the creation of Father's Day and Mother's Day, see Schmidt, *Consumer Rites.*

45. "Date Mix-Up May Ruin Father's Day," *New York Times,* 4 June 1925, p. 9.

46. "National Father's Day Project Has Languished Twenty Years," *New York Times,* 23 May 1926, p. IV-12.

47. "Father's Day Dawns—Over His Protest; Ties and Cigars to Be His Lot, Then Obscurity," *New York Times,* 19 June 1927, p. II-1; "Rose Market Quiet for Father's Day," *New York Times,* 17 June 1928, p. II-1.

48. Wendy Griswold offers this definition of a cultural object: "A cultural object may be defined as shared significance embodied in form. In other words, it is a socially shared meaningful expression that is audible, or visible, or tangible, or can be articulated." Wendy Griswold, *Cultures and Societies in a Changing World* (Thousand Oaks, CA: Pine Forge Press, 1994), p. 11. See also Wendy Griswold,

Renaissance Revivals: City Comedy and Revenge Tragedy in the London Theatre,
1576–1980 (Chicago: University of Chicago Press, 1986). To say that Father's Day
was recognizable in the 1920s does not mean that it had entered the perception of
all Americans, only that it had captured the attention of a significant number of
men and women and moved into the public realm. And the comparisons with
Mother's Day continued to be striking. Mother's Day, for one thing, meant a lot
more money in the business community's coffers. Said one florist in 1928, "[Fa-
ther's Day] has been nothing like Mother's Day last month. . . . I figure it out that
fathers haven't the same sentimental appeal that mothers have. You know how it is
yourself." See "Rose Market Quiet for Father's Day," *New York Times,* 17 June
1928, p. 1.

49. "This Is Father's Day, and Retailers Profit," *New York Times,* 16 June 1929,
p. II-6.

50. "Today Is Father's Day. Symbolized by the Dandelion, Which Thrives on
Abuse," *New York Times,* 21 June 1931, p. 21.

51. "Mother's Day, Inc.," *Time,* 16 May 1938, pp. 17–18; "Mother's Day Origi-
nator Acquitted," *New York Times,* 15 September 1925, p. 52. Technically, at least,
Mother's Day was "owned" by Jarvis. She managed not only to incorporate the
Mother's Day International Association, but also to register "Second Sunday in
May, Mother's Day, Anna Jarvis, Founder," as the organization's trademark. See
"Second Sunday in May. Mother's Day Finds Promoter of Idea Poor, Hospitalized,
and Still Bitter," *Newsweek,* 8 May 1944, p. 35–36. In legal response, the business
community contended that since Mother's Day had been approved by Congress,
it was "a day of public recognition of motherhood for all, not under the control of
one organization." "Mothers at Odds on Day," *New York Times,* 4 May 1924,
p. X-8. Schmidt reports in *Consumer Rites* (p. 268) that initially Jarvis cooperated
with merchants.

52. Krythe, *All About American Holidays,* p. 159. Dodd gave birth to a son
who, as an adult, worked for the National Park Service and, perhaps not coincidentally, at one point was named the District of Columbia's Ideal Father (p. 161).

53. The Commercial Factor in Father's Day and Mother's Day, as shown in the
percentage of Father's Day and Mother's Day articles in the *New York Times* that
centered on advertising campaigns, holiday sales, and the like:

Period	Father's Day		Mother's Day	
1900–1909	—	(0)	0%	(2)
1910–1919	0%	(6)	0%	(19)
1920–1929	53%	(15)	9%	(55)
1930–1939	72%	(60)	2%	(142)
1940–1949	46%	(120)	2%	(89)

54. "Fathers to Receive Honors Tomorrow," *New York Times,* 18 June
1932, p. 3.

55. "To Promote Father's Day," *New York Times,* 25 April 1934, p. 39; "Father's
Day Plans Made," *New York Times,* 6 June 1934, p. 30; "Daner Wins Display
Award," *New York Times,* 13 July 1934, p. 24.

56. "Plans for Father's Day," *New York Times,* 21 March 1935, p. 40; "Meet on

Father's Day," *New York Times,* 9 May 1935, p. 38; "Sunday is 'Father's Day,' " *New York Times,* 14 June 1935, p. 25.

57. *Father's Day 75th Anniversary Commemorative,* p. 6.

58. A council member once resigned because he was angry that a Father's Day poster showed a father with a cigar in his mouth instead of a pipe. Ibid., p. 7.

59. "Father's Day Ads Increase," *New York Times,* 19 June 1936, p. 37.

60. *Father's Day 75th Anniversary Commemorative,* p. 7.

61. Interview conducted 17 August 1989. One very simple yet important job that the council carries out is to remind people when Father's Day is. Unlike Christmas, which always falls on 25 December, Father's Day falls on a particular weekend. Thus, one year it may be on 15 June, the next year on 21 June, and so on.

62. "Plans for Father's Day," *New York Times,* 21 March 1935, p. 40; "Father's Day Orders Heavy; Promotion Wide," *New York Times,* 1 March 1938, p. III-8. See also Schmidt, *Consumer Rites,* p. 286.

63. The same deception operates in the commercialization of feeling. Flight attendants and other service workers are paid to "care for" customers, but the company for whom they work would prefer that they *appear* to be doing it out of the goodness of their heart. See Arlie Hochschild, *The Managed Heart: Commercialization of Human Feeling* (Berkeley, CA: University of California Press, 1983).

64. The group I am referring to is the National Committee for the Observance of Mother's Day, which George Hecht was asked to head in 1941 and which, like the National Council for the Promotion of Father's Day, represented a large conglomerate of business interests. In the words of the current Mother's Day Committee, "The National Committee for the Observance of Mother's Day was organized in 1941 to give cohesion to the Mother's Day movement, and to enhance its observance by the entire country." See "Tenth Anniversary Outstanding Mother Awards," p. 2. These national committees/councils were not the first organizations to promote Father's Day and Mother's Day. Other organizations did the same throughout the early twentieth century. For example, in 1933, "The American Mother's Day Committee [was] founded 'to develop and strengthen the moral and spiritual foundations of the American home and to give the observance of Mother's Day a spiritual quality representative of ideal motherhood.' " See Hatch, *The American Book of Days,* p. 440. This 1933 Committee may have been the precursor to the National Committee for the Observance of Mother's Day. What set the National Council for the Promotion of Father's Day and the National Committee for the Observance of Mother's Day apart, however, was the word *national.* These were organizations designed to mobilize support for Father's Day and Mother's Day on a country-wide scale. Looking at the Father's Day and Mother's Day movements in these terms, national economic mobilization for Father's Day preceded national economic mobilization for Mother's Day by six years, because the National Council for the Promotion of Father's Day was founded in 1935, while the National Committee for the Observance of Mother's Day was founded in 1941.

65. "Sell Ads for Father's Day," *New York Times,* 27 March 1936, p. 32.

66. "Father's Day Ads Increase," *New York Times,* 19 June 1936, p. 37.

67. "Fathers Have 'Their Day,' " *New York Times,* 22 June 1936, p. 21.

68. "More Family Reunions Urged by Queens Pastor," *New York Times,* 22 June 1936, p. 21.

69. "Million Spent on Father's Day," *New York Times,* 19 June 1937, p. 28.

70. "Father's Day Sales Rise. Men's Wear Volume Held Down by Greater Competition," *New York Times,* 20 June 1937, p. III-9.

71. "Some Fathers Have a Day. But Spotty Observance Here Is Indicated by Reports," *New York Times,* 21 June 1937.

72. P.W. (female), writing on behalf of the Father's Day Committee, to Angelo Patri, Box 33, 19 May 1937, Angelo Patri Papers, Library of Congress.

73. Angelo Patri to P.W., Box 33, 7 June 1937, Angelo Patri Papers, Library of Congress. Scribbled on P.W.'s letter was the phrase, "Too late."

74. "Father's Day Orders Heavy; Promotion Wide," *New York Times,* 1 March 1938, p. III-8.

75. "Father's Day Plans Pushed by Retailers," *New York Times,* 30 March 1938, p. 38.

76. "Wide Support Given Father's Day Plans," *New York Times,* 13 April 1938, p. 40.

77. "Council Organized for Father's Day," *New York Times,* 10 June 1938, p. 39.

78. "Father's Day," *New York Times,* 19 June 1938, p. IV-19.

79. Situated next to the 19 June 1938 article in the *Times* (see note 78 above) was a reproduction of a poster that was being used to promote Father's Day that year. It pictured a father sitting in an easy chair and being showered with gifts from his two young children, while mother looks on approvingly. The caption was, "Remember Dad." The question is, Who is orchestrating the presentation? The answer, I think, has to be the mother. The message to women: You, too, can enjoy the same kind of domestic tranquility and warmth that you see in this poster, *provided* you help your children purchase gifts for Father's Day.

80. The point, again, is that the business community, whether it recognized it or not, was benefiting from the legacy of the New Fatherhood movement. Consider again the 1938 poster (see note 79): What prevents a mother from seeing the advertisement as a commercial ploy, that is, *seeing through* the ad? It is the sanctification of fatherhood from nonbusiness interests. Similarly, the business community can create the most endearing ads to promote Christmas, but were it not for Christianity's sanctification of the day, Christmas would not be the financial windfall it is each year.

81. I am saying I "hypothesize" here, because I know the connections that I am trying to make are based in part on speculation. To firmly establish the connections, we would need time series data in order to meticulously correlate the growth of Father's Day and the growth of New Fatherhood , with attendant consideration of lagged effects.

82. "Trade Unity Held Vital to Recovery. Expanded Father's Day Drive Commended as an Example by N.R.D.G.A. [National Retail Dry Goods Association]," *New York Times,* 2 April 1938, p. 20.

83. For a discussion of how warfare lends prestige to a country's defenders, who are more often than not men, see Janet Saltzman Chafetz, *Gender Equity: An Integrated Theory of Stability and Change* (Newbury Park, CA: Sage, 1990), pp. 119–21.

84. "Gifts to Fathers Pour in Tomorrow," *New York Times,* 17 June 1939, p. 10; "100,000 Father's Day Posters," *New York Times,* 21 April 1939, p. 34; "Notes," *New York Times,* 10 June 1939, p. 24.

85. "Typical Father Wins Motor Car," *New York Times,* 19 June 1939, p. 8.

86. "Father's Day Tomorrow," *New York Times,* 15 June 1940, p. 17.

87. "Advertising News and Notes," *New York Times,* 12 June 1940, p. 40.

88. "Gifts and Messages Showered on Father," *New York Times,* 17 June 1940, p. 8.

89. "Father's Day Sales Rose 22%," *New York Times,* 21 July 1941, p. 24; "Father's Day Budget Widened," *New York Times,* 26 June 1942, p. 28.

90. "Opens Father's Day Drive. Council Releases 1941 Poster, Starts Fund Campaign Monday," *New York Times,* 27 September 1940, p. 34; "Mayor Unveils Poster," *New York Times,* 16 November 1941, p. 40.

91. "'Twas Father's Day For Boys of A.E.F. and at Exercises on Mall They Heard Their Sons Pledged to Defend the Nation," *New York Times,* 16 June 1941, p. 17.

92. "Proclaims Father's Day. Mayor Urges 'Proper Religious, Spiritual, Patriotic' Celebration," *New York Times,* 18 June 1942, p. 18.

93. "MacArthur Named 'Outstanding Father'; Detroit Worker Also Is Honored," *New York Times,* 17 June 1942, p. 24.

94. "M'Arthur Is Proud to Be a Father. Hopes Son Will Remember Him Not in Battle, but in Home," *New York Times,* 19 June 1942, p. 13. See also William Manchester, *American Caesar: Douglas MacArthur, 1880–1964* (New York: Dell, 1978), p. 334. The first five National Fathers of the Year, chosen by the Father's Day Committee, were all military or political figures: General Douglas MacArthur (1942), General Dwight D. Eisenhower (1943), General Mark W. Clark (1944), President Harry S. Truman (1945), Marine Al Schmid (1946). See "Father of the Year: Honors List, 1942–1989" (New York: National Father's Day Committee, 1989).

Chapter 9: Conclusion

1. Spock's book was published first in 1946 and revised in 1957, 1968, 1976, and 1985. The 1985 edition is a collaboration between Benjamin Spock, M.D. and Michael B. Rothenberg, M.D. Its official title is *Baby and Child Care,* but the cover reads *Dr. Spock's Baby and Child Care* (New York: Pocket Books, 1985). When Spock's book was initially published, it was titled *The Common Sense Book of Baby and Child Care* (New York: Duell, Sloan, and Pearce, 1946). A paperback version, published the same year by Pocket Books, however, was titled *The Pocket Book of Baby and Child Care.* The second edition of the paperback version (1957) and the third edition of the hardback version (1968) resorted to the simpler title, *Baby and Child Care.* This title was retained in the fourth edition (1976), and, save for what was printed on the cover, in the fifth edition (1985) as well. See Michael Zuckerman, "Dr. Spock: The Confidence Man," in *The Family in History,* ed. Charles E. Rosenberg (Philadelphia: University of Pennsylvania Press, 1975). The estimate of over 40 million copies is extrapolated from a figure of "over" 39 million copies that Spock provided in 1989. I am assuming that the book has continued to sell at a brisk pace. See Benjamin Spock, M.D., and Mary Morgan, *Spock on Spock: A Memoir of Growing Up with the Century* (New York: Pantheon, 1989). Some have said that Spock's book is "the all-time best-selling book in American history after the Bible." Shari L. Thurer, *The Myths of Motherhood:*

How Culture Reinvents the Good Mother (New York: Houghton Mifflin, 1994), p. xvii.

2. Janna Malamud Smith, "Mothers: Tired of Taking the Rap," *New York Times* Sunday magazine, 10 June 1990, pp. 32, 34, 38; Nancy R. Gibbs, "Bringing Up Father" [cover story], *Time*, 28 June 1993, pp. 53–61.

3. Spock, *The Common Sense Book of Baby and Child Care* (1946), pp. 15–16. Spock, *Baby and Child Care* (1976), p. 46.

4. For a discussion of the distinction between "implicit" and "explicit" history, see S. Thernstrom, "Yankee City Revisited: The Perils of Historical Naivete," *American Sociological Review* 39 (1965) 234–42. See also Robert K. Merton, "Three Fragments from a Sociologist's Notebooks: Establishing the Phenomenon, Specified Ignorance, and Strategic Research Materials," *Annual Review of Sociology* 13 (1987), pp. 1–28.

5. As we saw in chapter 3, not only were there some "baby doctors" (academic psychologists in particular) whose approach to fatherhood in the 1930s and early 1940s was more feminist than was Spock's approach to fatherhood in 1946 (or 1976), but even the changes observed in the more conservative *Infant Care* from 1914 to 1942 were more sweeping (in percentage of change) than the changes observed in the Spock manual during its time. People too often assume that manuals change because, and only because, of societal pressure, but the truth is that a book might change, or not change, from one edition to the next for any number of idiosyncratic reasons. The evidence indicates that Spock revised his book in response to feminism, but the influence was more direct and more personal than some might assume. In his memoir, Spock writes, "In the forties, I was a sexist almost like everybody else. When the women's liberation movement became active in 1969 and '70, it still took me a long time to acknowledge my own sexism and try to change my ideas. While I was attacking the war in Vietnam, I was being attacked by feminists on the rampage. I was no more sexist than the average man, I think, but since I'd written down so much, the feminists were able to put their finger on it." He then talks about how, in 1972 when he was running for president of the United States, he was asked to speak to the National Women's Political Caucus, to explain his views and those of his party (the People's Party) with regard to women's liberation and sexism in general. Although his party platform was, in his opinion, "emphatically feminist," he was not greeted warmly by the group. Several women left the hall when he got up to speak, and the feminist leader Gloria Steinem, who happened to be in the audience, vented her rage at him: "Dr. Spock, I hope you realize that you have been a major oppressor of women in the same category as Sigmund Freud!" Spock says it hurt his feelings to be called an enemy of women, and that after "three years of discussion with many patient women" he finally came to "fully understand the nature of [his] sexism" and "felt ready to begin, in 1973, the revision of *Baby and Child Care*." See Benjamin Spock and Mary Morgan, *Spock on Spock: A Memoir of Growing Up with the Century* (New York: Pantheon, 1989), pp. 247–48. What is interesting about this account is that it shows how sensitive Spock was to feminist criticism, and helps us to appreciate why the 1976 edition took such a feminist turn. Another male author, without equally strong feminist leanings, might not have changed his best-selling book the way Spock did, and the history of twentieth-century fatherhood (as seen through the pages of a single manual) would have exhibited a gentler thirty-year (1946–1976) slope.

6. Terry Strathman, "From the Quotidian to the Utopian: Child-rearing Literature in America, 1926–1940," *Berkeley Journal of Sociology* 29 (1984), p. 19.

7. See, for example, Philip Wylie, *Generation of Vipers* (New York: Farrar and Rinehart, 1942).

8. Anne Shannon Monroe, "We Want Daddies," *Good Housekeeping,* June 1930, pp. 51, 217, 218, 220.

9. I say "not entirely" because the father as male role model did suggest that there were contributions that men could make that women could not, which to some degree did devalue women. But the father as male role model also reinforced the notion that women had something special to contribute, that is, their femininity.

10. Two books which discuss how America's nostalgia for the 1950s has influenced family policy in the present are Stephanie Coontz, *The Way We Never Were: American Families and the Nostalgia Trap* (New York: Basic, 1992); and Arlene Skolnick, *Embattled Paradise: The American Family in an Age of Uncertainty* (New York: Basic, 1991).

11. See chapter 2, note 11, where I say that it is more appropriate to talk of *histories* of *fatherhoods* but that, following grammatical convention, I opted for the singular form. A number of histories of fatherhoods remain to be written. Little is known about the histories of fatherhoods in different racial, ethnic, and class groups, for example. And it would be wonderful if scholars took it upon themselves to write detailed histories of fatherhoods in the seventeenth and eighteenth centuries, or the 1950s and 1960s. Even within the circumscribed period that I chose to study, the 1920s and 1930s, I could do only so much with the resources I had. Thus, I did not focus on the modernization of fatherhood(s) in, say, the African-American community or Italian-American community (where my roots lie). I do hope, however, that others will do the research on these and other communities and report what they have found. Similarly, we need to know more about how the modernization of fatherhood(s) in the white middle class diffused to other classes. What was the process, the timing, the speed?

Index